1976

TEEN DAY

# Communication Is Power

# *Communication Is Power*

UNCHANGING VALUES IN A CHANGING JOURNALISM

Herbert Brucker

New York Oxford University Press
1973

**To tomorrow's journalists**

Communication is power, and exclusive access
to it is a dangerous, unchecked power.
Senator J. W. Fulbright, August 4, 1970

# *Apologia and Credo*

A REPUBLIC in which the people are the ultimate source of power must strive constantly, in the face of inevitable change, to democratize its communications.

Norbert Wiener once said that to live effectively is to live with adequate information. But if an adequate input of information is essential to each of us, so is an adequate outgo from each of us. Journalism by nature consists principally of broadcasting information and interpretation to the mass, whether through print, electronics, or other means. But it serves best if it also makes the governors—economic and moral governors as well as political governors—aware of what the governed think and feel.

Therefore journalism, the press, the media—whatever you call the mechanics of our communications—should perform both tasks. Our journalism does so. It is sometimes superb, sometimes dreadful, and mostly in between. One reason for its failures is the inherent difficulty of the task. Another is the fact that journalists, like everyone else, are fallible human beings. But difficulty lies also in the economic system that journalism shares with the rest of the private sector of our economy. Like the other businesses that get the world's work done, journalism must be a profit-making enterprise. But unlike all the others, it performs a public service without which self-government cannot exist. That puts upon it obligations other businesses do not share.

The pages that follow are drawn from half a century of experience. Over the years some of the theses here advanced first took shape as magazine articles or speeches. Because the common thread of journalism ran through them it seemed a good idea to pull them together in one place, simply updating them. But it soon became evident that updating was not enough. The business of telling the world what happens and why has entered an era of change by geometrical progression, change that feeds upon itself. This necessitated not only new illustrative material, but also inquiry into factors unknown until recently.

It is our lot, said Justice Holmes, always to be wagering our salvation upon some prophecy based on imperfect knowledge. It is the life work of the journalist to push that knowledge as far toward perfection as he can. May those who come after us be free to do just that.

H.B.

Cornish, N.H.
September 1, 1972

# By Way of Acknowledgment

I WISH TO thank the old Saturday Review, as built over the years by Norman Cousins, and the editor of SR's former communications section, Richard L. Tobin. They encouraged me to write some of the articles that appear, in modern dress, as some of the chapters in this book. Mr. Cousins also gave me permission to adapt what was said there to the present purpose.

My thanks likewise go to Nancy Weston, formerly of Stanford University, and to Margaret Abbott of Newport, N.H., for long hours of re-typing often messy copy.

Likewise I wish to thank many friends of newspapers and magazines, of news broadcasting and the academic world—notably my associates of the *Hartford Courant* and Stanford University—for many of the thoughts and values that appear in what I say as though they were my own. The entire responsibility is of course mine.

Most of all my thanks to go my wife, Elizabeth Spock Brucker, who endured it all when there were more interesting things we might well have been off doing.

Finally, I thank the following for permission to quote:

*The Atlantic Monthly*, "Carnival of Excess," by Charles Mc-

# *Contents*

# *Communication Is Power*

# 1

## Press Pass to History

### Sermons vs. Circuses

A STUDENT at Columbia University's Graduate School of Journalism once made this diagnosis of his future profession: "The trouble with newspapers is that they are made for people who need sermons, but want circuses."

That simple statement explains why many of us, in our better moments at least, are irritated by the press. A preoccupation with the odd and the evil, the violent and the macabre, is inherent in journalism. Two other factors limit journalism's perfectability. One is the perennially insistent pressure for speed. The other is the necessity of working through fallible human beings, whose preparation for serving as history's witnesses is not always the best.

For all that the newspapers of the past—like those of today, as supplemented by the words and images imprinted on film and tape—constitute a press pass to history. To a large extent yesterday's journalism is today's history. Just so today's journalism will be the dominant part of tomorrow's history.

It is also true that, more often than we realize, a reporter's account of the human circus at some milestone in history has a sermon wrapped up in it. Here, if not yet in full detail and ordered perspective, is not only a factual account of some spectacular or momentous happening, but also some hint of its significance.

### An Assassination

Take for example an event still near enough to be remembered by many, the assassination of President John F. Kennedy in Dallas on November 22, 1963. Or, for that matter, take the ironical repetition of that tragedy in the murder of his brother, Senator Robert Kennedy, in Los Angeles on June 5, 1968. You can recapture the incredible drama of these events by looking through the files of the newspapers published and the films exposed at the time. But it is more convenient to leaf through one of the news-books that retell these stories.

One such book is *Four Days: The Historical Record of the Death of President Kennedy,* compiled within a month of the event by United Press International and American Heritage Magazine. This large-format book is a recapitulation of the news reported on the spot from moment to moment. It is divided into chapters that relive, one by one, the days from November 22 through 25, when the story ended with the funeral in Washington. Chapter 1 opens with a few words and pictures to set the stage. It has such sub-headings as: "A Cheerful Morning in Fort Worth," "The Welcome in Dallas," and then simply "The Motorcade," and "The Sniper's Post." There follow the historic three shots, whose impact is pictured still in photos made from amateur moving pictures taken on the spot.

Next come photo-reproductions of the gray news-ticker copy that first alerted the nation and the world. These reports were sent in by UPI reporter Merriman Smith, dean of White House correspondents. He was riding in the press-pool car, the fourth car in the procession behind the open bubbletop carrying President and Mrs. Kennedy and Governor and Mrs. Connally.

At the moment the assassin fired, the UPI Teletypes in newspaper and broadcasting offices throughout the country were clattering out a report on a Minneapolis murder trial. The Dallas bureau interrupted with MORE DA 1234 PCS, indicating that this routine account would be continued later because now, at 12:34 p.m. Central Standard Time, Dallas had a hotter item. Then there clacked out the first hint of the news, as Dallas had it from Smith, reporting via radio-telephone from the press-pool car which was already careening after the President's car on the way to the hospital:

> UPI A7N DA
>    PRECEDE KENNEDY
> DALLAS, NOV. 22 (UPI)—THREE SHOTS WERE FIRED AT PRESIDENT KEN-
> NEDY'S MOTORCADE TODAY IN DOWNTOWN DALLAS.

Minneapolis tried to continue its interrupted account of the trial; Atlanta sought to come on with something from there. But New York headquarters squelched them both, and gave priority to Dallas:

> BUOS UPHOLD, DA IT YRS

(bureaus hold it, Dallas it's yours). Then:

> URGENT
> 1ST ADD SHOTS, DALLAS (A7N) XXX DOWNTOWN DALLAS.
> NO CASUALTIES WERE REPORTED.
> THE INCIDENT OCCURRED NEAR THE COUNTY SHERIFF'S OFFICE ON MAIN
> STREET, JUST EAST OF AN UNDERPASS LEADING TOWARD THE TRADE
> MART WHERE THE PRESIDENT WAS TO MA

By that time Smith had seen the blood-stained President and Governor, still in their car, before they were carried into the hospital. Through a telephone snatched at the hospital, he gave the first indication of tragedy:

> FLASH
> FLASH
> KENNEDY SERIOUSLY WOUNDED
>    PERHAPS SERIOUSLY
> PERHAPS FATALLY BY ASSASSINS BULLET

A Secret Service man at the hospital had told Smith, "He's dead."

Now that an alert had been broadcast to the world, Smith began dictating over his commandeered telephone an ordered account, ready for printing:

BULLETIN
      1ST LEAD SHOOTING
DALLAS, NOV. 22 (UPI)—PRESIDENT KENNEDY AND GOV. JOHN B. CON-NALLY OF TEXAS WERE CUT DOWN BY AN ASSASSIN'S BULLETS AS THEY TOURED DOWNTOWN DALLAS IN AN OPEN AUTOMOBILE TODAY.

THE PRESIDENT, HIS LIMP BODY CRADLED IN THE ARMS OF HIS WIFE, WAS RUSHED TO PARKLAND HOSPITAL. THE GOVERNOR WAS ALSO TAKEN TO PARKLAND.

CLINT HILL, A SECRET SERVICE AGENT ASSIGNED TO MRS. KENNEDY, SAID "HE'S DEAD," AS THE PRESIDENT WAS LIFTED FROM THE REAR OF A WHITE HOUSE TOURING CAR, THE FAMOUS "BUBBLETOP" FROM WASH-INGTON. HE WAS RUSHED TO AN EMERGENCY ROOM IN THE HOSPITAL. OTHER WHITE HOUSE OFFICIALS WERE IN DOUBT AS THE CORRIDORS OF THE HOSPITAL ERUPTED IN PANDEMONIUM.

THE INCIDENT OCCURRED JUST EAST OF THE TRIPLE UNDERPASS FACING A PARK IN DOWNTOWN DALLAS.

REPORTERS ABOUT FIVE CARS LENGTHS BEHIND THE CHIEF EXECUTIVE HEAR

MORE 144 PES

Thus, within ten minutes of the firing of the shots themselves, an accurate account of what had happened, as it was known at the moment, was flashed around the world.

Reporters on the scene, plus others rushed to Dallas by plane, took the unbelievable story from there as it unfolded. The UPI's version, assembled between the covers of this book, takes a reader today through it all over again, in often poignant words and pictures. From the shocked reaction, "My, God, what are we coming to?" of Speaker John McCormack in Washington, to the hunt for the killer in Dallas, we retrace instant history's way through the jumble of events. Patrolman Tippit is murdered in the street, and Lee Harvey Oswald is seized in the movie theater near by. Vice President Johnson takes the oath as President in the hot confines of Air Force One, with Jacqueline Kennedy, still in blood-spattered clothes, beside him.

So to Washington, where for the first time the new President speaks briefly to the nation, and the casket is borne to the White House. Then the vigil, the national mourning, as condolences pour in from the great of the earth and from simple citizens everywhere. The new President gets to work, the famous Kennedy rocker is carried from the White House. In Dallas the evidence against Oswald mounts.

After a rainy Saturday in Washington, Sunday dawned clear, with fall's soft brilliance. It was to be a day of solemn ritual. The casket, bearing the body of the youngest President the nation has ever elected, was marched slowly to the Capitol rotunda. There were touching scenes there, as when the President's young daughter, kneeling, slipped her hand under the flag to touch the casket. But that day, while the nation was watching the solemnities on television, the unbelievable happened again. While newsmen's cameras clicked and whirred Jack Ruby shot and killed Oswald in the basement corridor of the Dallas city prison. The pictorial record was complete to Oswald's grimace as the bullet tore through him. Finally on the fourth day, Monday November 25, came the dignity of the President's funeral in Washington, with the world's statesmen attending.

Even now it is hardly possible to look through this account, taken from the journalism of the elapsing moment, without having tears well up within once more.

*The New York Times* of the morning following the assassination ran an eight-column, three-line heading, rare in a paper that plays the news in accordance with its worth rather than its shock value. It said:

KENNEDY IS KILLED BY SNIPER
AS HE RIDES IN CAR IN DALLAS;
JOHNSON SWORN IN ON PLANE

The lead story is by Tom Wicker, the Time's White House man at that time. Like other reporters, he was in Dallas because he was covering the President's tour. His account too was history in a hurry, all its information gathered, checked, and organized into a smooth-flowing whole in a few hours. The basic fact of the Presi-

dent's death came first, then the circumstances, and what happened
after: the hospital, the last rites, the confusion, the actions of the
principals, the capture of Oswald, the swearing in of Mr. Johnson.
And so to lesser events of the day, ending with brief quotations
from the speech that President Kennedy was to have delivered at
the Merchandise Mart luncheon that noon.

There is a lesson for us here, to be remembered whenever we
wish to berate the press for the circuses it prepares and prints.
These on-the-spot histories from Dallas stand up in substantial accuracy today. After nearly a year of monumental investigation the
Warren Commission issued, in 888 pages based on 15 volumes of
testimony by 552 witnesses, its definitive report on what had really
happened and what lay behind it all. In the words of another *New
York Times* reporter, Anthony Lewis, it all came down to this:

> Washington, Sept. 27 [1964]—The assassination of President Ken-
> nedy was the work of one man, Lee Harvey Oswald. There was
> no conspiracy, foreign or domestic.
>
> That was the central finding in the Warren Commission report,
> made public this evening. Chief Justice Earl Warren and the six
> other members of the President's Commission were unanimous
> on this and all questions. . . .[1]

In the nature of things, journalism's immediate reports on complex and unexpected events do not always merit such precise confirmation as this from subsequent leisured and authoritative investigation. Nevertheless, here was testimony to the competence of
the press to give us accurate accounts of great events almost instantly. For in no substantial way did the painstaking Warren report differ from the stories Merriman Smith, Tom Wicker, and all
the others had fashioned under pressure of a deadline. And while
there are still those who cling to the notion that there must have
been some conspiratorial plot and organization behind Oswald's
act, to this day no one has yet brought forth even the tiniest bit of
evidence to that effect. Journalism's first report stands up, even in
the piercing brilliance of hindsight.

It is fair to say, then, that at least much of the time journalism gives us more accurate reports than we are willing to believe. At the same time there is reason for the existing popular skepticism as to journalism's reliability. Even Thomas Jefferson, who wrote some of the most stirring defenses of the press ever made, thought the better of it upon occasion. Lake the two Presidents before him and all who followed, he suffered from inaccuracies in reporting and, still more, from editorial venom. No wonder that at one exasperated point, toward the end of his presidency, he said:

> Nothing can now be believed which is seen in a newspaper. Truth itself becomes suspicious by being put into that polluted vehicle. . . . I will add, that the man who never looks into a newspaper is better informed than he who reads them; inasmuch as he who knows nothing is nearer to truth than he whose mind is filled with falsehoods and errors.[2]

Since Jefferson's time journalism's standards of fairness and accuracy have risen considerably. The item in today's newspaper may sometimes be inaccurate, of necessity or otherwise. But normally it does fix in time the basic facts of the vanishing moment. Especially is this so if we trouble to heed the ascriptions and qualifications that are written into the modern news story as a matter of course. When in the often fear-ridden early 1950s Senator Joseph McCarthy charged that some hapless victim was a Communist, it did not necessarily signify that he was. Nevertheless it was accurate to report that the gravel-voiced Senator had said he was.

### Fall of the Winter Palace

Turn through the yellowed, often crumbling newspaper files of the past, or scan them in the dim light of the microfilm reader, and you can see that the Dallas story was not unique, a fortunate freak. Despite inevitable errors and omissions, the news is history written down as it is made. The eight-column headline in New York's late, great *World* for Friday, November 9, 1917, reads as follows:

KERENSKY DEPOSED, FLEES PETROGRAD TO ESCAPE
THE REDS; SHELLED BY CRUISER AND FORT, WINTER
PALACE SURRENDERS[3]

This was the October Revolution, which established what became known as Soviet Russia and thereby set the stage for much
of the history of the twentieth century. The *World's* dispatch
began:

> Petrograd, Nov. 8—Maximalists have obtained control of Petro-
> grad and deposed the Kerensky government.
>
> Kerensky has escaped arrest by fleeing the capital and is be-
> lieved to be on his way to the front. Other members of the Minis-
> try have been arrested by the Revolutionary Committee.
>
> A delegation has been named to the Workmen's and Soldiers'
> Delegates, the Bolshevik body, to initiate peace negotiations with
> the other revolutionary and democratic organizations, "with a
> view to taking steps to end the bloodshed."
>
> Government forces holding the Winter Palace were compelled
> to capitulate early this morning under the fire of the cruiser Au-
> rora and the cannon of the St. Peter and St. Paul fortress across
> the Neva River. . . .
>
> At 2 o'clock this morning the Women's Battalion, which had
> been defending the Winter Palace, surrendered.
>
> The Workmen's and Soldiers' Delegates are in complete con-
> trol of the city. . . .

One of those present was John Reed, Harvard classmate of
Walter Lippmann, who had already reported the revolutionary
gyrations af Mexico's Francisco Villa. As often happens, this colorful reporter later retold the running story he had witnessed in a
book, *Ten Days That Shook the World.*[4] His account, which became a classic, put flesh on *The World*'s bare bones of fact:

> Wednesday, November 7, I rose very late. The noon cannon
> boomed from Peter-Paul as I went down the Nevsky. It was a
> raw, chill day. In front of the State Bank some soldiers with
> fixed bayonets were standing at the closed gates.
>
> "What side do you belong to?" I asked. "The government?"
>
> "No more government," one answered with a grin. "Slava
> Bogu! Glory to God!" That was all I could get out of him. . . .

Reed tells the tale as it unfolded minute by minute, taking one through the unrest, the occasional shooting and looting, and the uncertainty from moment to moment. At one point, riding in a truck with revolutionary soldiers, he picked up a proclamation that told the story:

### TO THE CITIZENS OF RUSSIA!
The Provisional Government is deposed. The State Power has passed into the hands of the organ of the Petrograd Soviet of Workers' and Soldiers' Deputies, the Military Revolutionary Committee, which stands at the head of the Petrograd proletariat and garrison.

The cause for which the people were fighting: immediate proposal of a democratic peace, abolition of landlord property-rights over the land, labor control over production, creation of a Soviet Government—that cause is securely achieved. . . .

So through the lengthening hours of that critical day. Finally, by night, Reed and his companions came to the Winter Palace, last refuge of Kerensky's authority, as that, too, was engulfed by the revolutionary flood. A line of sailors yelled furiously at the truck to stop:

It was an astonishing scene. Just at the corner of the Ekaterina Canal, under an arc light, a cordon of armed sailors was drawn across the Nevsky, blocking the way to a crowd of people in columns of fours. There were about three or four hundred of them, men in frock coats, well-dressed women, officers—all sorts and conditions of people. . . .

Like a black river, filling all the streets, without song or cheer we poured through the Red Arch, where the man just ahead of me said in a low voice: "Look out, comrades! Don't trust them. They will fire, surely!" In the open we began to run, stooping low and bunching together, and jammed up suddenly behind the pedestal of the Alexander Column.

Soon, however, the crowd was reassured by the presence of Red Guards, and the absence of all but a few soldiers. So over the barricades and on toward the palace:

. . . On both sides of the main gateway the doors stood wide open, light streamed out, and from the huge pile came not the slightest sound.

Carried along by the eager wave of men, we were swept into the right-hand entrance, opening into the great bare vaulted room, the cellar of the east wing, from which issued a maze of corridors and staircases. A number of huge packing cases stood about, and upon these the Red Guards and soldiers fell furiously, battering them open with the butts of their rifles, and pulling out carpets, curtains, linens, porcelain plates, glassware. . . . One man went strutting around with a bronze clock perched on his shoulder; another found a plume of ostrich feathers, which he stuck in his hat. The looting was just beginning when somebody cried, "Comrades! Don't touch anything! Don't take anything! This is the property of the people!" . . . Many hands dragged the spoilers down.

The account runs on through the milling uncertainties of the night. Imperial palace servants, still in their blue and red and gold uniforms, stood about nervously repeating from habit that it was forbidden to go in there. Moods changed and suspicion arose in spontaneous combustion. At one point Reed and his American companions were growled at by a soldier and collecting crowd, who suspected them of being Kerensky provocateurs. Only a revolutionary officer-commissar, who unlike the soldiers could read the Americans' passes from the Military Revolutionary Committee, got them out of the melee. So ends this day that signalled the takeover of the last center of authority by the Bolsheviki. Reed reported from the spot:

> We came out into the cold, nervous night, murmurous with obscure armies on the move, electric with patrols. From across the river, where loomed the darker mass of Peter-Paul, came a hoarse shout. . . . Underfoot the sidewalk was littered with broken stucco, from the cornice of the palace where two shells from the battleship *Avrora* had struck; that was the only damage done by the bombardment. . . .
>
> It was now after three in the morning. On the Nevsky all the street lights were again shining, the cannon gone, and the only

signs of war were Red Guards and soldiers squatting around the fires. The city was quiet—probably never so quiet in its history; on that night not a single holdup occurred, not a single robbery.

The tale, even though rewritten in a book, is still journalism—history written as it happens.

## A Noble Calling

The difference between journalism and history lies in this, that as the eventual chronicler picks over the literary rubble, to recreate what we have lived through, he has a perspective more sure, a vision more clear, than ours. What is mystery to us cannot be unraveled until a generation or two later, when all the accounts are in, including those locked up against contemporaries in hidden corners and in government or private vaults. Nor can we today have the hindsight of those who know what followed in what, to us, is still tomorrow. The British newspaper that reported the birth of a boy to Lord Randolph and Lady Churchill could hardly add that one of the great statesmen of the coming century had just been born. So it was again when an anonymous reporter wrote this dispatch from Sarajevo, on June 28, 1914. He could not tell the reader that the tragedy he was describing was the spark that would set fire to World War I:

Sarajevo, Bosnia, June 28 (By courtesy of the *Vienna Neue Freie Presse.*)—Archduke Francis Ferdinand, heir to the throne of Austria-Hungary, and his wife, the Duchess of Hohenberg, were shot and killed by a Bosnian student here today. The fatal shooting was the second attempt upon the lives of the couple during the day, and is believed to have been the result of a political conspiracy. . . .[5]

Nevertheless, *The New York Times* that night displayed the story, with photographs of the murdered royal couple, four columns wide on the front page. Thereby it gave readers of the day at least some notion of the import of the event.

Today the new tools of journalism—radio, still photographs, moving pictures, and television as recorded on tape—add color and verisimilitude to the printed word. Together they are the unrolling scroll of history. Children must still learn about Caesar or Lincoln from books. But now it is at least possible for them to see, in high school or college, films that reveal later figures on history's stage— for example Hitler or Stalin—much as they appeared to their contemporaries. The Vietnam war was reported on television in a way to give the home population, for the first time in history, some glimpse of the bestiality that war really is. Those films and tapes, too, are now part of the press pass to history that journalism offers.

What if there had been reporters carrying sound cameras at Salamis, at Vienna in 1529, or Yorktown, or Waterloo, or Gettysburg? Perhaps we could then know in more graphic detail than the written word allows what man's past was like.

Whatever the age, whatever the accompanying paraphernalia of civilization, it is always the journalism of the day that tells us most of what we know of it. Long before Gutenberg and his printing press there were reporters. Thucydides had lived through great times, those of Greece's apogee, in the fifth century B.C. Having known that day, writes Sir Alfred Zimmern, Thucydides desired to record it:

> . . . it was in midwinter, when the Long Walls had been dismantled and the Acropolis had housed a Spartan garrison, that he wrote his eulogy of the city in the form (what form could be more appropriate) of a speech over her noble dead. It is not, of course, the speech which Pericles delivered, or even, as the speaker hints, the kind of speech usually given on such occasions. There is too little in it about noble ancestors, and too much about the present day. But there is no reason to doubt that Thucydides had heard his hero speak, most probably more than once, over the city's fallen soldiers, and could recall in after years among his most sacred recollections, "the cadence of his voice, the movement of his hand," and the solemn hush of the vast audience, broken only by "the sobbing of some mother of the dead."

We may feel with confidence that he has given us, with the added color of his own experience, not merely the inner thought but much of the language of Pericles. So that here we can listen, as in all fine works of interpretation, to two great spirits at once; and when we have learnt to use our ears we can sometimes hear them both, Pericles' voice coming through, a little faint and thin after the lapse of the years, above the deep tones of the historian.[6]

No doubt it is out of scale to liken today's run-of-the-mill reporter to the Greek historian known through the ages. Yet they are alike in that they observe and write of events they have seen, and in so doing give us some understanding of the meaning of those events. This is not easy. Two historians who once put together a fascinating pageant of history, in the form of an anthology of news reports over nearly four centuries, thus analyze the task:

There is no simple formula for the reporter who must work under pressure and yet produce a story with staying power. But there are certain essentials it would be disastrous to ignore. To begin with, great reporting must reveal perception, disclose its creator to be the possessor of "the seeing eye and the hearing ear," capable of discerning the deeper implications in the event he has witnessed. Vespucci had this perception when he recognized that what he looked upon was a New World, a fact that Columbus died without ever realizing. Schumann had this kind of perception when he hailed Chopin's *Là ci darem* (which had been coolly received by the critics) with the words, "Hats off, gentlemen, a genius!"[7]

Perception or not, it is only through the reporter who was there that we can learn what it was like, whether somewhere back down the long hallways of time or across town yesterday. And just as today's photo-electronic reporters are storing up a treasure house of the sights and sounds of our own time, just so printed journalism has preserved for us more fragments of life than was possible when hand-written history, plus a few stones or artifacts, were all that could preserve the past. How else than through an early Fugger newsletter can we recapture some inkling of what life was like in

1587? Here is the closing passage of an account of the fate of the witch Walpurga Hausmännin, condemned to death for her lustful dalliance with the devil, and for the evil magic she had wrought through his powers:

> She was sentenced to be led, seated in a cart to which she is tied, to the place of execution, her body first to be torn five times with red-hot irons. The first time, outside the Town Hall, in the left breast and the right arm. The second time, at the lower gate, in the right breast. The third time, at the mill brook outside the hospital gate, in the left arm. The fourth time, at the place of execution, in the left hand. Considering that the condemned was a licensed and pledged midwife of the city of Dillingen for nineteen years and yet acted so vilely, her right hand, with which she did such knavish tricks, is to be cut off at the place of execution. After the burning her ashes are not to remain lying on the ground, but are to be carried to the nearest stream and dumped therein.[8]

So it is that journalism brings us sermons and circuses together. We sometimes forget, in our readiness to lap up the latest sensation, to see the fires and the looting and shooting in the riot, or the battle on the evening TV show, that, at its peak, reporting can have a function as pure, and a purpose as high, as that of the scientist or philosopher or theologian in search of the truth. The only thing that keeps this world of almost four billion confused, fearful, and hopeful individuals going is their knowledge of it and of one another. To the extent that this knowledge corresponds to the actual, tumultuous earth and its people it is possible to have government, peace, and prosperity. And journalism is the principal means of making the picture of the world in any citizen's head something more than a caricature of the real thing.

The reporter, whose business takes him to the cracks and seams and oozing sores of the social body, sees the little man in pain. He sees also the great of the earth, and the stuffed shirts who sometimes sit in the seats of the mighty. Often what he sees makes him cynical.

Yet he practices a calling that can be second to none in nobility. For the reporter who knows his job, especially if he has a boss who realizes that journalism is something more than a business, has it in his power to make the fresh winds of truth blow through the minds of men. It is in this that reporting has its greatness.

# 2

## Newspapers Shouldn't Play God

### Tell It as It Is

SHORTLY before Christmas, 1966, a precedent that had come down through the ages was broken. At that time of American escalation of the Vietnam war an American journalist, Harrison Salisbury of *The New York Times,* went to Hanoi to report the war from the enemy capital.

Not long thereafter Mr. Salisbury went to Russia. There a member of the Soviet intelligentsia told him that sending an American reporter to cover the other side of a war we were fighting had made some Russians "believe, for the first time, that the democracy of which you speak in America" is not propaganda but fact.[1]

Mr. Salisbury was the first of a lengthening line of American correspondents who reported at least fragments of the Vietnam war from behind the enemy lines. In part this was because in one sense this long, costly, and unsettling war wasn't a war at all. It hadn't even been declared. We weren't really fighting a war at all, in fact— just helping the good guys of Saigon contain the bad guys of communism. The confusion became the greater when President Nixon took over. With one hand he brought American ground forces

18

home, while with the other he escalated our air and naval war to an extent and ferocity from which even President Johnson had recoiled.

The fact that American and other western reporters were able to tell us some of the story of the war from Hanoi's side exacerbated our political divisions at home. The risk of transmitting enemy propaganda was obvious. Mr. Salisbury's early dispatches, citing Hanoi's unchecked casualty figures, did just that. Still, they punctured the official line that American bombing—heavier than that of World War II—caused few if any civilian casualties. By 1972 the White House and the Republican National Committee were attacking newspapers, wire services, and the networks as guilty of "bad journalism." They accused the media of serving the communist rather than the American cause.[2]

Despite such attacks the country as a whole took in stride this departure from war's accustomed one-side-only reporting. Here in truth was testimony to American faith in democracy. Whatever may have been our past attachment to Stephen Decatur's "my country right or wrong," in the modern day the public seemed to accept balance and accurate reporting as the greater good. Perhaps the reason is implicit in what Leon Daniel, UPI manager in Thailand, cabled when he was expelled from Bangkok:

> My opinion is that the Thais may have been angered by my frequent reports that the Thais fight in Laos for American money, which is hardly a military secret. The only story that I have ever been officially reprimanded for was one reporting the king's car broke down during the visit of Queen Elizabeth II.
>
> It is no secret that I have stepped on toes, both Thai and American, by my contention that Americans obliged to support a war ought to know more about it and to accomplish that newsmen must have access to bases. The U.S. maintains that since the bases are Thai-owned, the Thai government must grant permission for newsmen to get on them to cover the air war. I have maintained the U.S. could get me in if it didn't want to fight a war with nobody looking.[3]

*The New York Times,* again attacked for printing a dispatch from Haiphong, added in an editorial:

> The Administration . . . in effect . . . suggests that American newspapers have a duty to suppress all statements by the North Vietnamese Government as inherently false and to accept all statements by the United States Government as the beginning and end of truth.
>
> There are too many countries, in which that is precisely the definition of good journalism. Happily, the United States is not among them.[4]

Self-government is founded on the premise that the electorate must have access to all relevant information. Every organized society there ever was has had some form of journalism, to keep itself functioning. Democracy stakes its all on free journalism. Only if our citizens know the world they live in as it is can they cope with it.

That is why journalism must report what citizens or government or both may not want to hear, as well as what they do want to hear. Newspapers must not risk the blasphemy of playing God. They must not seek to lessen or to prevent some evil by withholding news of what has happened, or by playing it down or blowing it up. If they thus distort the truth, some evil worse than the one they seek to avoid may follow. The news is not a device to be turned on and off like a faucet, to achieve some end. It is an end in itself.

There are, of course, qualifications to this fundamental principle. Most newspapers will suppress news if there are convincing reasons indicating that, under the particular circumstances obtaining, the values of suppression promise to outweigh those of publication. Things like the names of youngsters in trouble with the law, or of victims of rape, are frequently withheld. The news of a kidnapping, or of arrangements for ransom, may be left unpublished when there is compelling reason to believe a life may be saved by so doing. When highjacking airlines became popular among political zealots and seekers after easy money the wire services, newspapers, and broadcasters were glad to cooperate with the airlines and pilots' associations, lest flamboyant or detailed reporting of one air piracy might inspire another. In the same spirit not only military preparations under censorship, but also sensitive peace-time negotiations between governments, may go unreported until they succeed or fail.

Nevertheless, the forces for suppression are more powerful by far than those for publication. Therefore the press must always push in a countervailing direction. If it does not, precious few others will.

For liberal democracies the need for information is acute. The tripartite government established by the American Constitution, for example, presupposes a citizenry well enough informed to make judgments on men and issues. Ex-President Madison said it well in a letter written in 1822 to the Kentucky politician William Taylor Barry. Though Madison was commenting on liberal appropriations made by the Kentucky legislature in support of public education, he is often quoted—and sometimes misquoted—by newspapermen, and with good reason:

> A popular Government, without popular information, or the means of acquiring it, is but a Prologue to a Farce or a Tragedy; or, perhaps both. Knowledge will forever govern ignorance: And a people who mean to be their own Governors, must arm themselves with the power which knowledge gives.[5]

### There Is No Bad News

In an election campaign in Connecticut Governor Chester Bowles, incumbent Democrat, was running for re-election. One October morning during that campaign I received at the *Hartford Courant,* in the same mail, two letters to the editor. One said, in part:

> It is certainly fortunate there are out-of-town newspapers for sale mornings in Hartford. The *Courant*—unlike its more cosmopolitan neighbors in New York City—conveniently withholds any news in any way detrimental to the Republican cause. . . .

The situation is deplorable and dangerous, when a newspaper, steeped in biased provincialism, deliberately withholds news of importance from the public.

A little further down in that morning's mail was an unsigned postcard that said:

Someone in your paper is getting paid to do Bowles publicity on your front page. Every time I get the paper our Chester is there grabbing headlines with speeches and statements and trips to Washington and other phony emergencies. And you're supposed to be a Republican paper. You had better wise up to what's going on in your office.

Here were two individuals who had looked at the same newspaper, at the same time, and had seen precisely opposite kinds of news in it. Both were examples of a basic fact of life—that the human being, looking out upon the infinite complexity of the world, cannot see it steadily and cannot see it whole. Instead, each of us sees the world as we want it to be, or have been indoctrinated to believe that it is or ought to be. We do this, moreover, without being aware that the picture of the world we carry about in our heads is not only vastly oversimplified, but actually distorted. We take it for granted that our private picture of the world is the truth, the whole truth, and nothing but the truth. This being so, we want passionately to have everyone else see the world as we do.

It is therefore natural that those among us who are in the seats of authority—whether in government, the church, business, labor, or anywhere else—find their task easier if everyone else sees the world, notably the affairs in their charge, as they themselves see them.

It has been an occupational disease of those in government to want to suppress information. They believe that by so doing they can achieve their aims without unnecessary complication or opposition. Suppression can keep them from being embarrassed if things go wrong. In this country, as in other political democracies, however, freedom of the press has long since been established, for the very purpose of preventing just this sort of suppression. There can be—or rather, there should be—no licensing or other censorship before publication. Because freedom of the press to say what it wants is the rule under the Constitution, government doesn't waste much time trying to suppress dissident voices. Instead it seeks to keep possible dissidents from finding out what is going on. It bottles up at the source whatever it wants to suppress.

In our private capacities we suffer a similar compulsion. We fear that harm will follow if other men are permitted to see anything besides what we think they ought to see. To us, any view other than our own is misguided.

This self-centered view of the world is the driving force behind all censorship, all the present and growing denial of the right to know. Curiously, it never occurs to us that we ourselves might suffer from exposure to the knowledge or doctrine, or book or picture, from which we seek to shield others. In our view the book may be obscene, the doctrine subversive. But even so, we are strong enough to withstand it. It is always the mass of our fellow men we want to save from what we ourselves are proof against.

When it comes to reporting the news we do not like it presented objectively, with the antiseptic and relentless cleanliness of science. Half a century in journalism has convinced me that most people's idea of objective news is news that is stained in the brilliant hues of their own prejudices.

So it was once when there was a proxy fight for control of the then New York, New Haven & Hartford Railroad. Jack Fitzgerald, financial writer for the *Hartford Courant,* went to New York to cover one round in the battle. In the process he had occasion to telephone Patrick B. McGinnis, the challenger who was seeking to win control of the railroad. As soon as Mr. McGinnis heard that a representative of the *Courant* was on the phone, he said, "I don't know whether I ought to talk to you." Asked why, he replied that it was because of "that editorial." Fitzgerald protested that he had nothing whatever to do with the editorial, which had expressed an

anti-McGinnis opinion. Mr. McGinnis went on: "I don't mind if
you fellows slant news stories, but you really shouldn't do that to
editorials."

This is, of course, a complete inversion of the standards of
American journalism. News stories are supposed to be fair and
square accounts of the facts, while editorials—analyses of significant or interesting or controversial facts—are expressions of opinion, and therefore subject to slanting.

To the layman, however, it hardly matters. Either news stories
or editorials can be offensive if they do not square with his own
view. No wonder, then, that even the best of newspapermen are
constantly belabored, from one side or the other, for what they
write. Here for example is an item published during a business re-
cession by the *Wall Street Journal*:

> Earl Burrows, secretary-manager of the Cleveland New Car Deal-
> ers Association, was asked how many members his organization
> had, how many dealers in his area had gone out of business re-
> cently, what his opinion of the outlook was. Declining to supply
> any kind of information on these subjects, he explained: "You've
> got no right to print pessimistic news. The only thing you should
> print is optimistic news."

Such a misunderstanding of what news is seems to be endemic
among laymen, and acute among those in authority. Each day
brings fresh examples. Consider this one from government:

> Washington, Nov. 13 (AP)—Secretary of Labor W. Willard
> Wirtz said today the nation's news media has ignored the prog-
> ress made by the Democratic administrations during the last six
> years and had concentrated, instead, on bad news.
> "I'm tired of it," said Mr. Wirtz, complaining there was too
> much emphasis on the Vietnam war, worry about inflation, Ne-
> gro riots, and slum problems.[6]

I recall an incident from the early days of the thaw that followed
the death of Stalin. One member of the first group of American
journalists to take advantage of the opportunity to tour Russia was

Rebecca Gross, editor of the *Lock Haven Express* in Pennsylvania. The articles she wrote about what she had seen with her own eyes included comments, both favorable and unfavorable, on life behind the Iron Curtain. She received protests from readers who had never been in Russia, but who assured her with heated conviction that her favorable comments were false. Even *Time* magazine, says Miss Gross, "implied we were a bunch of yokels who, obviously, had been taken in."[7]

It is true that an impressive case can be made by those who say newspapers should eliminate the negative and accentuate the positive. In 1969, when Vice President Agnew berated television and the press for their negative and—so he said—false interpretations of the news, he drew a popular acclaim so strong that it indicated something in our journalism was wrong. Perhaps what is wrong was summed up by James Keogh, a White House staff member who had been executive editor of *Time*:

> This is my concern: I fear that journalism is becoming more and more a destructive force. . . .
>
> Now I recognize that news is essentially negative—that bad news is news—and it has always been so. What bothers me is that in our revved-up era, bad news is traveling so fast and so far that the essentially-and-largely positive side of life is almost totally ignored.
>
> This negative tendency in reporting the news has been hurried and expanded by the growth of television as a major news medium. When news must be visual and must be crammed into an extremely limited amount of time, there hardly seems to be room for anything except the negative.
>
> I strongly suspect that the negative impact of news coverage in the past decade has done a great deal to build the mood of despair and helplessness that exists among too many people. . . . Every evening they watch these handsome, sincere young men on that screen telling them of terrible things, and they end up thinking that if everything is that bad, what's the use?[8]

One concludes that it is right to charge the press with taking the line of least resistance by publishing the bad news that the customers will always read, at the cost of overlooking good news that should also be reported. In fact various attempts have been made by individual newspapers and broadcasters to publish antidotes to what is normally considered newsworthy. In California there was even launched a syndicate, called For Goodness Sakes Inc., to distribute only good news. Papers using it reported a favorable reaction.[9] No doubt, then, it would be healthy if editors and broadcasters were to appoint good-news editors, whose mission it would be to dig out trends and events to right the balance.

Still, for the most part all such attempts miss the point: it is socially and politically necessary to have news reported completely and accurately, whether what is reported is good or bad. We seem unable to get it into our heads that, as the late Bernard Kilgore once put it, "There is no really bad news. It is misinformation and ignorance which cause trouble."[10]

## Act Now, Think Later

It is the newspaperman's common experience to be asked to withhold the name of a drunken driver who has had the misfortune to be picked up. I have been called in the middle of the night with such pleas. Or else the reporter is asked not to mention the fact that someone is getting a divorce or that some youth has gotten into trouble with the law. Always the request for suppression is backed by a hard-luck story, and often that hard-luck story is genuine. Publication will hurt the family, it will shame an innocent wife and children, it will spoil an otherwise promising career, it will prevent rehalibitation of a young man who without publication might be rehabilitated—and so on, through the whole catalogue of human misery.

The pattern is always the same. First, thoughtlessly, an evil is done. Then, inevitably, comes the request that the newspaper wipe out the evil, or at least lessen its effect, by concealing the fact that it has been done. People never seem to ask themselves beforehand what they are getting into. Instead they want the newspapers to protect them afterward, against the consequences of what they themselves have done.

Consider a story involving taste. Once a reporter for South Carolina's *Columbia State* dropped a story on the city desk. The item seemed routine—it was an account of the annual party and dance of a large amateur theatrical group. It said that members came in costumes representing the titles of popular songs. First prize, it reported, was won by Mrs. So-and-so, "who came as her very pregnant self, wearing a sign saying, 'I didn't know the gun was loaded.' "

The *State* printed the story as written. Should it have?

When I ask that question of non-newspaper friends they all reply in variations on a single theme. They contend that this was just a bit of incidental fun at a private party, and that, therefore, the paper had no business publishing it.

I disagree. No doubt it made little difference in the course of the city's affairs whether or not this particular fragment of the event was reported. Yet the principle involved is vital. A considerable number of the town's elite were there, and the meeting was important enough locally to get into the paper. For this reason it should be reported as it was, and not in a version bowdlerized for publication. To pick and choose what shall be published so as to achieve some desired effect—to try to play God—is to betray journalism's reason for being.

Particularly is this so when it comes to brushes with the law, including a first offense, such as a skylarking auto theft, or drunken driving. To the extent that truth is suppressed, society is insulated from reality. It may thereby be prevented from awareness of a growing evil that requires remedial action. And if people become aware that things can be kept out of the paper, they lose faith in that paper's credibility.

Above all, those with a personal stake in the news should never be permitted to judge whether or not it shall be published. It is, of course, true that there is a right to privacy. Indeed, one mark of civilized government is that it does not inquire too closely into the lives of its citizens. Privacy is important to society as a whole, especially as we develop ever more powerful engines of publicity. Inevitably, there is a clash between two values—the public's right to know, and the individual's right to privacy. Both are precious.

The individual's right to privacy was first isolated, and upheld as deserving protection in the law, almost a century ago, when the modern world began to cast its shadow over the simpler world of long ago. Louis D. Brandeis, later to became the famous Supreme Court justice, and Samuel B. Warren contributed an article entitled "The Right to Privacy" to the *Harvard Law Review*.[11] They noted, as one reason why the common law must be interpreted to envelop privacy, that "Instantaneous photographs and newspaper enterprise have invaded the sacred precincts of private and domestic life."

Since then much has happened, through court decisions and otherwise, to define and to buttress the right to privacy. For our purposes it is enough to note that even the original protagonists of the right recognized that private values must be measured against public need. They recognized that there were those "who, in varying degrees, have renounced their right to live their lives screened from public observation." Therefore, "The right to privacy does not prohibit any publication of matter which is of public or general interest." They explained:

> The general object in view is to protect the privacy of private life, and to whatever degree and in whatever connection a man's life has ceased to be private, before the publication under consideration has been made, to that extent the protection is to be withdrawn.[12]

Those suddenly thrust from obscurity into notoriety often resent the fact that details of their lives, once considered personal, should in flash be deemed public property. The President of the United States is a spectacular example. He and his family find themselves plopped into a goldfish bowl. Yesterday nobody paid much attention to them. Today the whole nation, perhaps even the world, is interested not only in the new President's policies but in the kind of necktie he wears, or his preference in cocktails. Just so the world's wife is interested in the First Lady's wardrobe and social graces, or lack of them.

A man who runs for public office invites this transformation. The king is always on exhibit. But unsought fortune or misfortune can make it happen to the least of us as well. Once long ago an unknown young airman named Charles A. Lindbergh was catapulted from nowhere into world fame by becoming the first to fly an airplane from New York to Paris, winning a $25,000 prize in the process. Without saturation press coverage of his achievement he would have remained a nobody. He owed the wealth and the fame that came to him to public knowledge of what he had done. Yet before long there developed a feud between him and the press. Later, in the heartache of the kidnap-murder of the Lindbergh baby, the relentless inquisitiveness of some of the press exceeded the bounds of decency. The whole affair led the Lindberghs to spend some years of voluntary exile in Britain.

Lord Dunsany, the Irish playwright of earlier years of this century, once spoofed the human crowd's preoccupation with inconsequential details about those who are precipitated into public notice. In a playlet called *Fame and the Poet,* he wrote of a young man who had srtuggled for years in the obscurity of his garret. One morning he awakes to find himself attended by an angelic figure representing Fame, who carries a trumpet. He is delighted that the world is finally paying attention to the truths he had sought to express. But he soon finds that the world doesn't care much about those truths. It is more fascinated by such things as the news, which Fame blares out to the cheering crowd outside, that he has eggs and bacon for breakfast.[13]

Irritating and distressing as it may sometimes be to get into the news, particularly if there is something unfavorable about it, there is a way we can protect ourselves against at least some of the hazards. A useful guide appeared in the 150th anniversary issue of a small New Hampshire daily, the *Keene Evening Sentinel*. Under the caption "Planning to be Arrested?" an editorial said:

> On the average of once a week the Sentinel is asked to keep something out of the paper. When it is pointed out that the request cannot be granted the attitude of the caller is that it's only pure cussedness on our part that prevents us from keeping his good name clear. . . .
>
> The news doesn't belong to us. It isn't our property to juggle. We don't make the news; we merely report it. If something you do or say is news we report it. . . . If something happens in Municipal Court we must print it. If we leave something out that should have been printed then we should leave out all cases. . . .
>
> We know of several persons who don't like us any more. Maybe they've stopped reading the Sentinel. We also know we've lost the advertising account of one local business because we printed something that we were requested to withhold. . . . Policy . . . calls for printing all the news that is news. Please remember this if you're planning to be arrested.

### Danger: Printing Press

The potentates and priests of old had little trouble controlling news. Legend tells us that a pharaoh could murder the messengers who brought him word of military disaster. A king could order a gossip's tongue cut off. As for a political troublemaker, he could be put out of circulation in a dungeon. Or, if like Sir Thomas More he was perversely stubborn about resisting the king's will, he could be executed.

The spread of printing after the middle of the fifteenth century changed all that. It made it possible for men to transmit to all the citizens fresh information and new insights, including the most subversive of ideas. In this way the ordinary man gradually came to see that it might be possible to change the world he lived in. Inevitably this undermined rule from above by church and state.

Indeed, the revolution that printing made inevitable destroyed the foundation upon which all previous ages had rested, and replaced it with a new and less stable one upon which our time still stands.

Those who were in positions of authority when printing began to nibble at their prerogatives feared that something like this might happen. It is not surprising, then, that an early American printer, William Nuthead, got into trouble. When he set up shop in Jamestown, Virginia, he issued nothing so dangerous as a newspaper. In the colonies that were the frontier of the western world it was a bit early for that. But Nuthead did undertake to print the acts of the colonial assembly. Authority, in the person of the Governor, was alarmed that the people should know in such precise detail what their rulers were up to. So he sent home to Britain for guidance. In due course Lord Howard of Effingham brought the king's word: No persons are to be permitted "to use any press for printing upon any occasion whatsoever."[14]

That was in 1684. Six years later, in Boston, on September 25, 1690, Benjamin Harris launched the first American newspaper. He called it *Publick Occurrences Both Forreign and Domestic.* Harris undertook to furnish his readers "once a moneth (or if any Glut of Occurrences happen, oftener) with an Account of such considerable things as have arrived unto our Notice." He also wanted to do something toward "the Curing, or at least the Charming of that Spirit of Lying, which prevails amongst us." Such a spirit inevitably prevails when a community must rely on gossip and rumor for an account of what has happened, instead of on some believable, easily available, permanent record, like a newspaper.

Unhappily, *Publick Occurrences* did not survive its first issue. It was squelched at once by the Governor and the Council of the colony, because it contained "Reflections of a very high nature: As also sundry doubtful and uncertain Reports." In a broadside proclaiming their "high Resentment and Disallowance," the Governor and Council "strictly" forbade anyone "for the future to Set forth any thing in Print without License first obtained from those that are or shall be appointed by the Government to grant the same." This was progress over Virginia. But it still reflected authority's determination to suppress any news it did not control.

So it was that when, in 1704, John Campbell started the first successful American newspaper, the Boston *News-Letter,* he was careful to get permission. He announced in large type, right under the title on the front page, that his sheet was "Published by Authority." Only so was it possible for his News-Letter to appear at all.

In the generations since then, the government's power to suppress or color the news to its taste before publication has, in theory at least, been abolished. The one exception is wartime. There has been a common assumption, at least until recently, that the national interest requires that any information relating to military plans and activities be hidden from the enemy.

Trouble arises from the inevitable temptation suffered by those in authority to stretch the censorship of military information to cover political matters as well. It is a short step from concealing the movement of troops or ships or weapons to concealing the fact that supplies are short, that policy is inadequate, or that a mistake has been made.

A further hazard, especially in this turbulent century, is the fact that the line between war and peace is often fuzzy. Gray areas like the cold war that followed World War II, and the wars that weren't wars in Korea and Vietnam, have given military and political authorities alike an itch to manipulate information before it goes, not only to the enemy, but also to the American people. There thus arose the practice that has been called managing the news.[15] This reflects, in modern dress, the identical desire to control the news before publication that the colonial governments had enforced against printers like Nuthead and Harris.

Even apart from the national security it has become more and more difficult, as government has grown ever more complex, to find out what government is doing. Accordingly newspapers, and news broadcasters and magazines, have taken up arms on behalf of what has come to be called freedom of information, or the public's right to know. They act out of self-interest. Yet they serve their readers as well, for the facts they seek to publish belong to the public and not to the government.

Recently there has come up a reverse twist in the perennial difficulty of getting news of what is happening out into the open. At stake in this new development is not the usual government suppression of news at its source. But it is suppression none the less, as an incident to government's attempt to enlist newsmen as unwilling aids in prosecuting crimes that its own agents have been unable to ferret out.

One manifestation is the shameful habit of some military authorities and crime-detection agencies of disguising their investigators as newsmen. Basic to the whole complex development is what a Twentieth Century Fund report, "Press Freedoms Under Pressure," said in 1972: "Questions of newsmen's access to news have so rarely been the subject of litigation that the very existence of a general First Amendment right of access remains in question." But events and conditions are moving toward a point at which such First Amendment rights need to be defined and affirmed.

The issue is by no means black and white. Still, it is disturbing that a 1972 Supreme Court decision in three cases has the indirect but nevertheless real effect of drying up information the public ought to have. At issue was the question whether three newsmen, the best known of them Earl Caldwell of *The New York Times,* had a First Amendment right to refuse to testify before a grand jury. Caldwell, for example, is a black who had published information obtained in confidence from unidentified Black Panthers. He obtained it only upon his promise not to reveal his sources. Nevertheless the state subpoenaed him to testify before a grand jury. He refused, on the ground that if he so much as went behind the grand jury's closed doors—even if he refused to testify there—no confidential source would trust him, or perhaps any reporter, in the future. Thus information important to the public would remain bottled up.

The Supreme Court majority denied this contention, holding that it is more important that newsmen testify upon command, just like all other citizens. In the background stands a changing world, thus summarized in Justice White's opinion for the majority:

> It is said that currently press subpoenas have multiplied, that mutual distrust and tension between press and officialdom have increased, that reporting styles have changed, and that there is now more need for confidential sources, particularly where the press seeks news about minority cultural and political groups or dissident organizations suspicious of the law and public officials.

Justice White brushed this argument aside as treacherous ground upon which to base a new First Amendment interpretation. Thus the issue remains to be reviewed in the future, because there can be little doubt that advancing social needs require protection under our historic principles. But that is for the future. First let us look back to the origins of the modern need to establish the public's right to know.

The drive for freedom of information had its origin in World War II. In 1945, before that war ended, the American Society of Newspaper Editors sent a three-man committee around the world in an attempt to persuade the world's governments that, when peace came again, they should break down barriers to the free flow of information across national borders. It was clear that these barriers had done much to bring on the wars of the past.[16]

By 1949 Basil L. Walters of the *Chicago Daily News,* at the time ASNE's Freedom of Information chairman, discovered that there were domestic as well as international iron curtains. He reported to his fellow editors:

> There is a growing tendency of some officials in some of the smallest governmental units, as well as the largest, to forget they are the stewards of the people and to act instead as though the taxpayers were their servants.[17]

Since then many a skirmish has been fought with officials who would keep from the public information about what they were doing in the public's name with the public's money. In 1958 the first federal freedom-of-information law was signed by President Eisenhower. The late Harold L. Cross, a dedicated lawyer acting on behalf of the American Society of Newspaper Editors, had discovered that when bureaucrats were challenged as to what legal right they had to keep the public's business secret, they scurried through the law books to come up with 5 U.S.C.A. 22. This was a statute dating back to 1789. It had simply established the new government's offices, in the course of which it had authorized regulations covering "the custody, use and preservation" of records and papers.[18] Therefore the 1958 law's one-sentence text read simply, "This section does not authorize withholding information from the public or limiting the availability of records to the public."

In 1967 a more formidable bill, which had been signed on July 4 the year before, went into effect. This federal public-records law sought to make all government documents and records available unless national security, invasion of personal privacy, or other overriding reasons, as specified in nine rather vague exceptions, permitted withholding them.[19] Nevertheless, the law represented progress. In the words of Attorney General Ramsey Clark, it established for the government these concerns:

> that disclosure be the general rule, not the exception;
> that all individuals have equal rights of access [to information];
> that the burden be on the government to justify the withholding of a document, not on the person who requests it;
> that individuals improperly denied access to documents have a right to seek injunctive relief in the courts [This was a notable change, because for the first time it put teeth into the right to know];
> that there be a change in government policy and attitude.[20]

It is a law precious to the continued health of self-government in a complex and confusing age. But government continues to flout it, and neither newspapers nor the public invoke it as often as they can and should.

In the 1950s and 1960s there was also a drive on the part of state journalistic groups to achieve, through state laws, public records and open meetings of bodies like town councils and school boards. Much remains to be done. What is at stake is well stated in the declaration of legislative intent of California's Brown Act:

> The people of this state do not yield their sovereignty to agencies which serve them. The people, in delegating authority, do not give their public servants the right to decide what is good for the people to know and what is not good for them to know. The people insist on remaining informed so that they may retain control over the instruments they have created.[21]

### Government's Right to Lie

The principle thus stated is incontrovertible. But trouble arises because government, the servant of the people, is also sovereign of the nation. It obviously cannot tell all as it goes along. Even President Wilson found out that the very first of his Fourteen Points, open covenants openly arrived at, could not be achieved in full. There must be room for private negotiation between governments, lest there be a public confrontation. For when national tempers are aroused, such a confrontation freezes the negotiators into positions from which they dare not retreat—as they must if they are to agree.

At the same time, there must be a limit, even in a time of war, to what a government may hide behind censorship. Its motives may be pure, and not colored by domestic political considerations. But if that government in its public pronouncements deceives the enemy, it at the same time deceives its own people. And all too often the enemy intelligence already knows what the home public does not.

In the early 1960s Arthur Sylvester, a former newspaperman

who had become Assistant Secretary of Defense for Public Affairs, asserted the right of government to lie. The issue had arisen in the wake of the Cuban missile crisis of 1962, when the world stood on the brink of nuclear incineration. Five years later, in a magazine article, Mr. Sylvester was still defending his thesis. As the Defense Department's spokesman, he wrote, he had held that the truth was indeed the indisputable requisite of a government information program. But, he added, he had also held

. . . that on occasions (such as the Cuban missile crisis) when the nation's security was at stake, the Government had the right, indeed the duty, to lie if necessary to mislead an enemy and protect the people it represented.

In explanation, Mr. Sylvester cited the fact that the crisis had arisen because aerial surveillance had provided irrefutable proof that Russia was installing nuclear missiles in Cuba. President Kennedy, interrupted while on a political tour, returned from Chicago to Washington under a covering announcement that he had a cold. Mr. Sylvester further quoted this Pentagon statement, which he had authorized a few days after the President's return:

A Pentagon spokesman denied tonight that any alert has been ordered or that any emergency military measures have been set in motion against Communist-ruled Cuba. Further, the spokesman said, the Pentagon has no information indicating the presence of offensive weapons in Cuba.[22]

The man who issued the release, Mr. Sylvester added, did not know that the second sentence at least was flatly untrue. But Mr. Sylvester knew, as of course did his superiors.

Those of us who lived through that week, when we wondered each day if we would be alive the next, are not likely to forget it. Still, could not the Pentagon release have said, accurately enough, that the anonymous, ignorant, Pentagon spokesman "had no information" about the offensive weapons in Cuba, thus saving the government itself from a lie?

In view of the stakes, perhaps it is a small point. Besides, it is not the world-shaking crises that make Americans question the candor, indeed, the simple honesty, of their government; rather it is the day-to-day conduct of business. And this has been notably so in the years since World War II.

Certainly, in the mid-1960s it was the seemingly deliberate shading of the truth, to present a picture of the Vietnam war that was more favorable than the facts justified, that helped to deepen the national doubt and frustration. All too common were statements like this one, made by another Assistant Secretary of Defense, Phil G. Goulding:

> The very suggestion that the government could conspire to withhold the news from people, and that the news media are so replete with irresponsibility that the people could be misled by a combination of deliberate government distortion and second-rate reportorial effort, is ludicrous. . . . I emphatically reject the allegation that the Department of Defense is not fulfilling its responsibilities to the American people.[23]

Maybe so. But it was possible for Wes Gallagher, general manager of the Associated Press, to bring together an array of quotes by Administration spokesmen and contrast them with known facts to show the opposite. These were statements designed to convince the American people, and the world, of the fact with which this chapter began, namely that the Administration was lying when it stated that, as the bombing of North Vietnam was gradually escalated, only military targets, and not civilians, were hit.

Secretary of Defense McNamara said that "The pilots were especially briefed to avoid civilian areas," and that "We have not hit Hanoi or Haiphong, we have hit oil-storage facilities." Vice President Humphrey said the bombing was carried out "so as to avoid civilian casualties." Senator Dirksen was "absolutely astounded at the real precision result." Nevertheless, Harrison Salisbury, and also the late William Baggs of the *Miami News,* both of whom were on the scene, found that civilian casualties had been heavy—

as is inevitable in any such bombing. Mr. Gallagher was able to conclude:

> How much different the picture would have been these past two years if the Administration had said the bombs were directed toward military targets but "inevitably some of them fell outside the area and probably caused civilian casualties." Such repeated statements would have been accurate, truthful, and believed. And Salisbury and Baggs' articles on the bombings would not have had the world impact that they did.[24]

Within a few months Roger Tatarian, Mr. Gallagher's opposite number in United Press International, was able to cite some UPI dispatches that tell a similar story. In abbreviated form, his account in the *UPI* Reporter (May 4, 1967) reads:

> January 23, 1967, from Saigon:
> The United States, barring a dramatic change in the direction of the war, will order the bombing of MIG jet bases in North Vietnam within the next few weeks, a highly placed source said today.
> He said the proposal, described as a "slight" escalation of the air war, awaits only final approval from President Johnson.
> "The war could be over in one month if we could hit what we consider the key military targets in North Vietnam," he added.

> January 24—Defense Secretary Robert McNamara, testifying before a Senate appropriations subcommittee, and referring specifically to the UPI dispatch of the day before:
> "Now I doubt very much that a high U.S. official made either one of those statements, and in any event, whether he did or didn't, both of them are absolutely wrong. Now this is the kind of incorrect and irresponsible press coverage that occasionally plagues us. . . ."

> April 24—UPI dispatch from Saigon:
> American planes today bombed Communist MIG interceptor bases in North Vietnam for the first time, U.S. spokesmen said. The U.S. Air Force jets hit bases near Hanoi.

Subsequently, the unauthorized publication of the Pentagon Papers in 1971 raised the question of government lying in more acute form. But, even without so glaring an example, it is difficult to escape the conclusion that, if a people is to find its way through an increasingly complex and interrelated world, it must have a government that does not lie.

## You Never Can Tell

There is a deeply moral reason why the press should seek continuously and relentlessly to pry out information and publish it, no matter who wants to stop it. For one can never tell in advance whether the results of publication will be good or bad. Two examples, one from private affairs and one from public affairs, indicate why.

One October night, in the years in which the hippie cult became part of the American scene, the eighteen-year-old daughter of a wealthy suburban family was found brutally beaten to death in the cellar of a New York tenement. Beside her body lay the equally bloodied corpse of a hippie youth with whom she had been associating.

The event shocked the nation because of the lurid light it turned on the hippie world, and on the fascination that somewhat sleazy world held for the children of the affluent. *The New York Times,* having first recorded the double murder in a standard news report, then set about reporting the event in depth. The resulting article was based on a detailed investigation of the young girl's life, both in her suburban home and in the hippie community. The account, which was later awarded a Pulitzer Prize, drew its strength from the juxtaposition of the two, for the separate versions of the identical circumstances made it plain that parents and daughter had lived in different worlds, each ignorant of the other.

To reveal this truth, however, required probing deeply into matters that, in normal circumstances, would have been private and personal. Inevitably, there were those who felt that it was as shameful as it was unnecessary for a newspaper to pry thus deeply, especially because in so doing it reopened private wounds. Laymen often charge that newspapers thus poke their noses into personal dirt simply to titillate their readers, the better to sell papers. This overlooks the fact that if the papers didn't sell, our basic supply of information about the world would be cut off. And if it were, it would be impossible for our system of self-government to function. But leaving that aside, consider only the difficulty of assessing in advance of publication the social value of this particular report.

It happened that the usual layman's resentment at journalistic probing into a family's grief was spelled out in a letter to another paper at about the same time. This paper, the weekly *Great Neck Record,* had published details about the life of another runaway, a fifteen-year-old girl. This, the letter-writer complained, was "irresponsible journalism designed to damage rather than clarify and enlighten." He went on:

> It is not relevant to discuss what motivated the child to leave home. . . . Why [does] a respected newspaper choose to go along and invade the privacy of a child and her very personal problem? . . . The press has done a great injustice to this family, who in the final analysis have to resolve their own conflicts together as a family unit. The newspapers cannot help them.[25]

Contrast this with another letter to the editor, written at about the same time, which appeared in *The New York Times.* This one, by another fifteen-year-old girl, was prompted by publication of the in-depth inquiry into the double life of the murdered girl:

> I was one of those kids who envied the hippies. I always wanted to try things like LSD, marijuana, pot, Methedrine and a lot of other things like that. I would always read about "the villagers" and agree with anything they said, no matter what it was. I hated Johnson because they hated Johnson, and his foreign policy because they hated his foreign policy.
>
> I started playing the guitar and sang folk songs because it was what "they" were doing. I started smoking because who ever heard of a "hippie" who didn't smoke? My friends and I would always sneak off to the Village without our parents' permission.

We went on peace demonstrations (without our parents knowing) and wore jeans and sweatshirts and walked around with guitars slung over our back. We wore our hair parted in the middle (even though it didn't look good on us) and walked around barefooted. . . .

[I] dreaded to come home to a house where nobody treated me as a human being, where I had no say in anything because I was a "child" and they were "adults," where I could not voice my opinion or contradict someone because it was "disrespectful." I dreamed of living [in the Village], with people who I liked and who wouldn't care what you did, or how you dressed, or how you looked. I could do what ever I wanted and nobody would ever mind or care.[26]

The young letter-writer went on to say that it had been the in-depth Times story of the murdered girl and her hippie friend that had started her thinking "about how this girl could have really made something of herself if she hadn't run away":

And then I thought of how I want to make something of myself. How I want to accomplish something and be something in life. And I thought of how the Village would ruin it all. I thought of how the drugs that I always wanted to try "for kicks" would have really ended it. I thought of how they were really an escape from reality, with no meaning at all.

And then I thought who really wants to escape from reality unless you have something to run away from. Unless you make something to run away from. Like I did.[27]

The fact that one youngster was brought to her senses by a report on the tragedy of another does not prove that publication is always right. But one cannot spend years in newspaper work without coming upon enough varied experiences of the kind to make an overpowering case for publication over suppression.

The same principle can be applied to larger matters: the Bay of Pigs invasion of Cuba, in April 1961. One can of course never re-run history, like an old movie with enough new scenes substituted to make possible a different ending. But it is likely that this disaster in the early days of the Kennedy administration would never have taken place had the newspapers pried and published. The record shows that at first the press was too lethargic, and then at the end too patriotic, to disclose what it had learned and thereby to forestall a tragic national mistake.

The story, which involved a considerable number of newspapers and magazines, is a fascinating one.[28] It had gradually begun to appear, through various isolated publications beginning with an editorial in the *Nation,* five months before the invasion, which said that the C.I.A. was recruiting dissident Cubans in Miami, and training them as guerrilla fighters at a secret base in Guatemala. In *A Thousand Days,* Arthur M. Schlesinger, Jr., tells how the threat of premature publication came to the White House in the form of proofs of a proposed *New Republic* article, called "Our Men in Miami":

> It was a careful, accurate and devastating account of C.I.A. activities among the refugees. . . . Obviously its publication in a responsible magazine would cause trouble, but could the Government properly ask an editor to suppress the truth? Defeated by the moral issue, I handed the article to the President, who instantly read it and expressed the hope that it could be stopped.[29]

The article was stopped, without further question—a patriotic act, wrote Mr. Schlesinger, that "left me oddly uncomfortable."

Soon thereafter, *The New York Times* received its own dispatch from Miami. This not only described the recruiting drive there, but reported that a landing in Cuba was imminent. Mr. Schlesinger continued:

> Turner Catledge, the managing editor, called James Reston, who was in his week-end retreat in Virginia, to ask his advice. Reston counseled against publication: either the story would alert Castro, in which case the *Times* would be responsible for casualties on the beach, or else the expedition would be canceled, in which case the *Times* would be responsible for grave interference with national policy. This was another patriotic act; but in retrospect I have wondered whether, if the press had behaved irresponsibly, it would not have spared the country a disaster.[30]

No doubt retrospect makes us all wonder whether publication would have been wiser than silence. But at the time there were few doubts in official quarters. Soon after the fiasco, President Kennedy addressed the annual convention of newspaper publishers in New York. He urged the newspapers "to re-examine their own responsibilities." It was not enough, he said, to ask of each event, "Is it news?" In the cold war, just as in a shooting war, one should also ask, "Is it in the interest of national security?"

Clifton Daniel of *The New York Times,* in his subsequent account of the affair, reported that soon thereafter, in a meeting with a few officials of the editors' and publishers' associations, Mr. Kennedy ran down a list of what he called premature disclosures of security information. His examples were drawn mainly from the *Times.* But, added Mr. Daniels:

> While he scolded the *New York Times,* the President said in an aside to Mr. Catledge, "If you had printed more about the operation you would have saved us from a colossal mistake."
>
> More than a year later, President Kennedy was still talking the same way. In a conversation with Orvil Dryfoos [then publisher of the *Times*] in the White House on Sept. 13, 1962, he said, "I wish you had run everything on Cuba. . . . I am just sorry you didn't tell it at the time."[31]

In October 1962, a year and a half after the Bay of Pigs, came the Cuban missile crisis. This time a more experienced President, and the same newspaper, once more withheld information. But there was a difference. For here the government was not plotting a clandestine adventure of dubious morality and little promise. It was seeking to pull the world back from the nuclear abyss. The motive for secrecy was to keep Premier Khrushchev from learning that Washington knew he was placing offensive missiles in Cuba, until such a time as President Kennedy could make a public announcement under conditions carefully contrived to avoid catastrophe. And this time it worked.

The issue of publishing vs. not publishing is one that can never be resolved. There are no absolutes here, any more than there are anywhere else. But the lesson to be learned is, once again, that the all-but-universal desire to suppress is usually wrong.

### Failure in the Fourth Estate

Whenever I tell non-newspaper friends that suppression is wrong, they come back with the charge that newspapers themselves do a fine job of suppressing whenever it suits them. They grant that government must not be allowed to manage the news, but they seem more concerned that newspapers themselves manage the news. As for the necessity of invading privacy in the public interest, they complain that the press picks and chooses whose privacy to invade.

There is truth in all these charges.

Take the press's prying into privacy. The layman is likely to say that the newspapers don't print everything, do they? When Mr. and Mrs. Nobody are divorced there is scant mention, unless there is something juicy about it. But when a prominent couple is divorced, they make the front page. All up and down the line newspapers select what to print, and what to display. If that isn't managing the news, what is it?

This point of view overlooks the nature of news. In over-simplified terms, news is simply a report about something that interests people. That's the way it is, and don't blame the newspapers if mankind is bored stiff with the fact that a clergyman has lived happily with his wife for forty years, but comes running all agog if he splits her head open with an ax. The first is not news; the second is. News values are made by the old Adam in us all, not by newspapers and not by what might be in Utopia.

Nevertheless, it remains true that some private doings are published, others are not.

As for digging out the truth about government, those who are themselves in government are likely to point out that the press doesn't always come up with the truth itself. After leaving the White House Theodore C. Sorensen, close adviser to President Kennedy, said just that in devastating terms. It had been part of his job there, he said, to get information by reading diplomatic and intelligence reports. But since returning to private life, he had a feeling of isolation from what was going on:

> In the White House I felt sorry for those who had to make judgments on the basis of the daily newspapers. There's a large difference between reading diplomatic cables and intelligence reports, and sitting in your living room reading the papers.[32]

That other Kennedy adviser already quoted earlier as a witness for the press, Arthur Schlesinger, Jr., had been even more severe in a 1962 appearance before the American Historical Association. After participating in important government decisions, he said, he could never "take the testimony of journalism in such matters seriously again." Their relation to reality, he added, "is often less than the shadows in Plato's cave."[33]

No doubt. But it is the experience of reporters, and perhaps of lawyers and historians as well, that eyewitnesses are notoriously fallible. In my early days I covered fires and other accidents, and I learned that those who have seen an event with their own eyes often give sharply conflicting versions of what happened. This is also true of those privileged to see important events from the inside. The famous experiment at the Congress of Psychology in Göttingen offers statistical evidence that trained observers are little better than Joe Doakes when it comes to reporting accurately what they themselves have seen.[34] And if there is journalistic criticism of what insiders in government or elsewhere have done, those insiders may paint their version of the truth in colors more favorable to their own probity and insight than the facts justify. Self-interest is ever ready to seduce them to the view that the newspapers have gotten things wrong again—and no doubt willfully.

To those of us who have spent our lives in journalism, this is a two-way street. The press is not always wrong, but it is not always

right, either. Newspapers are manned by human beings, and so
are no more perfect than any other human institution. This is the
more regrettable because of the sensitivity of their task. Theirs is
the only private business there is that has a special protection in
the Constitution, and that protection gives them a responsibility no
other private business has. Freedom of the press was not embedded
in the Constitution to make life easier or more profitable for newspapers and their owners, but to enable them to give the public
accurate information. In this way they often fail. Yet the press,
which likes to hold itself up as a crusading angel bearing the torch
of truth, is curiously blind when it comes to reporting its own sins.

The *Wall Street Journal,* which in recent decades has made itself a national institution by consistently doing the fearless searching and reporting all of us talk about, once devoted five columns
to an inquiry into the ethics of the press. The first few paragraphs
indicate the kind of thing the rest of the article documented, nam-
ing names, and citing chapter and verse:

> In Boston and Chicago, newspaper investigations into suspected
> hanky-panky suddenly are aborted. In one case, a subject of in-
> quiry turns out to be a stockholder of the paper and friend of the
> publisher. In the other, the investigation threatens to embarrass
> a politician who could help the paper in a building project.
>
> In California, a batch of small newspapers run editorials en-
> dorsing the Detroit position on auto safety. All are worded simi-
> larly. An incredible coincidence, this identity not only of opin-
> ion but of phrasing? Hardly, for all the articles are drawn from a
> single "canned" editorial emanating from an advertising agency
> in San Francisco.
>
> In Denver, the advertising staff of a big daily wrestles with an
> arithmetic problem. A big advertiser has been promised news
> stories and pictures amounting to 25% of the ad space it buys;
> the paper already has run hundreds of column inches of glowing
> prose but is still not close to the promised allotment of "news"
> and now is running out of nice things to say.
>
> All this hardly enhances the image of objectivity and fierce in-
> dependence the U.S. press tries so hard to project. Yet talks with

scores of reporters, editors, publishers, public-relations men and others reveal that practices endangering—and often subverting—newspaper integrity are more common than the man on the street might dream. Result: The buyer who expects a dime's worth of truth every time he picks up his paper often is short-changed.[35]

Few newspapermen needed the examples that followed to convince them of the substantial accuracy of this statement. Most of us have encountered plenty of examples in our own experience.

I recall an able reporter who became a public-relations man for the insurance industry, so that he might have a more generous income than that which reporting offered. When he left his paper, I chaffed him for having sold his soul. And it is true that many newspaper men turn down the bigger salaries they can often command elsewhere because, despite everything, they feel that journalism brings satisfactions no other career can offer. Even so, my young friend was able to make a persuasive case that, in plugging the insurance industry before the public, he was no more prostituting himself than he had on occasion as a reporter, by direction of his superiors.

A single example from the *Wall Street Journal's* chamber of horrors is enough to illustrate the kind of thing that happens. The *Boston Herald* boasted a Research Bureau whose purpose was to probe crime, corruption, and social injustice. Three of the Bureau's top-flight reporters began smelling around a complex stock transaction that had attracted the attention of both the Securities and Exchange Commission and the U.S. Attorney in New York. It seemed that one Joseph Linsey, a well-known Boston businessman and philanthropist, was involved in businesses that had underworld connections, including Cosa Nostra. But when the reporters set about digging for the truth, they were called off by their own publisher. One of them explained later:

> We certainly never accused Linsey of anything, nor did we have any evidence that he was involved in anything illegal. But we thought his apparent association with some rather well known mobster types made him worth looking into. Things became in-

tolerable when they wouldn't even let us interview someone about an important story. We resigned because it's clear the paper isn't interested in serving the public.[36]

Asked about this by the *Wall Street Journal,* the *Herald*'s publisher at that time, George E. Akerson, said that newspapers weren't the proper forum for such a discussion. The *Wall Street Journal*'s account went on:

Evidently other Boston papers seem to agree with this statement, one that probably would startle legions of journalists taught to believe that the newspaper *is* the natural forum for practically every matter of fact or opinion. Not a word about the happenings at the *Herald* has appeared in other Boston dailies—even though the Drew Pearson-Jack Anderson syndicated column has outlined them twice already. The *Boston Globe,* which ordinarily runs most Pearson-Anderson columns, printed neither of these.[37]

It is easy to stand outside and cast stones. The merger of Boston's morning *Herald* with its evening *Traveler* and its subsequent death from failing income is in itself a sign of the pressures that work against journalistic integrity. And it is the weakling, not the paper with healthy circulation and advertising income, that is pressed toward compromising the truth.

Those who bear the responsibility for keeping a newspaper going often point to the socio-economic changes that have strangled papers wholesale. Between 1910 and 1965 the nation's population grew from 92 million to 200 million, while, in the same period, the number of America's dailies shrank from 2600 to 1760. The threat of extinction is a powerful pressure, and it inclines a publisher not to offend his stockholders, or the business establishments upon which his paper is dependent for its life, or indeed anybody else. One can point to the disappearance of newspapers in New York, Chicago, Los Angeles, San Francisco, and many another city to make it plain that the going is not easy.

Nevertheless, one suspects that those newspapers that go under do so for other reasons than printing the truth. In fact, there is reason to believe that one of the things that keeps a paper alive

is the respect it earns from its community by being able, courageous, and honest. Journalism's moral failures arise primarily because, as the *Wall Street Journal* put it, "It is the publisher himself
who lays down news policies designed to aid one group or attack
another." And finally:

> . . . it seems apparent that a double standard exists at many
> papers; reporters and editors are expected to eschew practices
> that might compromise the paper's integrity, while the paper it-
> self, by actual policy or common practice, distorts the news to
> suit advertisers or literally hands over news space to them.[38]

One sees the same influences at work in ways less crass. Those
responsible for the success of a newspaper are tempted to let the
advertising and circulation revenue flow in, as it must now that most
of our dailies are monopolies, and not to disturb so comfortable a
situation by stirring up the animals.

Thus the public was no doubt served well enough by the fact
that in 1967 the United States Senate, for the sixth time in its history, censured one of its members, Thomas J. Dodd of Connecticut.
But that censure was prompted less by a fearless and independent
press than by others. One critic, Robert H. Yoakum of Lakeville,
Connecticut, who researched the lethargy of Senator Dodd's home
press was able to document two persuasive articles on the subject.[39]
But these articles, far from stimulating a *mea culpa* from the state
press, brought down an angry journalistic buzz. Looking on from
the outside, one concludes that Mr. Yoakum was right when he said:

> Dodd was not censured because of an alert or aggressive press
> any more than he was censured because of an honest or reformist
> Senate. He was censured because four of his employees removed
> and copied nearly 6000 papers from his files to document their
> charges against him, and because Drew Pearson and Jack Ander-
> son, to whom the copies were given, hammered away at him in
> more than 70 columns.[40]

After it was all over Mr. Yoakum was still able to say, "Not one
item in my stories has been refuted."[41]

There are eminently human reasons for a newspaper's reluctance to expose or denounce unsavory doings close to home. They were set forth by Jenkin Lloyd Jones of the *Tulsa Tribune,* in a talk on editorial writing to his colleagues in the American Society of Newspaper Editors:

> In 1860 Horace Greeley once sent these words of advice to a young friend of his about to start a newspaper:
>
> "Remember," he said, "that the subject of deepest interest to the average human being is himself. Next to that he is most concerned about his neighbors. Asia and [the] Tongo Islands stand a long way after these in his regard."
>
> I am sure Greeley wouldn't suggest, nor would I, that editors should hesitate to comment on affairs far afield. That is both a privilege and a duty. But unless the editor can convince his readers that his local ideas are worth reading he is not going to create much interest in his long-distance observations. . . .
>
> The tragic fact is that many an editorial writer can't hit a short-range target. He's hell on distance. And there's a lot that is comfortable about this distance. It takes guts to dig up the dirt on the sheriff, or to expose a utility racket, or to tangle with the governor. They all bite back, and you had better know your stuff.
>
> But you can pontificate about the situation in Afghanistan in perfect safety. You have no fanatic Afghans among your readers. Nobody knows any more about the subject than you do, and nobody gives a damn.[42]

This salty comment gave the trade the word Afghanistanism.

I think it fair to say that the morals of the American press today are higher than they have ever been. But there is still room for improvement in journalistic ethics. Besides, newspapers are often less aggressive than they used to be. Therefore every newspaper ought to nail to the wall of its newsroom, in a place where no eye can avoid it, this motto: *There Is No Sacred Cow in This Room but the Truth.* It would be a handy device for a reporter to point out to his editor, now and again, and still more for an editor to point out to his publisher.

Perhaps journalism can find a model in psychiatry. I recall an experience I had early in my days as an editor. Medical and lay authorities from Hartford Hospital came in one day to say that a prominent psychiatrist in town had killed himself by jumping out of a window. He had patients who were themselves unstable, and it might break the delicate strands that held them to sanity if the papers published the fact of his suicide. We had to report his death, no doubt, but could we not simply say he had died suddenly? They reinforced their appeal by telling me they had already obtained the agreement of the *Hartford Times,* the opposition paper, not to call it a suicide if the *Courant* did not.

I have since wondered whether they may have first said the same to the *Times,* whose press time was nearer, about us. Anyway, it happened that there were no front-office authorities, or other wiser heads, in the office that day. So, though puzzled and reluctant, I went along with the request. But I wonder. As I understand it, modern psychiatry itself is based on trying to get us all to face up to reality, no matter how unpleasant it may be. Why should society ask the press to protect it against an honest picture of itself, warts and all?

Certainly society's ills cannot be cured by newspapers. It can be done only by long-time action by the appropriate agency, whether government, the schools, the church, the family, or what not. We become angry if the water we drink or swim in, or the air we breathe, is polluted. Why should we feel differently about the information we get about the world we live in?

To suppress, to pull punches, for a moral end is just as immoral as to do it for an ignoble end. Once a paper bends to serve some cause other than the truth, it has crossed the line into Goebbels journalism, or Soviet journalism, where the news is considered to be not so much an honest and accurate report as a social weapon.

When you come right down to it, today's newspapers can take as their standard that of Benjamin Harris of *Publick Occurrences,* that very first American newspaper. Let them stick to giving "an

Account of such considerable Things as have arrived unto" their notice. Only today's newspaperman will tell you he cannot wait for events to arrive unto his notice. With all the pressures for suppression—whether from government, business, private citizens, or from within the press itself—the events no longer come to him. So let newspapermen go out to get as best they can the facts about "such considerable Things" as are happening, and then print them just as they are.

# 3

## *What Is News?*

### Blood, Broads, and Money

A YEAR and two summers out of college, in the fall of 1922, I found myself a student again. Accidentally put on the trail of newspaper work, a career that had never occurred to me, I had enrolled in Columbia's School of Journalism.

The idea soon took. Here was something to spend your life in. News made the world go round. People had to have it fresh every day. And while one could listen to that new plaything, radio, through earphones, it had not yet developed journalistic powers. The only way to get the news was from newspapers. And what was news? If you had a nose for it, you could smell it at once. The standard definition was the one probably originated by John B. Bogart, city editor of Charles A. Dana's *Sun,* in 1880: "When a dog bites a man, that's not news, but when a man bites a dog, that's news."

There is truth in the man-bites-dog formula. No matter what laymen may say newspapers should print, what the human animal will actually read by way of news does not stray far from the unusual, the shocking, and the spectacular. However you track down and measure people's reading habits—and there are now reasonably accurate methods—the statistics confirm what one of our Columbia professors, Walter B. Pitkin, taught: what interests people primarily, apart from their immediate personal and local concerns, is action, sex, and wealth. Or, as others put it, blood, broads, and money.

Perhaps one can best understand what news is today, and best evaluate the competence of the press in reporting it, by noting the changing standards according to which news was and is written. The first point to note is that for a century and more American newswriting has differed, at least until recently, from all other forms of writing.

The reporter's first commandment is to get the facts. And what are the facts? Why, the Four Ws: What, Where, When, and Why. Others score them as five, adding Who, which might just as well be lumped into What. Still others add a sixth element, How, which is implicit in the original four. No matter, it all comes down to the basic, verifiable, structure of any event or situation.

How is this essential information to be conveyed to the reader? By compressing the whole of it into an opening sentence, or brief paragraph. The idea is to hit the reader between the eyes, right in the beginning, with the sum total of what has happened. Consider this 1919 model:

> Oyster Bay, N.Y. Jan. 6 (AP)—Col. Theodore Roosevelt, twenty-sixth President of the United States, who died at his home on Sagamore Hill early today, will be laid to rest without pomp or ceremony in Young's memorial cemetery in this village Wednesday afternoon.

Compressing the essentials into a single sentence in this fashion may make a lump not easy to digest, but it does tell the news in a hurry.

Once the lead is out of the way, you construct the rest of your story in the shape of an inverted pyramid. The facts are given in descending order of importance, a process that gradually makes clear, through revealing detail or quotation or both, the outlines of what happened. The paragraphs, however, are separate building-blocks of information. They are assembled not to make a connected narrative, but according to their rank on the man-bites-dog scale. And so to the end, where the story simply dies of inanition.

The inverted pyramid was developed gradually, during the late nineteenth and early twentieth centuries. It was practical considerations that forced this sharp departure from normal literary construction, which puts the climax toward the end, instead of at the beginning. The emphasis on street sales of newspapers made for fast-moving leads, with big, punchy headlines over them. Then, too, as industrial society advanced, and increased advertising plus crowding events made the papers fatter, they found themselves serving up a richer smorgasbord of information than any single individual cared to digest. Not everyone was interested in all of the general news—local, national, and foreign—let alone specialties like sports, finance, society, entertainment, and all the rest. With so much to choose from, the reader needed a guide to what might interest him. The headline and Four-W lead did this for him. He could tell at once what an item was about, and skip it if he chose. Thus the formula was developed naturally, in response to need. It became a reliable, solid, and universal container into which to pour all shapes and sizes and kinds of news.

It had, and still has, a further practical advantage in the last-minute rush in the composing room, where the news, by now in columns of type, is put together. If an inverted-pyramid story is too long for the space available, the printer and the make-up editor can cut out a paragraph, or two or three, without sacrificing anything vital. The system works wonderfully, unless the truncated item now ends with "The Governor said:" or something of the kind. Finally, the building-block structure of the inverted pyramid makes it easy to insert in the original account, for later editions, added facts as they come in. This has to be done every day, especially on evening papers, in reporting events that are still unfolding.

All this does not change the fact, however, that the inverted-pyramid news story has become, for all but the biggest and most breathless news, an ideal device for inducing people not to read a newspaper. It also offers other difficulties. Stephen Leacock, the McGill University political scientist who was more widely known as a writer of humor, once lampooned the inverted pyramid in a magazine article purporting to analyze the difference between the British and the American press.[1] Though his spoof is somewhat musty after half a century, it still has validity. Mr. Leacock assumed similar happenings in the two countries, the suicide of a congressman and that of an M.P. His American version, which is only a slight caricature of the dangling clauses to which the Four-W lead is prone, begins as follows:

> Seated in his room at the Grand Hotel, with his carpet slippers on his feet and his body wrapped in a blue dressing gown with pink insertions, after writing a letter of farewell to his wife, and emptying a bottle of Scotch whisky, in which he exonerated her from all culpability in his death, Congressman Ahasuerus P. Tigg was found by night-watchman Henry T. Smith, while making his rounds as usual, with four bullets in his stomach.

In contrast, Mr. Leacock wrote, a first-class London paper would take a radically different tack:

> The heading would be "Home and General Intelligence." That is inserted so as to keep the reader soothed and quiet, and is no doubt thought better than the American heading "Bughouse Congressman Blows Out Brains in Hotel." After the heading "Home and General Intelligence," the English paper runs the subheading, "Incident at the Grand Hotel." The reader still doesn't know what happened; he isn't meant to. Then the article begins like this:
> "The Grand Hotel, which is situated at the corner of Millbank and Victoria Streets, was the scene last night of a distressing incident."

The reader, Mr. Leacock explains, wonders what it is all about as the story wanders on, explaining all sorts of irrelevant details, such as that the hotel probably dates from the Georgian period, is quiet and serves as meeting place for the Surbiton Harmonic Society, and so on, down to the details of its clientele and cuisine. Only much later does the tale close in on the news:

> "Among the more permanent of the guests of the hotel has been numbered, during the present Parliamentary session, Mr. Llewyllyn Ap Jones, M.P. for South Llanfydd. Mr. Jones apparently came to his room last night at about 10 p.m., and put on his carpet slippers and his blue dressing gown. He then seems to have gone to the cupboard and taken from it a whisky bottle, which, however, proved to be empty. The unhappy gentleman then apparently went to bed. . . ."
>
> At that point the American reader probably stops reading—thinking he has heard it all. The unhappy man found that the bottle was empty and went to bed—very natural; and the affair very properly called a "distressing incident," quite right. But the trained English reader would know that there was more to come and that the air of quiet was only assumed, and he would read on and on until at last the tragic interest heightened, the four shots were fired, with a good long pause after each for discussion of the path of the bullet through Mr. Ap Jones.

### The Charge of the Light Brigade

Useful as it is, the inverted-pyramid news story does not always do its job of transferring some fragment of the world outside into the head of the citizen. One reason is that its hind-end-foremost approach is dull, and it gets duller as one proceeds. It is often irritating as well, because of its inevitable repetitions. Hence over the years newspapermen have become increasingly dissatisfied with it. Surely, in a confusing world dominated by the evening TV news show, the newspaper should be capable of something more dynamic and meaningful. Many of us have agreed with Louis Lyons, former Curator of the Nieman Fellowships at Harvard, who recommended the formula of the Queen in Alice in Wonderland: "Begin at the beginning and go on to the end."

This is hardly a new idea, because this is where newswriting naturally began. Take the classic report on the battle of Balaklava, sent from the scene to the London *Times* by its correspondent in the Crimea, William Howard Russell.[2] This dispatch gave Britain first word of the action subsequently immortalized in Tennyson's "Charge of the Light Brigade." Reading Russell's account, one notes that some of Tennyson's lines were taken almost verbatim from it.

The battle in which someone blundered took place October 25, 1854. Russell's account, published in London November 13, was graphic. As he explained in it, he was standing on a hill that overlooked the battlefield, and he was able to witness the entire action as plainly "as the stage and those upon it are seen from the box of a theater."

Stephen Leacock's tale of the suicide of Mr. Ap Jones was evidently not far off as an example of British newswriting on the model inherited from Russell's day. Russell's real-life account also began in ominous quiet:

> Heights Before Sebastopol, October 25 [1854]—If the exhibition of the most brilliant valor, of the excess of courage, and of a daring which would have reflected luster on the best days of chivalry can afford full consolation for the disaster of today, we can have no reason to regret the melancholy loss which we sustained in a contest with a savage and barbarian enemy.

Note that while the dateline does give the When and Where, the lead itself merely hints at the What and Why. There is a vague warning of disaster, and that does arouse interest. After this opening paragraph, however, Russell backs off instead of telling what happened. His second paragraph reads:

> I shall proceed to describe, to the best of my power, what occurred under my own eyes, and to state the facts which I have heard from men whose veracity is unimpeachable, reserving to myself the exercise of the right of private judgement in making public and in suppressing the details of what occurred this memorable day.

Russell first sets the stage, describing in detail the vast scene, and the disposition of friendly and hostile troops upon it. It takes many a paragraph to get to the point at which action begins. But such preliminaries help the reader to grasp the enormity of the event that made all the world wonder, and to see, as in a kind of verbal TV, the unfolding action that brought disaster to the six hundred.

Once the events of the day begin to march across the mind's eye, tension gradually mounts until it is hardly possible to stop reading. The "thin red streak topped with a line of steel" makes its fore-doomed attack. We ourselves ride into the Valley of Death, until at length we can see the sabers swing in the dust amid the Russian guns. And so through the grisly retreat, as some, but not, not the six hundred, ride back: "At 11:35 not a British soldier, except the dead and dying, was left in front of those bloody Muscovite guns." Russell ends with a basic fact that belongs in or close to the lead in the inverted-pyramid style: of the 607 Dragoons, Hussars, and Lancers who attacked as ordered, theirs not to reason why, only 198 came back.

The account not only makes more gripping reading than would an inverted-pyramid account, but in the end it gives the reader a sharper comprehension of what happened. It is a graphic specimen of the kind of reporting that Russell sent back to a *Times* then at the height of its authority. It was reporting that brought Florence Nightingale and the beginnings of modern medical care to the battlefield, and led to the overturn of the Aberdeen government that had presided over the tragedy.[3] Whatever the failures of British arms and political leadership, this was journalism at its finest.

### From Propagandist to Reporter

In the two generations stretching from the Crimean War to World War I, narrative reporting like Russell's was gradually elbowed out of American journalism by the inverted pyramid. But if this stylized kind of newswriting lost something in color and dramatic impact, it had an advantage in addition to those already noted. It became one of several natural forces that gradually established the standard of impartial or objective news.

In colonial days, to be sure, American printer-journalists were objective enough by the standards of the time. They did little but copy one another's accounts "of such considerable things as have arrived unto our Notice." The news thus cribbed from papers imported from Europe and the other colonies might be late, but it was the only way early Americans could keep up with Europe's wars and dynastic changes, or the major developments in other colonies scattered along the Atlantic seaboard and in the West Indies.

The Revolution changed such easygoing habits. It did so because pamphleteers like Thomas Paine and Samuel Adams found that news, judiciously slanted, can serve as a weapon. When, for example, the Redcoats took control of Boston, the patriot-printer Isaiah Thomas fled to Worcester with his *Massachusetts Spy*. In it there soon appeared what remains today a recognizable account of the ride of Paul Revere and his fellow scouts, and of the shot heard 'round the world. But what there was in the way of fact was all but obscured by incitement to rebellion. The news report began with this exhortation:

Americans! Forever bear in mind the BATTLE OF LEXING-TON;—where British troops, unmolested and unprovoked, wantonly, and in a most inhuman manner fired upon and killed a number of our countrymen, then robbed them of their provisions, ransacked, plundered and burnt their houses! Nor could the tears of defenceless women, some of whom were in the pains of child-birth, the cries of helpless babes, nor the prayers of old age, confined to beds of sickness, appease their thirst for blood!—or divert them from the DESIGNS of MURDER and ROBBERY![4]

The power of this technique was not lost upon the politicians of the early decades of the Republic. The result was that, by the time the nineteenth century began, reporting was little more than partisan propaganda. Consider this bit from the *Connecticut* (now Hartford) *Courant* of 1800, written by a frequent contributor, a political polemicist who signed himself Burleigh:

> Neighbors will become the enemies of neighbors, brother of brother, fathers of their sons, and sons of their fathers. Murder, robbery, rape, adultery, and incest, will openly be taught and practised, the air will be rent with the cries of distress, the soil soaked with blood, and the nation black with crimes.[5]

What threatened so horrendous a fate was the impending election of Thomas Jefferson as President. Small wonder that in 1828 ex-President James Madison, looking back upon his own experience with non-objective news while in office, should write:

> Could it be so arranged that every newspaper, when printed on one side, should be handed over to the press of an adversary, to be printed on the other, thus presenting to every reader both sides of every question, truth would always have a fair chance.[6]

The late historian of American journalism, Frank Luther Mott, called the first third of the nineteenth century the dark age of American journalism. This was the period, following Jefferson's breaking of Federalist rule, in which partisan politics began to assume its modern habits and traditions. It was about this time, too, that journalism began its long and still incomplete pilgrimage from news as partisan propaganda to news that is objective.

One contributing factor was the coming of the penny press, of which the New York *Sun,* founded in 1833, was the first to succeed. The penny press was invented to serve up news to the newly literate lower classes, taught to read by the spread of popular education. Here was a market for a new kind of news, news told for its own sake rather than for its political or economic message. Penny-press news was made up largely of items that interested to the lowest common denominator in the population, rather than the mercantile and political fare that appeared in the established six-penny papers.

Thus began the habit, still with us today, of regarding trivial happenings as news. Pioneers such as Benjamin H. Day and James Gordon Bennett began gathering tidbits in the police courts and firehouses, in hotels and public institutions. They searched the highways and byways of society for anything bizarre or spectacular. Tinsel though much of this news was, it had the merit of being reported without regard for any value it might have as partisan propaganda.

A little later came the early and often short-lived press associations, central agencies for gathering news and distributing it to individual papers, which did not reach their modern stature until the turn of the century. The economy of shared expenses forced individual publishers to pool their efforts. In New York, where the practice began, a single boat would go down the bay to meet incoming vessels, each with its bundle of newspapers from abroad. This was obviously less costly than having each proprietor send his own men down in a race that, nevertheless, had its competitive advantages.

As the country expanded, covering it became too vast and costly for all but a few unusually successful papers. The telegraph made it possible to gather political and other news from afar, but it was a luxury. Here was another reason for a press association that could collect the news once, and then distribute it equally to subscribing journals. But because these papers came in all partisan hues, the press-association reporter was forced to confine himself to the facts. If, for example, he filed an account of what the prairie politician Abraham Lincoln had said on the stump in Illinois last night, he had to be content with boiling down the speech itself. He might add the verifiable facts about setting and circumstances. But he could not embroider his account in partisan colors if he was to please all the politically variegated newspaper proprietors who were his clients.

In the same way, in the decades after the Civil War, there began to be occasion to gather news originating in the growing industries of the country. Here, to be sure, there might be temptation to slant the news in favor of the robber barons of the day, or toward labor. Still, some of the country's growing pains were reported for their own sake, rather than for possible partisan impact.

Two other factors also pushed American journalism toward objectivity. One was the decline of sensationalism, which made possible a more accurate and meaningful presentation of the news than that of the fabled midwesterner Wilbur F. Storey, whose aim was "To raise hell and sell newspapers."

Since that time television and radio, for all their sins, have been largely responsible for the declining emphasis on gee-whizz news in print. Because we normally get first word of what has happened from the car or kitchen radio, or from the evening news show, the street sales that used to put a premium on big headlines and lurid exaggeration have shrunk to insignificance. By the late 1960s, the American Newspaper Publishers Association was saying:

> The old charge that newspapers indulge in sensationalism to increase circulation received a strong refutation from a recent Associated Press survey on coverage of the Candace-Mossler-Melvin Powers trial in Miami. Of 30 morning and 30 afternoon papers surveyed on a day picked at random—most of them selected because they have large editions, large newsholes and a wide variety of news services—21 didn't even carry the story. Of the 39 that did carry it, only seven put it on page one.
>
> The charge of sensationalism to sell newspapers is frequently a throwback to the days of competitive newspaper selling on street-corners. Today circulation studies show that most newspaper circulation is home delivered. Therefore features in that day's editions could have little effect on circulation.[7]

Home-delivery readers of today may be just as avid for stories about blood, broads, and money as the newsstand patrons of the 1920s. But repeated statistical surveys reveal a decline in newspaper sensationalism that is probably greater than most critics of newspapers have noticed.

The remaining sobering factor in presentation of the news has been the penetration of education down through successive layers of the population. I did not realize, when I was graduated from East Orange High School in 1917, that I was one of a favored few. There were, as I recall it, 2000 students in that four-year school, which made it seem obvious to me that everyone went to high school. But in fact we were a privileged minority. Through the years, Americans have enjoyed a rising level of popular education, and still higher levels are to come. One Census Bureau forecast says that by 1975 only 11.1 per cent of our people will quit school after the first eight years. Another 36.7 per cent will finish high school, and 12.5 per cent will complete four or more years of college. The others will fall somewhere between: for example, another 10.4 per cent will have from one to three years of college before calling it quits. The newspaperman no longer has to write for the man with the mind of a twelve-year-old, who was supposed to be the universal reader when I became a reporter. This does not necessarily mean that news is presented objectively. But, like the decline of the need for sensationalism, it helps.

In Europe, journalism has had a different history. In the first place, European newspapers clung longer than ours to partisan news. The death of a prominent man, a political speech, a change of government, or whatever, is often still announced in a few press-association words. Then an expert in the field concerned, rather than as with us a reporter under orders to be objective, explains the significance of what has happened. And no one takes it amiss that he tints his analysis in colors that match his paper's outlook.

Then too the fact that Europe's nation-states are smaller by far than the United States, and live elbow-to-elbow on a crowded continent, has had its effect on its journalism. National rivalries pushed Europe's various national news agencies into being little more than house organs for the home government. All of them, however, were dominated by Britain's Reuters, France's Havas, and Germany's Wolff. These were all-powerful news monopolies that had divided the world outside North America among themselves, with Reuters on top. The empire-slanted news that came out of this system bore its share of responsibility for World War I. At Versailles in 1919 a few far-seeing journalists urged a free flow of news across national boundaries, so that historic enemies, Frenchmen and Germans, for example, might see a dispute between their two governments in terms of the same set of facts. But the leaders at the peace conference paid little heed.

Despite considerable improvement since then, especially after World War II, we are still short of the ideal of newspapers that give citizens on both sides of a national boundary the same view of a potentially explosive event. Totalitarian states make a virtue of controlling the news to give their nationals only a desired picture. The rest of us, even though we have a tradition of objective news, find it hard to escape an outlook on the world that reflects our own national interests.

Europe's nineteenth-century habit of imperially monopolized news prompted the late Kent Cooper, general manager of the Associated Press, to say in 1942 that the ideal of truthful and unbiased news was "the finest moral concept ever developed in America and given the world."[8] It may not have been quite that. The standard of factual news, told for its own sake, was achieved independently by a handful of Europe's better papers before World War II. Nevertheless, the concept of news as something precious for its own sake, to be reported as accurately and honestly as can be, remains journalism's highest goal. To the extent that we have it, the press becomes a genuine Fourth Estate, serving impartially all the other estates that make up the body politic.

### But What Does It Mean?

Those of us who went into journalism in the first half of the century had the standard of objective news drilled into us. We found it good. Here was an infallible compass, pointing the way to the truth. Just the facts, Ma'am, just the facts. Anything beyond that might stray into opinion, and that must be left to the editorial page.

Alas, as the years went by it turned out that the compass needle of objectivity sometimes went astray. For to confine the reporter to that part of the iceberg above the surface—that is, to those facts about an event that are verifiable—risks leaving out supplemental matter that may be essential to an understanding of the whole. To be unbiased, the news writer must cling to the rules of objectivity. But doing that may keep him from reporting what happened in perspective. Therefore he is left with an incomplete report. And how can that be genuinely objective?

The distinction between surface news and its background was first made long ago, in the social ferment let loose by that cataclysm on which the twentieth century is founded, World War I. Newspapermen became concerned because the old man-bites-dog concept of news failed to give the public the essential meaning and significance of what was going on in an increasingly complex world.

The answer was interpretive news. In a book published in 1937 I made what was then a fresh observation:

> To report [in times past] . . . meant simply to recite the facts. Anyone could understand them without help from Walter Lippmann. . . .
>
> Nowadays, what with the WPA, sit-down strikes, fascism, dust storms, wars that are not wars, the A plus B theorem, silver nationalization, the Comité des Forges, import quotas, Father Coughlin, cosmic rays, nonintervention agreements to screen intervention, and unemployment, news is different. There must be interpretation.[9]

A convenient birth year for interpretation might be 1923, when *Time* magazine was founded. The thesis of its youthful inventors, Briton Hadden and Henry R. Luce, was that the bare bones of the news, as reported in scattered snippits by even the best of the dailies, were often meaningless. It was necessary to organize the news into a coherent pattern that gave it meaning and color. Because this diagnosis was sound, newsmagazines have long since become part of the journalistic establishment. In the early years, daily newspapermen found *Time* suspect, because it lived off the sweat of their brows, simply pulling together in rewritten condensation the scattered items they had labored to dig out.

Long since, of course, newsmagazines acquired their own reporters, their own bureaus and stringers around the country and the world. And they now search out news of their own that often makes stories for the daily press, instead of the other way around.

Moreover, *Time,* for one, soon developed a style of writing that, despite the odd and irritating quirks that were long its trademark, often presented a more graphic and colorful picture of an event than that produced by the ritualized inverted pyramid technique. One trick was to give the reader a picture-in-words of the event described, again a kind of verbal TV. This is, of course, but an extension of the practice known to good writers through the ages, that of incarnating whatever is written in such concrete and specific detail that it appears to have physical reality in the reader's mind. Was it not Chekhov who told an aspiring writer that, if he were describing a housewife tossing a coin out of the window to an organ grinder in the street below, "Let me see and hear that penny *hopping* and *chinking* on the sidewalk"?

There is more to interpretation, however, than style of writing and interval of publication. The better dailies, and the wire services, have long since learned both. They are increasingly turning from the one-day-wonder, bing-bang-biff stories of the old days. They still distribute, as they must, the factual record of each day's events but they also detach reporters, or even teams of them, from the daily beat to produce carefully researched copy resembling a magazine article more than a spot-news item.

Even so, one may question whether this development has gone far enough. Newspapers still tend to wait for a riot or some other social explosion to happen before reporting it. The modern world requires that the historic journalistic function be expanded into constant probing into the dark corners of society, to discover and report conditions that may eventually erupt in some hard-news disaster.

The *Wall Street Journal* remains a continuing example of what all dailies can do. Before World War II the Journal was a specialized, daily trade paper of 40,000 circulation. It was useful to the financial community, but boring to others. Today, more than a million copies are distributed nationally, in four regional editions, printed simultaneously in seven plants around the country. Interpretive reporting, as pioneered chiefly by the late Bernard Kilgore, caused the transformation.

The change, which applies to everything in the paper except its statistical tables, is most readily visible in the magazine-type, in-depth stories on the front page. They are readable accounts of something interesting and significant. But again, there is more to it than style:

> One of the chief changes in the *Journal* was the broadening of its concept of what constitutes "business" news, or, rather, what constitutes news of importance or interest to its readers. In the *Journal's* view, business news embraces everything that somehow relates to making a living. And *Journal* coverage of such news is shaped by a belief that to understand or explain business, it's necessary to look at what people are doing, thinking, and feeling about matters that are seemingly remote from "business," but that influence it directly.[10]

Not least attractive to readers is the fact that the *Journal's* management is bolder than most about stepping on toes that ought to be stepped on. A free press should poke courageously into hidden places, so that the citizen may see the world as it is, skulduggery and all, and demand remedial action when and where it is indicated. Yet all too many of our newspaper owners and publishers and editors pull their staff's punches—either directly or, more likely, simply because the staff members know what is expected of them. This despite the example of the *Wall Street Journal's* spectacular commercial success, one reason for which is its pride in being "above all independent when reporting any aspect of the business community" it serves.[11] This enables it to tell the news as it is, rather than as the paper's bosses or prominent customers might wish it to be. Besides:

> As other newspapers have found, readers and news sources soon recognize a paper's willingness to probe sensitive story subjects, and this knowledge in itself brings forth tips that lead to still more exposés.[12]

One result is that the small businessman or housewife who starts reading the *Journal* to keep an eye on investments may remain a fascinated general reader. And this may cost some standard newspaper a subscription.

A long chain of experiences brought about the transition in American newswriting from Four-W accounts of surface events to the fully rounded reports that are the best of today's journalism. One came in 1924, when thoughtful observers were struck by a lurid drama whose aftermath almost accidentally revealed the inadequacy of reporting merely the spectacular in the passing show of events. At the time the New York press found colorful fare in tales out of the Prohibition-and-gangster era. One such real-life whodunit ran from January to April, as the Bobbed-Haired Bandit, as the headlines called her, struck again and again in a series of Brooklyn and Bronx holdups. In due course, the young gun moll who had terrorized the city was caught. When she was sentenced, the papers had handed to them a probation officer's carefully researched, factual report on the entire life of the ex-bandit. It showed that this supposedly hard-bitten female, Celia Cooney, was nothing but a frightened child, a bit of human flotsam condemned from birth never to have a chance in life. The facts, as dug out by someone other than a reporter, and illumined by a brilliant editorial in *The World* by Walter Lippmann, were devastating in revealing the reality hidden under the surface of crime, and the failure of society in coming to grips with that reality. These facts were equally devastating in revealing how much that was both fascinating and important the papers were missing.

This experience, and others like it, prompted newspapermen to speak increasingly of the need to get the news behind the news. They found multiplying examples of that need in the confusing social, economic, and political aftermath of both world wars. But it was not until the early 1950s that the nation experienced a trauma that left no doubt whatever that surface news is not enough.

Senator Joseph McCarthy of Wisconsin, emerging suddenly from political obscurity, spread a miasma of fear and suspicion over the land by abusing the standard of objective news. He had found, almost by accident, that a widespread if irrational fear of communism, endemic in those days and still palpable today, was loaded with political pay dirt.

The papers, clinging to their painfully acquired rule that opinion must not creep into the news, seemed unable to cope with this new and treacherous kind of story. If McCarthy charged that there were eighty-nine card-carrying Communists in the State Department, the wire services reported it and the papers printed it. No reporter or editor let his suspicion that McCarthy was lying deflect him from his obligation to report factually what a United States senator had said.

Although conscientious newspapermen were distressed at McCarthy's clever misuse of their own ideals, nobody did much about it. Palmer Hoyt, then editor and publisher of the *Denver Post,* did, however, issue a memorandum to the managing editor and staff, specifying techniques that might lessen the harm done by McCarthy's pyrotechnics without relapsing into counter-propaganda. His key point was this: "News stories and headlines can be presented in such a manner that the reading public will be able to measure the real worth or value and the true meaning of the stories." Ways and means ranged from adding to the stories factual reminders that the senator's past attacks had eventually been proved false, to giving a more modest display in headline and position than such spectacular charges might normally receive. In general, "The *Post* will not consider any story complete and covered until rebuttal and answering statements are printed."[13]

The late Elmer Davis, a newspaperman and radio commentator who was more sensitive than most to the damage being done, denounced what the newspapers were doing as deadpan reporting. Still, the remedy was elusive. A paper, Mr. Davis noted, could hardly precede its front-page account of the senator's latest blast with some such notation as, "For the truth about what you read below, see tomorrow's editorial page."

Two values, each precious, are involved in what remains a continuing difficulty. One is the necessity of reporting factually what happens, without prejudicing the reader by indicating what you think about the event, or think ought to be done about it. The other is that a newspaper should not let a mountebank, or a President of the United States for that matter, get away with putting over an untruth simply by issuing it from an official source rated as newsworthy. Even Soviet Russia learned to take advantage of our journalistic mores in just this way.

So the reporter and the editor must learn to interpret. Again to quote Mr. Davis:

> The good newspaper, the good news broadcaster, must walk a tightrope between two great gulfs—on one side the false objectivity that takes everything at face value and lets the public be imposed on by the charlatan with the most brazen front; on the other, the "interpretive" reporting which fails to draw the line between objective and subjective, between a reasonably well-established fact and what the reporter or editor wishes were the fact. To say that is easy; to do it is hard.[14]

It turned out to be even harder for television, the new medium of information, to walk the tightrope. During the Vietnam years Eric Sevareid cited an example:

> Buddhists staged some riots in Saigon and Da Nang. The TV cameras wheeled up. They focus, of course, on whatever is more

dramatically in motion. They act like a flashlight beam in the darkness. Everything else around, however vital to the full story, is lost in the darkness and ceases to exist. The pictures could not show you that a block away from the Saigon riots the populace was shopping, chatting, sitting in restaurants in total normalcy. The riots involved a tiny proportion of the people in either city; yet the effect of the pictures in this country, including in the Congress, was explosive. People here thought Vietnam was tearing itself apart, that civil war was raging. Nothing of the sort was happening.[15]

Yet television is not the only medium to stumble in its attempts to report the truth. The inherent difficulty in all journalism is that one must report, in terms of solid blocks of Four-W fact, the subtle, fluid, dynamism in man's affairs, the nuances of things felt rather than seen. Again from Vietnam, one wire-service reporter, Mike Feinsilber of UPI, wrote a single sentence that encapsulates the problem: "I was in Saigon for seven months, long enough to reinforce all my dovish tendencies and to learn how difficult it is to report the surrealities in rational terms."[16]

Reporting Vietnam caused many a journalist to search his soul. Michael J. Arlen of *The New Yorker* wrote a long analysis of what was wrong. His point was summed up in the headline on his article: "THE AIR: Television and the Press in Vietnam; or, Yes, I Can Hear You Very Well—Just What Was It You Were Saying?"[17] Arlen's complaint is not easy to summarize. Its burden is reflected in his comment that just about the first thing anyone asks a returning visitor is, "What's *really* going on there?" He charged that the press failed to communicate the reality of the Vietnam war, and that this was not an isolated phenomenon:

It isn't, perhaps, that the world is deeper in chaos than it used to be but that the element of chaos which has always been there in life, which really *is* life (after all, there were minority groups and emerging nations in the eleventh century, too), is now coming more and more out from under wraps. . . .

We have this great arrogance about communications. We've

given up much of our capacity for first-hand experience—certainly for first-hand sensory experience—cheerfully peering out at
the world through lenses, electronic tubes, photographs, lines of
type. And we've also, at a time when the ability of a people to
order and enhance its existence depends increasingly on its ability to know what is really going on (no more milling around in
front of Whitehall to find out what really gives with Kitchener
in the Sudan)—we've also given up the ideal of knowing first
hand about ourselves and the world in favor of receiving sometimes arbitrary and often nearly stenographic reports through a
machine system we call "communications," which for the most
part neither recognizes the element of chaos in the world for
what it is nor is able to make contact with it except on a single
narrow-beam wave-length.[18]

The trouble was, Mr. Arlen added, that newspapers and TV
tried to cover the war the way they covered fast-breaking news at
home, despite the fact that "Vietnam isn't a fast-breaking news
event most of the time." Reporters, conditioned by their trade to
"reorder actuality into isolated hard-news incidents," seemed somehow to miss the essence of it all. The result is that the tumultuous
reality of life emerges in *The New York Times* as "somehow ordered and dignified."

Or, as one *Times* alumnus put it, journalistic truth is "a truth
that is limited but verifiable."[19] One might turn that around, and
say that journalistic truth, being restricted to that which is verifiable, has only limited capacity to report a world that is infinitely
subtle and complex.

### Man Bites Four Ws

The possibility that the world has become so vast, so chaotic, and
at the same time so hard to know that journalism is incapable of
reporting it is disturbing. For journalism is the unofficial fourth
branch of our tripartite government.[20] If it fails, then self-government fails.

Perhaps we have not reached that point. After all, the daily papers, and radio and TV, never were anything more than informational first aid. The full story about any event is never told at the time it happens. It only comes out later, as magazines, documentaries, research reports, personal memoirs, and books fill in the details. In the end, long after the generation that had to cope with the event is dead, the historians have their final, if still fallible, word.

Still, the question remains: How can today's journalism best fulfill its mission of giving an adequate first report on what is going on?

Half a century ago, even a decade ago, everyone agreed with what had been taught those of us who went into newspaper work in the first half of the century: objective news—an accurate, unbiased account of the facts—was journalism's purest gem.

It was, and it still is. Curiously, however, objective news has become anathema to today's young activists in journalism, to some among the rising generation of university intellectuals, and to others who should also know better. They do not see the issue in terms of what is at stake—unprejudiced news. Ignoring this crucial point, they denounce objective news as an impossibility. To them the attempt to write the news impartially, in terms of the observable facts, is at best an obsolete convention that misses the point. At worst, it blocks progress toward a better world.

This latest *Weltanschauung* is bigger than journalism. In the universities, too, it became fashionable to denounce as false the academic standards of scholarship that were evolved through the centuries, on the plea that because total objectivity is unattainable it is a myth. Young professors as well as young journalists dismiss this infinitely precious concept by saying, "There is no such thing as objectivity." But, as Yale's Kingman Brewster said at the time:

> Cynical disparagement of objectivity as a "myth" seems to me both naïve and irresponsible. Any claim of novelty to the observation that men are fallible at best, corruptible at worst, is naïve.

Its irresponsibility lies in the conclusion that since the ideal is unattainable it should not be held up as a standard to both practitioners and critics.[21]

The new attitude struck me with force when I noted that able young newsmen, applying for an academic sabbatical at Stanford, repeatedly volunteered the information that their goal was something nobler than objective news. This, from one of them, is typical:

It is a great misfortune that many of us in the profession fail to utilize these tools [immediacy and spontaneity], and too frequently deny ourselves the full power of the moment in reporting an event because of our peculiar, and at times perverted, devotion to that which we have mislabeled objectivity.

Even some among the journalistic brass joined the attack. Bill Moyers, who left President Johnson's inner councils to become for a time publisher of *Newsday*, says he learned at the White House that "of all the great myths of American journalism, objectivity is the greatest. Each of us sees what his own experience leads him to see."[22]

The late Ralph McGill of the *Atlanta Constitution,* one of the more enlightened of his generation of editors and publishers, often charged that American journalism did not inform the public as it should "for the simple reason that we have been taught to worship a word—objectivity. Truth, I want. But not objectivity. . . . There isn't any such thing as objectivity, and cannot be any such thing."[23]

Again Cecil King, the former British press lord, denounced "the fetish for objectivity, the fear of editorializing" in the American press. Our reporters, he said, "divest news of its own inherent drama. They cast away the succulent flesh and offer the reader dry bones, coated with an insipid sauce of superfluous verbiage."[24]

Perhaps the best way to untangle all this is to define terms. The dictionaries, not surprisingly, do not support the attack on objectivity. Objectivity is the state, quality, or relation of being objective. And objective means "uninfluenced by emotion, surmise, or personal prejudice." It has to do with that which is "based on observable phenomena, presented factually."

One concludes that objective news is news written as something apart from the observer and his feeling about it, something like the *Ding an sich* of the Kantian epistemology. There is little semantic authority to support those who say they want to be fair rather than objective. To be objective is, by definition, to be fair.

But if objective news is simply impartial news, why all the fuss? Why the animosity against it on the part of some of today's more thoughtful journalists?

Actually, the critics of objective news do not seem to be as much against objectivity as they make out. They have fallen into a semantic trap, and they simply use that term as a convenient club with which to strike at what really disturbs them. And that is journalism's incapacity for instant truth, notably its failure to confirm their own subjective view of the truth. They are particularly restive at the inverted pyramid, with its bulldozer lead and building blocks of surface fact. It must then be the Procrustean bed of our American rules for newswriting, not objectivity itself, that irritates the critics of objectivity. But then, this is nothing new. Only the intensity of emotion behind it is new. The whole development of interpretive reporting since World War I has been a reaction against news forced into the Four-W mold.

The first indictment against objectivity of which I am aware was made as long ago as during World War II. Kenneth Stewart, now retired as a journalism teacher at the University of California at Berkeley, after previous professional experience that included the Sunday *New York Times* and *PM,* put it into a book that has a contemporary ring despite the fact that it was published nearly three decades ago. He quoted a fellow newsman:

> "I'm afraid I haven't got any high-flown theories about journalism," says Victor Bernstein. "All I know is that I never go out on a story without a bias. This bias is predicated on the belief that most people are not getting what's coming to them. This bias does

not lead to a distortion of fact. It does encourage me constantly to look for explanations behind the facts. My hunch is that so-called 'objective journalism' is something like the policy of non-intervention in Spain; it means holding back, so that the strong can kick the weak around without opposition."[25]

There is here that same concern for the political or social impact of the news, rather than respect for scrupulous neutrality in reporting it, that distinguishes the modern crusade against objectivity. Mr. Stewart wrote that what irritated him about *The New York Times* was not its professed aims so much as its insistence that the facts alone are enough:

If you mean by objectivity absence of convictions, willingness to let nature take its course, uncritical acceptance of things as they are . . . the hell with it. If you mean by objectivity a healthy respect for the ascertainable truth, a readiness to modify conclusions when new evidence comes in, a refusal to distort deliberately and for ulterior or concealed motives, a belief that the means shape the end, not that the end justifies the means, all well and good.

Draw a fine distinction between conscious coloration and deliberate distortion. You have no right to force the facts to fit into a pattern, but if they fall there naturally, then make the most of it.[26]

There is something here that induces a queasy feeling in one who believes that the news writer should strive to keep himself out of what he reports. Those who denounce objectivity always seem to be looking over their shoulder at the effect of what they write, rather than straight at the truth as best they can find it out, no matter what its consequences may be. There is a risk, I think, that what is deliberate distortion when our wicked opposition does it is only conscious coloration when we ourselves do it.

It is of course true that deadpan reporting, like any other incomplete or sloppy reporting, is likely to miss the point. One critic of objective news, Nicholas von Hoffman of the *Washington Post,* argues that the world has changed so much that reporting under the old rules bends the truth out of shape:

. . . the Four Ws do not describe reality for modern, particularly college-educated, Americans.

They don't see an event as a discrete act. Rightly or wrongly, they're so permeated with psychological and sociological understanding that for them an event is a complicated environmental sphere of thought, experience, mood, and motif.[27]

Mr. von Hoffman goes on to say that history is playing tricks on us:

Important news events are beginning to lose their Four-W characteristics. The most recent example [he wrote in 1969] is Woodstock where a third of a million people turned out for a concert which nobody could hear and no music reviewers did a criticism of. *The New York Times* handled the story in a Four-W way, as it would a Jets-Giants game, with the result that it misled everyone, including its own editorial page. The editorial page has reversed itself and the paper has printed God knows how many thousands of extra column inches trying to catch up with its own manhandling of the material. It has yet to do it because it's still trapped way back down there in the Ws.[28]

Such complaints cannot be dismissed as nothing but a reflection of the New Journalism's naïve blindness to the risk of a return to slanted news. The charge brought by the activists is that a new approach is necessary because the old journalism doesn't tell the truth. They insist that the chronicling of our time must rise above the evils of existing journalism. They envision a glorious new day in which they will put into words, and pictures and sounds, a truth too subtle, too noble, to be within the powers of the wage-slaves of the standard press, the squares "trapped way back down there in the Ws."

Sometimes, to be sure, the complaint is simply the old familiar one that must go back to man's beginning: Because you don't report the truth as it has been revealed to me your report is false. Here is one of innumerable examples:

Any writer or observer, writer or not, is going to see some things and ignore other things. . . . The selection process at this point is enormous; so to report something "objectively," such as the activities of the President in Washington, is really to distort the story. What is the *meaning?* When the President speaks about Laos, if the commentators don't ultimately end up using the words, "The President lied tonight on television about Laos," they are not telling the truth.[29]

The answer to such strictures must be a "Maybe yes, maybe no." I for one agree wholeheartedly on Laos and the rest of Indochina, as most of the country apparently has since 1968 at least. But simply to report what the President says or does, and then to call him a liar, does not make for complete and competent reporting. The truth comes in infinite shades of gray as well as in black and white.

Sometimes, however, the New Journalism seeks its ends by more sophisticated means. It rearranges facts—and often adds supposed facts that don't exist—to synthesize a whole that is bigger than life-size. The goal is to present a picture more real than the grubby facts themselves. Consider this specimen from a comprehensive analysis of the new technique:

New York—Redpants is a hustler from Detroit who wears Gucci shoes. She once worked for a pimp named Sugarman, and she gets a lot of business by hanging around the Waldorf-Astoria here, where a friendly guard looks upon her with fondness and sympathy.

Her story, tragic and absorbing, was told recently in New York magazine. Staff writer Gail Sheehy had apparently become as close as a sister to the prostitute, and the resulting story was one of the most readable articles ever to appear in the readable young publication. Readers were given a real insight into a world most don't know.

Miss Sheehy painted a vivid picture. Leading the john up the warped stairs of the Lindy Hotel, a second-floor fleabag several blocks down from the Waldorf, Redpants looks as awkward as she feels. Behind the desk is a beefy man in a mustard undershirt, his arms blue with tatoos. He smiles at Redpants by way of a welcome into the fold.

" 'That's $7.75, pal.' The john fills out a registration card.

Halfway up the staircase the couple is stopped by a shout from the tatooed man.

" 'Hey, you're man and wife, right?' Redpants giggles. 'Right.'

The article is filled with such fascinating detail, but there is one detail Miss Sheehy left out:

Redpants didn't do and say a lot of the things Miss Sheehy ascribed to her.

Redpants is what's known as a composite character. Miss Sheehy spent weeks interviewing real hustlers and pimps, and then she combined the salient details of their lives into the characters of Redpants and Sugarman. So the story was true, sort of, but then again it wasn't. The reader, however, was not told any of this.

It's all part of the New Journalism, or the Now Journalism, and it's practiced widely these days.[30]

This kind of thing *is* practiced widely, because it sells. It permits a kind of writing that grips the reader with more color, more concrete detail, more drama—indeed, sometimes more inmost thoughts of the people written about—than exists in the world as it is. So we get a report—if one can call it that—that is more real than the real thing.

Some of today's most successful writers led the way in using this technique. Perhaps it all began with Truman Capote's *In Cold Blood,* the fictionalized account of grisly but real murders. Or perhaps the prototype was *A Night to Remember,* the minute-by-minute recreation of the sinking of the Titanic that read like fiction. By now the leading practitioners of the art have become models for younger aspirants: Norman Mailer on the steps of the Pentagon, or at the political conventions; Gay Talese telling the story of *The New York Times,* or the Mafia, in such revealing intimacy that you wonder if the people written about were themselves aware of what they are described as thinking and feeling. Then there are Jimmy Breslin, Tom Wolfe, and a multiplying host of others.

Such journalism not only makes gripping reading but on occasion it may, like poetry or the other arts, actually give the reader an insight that an account of measurable facts could not. In the hands of topflight artists a little imaginative touching up, based on a painstaking, infinitely detailed digging into the facts, may permit an understanding more penetrating than even a masterful account of the facts as they are. In the hands of the few, therefore, the New Journalism may have value beyond the fact that it sells. But for the rank and file of journalism, the men and women of lesser capacity and less patience than the headliners, one wonders. Do they not settle for the technique without bothering with the endlessly meticulous research?

Beyond that there remains a risk, even in the hands of the best. For much of the New Journalism is not journalism at all, but contemporary historical fiction. Granted, it may show us truths we might otherwise miss. But it too can lie.

What this long and sometimes frustrating debate comes down to is the attempt to analyze and define reporting, as distinct from other kinds of writing. When one tries to puzzle out what the New Journalists are really trying to urge upon us it seems to be what one apologist calls "individual truth-seeking." Thus to set the individual free to pursue the truth as he sees it is surely noble in motive and far-reaching in purpose, as President Herbert Hoover once said of Prohibition. But is it reporting? If journalism's reason for being is to transfer the great world outside into the head of the citizen, then journalism must be what Macauley called Parliament's press gallery early in the nineteenth century, "a fourth estate of the realm." This means that, ideally, journalism is a neutral agency not associated with any of the other estates that make up the body politic. The journalist's mission becomes that of telling us what's going on as completely, accurately, honestly, and dispassionately as possible. And that is objective reporting.

## Something Is Wrong

If there is a risk that the New Journalism will take us away from the truth, rather than closer to it, that does not do away with the fact that under today's conditions the old journalism runs the same risk. The newspapers and news broadcasts of the 1970s are not quite the mirror of society we like to think they are.

In Anglo-American history the free press evolved to become critic not only of government, but of all society. As such, it ferreted out and published truths that the authorities did not want published. And, as the Pentagon Papers showed, it still does. But, at the same time, our press has itself taken out membership in the Establishment, and so feels inner pressures that make it pull some of its punches.

Against this fact one can set another, which I have examined elsewhere[31]—namely, that the concept of objective news has in good part compensated for the loss suffered in the sharp decline in the number of newspapers in proportion to population. Nevertheless, it does seem that it is now time for one of those swings in the habits of journalism that have marked its past responses to changing times.

There is, in the first place, what Mr. Moyers calls "the subjectivity of our objectivity." Still more important is the fact, familiar to anyone in the trade, that behind the screen of supposedly impartial reporting, newspapers do, from time to time, obscure some essential truth. Whether the tendency is deliberate or not hardly matters.

A single example should illustrate. In the wake of that milestone in American history, the 1968 Democratic convention in Chicago, a correspondent of the *Christian Science Monitor* reported that a maverick publication was pushing Chicago's big-time press into change. *Hyde Park-Kenwood Voices,* which the writer characterized as "a sprightly tabloid published monthly in the South Side University of Chicago area by two admittedly crusading journalists," was the prime mover: "Many newsmen here believe that the strident, muckraking opposition of the *Voices* may well be forcing the city's five metropolitan dailies into adopting a more critical stance toward the Daley administration than has been the case in the past." One might say much the same for the *Chicago Journalism Review*, a plainly biased critique of Chicago's big papers written by staff members of those papers, because they believe their bosses are not covering the town with a sufficiently critical eye.

Nationally, the misnamed underground press, for all its offensive manners and childish relish for the language of the outhouse, serves much the same purpose. There have, of course, always been gadfly agitators on the fringes of journalism, like the abolitionist Elijah Lovejoy, who helped bring on the Civil War and end slavery, and was martyred for his pains. Such correctives from zealots not in the main stream of journalism are often healthy. But they are no model for the standard press, precisely because they make no pretence of objectivity. In fact they glory in their prejudice on behalf of whatever cause is, in their minds, more important than all else.

Perhaps there is something wrong with today's established, mass-media journalism; nevertheless, it seems to me dangerous to believe that turning our backs on objectivity is the cure. Such a cure would be worse than the disease. Surely, those who denounce objective news should stop and think, before American journalism reverts to the primitive propaganda from which objectivity rescued it.

I gained some insight into the attitudes of the new journalists from a young friend, a Chicago newspaperman who seemed to consider objectivity a device invented by the power structure to uphold a status quo that needs tearing down. If I understand him correctly, the model for the modern journalist should be the one Leon Trotsky prescribed for the historian. In the preface to his three-volume History of the Russian Revolution, Trotsky wrote that the serious reader does not want what he called "a treacherous impartiality." To Trotsky, impartiality offers the reader only "a cup of conciliation with a well-settled poison of reactionary hate at the bottom." Far better is "a scientific conscientiousness, which for its sympathies—open and undisguised—seeks support in an honest study of the facts, a determination of their connections, an exposure of the causal laws of their movement."

If this is right, the historian should be a combat correspondent, a soldier in one army rather than an observer of both. Indeed, Trotsky warns that he must under no circumstances "stand upon the wall of a threatened city, and behold at the same time the besiegers and the besieged."[32] Which side should he fight on? Why, the right one, of course. And how do you know which is right? It is the one toward which your own subjective outlook, made up of indoctrination, environment, and emotions, pulls you.

History cries out that this is a false doctrine. Eyewitness reports are obviously invaluable, both to history and to journalism. But they hardly give the whole truth. To preach so treacherous a partiality for the journalist is to preach a return to the polemics that passed for news before the concept of objectivity was born. How sad, how wasteful, that each generation must learn afresh what its predecessors bequeathed to it, after having themselves learned it at great pain.

The notion that the reporter must himself mount the barricades is not revolutionary, but reactionary. Nevertheless, the True Believer, as isolated and dissected by Eric Hoffer, may be found in the ranks of newsmen as well as throughout the general public.[33] He insists, passionately, that *his* truth is the only truth. America's activist reporters and Soviet Russia's veteran newsmen are as one in this. "There is only one truth," Soviet editors say repeatedly. "When you print what you call both sides, one side is untrue and you spread the untruths."[34]

How much more accurately is mankind's experience caught up in the statement in Milton's *Areopagitica*, that truth "may have more shapes than one." Truth is usually lost somewhere in the dust of battle between clashing forces, each of which may hold some fragment of it. That is why it is best if the reporter does not choose among them when on the job. He who is convinced he is in possession of the ultimate truth is not qualified to be a reporter.

It is of course argued that he must choose. As Walter Lippmann once put it:

> It is all very well to say that a reporter collects the news and that the news consists of facts. The truth is that in our world the facts are infinitely many and that no reporter could collect them all,

no newspaper print them all, and nobody could read them all. We have to select some facts rather than others, and in doing that we are using not only our legs but our selective judgment of what is interesting or important or both.[35]

The crucial question, however, is not the need for selection, so much as our response to that need. Should the reporter say to himself, "Why bother even trying to be objective—I might as well slant things my way?" Or should every journalist, aware of the danger, redouble his zeal to approach objectivity just as closely as he can?

Time, as Justice Holmes reminded us long ago, has upset many fighting faiths. Therefore, a news story should report that which the reporter "loathes and believes fraught with death" as honestly and accurately and completely as that which supports his dearest wish. Again to quote Elmer Davis:

> All of us in the news business ought to remember that our primary responsibility is to the man who buys his newspaper, or turns on his radio [today he would have added TV], expecting us to give him in so far as is humanly possible not only the truth and nothing but the truth, but the whole truth.[36]

Not long ago one newspaperman wrote, "I sometimes think . . . that if the twentieth-century American press had to report the Crucifixion of Christ, the second paragraph would be a straightforward judicial explanation from Pontius Pilate." Perhaps so. But newspapermen are reporters, not Apostles. To report the crucifixion objectively would require including, along with the gospel message, whatever details reportorial questioning might have pried out of Pilate.

The problem of what to report and how to report it will never be solved, because the line between fact and the subjective view of that fact remains elusive. Despite this today's reporters and editors should keep the flag of objectivity flying high. To do so will give a more honest and accurate view of this confusing world than we can get from a latter-day Trotsky, or any other partisan on any side, who masquerades as a reporter while actually giving us his private notion of what's what.

## A Test of Objectivity

The newspaperman who believes that there is no higher calling than reporting can make a practical test of whether a news story is objective or loaded. Indeed, the careful reader can do the same.

It is true that we all tend to see a report that matches our own prejudices as objective. Still, a certain amount of education and experience do not leave us defenseless. Here is a test, a journalistic litmus paper, that shows whether a given report is corrupted with the acid of opinion, or neutralized with the alkali of objectivity:

Does the news story, whether interpretive or straight, leave the impression that it presents the facts on both sides of any event, issue, or controversy? Does the reporter write in the dispassionate spirit of the scientist, or is he openly or subtly plugging a cause? In fact, can you tell which side the reporter himself is on? If you cannot, then his report is objective.

But what of his bosses? Today's journalistic establishment is often accused of giving false or partisan reports. And all too often there is reason for the charge. But the failure may be less one of deliberate slanting than of failing to understand what objectivity requires in the modern day.

A basic source of trouble is the surviving tendency of our press and our broadcasters to see news in terms of what an official source says or does—whether that source is the White House, General Motors, or the least significant one in town. If one regards what someone of prominence says or does as news, why then one tends to let it go at that. But letting it go at that is *not* objectivity. The chances are that the official doctrine or official action is at best only part of the story, and at worst distorted if not downright false. Therefore, if a report is to be objective, something must be added to it.

Look at it as you will, the motive of striving to get the whole story is what matters. Interpretive reporting does not consist in editorializing, in expressing an opinion as to what the facts mean. Rather it is a matter of digging and digging, within the limits of time and space available, for all facts—not only those on top of the iceberg, but those down under the surface as well.

I have before me a clipping from the front page of the *San Francisco Chronicle*.[37] It bears the headline, "The Reagan Recall Fizzles." The story reports that a drive to recall California's governor failed. Political opponents had resorted to California's mechanism of recall, a kind of election-in-reverse, in hope of unseating Governor Ronald Reagan only two years after he had come triumphantly from nowhere to win his first four-year term.

In discussing the event with reporters Governor Regan, understandably enough, was elated that the recall had failed. But he took the occasion to berate the reporters. "I've had faith in the common sense of the people of California, and that faith is vindicated," the Governor is quoted as saying. "The fact that it [the recall] died an ignoble death gets much less attention from any of you than the efforts to put it over received."

After having paid his respects to objectivity by quoting this remark Michael Harris, the *Chronicle* reporter, added:

> The Governor did not tell why he had the impression his triumph had been suppressed. The seven afternoon papers in California with circulations over 100,000 all reported yesterday's figures [on the recall vote] with prominent headlines on the first page. None of the seven had given the recall drive itself equal prominence.

Gratuitous insertion of this information into a report on what the Governor had said might be considered editorializing, in that it presented a point of view opposed to that of the Governor. Parenthetically, one might note that this is precisely the view held by President Nixon and Vice President Agnew. To them, as to many another officeholder, the press should be a vast public-address system, through which those in high places may tell the public what they wish, without any TV commentators, reporters, interpreters, analysts, or others saying something different. But the point in this California example, as in all others like it, is this: *the reporter was not expressing an opinion.* He was supplementing what the Governor said with added facts that were unquestionably pertinent to an understanding of the incident.

No doubt the view of the world we get by peering out at it each day through the evening news show, or even *The New York Times*, is not reality in all its subtle depth and breadth. Moreover, reporters do at times view the same event differently, and report it differently. They are only human. It is indeed fortunate that, despite the trend toward monopoly, American journalism does not yet speak with a single voice. Where differences in first reports do occur, follow-up stories soon make the truth recognizable.

It is, in short, nonsense to say that there can be no such thing as objectivity. Any newsman qualified for his calling and tempered by experience can tell the difference between a slanted story and a fair one. Objective reporting is nothing more than what good reporting has always been: the work of a disciplined professional who has tried his damnedest to get the whole story, and then to present it accurately and honestly without letting his own bias creep into it.

# 4

## *Making News by Covering It*

### Get the Cameras!

"THE whole world is watching! The whole world is watching! The whole world is watching!"

This taunt, chanted rythmically as an obbligato to the televised sights and sounds of battle at the barricades, is an unforgettable part of the 1968 Democratic National Convention in Chicago. The street demonstrators had good reason to shout their battle cry, as police batons and boots and knees—and motorcycles—bruised and bloodied their skulls and bodies. For the world was indeed watching, and the police knew it. The knowledge fired Mayor Daley's blue-shirted warriors with a resentment and malice they might not have felt had they been unobserved.

It was the modern journalist, armed not only with pad and pencil but also with tape recorders and cameras, lights, and all the other impedimenta of radio and television, that enabled the world to see what happened as it happened. It was an object lesson revealing something new in the world: Massed battalions of reporter-technologists actually change the news they cover by covering it. No longer are they neutral observers on the sidelines. Without intending any such thing, they have become a third force in human

90

conflicts, a force that changes the outcome from what it might have been had they left it unreported.

Chicago in 1968 became a spectacular example of this new journalistic phenomenon, because what took place in its streets and parks and downtown hotels those hot August nights and days was as significant as the political nightmare inside the Stockyards Amphitheater that was the occasion for it all. In one camp was protesting youth, assembled from all over the country. Among them, beyond question, were provocateurs and revolutionaries, zealots intent on tearing down society. But the overwhelming majority seem to have been nothing more than young people protesting, with good reason, the fact that their country was betraying the ideals it professed to honor.

The other camp was dominated by the shadow of the absent, recently abdicated Lyndon Johnson. In its ranks were political representatives of an older generation, many of them unhappy at what they themselves were doing. The presidential candidate they chose, as foreordained by the political realities that played their part in the protest, was the ex-hero Hubert Humphrey. At Chicago he was smaller than life size, a mockery of what he had been for twenty years, because he could not bring himself to declare his independence, on the central issue of Vietnam, from the man who had made Vice President. But even more important than he to the clash was that surviving outcropping from an earlier stratum of American political geology, Richard Daley, Mayor of Chicago since 1955.

The Democratic establishment not only flew the banners of law and order; it controlled the official machinery. It commanded Chicago's 12,000-man police force, which was backed by 6000 men of the Illinois National Guard wielding bayonets, plus an airlifted 6000 U.S. Army regulars, armed among other things with flame throwers and bazookas.

Between them the two camps played out a national drama that rumbled with the overtones of civil war. But what matters here was the way in which the third force of journalism rewrote that drama from what it set out to be.

One newsman who was there said later: "On Sunday and Monday nights, August 25-26, Chicago policemen conducted a deliberate, unprovoked attack against the working press. This was not a series of accidental, scattered incidents, but a concerted effort to drive us from the streets." He quoted a colleague, who said, "You didn't have to do anything to be assaulted; you merely had to be there."[1]

The fact that the police attacked the press, deliberately and with sanction from above, is documented in a report to the National Commission on the Causes and Prevention of Violence, prepared by a 212-member staff under Daniel Walker, corporation lawyer and president of the Chicago Crime Commission.[2] Its conclusion was that what happened "can only be called a police riot." The eyewitness accounts of the five-day street battle were sickening; and they included police punishment of the press that had made it possible for the whole world to watch.

The Walker report noted that there was at least a partial excuse for police violence against the press:

> Camera crews on at least two occasions did stage violence and did fake injuries. Demonstrators did sometimes step up their activities for the benefit of TV cameras. Newsmen and photographers' blinding lights did get in the way of police clearing streets, sweeping the park and dispersing demonstrators. Newsmen did, on occasion, disobey legitimate police orders to "move" or "clear the streets." News reporting of events did seem to the police to be anti-Chicago and anti-police.[3]

But, asks the report: Was the response appropriate to the provocation? It lets the facts speak for themselves:

> Out of 300 newsmen assigned to cover the parks and streets of Chicago during convention week, more than 60 (about 20 per cent) were involved in incidents resulting in injury to themselves, damage to their equipment, or their arrest. Sixty-three newsmen were physically attacked by police; in 13 of these instances, photographic or recording equipment was intentionally damaged.[4]

What the policemen's passion to destroy evidence against themselves meant, in terms of human injury, smashed equipment, and
confiscated film, is hinted at in these excerpts from the Walker
report:

> It was on these nights that the police violence against media rep-
> resentatives reached its peak. Much of it was plainly deliberate.
> A newsman was pulled aside on Monday by a detective acquaint-
> ance of his who said: "The word is being passed to get news-
> men." Individual newsmen were warned, "You take my picture
> tonight and I'm going to get you." . . .

A network cameraman reported that, on the same night:

> I just saw this guy coming at me with his nightstick and had the
> camera up. The tip of his stick hit me right in the mouth, then I
> put my tongue up there and noticed that my tooth was gone. I
> turned around then to try to leave and then this cop came up be-
> hind me with his stick and he jabbed me in the back.
> All of a sudden these cops jumped out of the police cars and
> started just beating the hell out of people. . . .
> Another policeman was running after me and saying, "Get
> the fuck out of here." And I heard another guy scream, "Get
> their fucking cameras." And the next thing I knew I was being
> hit on the head, and I think on the back, and I was just forced
> down on the ground at the corner of Division and Wells.
> If the intent was to discourage the coverage, it was successful
> in at least one case. A photographer from a news magazine says
> that finally, "I just stopped shooting because every time you push
> the flash, they look at you and they are screaming about "Get
> the fucking photographers and get the film."[5]

### How to Start a Riot

The significant factor in the power of the press to alter what is
happening, by reporting it, is wrapped up in the complaint Chicago's policemen kept making to newsmen: "If you didn't give 'em
[the demonstrators] publicity, they wouldn't be here."

Long before Chicago, campus radical leaders had learned that they could manufacture news by planning a protest and then inviting TV and the press to cover it. It becomes common for bearded demonstrators to stage a mass scene at noon and then to watch themselves on TV that night.

Inevitably this raised the question whether journalism should deliberately reshape its reflexes, its normal news judgments, because of the effect its presence on the scene might have on what took place. And while campus mob scenes were bad enough, ghetto explosions were worse. This prompted some editors to come up with a solution. "Downplay their stupidity," wrote Felix McKnight, Texas editor and a former president of the American Society of Newspaper Editors, to his fellow editors. His diagnosis, if not his cure, is hardly arguable:

> I wince when I think of the mileage Stokely Carmichael has received from the news media. This dangerous man—and we damn well know he is dangerous, and usually three cuts below minimum news-acceptance standards—is permitted to mouth his way from one street insurrection to another under the protective cloak of a free press and free speech.
>
> And what's our reward for the high-principled backbending on behalf of a traitor who long since should have been charged with acts injurious to this nation? Hundreds dead, billion-dollar destruction, a widening breach between black and white that has taken us back to pre-Civil War days, and fear that has never been known in the United States.
>
> We gave Carmichael a platform and he preached hatred and killing and burning from television microphones and newspaper front pages. We gave him his inning and society has been brutally flogged.
>
> Next came another inciter who openly harangued his followers to "kill Whitey," burn the town, and establish Black Power, whatever that is. I speak of a total unknown who has become a national figure because we made him one—H. Rap Brown.[6]

Another troubled editor was Jenkin Lloyd Jones of the *Tulsa Tribune*. He made the point that "the technique [of commanding press attention] is calculated, polished, and being used with increasing frequency."[7] And Whitney Young, Jr., director of the National Urban League, agreed. The press had created Stokely Carmichael, said Mr. Young: "His following right now amounts to about 50 Negroes and about 5000 white reporters." The fact is inescapable: a moderate never gets the attention a firebrand does.

## The Roots Go Deep

Not until the mid 1960s did ghetto riots and campus revolutions make the present generation of Americans aware of journalism's power to change events by reporting them. Actually, however, the roots of this power can be traced far back into history. And today the same power spreads far beyond the spectacular events that brought it to our attention.

In societies less complex than ours, the same individual can be both protagonist of a cause and chronicler of it. The contemporary activist reporter, who sees journalism not as a neutral observer so much as a handmaiden of revolution, is but a reversion to Mirabeau, Marat, and the other agitators of the French Revolution. These earlier activists reinforced the impact of their deeds by spreading word of them through newspapers that were first of all propaganda organs.

The French revolutionists in turn had found their model in the pamphleteers of the American Revolution—Sam Adams, Thomas Paine, Isaiah Thomas, and the rest. These men earned their niche in history by being at once leaders in the struggle for independence and propagandists for it. Historians tell us that at the time of the Revolution only one-third of the American colonists were patriots. Another third were Tories, while the final third resembled the modern types who don't want to get involved. How much did Sam Adams help the rebel cause merely by calling a street fracas, in which the Redcoats were provoked into killing four men, the Boston Massacre? Without such fiery journalism George III might have carried the day.

History is crowded with examples of how publicity can change the course of events. The phenomenon is most readily visible in times of violence, as during the Civil War, when a lack of censorship enabled reporters, in their zeal to cover the news, to tip off the enemy to supposedly secret battle plans. I believe it was General Sherman who said, on hearing that three reporters had been killed by a shell, "Good, now we'll have news from hell before breakfast."

Less spectacular events and developments, however, are also subject to alteration by being reported. In recent years, when concern over the use of drugs by American youth was rising, the magazine *Science* commented:

> It is characteristic of youth to rebel against accepted values and to test himself and his environment, often to the point of no return. Nevertheless, the use of psychedelic drugs would not have become so widespread had not the press glamorized them. Frank Barron has said: "The chemical substance most instrumental in the spread of the psychedelic movement is printer's ink. . . . The slick-paper picture magazines of large circulation . . . have used a device . . . : they deplore the excesses that they are at pains to picture and they warn of dangers while at the same time suggesting the appeal of what they dramatize."[8]

One might say that the problem in its modern form began with the trial of Bruno Richard Hauptmann, kidnapper and murderer of the Lindbergh baby, in Flemington, New Jersey, in 1935. About 300 reporters virtually took over the courtroom. Radio broadcasters were there with their wires and microphones. And a horde of news photographers, even though they used the new flash bulbs that were a considerable improvement over the mephistophelian open flash, nevertheless made themselves equally obnoxious.

The world read and listened with relish, for here was drama. But the fact that this journalistic extravaganza centered upon a man on trial for his life aroused thoughtful leaders of bar and bench and press. Here was the origin of the long battle over free press and fair trial that is only now on the way to settlement.

Throughout, camera and microphone have been the chief offenders. No pad-and-pencil reporter could cause a scene like this one, at the 1964 Republican Convention in San Francisco:

> . . . I have not forgotten watching Robert ("Shad") North-shield, a top NBC News executive, sending Vanocur, McGee, and Chancellor onto the floor of the Cow Palace at the start of the Goldwater convention. As they threw their legs over the railing and went out there like a fresh hockey line, the amiably flamboyant Coach Northshield intoned, "I have the feeling this is the lull before the lull. But if it gets deadly, we are prepared to make our own show."
>
> Later, as everyone knows, Chancellor was arrested for refusing to be cleared from the floor. After interviewing his captors, he was bodily removed, signing off for posterity, "This is John Chancellor, somewhere in custody."
>
> The incident was an extreme example of the kind of electronic journalism that provokes the charge that television does not so much cover a convention as it covers itself covering a convention.[9]

Earlier, when the Eisenhower administration for the first time admitted television to presidential press conferences, newspaper reporters ceased to be reporters. They became actors in a performance played before the nation. Nor is the impact of electronic journalism upon the news confined to high places. By the early 1960s it had become standard practice for newspaper reporters to be shunted into the background, while the TV crews took over. The sight-and-sound reporters stood front and center, side by side with the person interviewed, chucking him under the chin with extended microphone. If the event was sufficiently gaudy, covering it became a mob scene in which half a dozen mikes were thrust into the teeth of the arriving statesman or numbed victim of disaster. One reporter who covered the New York airports marked the change by complaining, in *Editor & Publisher*, that whenever the great arrived at an airport he and his kind were pushed aside by Secret Service men and other officials, while the broadcast journalists, gear and all, were ushered to the ramp:

The old traditions which sought to keep press interviews of all types within bounds and on a dignified and professional basis began to go out of the window.

There was the microphone squad rush and the blunt, cross-examining technique:

"Are you going to run for re-election?"

"Are you sorry you killed your wife?"

"How do you feel, now that you are free after 35 years' imprisonment?"

No follow-ups. Just questions—pointed, helter-skelter, on the run.

The writing press stood by and, instead of doing the interviews, began to cover the interview riots.

This kind of thing is inevitable, because, while broadcasting is show business first and journalism only incidentally, it has a compulsive immediacy that written journalism cannot match. The element of theater inherent in broadcast journalism prompts some in the newspaper ranks to dissociate themselves from the electronic tail that now wags the journalistic dog. But history cannot be undone. The press, or journalism, or the media are all one. And the public, making no distinction between them, visits the sins of one upon the heads of all. "You're all the same, and all to blame," I was told repeatedly and vehemently at the time of President Kennedy's assassination. It was the same when Vice President Agnew took off after both television and the press in the fall of 1969. And so it is whenever some public crisis is made the more disorderly by the newsmen who cover it.

The tragedy at Dallas was trauma enough in itself. Two days later, incredibly, it became even more sickening. The murderer was himself murdered while in custody of the police, and before the whole nation's eyes at that. It was immediately apparent that newsmen, serving the public's need to know, were in good part responsible. The American Civil Liberties Union lost no time in pointing an accusing finger:

In our view, Oswald's killing is directly related to the police capitulation to the glare of publicity. Having surrendered to the public clamor during the preceding two days, the police arranged Oswald's transfer from the city to the county jail to suit the convenience of the news media and thereby exposed Oswald to the very danger that took his life. Minimum security considerations would dictate that the transfer of this prisoner at least ought not, in effect, have taken on the quality of the theatrical production for the benefit of the television cameras.

In due course the Warren Commission, covering the same ground with meticulous thoroughness, agreed. "The promulgation of a code of professional conduct governing representatives of all news media," it concluded, "would be welcome evidence that the press had profited by the lesson of Dallas."[10] To that end the commission made this the final recommendation of the dozen it proposed:

> The Commission recommends that the representatives of the bar, law enforcement associations, and the news media work together to establish ethical standards concerning the collection and presentation of information to the public so that there will be no interference with pending criminal investigations, court proceedings, or the right of individuals to a fair trial.[11]

The problem cuts deep. Soon after President Kennedy became the fourth President to be murdered of the 34 individuals who had held the office by this time, there followed the assassinations of Martin Luther King, Jr., and Robert Kennedy. So spectacular a repetition of tragedy prompted the *Wall Street Journal* to ask, in an analytical article, whether the press inspires assassins. Its answer was that it does:

> Whatever Oswald's and Sirhan's motivations, both men suddenly achieved world-wide notoriety. Instantly, too, the news media conferred a kind of celebrity status on them, monitoring every move, transcribing every public word, vying to purchase the revelations of relatives.[12]

The insecure, frustrated, anonymous loners from whose ranks the murderers of public figures seem to come evidently find relief from neglect in their sudden notoriety. "Now everybody will know who I am," said Lee Harvey Oswald to a police captain after his capture. So too Sirhan Sirhan, murderer of Robert Kennedy: "They can gas me, but I am famous. I achieved in a day what it took Kennedy all his life to do."[13] And again, when in 1972 a campaigning Governor Wallace of Alabama was cut down by bullets intended to kill him—once more before the television cameras—the morose young busboy and janitor who shot him turned to the captors leading him away and asked, "How much do you think I'm going to get for my autobiography?"[14]

A professor of criminal law, quoted in the *Wall Street Journal* article mentioned above, held that this kind of assassin seeks some identity, some achievement, that life has hitherto denied: "The [attention of the] media is their reward, and what the criminal law does to them afterward is quite secondary," he said. It is the same with the occasional mass murders that seem to be contagious:

> The killing of eight nurses in Chicago is followed by the sniper-slaying of fourteen people at a Texas university and by the murder of five women in an Arizona beauty parlor by an 18-year-old boy; the boy told authorities he got the idea by reading about the earlier crimes.[15]

The impact that news coverage has on events of all kinds leaves us with a dilemma of vast proportions. Consider, for example, the 1959 visit of Premier Khrushchev to the United States. During the tour across the country there occurred what became known as the Battle of Coon Rapids. This was a near-riot on the Roswell Garst farm in Iowa, caused by the unnecessary and overwhelming number of television, radio, photographic, and newspaper reporters on hand. Contemporary accounts had it that on the tour CBS alone used 65 cameras and 375 cameramen and technicians, besides the ten top reporters and commentators who traveled with the visiting Premier.

This army of newsmen made it certain that none of the Khrushchev trip could really be orderly. But on the Garst farm the reportorial disarray became extreme. Photographers roosted in trees, in barn lofts, in upstairs windows, in haystacks. "You couldn't get a coherent quote," said John Crosby, the New York *Herald Tribune*'s syndicated TV columnist. "You tried to ask a question but were pushed out of the way before you could finish." No wonder Mr. Garst, host on the occasion because he had himself visited Soviet farms, began hurling silage at the locust swarm of newsmen. No wonder he delivered some well-placed kicks to not only the principal offenders, but seasoned and responsible reporters.

James Reston of *The New York Times*, a veteran of the battle, wrote on his return: "We didn't cover the Khrushchev story, we smothered it. We created the atmosphere of hysteria. We were not the observers of history, we were the creators of history."

Another veteran of this and other mob scenes along the way, as when reporters made a shambles of the San Francisco supermarket Khrushchev suddenly decided to inspect, was the late Alexander F. Jones, editor of the *Syracuse Herald Journal*. He wrote:

> Before the trip was over I was ducking my press badge. I did not want people to know I was one of the mob of human locusts which acted like a bunch of reform school characters suddenly released.
>
> These big stories are becoming nightmares. With the advent of television, involving all the equipment it does, and the Capone gangster manners of many of the cameramen, the free press apparatus has grown to the point where it is impossible for anyone to think. . . .
>
> I have always been proud of being a newspaperman, but on my return from this trip I felt that anything that happens to us in putting us where we belong from the standpoint of our manners and deportment is deserved.

The principal difficulty grows out of the sheer number of newsmen that a teeming and technological society sends to cover spectacular events. The reason for these unprecedented numbers is first of all the fact that modern technology has transformed what used to be a handful of newspaper reporters into an army of technicians.

Then, too, there is affluence. Through the decades that followed World War II more newspapers than ever before began to send more reporters than ever to scenes that caught the public fancy. And there they were joined by the legions of television technicians that had not existed before.

Nowadays, too, spectacular stories are likely to add a troupe of foreign reporters to the native pack. We have come far from the day when a few foreign correspondents maintained diplomatic residence in Washington and covered the country by reading the papers. In the same way the owners of small-town dailies, which still hardly bother to send a reporter into the next county because the wire services cover that well enough, like to go on the more glamorous assignments themselves. But why should it be necessary to admit the *Podunk Press* just because its publisher and his wife take a notion to see a spectacular trial in person, or to go along for the ride on the latest junket to Moscow? Why admit every Tom, Dick, and Joe Doakes of dubious qualifications who can wangle press credentials?

Necessity sometimes forces a sharp diminution of the journalistic hordes to a select handful, or even a single reporter, who must cover for all the rest. This is pooling, which newspapers instinctively and properly resist. Sometimes, say, when it is a question of getting a handful of reporters on a carrier recovering astronauts, or to a difficult or remote spot, lots are drawn or turns are taken. But this may have unfair results. It might mean that the representative of the *Bingville Bugle* or Station BLAH gets a front-row seat at history, while the reporters from great newspapers, and from the wire services that cover for everyone, are left back on the beach. After the Kennedy assassination in 1963, Wes Gallagher, general manager of the Associated Press, put the defects of pool coverage into these words:

> The Associated Press represents not only hundreds of newspapers and radio and television stations in this country but thousands abroad. The same situation exists for the UPI and Reuters. Most

of these members are solely dependent upon the press associations for their news and would in no case be in a position to send their individual reporters.

The Associated Press will have to provide on the Ruby trial, for example, continuous, almost word-for-word coverage, frequent leads to meet deadlines in every section of the world, and a running colored description of the trial as a bare minimum. There will be hundreds of special requests to handle. Such coverage cannot be executed by one man in a pool position, nor could it be executed by three or four non-AP reporters serving as pool observers, because they simply are not familiar with the needs of our type of coverage.

It's a good point. So is the fact that any limitation of any kind on reporting risks letting the failures and injustices of society, which a free press is supposed to unearth, remain hidden. The tortuous process of digging into an Army cover-up that finally got news of the 1968 massacre at Vietnam's My Lai before the nation shows that there can be too little reporting as well as too much.[16]

Therefore, if there is room for but one reporter on a World War II bombing mission over Berlin, or for none at all when President Johnson takes the presidential oath in the jet that is to take him and the body of his predecessor back to Washington, then so it must be. But it need not be so at a presidential inauguration, or at any other event—perhaps even a campus explosion—that takes place where there is elbow room.

Between the extremes of too-tight pool coverage and the mob scene in which the press pushes the event itself out of the way there is room for a rule of reason. Here is another responsibility for a press that is fierce in defending its freedom, but unenthusiastic about any restrictions on getting the news. First, the press in all its forms must be aware of the danger inherent in mass coverage, which can be a danger to itself as well as to justice and public order. Second, the press must learn to do something about that danger in advance whenever trouble casts its shadow before. Just as the press is learning that there are standards it must observe in reporting crime, so it must remember that it is the reporter of history, and not the maker of it.

There is no easy answer, and there can be no blanket rule. But whenever there is time to think ahead, responsible editors can, if they will, adjust their coverage to the situation in hand. Before each paper or station or network individually turns out the guard, each responsible editor should ponder this question, asked by J. Russell Wiggins when he was editor of the *Washington Post*:

> No one wishes to stifle the sort of reportorial rivalry that is the life blood of competition and the spur to news and editorial excellence. But who has ever watched a Presidential or a Cabinet press conference, witnessed a fire or a flood, chronicled a political speech, or covered a disaster without vaguely wondering just how many lads it takes to watch one rat hole?

### Pass a Law

What it comes down to is that we are damned if we do and damned if we don't. Most newsmen want to be responsible about reporting the news. Yet their first responsibility is to get the news. And if they charge full steam ahead to report some big or bizarre or frightening happening they may bend it or even trample it out of shape.

Americans, who always seek quick, decisive solutions, tend to say, "There ought to be a law!" Or, if the First Amendment says there shall be no law, then let Vice President Agnew threaten the media until they behave. However it is done, stop this evil.

On the face of it, there is an obvious cure. If news coverage can build anonymous nobodies into national menaces, if it pours fuel on the flames of discontent, why the thing to do is to stop news coverage of explosive matters. It sounds plausible. Take this suggestion, made to the networks and wire services by a private citizen from Florissant, Missouri:

What I propose is a one-month moratorium on news of ANY campus unrest. Without the publicity that nurtures them, the campus riots would simply wither away.

The ideal time for such a moratorium would be the month of October, because most colleges don't really get into gear before then. Surely, the people who plan the college riots will be using the entire summer to get their forces ready to stir things up early in the school year. YOU can nip these riots in the bud simply by not reporting them.

One suggestion—if you take this idea seriously. You can't announce the news moratorium until September 30. Announcement of it before then would only result in a decision by the rioters to "cool it" until November.

Sure, local newspapers, radio and TV stations would "scoop" you by carrying campus news anyway. But you might appeal for cooperation by those who would be of a mind to go along with the moratorium.

Here's your chance to show that you are more interested in the welfare of the nation than in merely reporting its steady decay.[17]

This again is the layman's perennial cure for whatever journalism does that he doesn't like: censorship. Here we need consider it only as it applies to journalism's impact on the events it covers. And the answer to censorship is what it must always be: It is the lesson of the centuries that censorship risks evils greater than the ones it is supposed to cure. Roger Tatarian, formerly vice president and editor of UPI, answered the suggestion for a blackout on news of campus riots in this way:

The gentleman from Florissant might applaud us when we did *his* bidding. But suppose we also started to do the bidding of someone whose motives he despised and deplored? The time for him to start mistrusting the media would be the very moment they agreed to his suggestion and assumed for themselves a special mandate to tamper with the truth. . . .

For millions of people in this country and additional millions overseas, we are the only source of information of events outside their immediate localities. So our job now, as ever, is to be a faithful stand-in for those who cannot witness these distant events for themselves. . . .

The test of our work is whether our reportage enables them to reach the same general impression that the event itself would have given them.[18]

Censorship doesn't work because it doesn't get at the source of the trouble. There have been times when conscientious newsmen went along with civic leaders who had persuaded themselves that sticky situations might be less sticky, or might even be avoided altogether, if news of them were suppressed. For example, when integration began to force its way into Dallas, both newspapers in town agreed to a blackout on the first steps toward it. And at the time they were satisfied that the community benefitted. In another city, lunch counters were integrated without incident under a similar blackout, and again the civic leaders responsible were pleased. As one of them said: ". . . I am convinced that if these matters had received normal news treatment, the alarm would have sounded among the Ku Klux Klan and the redneck types, and that they would have been there with their baseball bats and ax handles; extremists among the Negroes would have responded in kind."

No doubt. But as a discerning student of journalism's role in society—William Rivers of Stanford University—has pointed out:

It is dismaying to contemplate journalists, who should be committed to breaking through walls of secrecy, helping to build them—especially in the company of civic leaders, many of whom are eager to promote business friendships that lead to country-club journalism. Journalists who march beside the First People of a community can neither see nor report the broad sweep of community life. Without a persistent and questioning journalism, civic leaders and public officials are unlikely to push the police into upholding the law when the Ku Klux Klan and the redneck types appear with their baseball bats and ax handles. If they are not held to account, the First People are all too likely to consider the Negro response to bats and ax handles the deplorable actions of "extremists."[19]

Then again, if in one situation censorship does seem to do its job, in others it does not:

In Detroit, there was a general and voluntary embargo of news on that summer Sunday when the most destructive race rioting of last year [1967] began. The incident that triggered it occurred early Sunday morning, but broadcasters didn't air any coverage until late in the afternoon.

"When there is an honest-to-God problem, you must inform the public," he [Richard Marks, director of Detroit's Community Relations Commission] insists, claiming that the Negro community quickly knew of the trouble anyway, via the grapevine. "Without the media giving them the full story," says Mr. Marks, "there was a distorted belief that the police weren't even trying to stop looters."[20]

Even the (Milton) Eisenhower Commission on Violence, whose task it was to suggest ways of avoiding it, learned that for the press to soft-pedal reports of violence is a dereliction of duty: "Unless we propose to emulate the ostrich, we must expect—indeed the public has a right to demand—that the press will report the day's intelligence including that which is violent. As with other events, when there is violence, the public has a right to know it."[21]

The Kerner commission came to the identical conclusion:

Indeed, we believe that it would be imprudent and even dangerous to downplay coverage in the hope that censored reporting of inflammatory incidents somehow will diminish violence. Once a disturbance occurs, the word will spread independently of newspapers and television. To attempt to ignore these events or portray them as something other than what they are can only diminish confidence in the media and increase the effectiveness of those who monger rumors and the fears of those who listen.[22]

Nathan Glazer, the sociologist, notes that while newsmen put Negro radicals on camera because they make more exciting subjects than moderates, this is not what makes radicals:

One might conclude ironically that just as liberal white newsmen soberly reporting the words of Joe McCarthy helped create McCarthyism, so too, liberal white newsmen have helped create the dominance of Negro militancy and radicalism in the community. But I shy away from ascribing this kind of independent role to the news media, whether in the creation of McCarthyism or in the success of the black militants. In both cases more substantial social forces have been interwoven with the vagaries of politics and the nature of the mass media to lead to the domination of the extremists.[23]

It may be true that the Rap Browns and Stokely Carmichaels, the Huey Newtons, Bobby Seales, and George Jacksons, have more followers among white newsmen than among ghetto inhabitants. Even so, a blackout on news of them would not get rid of the rage of the black community, which has been building up for a century and more. The radicals did not make that rage, they merely exploit it. For again, as the Kerner commission said, the media are not a cause of riots, "any more than they are the cause of other phenomena which they report."[24]

It was not the reporting of inflammatory events, but rather the lack of reporting, that let loose the Newark riots of 1967. A troublesome and troublemaking black taxi driver was picked up by police, an event leading to hysterical reports that police were beating him and even that they had killed him. When his arrest was reported to the company that employed him, taxi drivers all over the city heard it on their radio telephones. This was enough to set off a disaster in a city already as tense as a Leyden jar before discharge. Rumors always fly when there is a vacuum of authentic, believable news. Growing with each excited repetition, they spread like a forest fire before the wind.

Moreover, accurate reporting can not only undercut rumor, it can do positive good. A report by Stanford University psychiatrists holds that censorship of the uglier consequences of violence in television, fictional as well as real, is a disservice to society:

> Ironically, the viewer is deprived of the one aspect of violence that might discourage violence. The censor cuts out the ugly consequences, the victim's pain and agony, and the wanton destruction of life. This restricts the viewer from determining the value of violent acts, since the full impact and range of consequences are not presented for appraisal.[25]

Dr. Glazer, quoted above, is not the only one who has pointed to the similarity between the press buildup of Senator Joseph McCarthy and the press buildup of ghetto and campus firebrands. I well remember how, in the oppressive climate of McCarthyism, I was told that if only newspapers did not report the Senator's lies, the distrust and suspicion that covered the country like a noxious vapor would evaporate. Yet it was the reporting of McCarthy that ended McCarthyism. In particular, it was the direct look at him in action, through, among other things, the thoroughly televised Army-McCarthy hearings, that let the country see him as he was. And that led to his downfall.

You can no more separate news coverage of a spectacular event from the event itself than you can get rid of a man's shadow. Therefore the wise course is neither to overplay violence nor to hide it. As the sociologist Otto N. Larsen, author of *Violence and the Mass Media*, told the American Society of Newspaper Editors:

> The basic issue is not the elimination of violence from the mass media. The case rests more on *how* rather than on *whether* it is presented.[26]

Well, how should it be presented?

## We Are Not Helpless

If neither censorship nor any other device gives us a ready solution, we are nevertheless not helpless. There is a middle road between trying to cure an evil by suppressing news of it, and letting news coverage take its unthinking, unrestrained course. This middle road requires no government action, no move by society as a whole. It does require thought, energy, and action on the part of journalists.

A convenient starting point is what the Kerner commission found to be the effect of the mass media on ghetto riots.

> First, that despite instances of sensationalism, inaccuracies, and distortions, newspapers, radio, and television, on the whole, made

a real effort to give a balanced factual account of the 1967 disorders.

Second, that despite this effort, the portrayal of the violence that occurred last summer failed to reflect accurately its scale and character. The overall effect was, we believe, an exaggeration of both mood and event.

Third, and ultimately most important, we believe that the media have thus far failed to report adequately on the causes and consequences of civil disorders and the underlying problems of race relations.[27]

If that seems to be no more than a slap on the wrist, it is nevertheless an indictment. Journalism, being like all human institutions imperfect, is no doubt condemned always to be running behind in performing its task of bringing the world to the citizen. But, even allowing for that, journalism can do better than it has so far.

Typical of what happens when nobody is paying attention is an incident that took place when the first of the modern ghetto riots laid waste the Watts area of Los Angeles in 1965. After it was over Thomas Bradley, a Los Angeles city councilman, told of a meeting in Athens Park attended by several hundred black community leaders who, with a single exception, offered constructive ways of dealing with the outbreak of violence:

> The one exception was a 16-year-old boy who made threats that the burning would spread to the white community and made several irresponsible statements. The other people in the audience shouted him down, but this was the one and only phase of the entire meeting which was carried by the communications media.[28]

This was not an isolated incident. The Kerner commission points to repeated journalistic failures that made riots worse. There were scare headlines not supported by the stories that followed them, false information accepted from beleaguered officials without critical check, a tendency to portray the troubles as race riots when the casulties were virtually all black, and vastly exaggerated reports of damage.[29]

Again, a Detroit radio station broadcast a rumor, based on a telephone tip, that Negroes planned to invade white suburbia the next night. They didn't. In Cincinnati reports were published that white youths had been arrested for possessing a bazooka, usually without mention of the fact that the weapon was inoperable. In Tampa a newspaper fanned trouble by news column speculations like this one, made when a state's attorney held the fatal shooting of a Negro youth justifiable homicide: "There were fears today that the ruling would stir new race problems for Tampa tonight." A West Coast paper ran a headline reading "Rioting Erupts in Washington, D.C. Negroes Hurl Bottles, Rocks at Police Near White House." All the story itself said was that teenage Negroes broke windows and threw bottles and stones at police and firemen downtown, a mile or more from the White House.[30] Individual newsmen sometimes staged events to get action they could photograph, as when one of them coaxed a Negro boy into throwing a rock at the camera.[31] Typical of the whole was this after-the-fact comment by a newspaper editor:

> We used things in our leads and headlines during the riot I wish we could have back now, because they were wrong and they were bad mistakes. . . .
> We used the words "sniper kings" and "nests of snipers." We found out when we were able to get our people into those areas and get them out from under the cars that these sniper kings and these nests of snipers were the constituted authorities shooting at each other, most of them.[32]

Journalism must struggle perennially to report what happens in a way sufficiently colorful and dramatic to induce the public to read it, while yet not betraying the truth. But journalists should have learned since May 17, 1954—the day of the Supreme Court's decision that separate schools are inherently unequal triggered all that has followed—that racial tensions require kid gloves.

The fact is that the old, police-beat standards of reporting inherited from the past will no longer do. Reporting tensions and troubles between the races requires a discipline and maturity that

newsmen earlier in the century never dreamed of. So unexpectedly
devastating was the Burn, Baby, Burn experience of Watts in 1965
that John McCone, former head of the CIA, was named to head a
commission of inquiry. Its exhaustive report included a brief suggestion that journalists should "consider whether there might be
wisdom in the establishment of guidelines, completely voluntary,
on their part, for reporting of such disasters." Thereafter, as the
riots multiplied, guidelines multiplied in their wake. Troubled cities
adopted them. Nationally, the wire services, networks, and some of
the larger newspapers laid down rules of their own.

Those issued by the Associated Press in 1965, and updated in
1967, are a good example. This staffer's catechism begins with
Joseph Pulitzer's three rules for reporting: 1. Accuracy. 2. Accuracy. 3. Accuracy. Then it becomes specific:

1. *Be Precise*. Tell exactly what happened without embellish-
ment. The presence of a crowd of 1000, including Negroes and
civil rights demonstrators, and a police force of 1000 does not
mean that 1000 police battled 1000 demonstrators. The chances
are that the crowd included a few angry militants and most of the
others were spectators; and that only a few of the police did any
battling. . . .

Choose your words carefully. If it's a minor disturbance, don't
call it a riot. But if a full scale riot develops, say so. . . .

2. *Credibility*. The source of your information is most important. We don't rush out with rumors of impending trouble. We
don't rush out with a story about a disturbance on the basis of a
single telephone call. Agitators love to give false information.
Well intentioned persons let emotions sway their better judgment. Check and doublecheck.

If a crowd gathers, don't be an alarmist with a story that "tensions mounted steadily." Don't assume that a crowd of Negroes
or whites is a mob or a potential mob. Get someone to the scene
fast, but wait for the action and tell it as it is. . . .

3. *Damage*. We report what qualified and responsible officials
say, but we do not state it as fact. . . .

4. *Perspective*. We don't reach for headlines by throwing a
story out of focus with an isolated cry of "Get whitey" or an isolated shooting. . . .

· 5. *Background.* Austin Scott, another task force member, states it well:

"All disputes have a history and we should know enough about the town to say what it is. . . .

"If the reporter finds that most of a crowd is angry, or most of the Negro community is troubled, he should say what it is angry at, or why it is troubled."

Spell it out. Don't generalize. Get both sides of any grievance.

6. *Staffing.* Get men to the scene at the first hint of trouble. There is no substitute for the eyes, ears, and wits of our own staffers. . . .

7. Don't describe every Negro who speaks up as a "civil rights leader." A leader has a definable following. One who does not, for example, is comedian Dick Gregory, who is a civil rights activist or militant.[33]

Yet responsible reporting of violence, even under the most stringent of guidelines, is not enough. Something more fundamental is also required. For, as the Kerner commission noted, its major concern was "not in riot reporting as such, but in the failure to report adequately on race relations and ghetto problems and to bring more Negroes into journalism."[34]

The need is to report situations and developments and conditions through the long months or years or even decades before anything overt happens. Because nothing spectacular was going on, journalism left us largely unaware of these long periods of incubation which set the stage for the seemingly spontaneous explosions that shocked the nation when they erupted without apparent reason.

Basically, the journalist must dig painstakingly for news where none seems to exist, by means of highly skilled, interpretive reporting. The Kerner commission says that the communications media, when they reported urban riots, failed to communicate:

They have not communicated to the majority of their audience—which is white—a sense of the degradation, misery, and hopelessness of living in the ghetto. They have not communicated to whites a feeling for the difficulties and frustrations of being a Negro in the United States. They have not shown understanding

or appreciation of—and thus have not communicated—a sense of
Negro culture, thought, or history.

Equally important, most newspaper articles and most television
programming ignore the fact that an appreciable part of their
audience is black.[35]

The commission repeatedly stresses this point. And so slow is
the white majority in becoming aware of it that it is worth stressing:

The ills of the ghetto, the difficulties of life there, the Negro's
burning sense of grievance, are seldom conveyed. Slights and in-
dignities are part of the Negro's daily life, and many of them
come from what he now calls the "white press"—a press that repeatedly, if unconsciously, reflects the biases, the paternalism, the
indifference of white America.[36]

The cure? It seems obvious. Here is how the commission spells
it out:

It would be a contribution of inestimable importance to race
relations in the United States simply to treat ordinary news about
Negroes as news of other groups is now treated.

Specifically, newspapers should integrate Negroes and Negro
activities into all parts of the paper, from the news, society and
club pages to the comic strips. Television should develop programming which integrates Negroes into all aspects of televised
presentations.[37]

At the time of Watts one resident summed up the white man's
journalistic habits in a sentence: "We only see you guys when you
can show us at our worst." And surely, as a black reporter put it
after the 1967 riots, "The most inflammatory thing is not to report
the variety of sounds coming out of the Negro community." What
we have had, and to too great an extent still have, is what William
L. Rivers of Stanford called "Jim Crow Journalism."[38]

If one backs off to see the whole forest of journalism's difficulty,
one sees that the task of reporting becomes more subtle, more complex, all the time. It can be discouraging, as when a paper or a
broadcaster goes to trouble and expense to dig into something that

lies behind the excitement of the moment, only to find that most of its readers or viewers pass it by. But that's the way it is. Perhaps the fault really lies in the conditions under which modern man lives. Most of us seem to feel that, in this tumultuous world, we cannot even keep track of, let alone try to understand, all that happens. True enough, no doubt. And it gets worse with each passing year. Yet journalism has no alternative but to try to make the individual see at least the things that matter. As the Kerner commission says at the end of its section on the media:

> To editors who say "we have run thousands of inches on the ghetto which nobody reads" and to television executives who bemoan scores of underwatched documentaries, we say: find more ways of telling this story, for it is a story you, as journalists, must tell—honestly, realistically, and imaginatively. It is the responsibility of the news media to tell the story of race relations in America, and with notable exceptions, the media have not yet turned to the task with the wisdom, sensitivity, and expertise it demands.[39]

The challenge is even bigger than that, because not only race but a whole sea of other troubles as well, require reporting in depth and dimension not dreamed of before. But if journalism learns that it has to anticipate the events it reports, and devotes its full resources to digging constantly under the surface for what may be going on there, it will be doing all we can ask of it.

# 5

# *Reporting Crime*

### Incident in Denver

IT WAS an August day in 1970. President Nixon, on his way back to Washington from his San Clemente White House, had stopped over in Denver for a meeting on crime control with 100 State and Federal officials.

Before the meeting the President talked with the press on the subject uppermost in his mind in that election year: crime. One thing that was wrong, he said, was the way in which the young, and perhaps adults as well, tended to glamorize vicious criminals. Press and broadcasters kept publishing accounts of crime and trials. But the American public, instead of upholding the system that guaranteed fair trial and so protected the accused as well as society, tended to see the criminals as victims of oppression, and the judges as villains.

Warming to his theme, the President explained that things were different in "Chisum," the John Wayne movie he had just seen at San Clemente. In these simple westerns the good guys won, the bad guys lost. Not so in real life. In the West Coast papers he had seen, for example, big headlines day after day about the trial of the bearded cultist Charles Manson, and three female followers, for the murder of the actress Sharon Tate and six others. Constant exposure by press and television helped glorify those on trial and make heroes of them. Yet, said the President, "Here is a man who was guilty, directly or indirectly, of eight murders without reason."[1] (He said eight rather than seven because Manson himself stood accused of still another murder.)

The comment was one such as any of us might have made. Testimony in the trial over the weeks, detail by detail, had left little doubt that the accused had indeed engaged in an unbelievable orgy of killing, for no apparent reason. Yet the President, himself a lawyer and the country's foremost champion of law and order, had grievously undermined the system of law he was seeking to uphold calling Manson guilty of murder. Reporters nearly bowled over the President in their rush to file their stories. But neither Attorney General Mitchell, who had stood at Mr. Nixon's side when he had made the comment, nor the rest of the presidential entourage seemed to sense the enormity of the presidential gaffe.

Press Secretary Ronald Ziegler soon issued a "clarification." It didn't clarify, because it did not take back the President's words.

In Los Angeles, the trial itself was in turmoil. Defense attorneys requested a mistrial on the ground that the President's verdict of guilty had made fair trial impossible. And so tumultuous was the reaction around the country—the more so because there had not been a swift, candid retraction of the Nixon statement—that Air Force One had to circle Andrews Air Force base for half an hour that evening while the President himself whittled out a statement. It began by saying that the President's words, "may continue to be misunderstood," but then came right out with it:

> To set the record straight, I do not know and did not intend to speculate as to whether the Tate defendants are guilty, in fact, or not. All of the facts in the case have not yet been presented. The defendants should be presumed to be innocent at this stage of the trial.[2]

Even that didn't end it. Next day one of the defense attorneys left a copy of the *Los Angeles Times* on the counsel table, where Manson could reach it. He picked it up and studied the back page in such a way that the front page was turned toward the jurors. They could not help seeing the headline, in enormous type:

MANSON GUILTY,
NIXON DECLARES[3]

The lawyer responsible for bringing the paper in—which the sequestered jury would not have seen otherwise—got three days in jail for contempt. But Judge Older, having in mind the loss to the state and to justice if the long trial had to be gone through all over again, polled the jurors and alternates individually. Finally he was satisfied that the presidential slip would not divert the jurors from basing their verdict exclusively on the evidence presented in court. Later he denied a renewed defense motion for mistrial, though the three young women defendants rose in court and chanted in unison, "If President Nixon thinks we're guilty, why go on with the trial?"[4]

The incident is significant because it is a spectacular example of a difficulty that plagues both justice and journalism: How can crime be reported to the public without at the same time prejudicing jurors, or those who will be jurors, by persuading them of the guilt of the accused before his trial is over—or perhaps even begun?

## The Conflict

Two basic rights are involved, and each, considered by itself, is of overriding importance. Yet, in practice, neither must be allowed to triumph over the other, for without both the civilized life toward which man has struggled through the ages could not survive. That is why both rights are written into the Constitution, as part of the Bill of Rights that was a condition of acceptance of the Constitution itself.

The First Amendment says simply, "Congress shall make no law . . . abridging the freedom of speech, or of the press. . . ." If that sounds innocuous, it is nevertheless of stupendous importance to us all. For the struggles of past centuries make it plain that eternal vigilance against any and all censorship is essential if the people are to know enough to keep control of their own affairs. That is why this country, throughout its history, has insisted that its press be free to print anything it likes, subject only to being responsible for abuse of that freedom.

When it comes to news of crime, and the risk of prejudicing the administration of justice, the American bar and bench show little interest in such freedom. In fact they tend to the opposite extreme, to the point of reminding one of the Maine skipper of wooden-ship days who refused to take in sail during a howling gale. At last the first mate, on behalf of sailors who feared for their lives, screwed up his courage and, through whistling wind and crashing wave, suggested precautionary measures.

"Mister," replied the skipper, "All I want from you is silence—and damn little of that."

Judges and lawyers have reason to ask for silence, for they are concerned with keeping trials fair. The free-press/fair-trial conflict is, as often in man's affairs, a clash not between right and wrong but between two rights.

The right to a fair trial is safeguarded by the Sixth and Fourteenth Amendments. These Amendments, like the First, seem obvious to the point of platitude. "In all criminal prosecutions," begins the Sixth, "the accused shall enjoy the right to a speedy and public trial, by an impartial jury. . . ." And the Fourteenth, that Civil War grab bag of 1868, adds: "Nor shall any State deprive any person of life, liberty, or property, without due process of law; nor deny to any person within its jurisdiction the equal protection of the laws."

These rights take on meaning when one translates them into experience. The history of mankind is in large part the history of injustice. Many a man has been unjustly condemned to disgrace, suffering, or even death, on the basis of insufficient or false evidence if not indeed plain malice.

This is why the upholders of fair trial insist that it is not necessary to publish everything right away. To be sure, they feel that the free press is important, and the public should not be kept unduly in the dark. But let's keep the administration of justice neat and tidy. We cannot have a safe and decent society unless that society is scrupulous in handling crime and punishment. Therefore let's trust the authorities to do things right. When justice is at stake, we should publish only the barest bones of fact, and let the full story come out later.

This attitude prevailed in that unhappy time after Senator Edward Kennedy drove off the bridge at Chappaquiddick, and Mary Jo Kopechne was drowned. Throughout the kid-gloves inquiries that followed there was a tendency to keep official proceedings under wraps. The result is that to this day there is something unsatisfactory about the event, an uneasy sense that the whole truth may still not be known.

The free-press/fair-trial clash thus leaves us on a seesaw. For if secrecy and concealment of the whole truth are unhealthy, the fact remains that the administration of justice must be kept as uncontaminated by outside influences as possible. Listen to a few sentences uttered a century and a quarter ago by Rufus Choate, the redoubtable courtroom advocate. Speaking before a Massachusetts State Convention, on July 14, 1853, he laid down this prescription for a judge:

> In the first place he should be profoundly learned in all the learning of the law. . . . In the next place he must be a man, not merely upright, not merely honest and well intentioned—this of course—but a man who will not respect persons in judgment. . . . He shall know nothing about the parties; everything about the case. He shall do every thing for justice; nothing for himself; nothing for his friends; nothing for his patron; nothing for his sovereign. If on one side is the executive power and the legislature and the people—the sources of his honors, the givers of his daily bread—and on the other an individual, nameless and odious, his eye is to see neither great nor small, attending only to the

"trepidations of the balance." If a law is passed by a unanimous legislature, clamored for by the general voice of the people, and a cause is before him on it in which the whole community is on one side and an individual, nameless or odious, on the other, and he believes it to be against the Constitution, he must declare it— or there is no judge.

We cannot all be judges. But we can all be jurors, or at least citizens sensitive to the "trepidations of the balance" of justice. Choate's words, though spoken in a different context, give fire and meaning to those two words, "fair trial."

Having in mind the value involved on both sides, one concludes that the conflict between free press and fair trial is inevitable. Presumably that conflict will last as long as man himself does. But then, there are ways of living with it.


### Trial by Newspaper

Today's free-press/fair-trial conflict began to take shape in 1831. At that time, however, it was not publication of prejudicial matter that was in question. What happened was this. A judge took umbrage at a legitimate, and indeed, necessary, newspaper function, the criticism of a decision he had rendered. So irked was he that he put the offending writers in jail for contempt of court. But this was so raw that Congress passed a law limiting the contempt power. Henceforth judges in federal courts might punish only acts committed in the court itself, or so near as to threaten justice.

Since then many a judge has bristled with indignation at newspapermen who dared question a decision of his. But there is little risk to writers and editors as long as the comment is not published before a trial is over. And American newspapermen, unlike their colleagues in Great Britain, are usually safe from jail for contempt even when what they write does prejudice fair trial.

Those heady days in which this century took shape, the 1920s, provided several spectacular examples of why there is a clash between bar and press. There was the 1923 Hall-Mills case, which revolved around the murder of an Episcopal rector and a choir singer in a New Jersey lover's lane. Tabloid journalism fanned the dying embers of the case into a second trial that made reams of lurid, if sometimes insubstantial, copy. There followed the sordid circus of the Grey-Snyder trial, complete with a sneaked front-page picture in the *New York Daily News* showing the convicted Ruth Snyder at the moment of execution in Sing Sing's electric chair.

There followed, in 1935, the Hauptmann trial, a prime example of how news coverage of an event can change the event itself. Bruno Richard Hauptmann, a taciturn Bronx carpenter, was brought to trial for the kidnap-murder of the infant son of Charles A. Lindbergh, who had become a world hero eight years earlier by being the first to fly from New York to Paris for a long-standing $25,000 prize. One reporter who was there thus described the scene in and about the Hunterdon County Courthouse in Flemington, New Jersey:

> The floating reportorial army, spectacularly augmented to give Americans every scrap of news concerning Bruno Richard Hauptmann's trial, has taken complete possession of this sleepy little town. . . . At least 700 reporters, photographers and communications men [telegraph and radio technicians] are here.[5]

It wasn't only the press and members of the bar who violated their professional ethics and turned this life-and-death trial into a spectacular caricature of justice:

> No less than 300 reporters, many of them star reporters, some of them famous novelists turned reporter for the trial—Walter Winchell, Edna Ferber, Arthur Brisbane, Fannie Hurst, Damon Runyon, Kathleen Norris, Alexander Woollcott, Adela Rogers St. John—were coming to Flemington. Also, great figures of the stage and screen, United States Senators, crooners, concert singers, social celebrities; and of course, people who never missed any important event—a World Series, a prize fight, a murder trial—had announced that they would attend. . . . Foreign accents were heard. Raoul de Roussy de Sales was in Flemington, sent by

*Paris-Soir,* and Lionel Shortt of the *London Daily Mail,* and Dixie Tighe of the *London Daily Express.* A great criminal lawyer, Samuel Leibowitz, had been engaged by a radio network to comment on the progress of the trial, and professional colleagues, no less familiar with the law's intricacies, were to analyze the events in the courtroom for rival networks. . . . This was to be the trial of the century. And the world was not to miss a word of it.[6]

Walter Winchell, the columnist, was not alone in finding Hauptmann guilty before the trial began. Typical of the whole was an incident that surfaced again in 1970, when Colonel Lindbergh's 1938-45 journal was published. Representatives of a free press broke into a Trenton morgue and wrenched the cover off the coffin containing the body of the murdered baby, to get a photograph to help sate the insatiable appetite of the crowd.[7] Later a second Lindbergh child was hounded on his way to nursery school. Once a makeshift curtain dropped from the back of a truck parked near the school and two tubes, like glinting eyes, focused on the child before the truck sped away. Another time a car forced the car containing a teacher and the child to stop at the curb. The teacher drew the little boy close as the photographers thrust their cameras into the window. It was not another kidnapping, just a news-photo syndicate at work.[8]

The American Bar Association's annual report for 1937 called the whole extravaganza "perhaps the most spectacular and depressing example of improper publicity and professional misconduct ever presented to the United States in a criminal trial."[9] There followed a split between bar and press that is only now being healed.

Through the mid-century decades, spectacular cases kept leading to spectacular abuses. One such was the 1954 trial and conviction of Dr. Samuel H. Sheppard, socially prominent Cleveland osteopath, for the murder of his pregnant wife. His story was that an unknown, bushy-haired intruder had broken into the house in the night, killed his wife, and knocked him out after a tussle.

Because there were no other suspects, attention centered on Dr. Sheppard from the first. Even so, despite some early questioning there was no arrest. Eventually, when nothing much happened, the papers began to ignore the case—except for the *Cleveland Press*. Its dynamic editor, Louis B. Seltzer, wrote front-page editorials that, while careful to call Dr. Sheppard a suspect, nevertheless pointed toward him as the probable murderer.

The captions over these editorials were classics in prejudicial journalism. The first one said:

### SOMEBODY IS GETTING AWAY WITH MURDER

The text began: "What's the matter with law enforcement authorities of Cuyahoga County?" It went on to say that Dr. Sheppard was surrounded by family and friends who would not let prying police and other authorities near. It ended with this: "It's time that somebody smashed into this situation and tore aside this restraining curtain of sham, politeness, and hypocrisy, and went at the business of solving a murder—and quit this nonsense of artificial politeness that has not been extended to any other murder case in generations."[10]

The Bay Village City Council, governing body of the tight little suburb in which the Sheppards lived, was thereby prodded into taking the investigation from its own police and turning it over to Cleveland's homicide squad. But still nothing happened. So there followed a second editorial. It was headed,

### WHY NO INQUEST? DO IT NOW, DR. GERBER

This galvanized Dr. Gerber, the coroner, into getting around to an inquest, which was turned into a televised circus but again produced nothing. Dr. Sheppard went back to the seclusion of the family-operated osteopathic hospital. There followed still another editorial, all across the top of page one, under a heading that became famous as an example of what the press should not do:

## QUIT STALLING—BRING HIM IN

That night Dr. Sheppard was arrested. He was indicted, found guilty of second-degree murder, and sent to the state penitentiary. Eventually the Supreme Court reversed this conviction, on the ground that prejudicial publication had prevented fair trial. A second trial acquitted Dr. Sheppard.

The tale is retold in the opinion Justice Tom Clark delivered for the Supreme Court, eight to one, with only Justice Black dissenting.[11] This formal account cites examples of the endless comment and supposed evidence that was fed to papers and television—to which the jury had untrammeled access—though much of what was published never was admitted as evidence in court. The chief trouble, however, was chargeable less to the press than to the trial judge. Justice Clark pointed to one basic factor in these words:

> With this background the case came for trial two weeks before the November general election at which the chief prosecutor was a candidate for municipal judge and the presiding judge, Judge Blythin, was a candidate to succeed himself.

Justice Clark's opinion is largely a catalog of errors that allowed prejudicial matter, published outside the court, to contaminate the trial itself. It all violated "the undeviating rule of this court" as it had been laid down by Justice Oliver Wendell Holmes in 1907:

> The theory of our system is that the conclusions to be reached in a case will be induced only by evidence and argument in open court, and not by any outside influence, whether of private talk or public print.[12]

The Supreme Court found it to be fact, wrote Justice Clark, that "Bedlam reigned at the courthouse during the trial and newsmen took over practically the entire courtroom, hounding most of the participants in the trial, especially Sheppard." When the Court said this, twelve years after the event, nine reporters who had covered the trial protested in a letter. "The description of a 'carnival atmosphere,'" they wrote to the Supreme Court, "has slowly been moved from a description of the inquest three months before the trial to the trial itself." During the actual trial, they declared, there had been "an admirable state of decorum." But the Supreme Court, having spoken, ignored the possibility that it might itself have been caught off base.

Today the Sheppard case survives as a textbook illustration of what happens when the First Amendment, with its deliberately wide margin for error, is allowed to override the Sixth Amendment's requirement of an impartial jury. It is to be noted, however, that it does not follow, as many of bar and bench concluded, that the press should therefore be restricted. Not once in his opinion did Justice Clark so much as hint at such a thing. His opening sentence pinpointed the question before the Supreme Court as "whether Sheppard was deprived of a fair trial . . . because of the trial judge's failure to protect Sheppard sufficiently from the massive, pervasive and prejudicial publicity that attended his prosecution." Indeed, Justice Clark noted that "a responsible press has always been regarded as the handmaiden of effective judicial administration, especially in the criminal field."[13] Throughout the opinion he laid down the rule that it is the responsibility of the courts themselves, not the press, to insulate trials against prejudice:

> . . . where there is a reasonable likelihood that prejudicial news prior to trial will prevent a fair trial, the judge should continue the case until the threat abates, or transfer it to another county not so permeated with publicity. In addition, sequestration of the jury was something the judge should have raised *sua sponte* with counsel. If publicity during the proceedings threatens the fairness of the trial, a new trial should be ordered. But we must remember that reversals are but palliatives; the cure lies in those remedial measures that will prevent the prejudice at its inception. The courts must take such steps by rule and regulation that will protect their processes from prejudicial outside interferences. Neither prosecutors, counsel for defense, the accused, witnesses, court staff nor enforcement officers coming under the jurisdiction of the court should be permitted to frustrate its function. Collaboration between counsel and the press as to information affect-

ing the fairness of a criminal trial is not only subject to regulation, but is highly censurable and worthy of disciplinary
measures.[14]

Here every stricture is directed against judge and counsel, not
against the press. Nevertheless bar and bench still point in horror
to the Sheppard case as a monument to press irresponsibility, and
some newspapermen agree. Yet one cannot get a balanced view of
the two rights involved if one lets it go at that. For one must ask
what would have happened if the *Cleveland Press* had not hounded
Dr. Sheppard into arrest. As far as anyone knows, nothing. The
basic fact about the Sheppard case, often forgotten, is this: Somebody *did* get away with murder.

Examples of why it is often a public service to publish, even at
the risk of prejudicing a subsequent trial, keep reappearing. I recall a time when Hartford, indeed, all central Connecticut, was terrorized by a series of six murders and several related violent crimes
in various communities. The deaths and injuries were part of a
chain of holdups and robberies that lasted from mid-December
1956 to the end of February 1957. Not only were the holdup victims—a tailor, a package-store owner, a druggist, and the like—
shot to death, or beaten, or both, but so was any hapless customer
or bystander, apparently lest a single witness survive.

At first it was assumed that but one bloodthirsty criminal was on
the loose. Gradually a pattern emerged, and it became evident that
a pair of murderers were at work. Typical of the sudden death that
kept striking out of the blue was the holdup of a North Haven shoe
store. Two young men entered the store before it closed for the
evening, and the taller one asked to see a pair of shoes, size 12.
Seconds later he pulled out a pistol and beat the proprietor over
the head with it. Just then a customer and his wife from nearby
Meriden happened in. The bandit ordered them to kneel on the
floor, and forthwith shot both dead with bullets in the back of the
head.

Twice an intended victim was shot or beaten and left for dead, only to recover. Nevertheless the police seemed helpless. Because the take from the holdups was small, there was nothing to account for the wide-ranging terror but a lust to kill. One could almost feel public apprehension rise from day to day. Perhaps a million people in the central part of the state began to wonder whether they might be the next to be murdered.

Seventy-five days after the terror had struck, when a gas-station owner and a customer were shot dead, relief came. It was the six-foot-three bandit's request to see size 12 shoes that trapped him, because the shoe store owner lived to tell the tale. It turned out that the killer had a previous record, including a stay in the death house for a 1950 holdup murder, from which he had been freed on a legal technicality only the year before.

Once the state police began to close in on the two murderers, what is denounced as trial by newspapers took place. This, inter-acting with the spontaneous public alarm over it all, later became occasion for a defense move for a change of venue. But at the time, when fresh deaths were expected daily, and when in fact they came unpleasantly often, nobody cared about prejudicing the rights of those who might subsequently be tried for so ghastly a series of crimes. Everyone cared about having the guilty ones found and put out of circulation. Inevitably there was a vast, almost palpable sigh of public relief when the state police finally got their hands on Joseph L. Taborsky and Arthur Culombe, the two social misfits responsible for the murder spree.

As far as the public was concerned what mattered was making certain that the arrested suspects were indeed the ones responsible. Everyone accepted as only right the publication of every fresh fact about the murders and attempted murders, the suspects, their ar-rest, previous criminal records, and anything they might say that might confirm the fact that the public would henceforth be safe.

What was published left no doubt. Witness after witness identi-fied the two men. After nearly a week of questioning by the state police (with little published as to the methods of questioning), first

Culombe, the accomplice, and then Taborsky, the principal, whose lantern jaw had earned him the nickname, "The Chin," confessed. This satisfying fact was made known by the commissioner of state police himself. A front-page picture in the *Hartford Courant* showed Taborsky re-enacting one of his crimes. All this, plus Taborsky's confession of the earlier murder, was trumpeted to the public on page one. As far as the public was concerned, trial by newspaper had settled it. The subsequent legal trial was but a formality to ratify what the facts as published had plainly told.

And so, indeed, it was. Taborsky eventually gave up the legal struggle, re-entered the death house, and this time came out dead. Culombe kept up the legal battle and got life imprisonment. No matter how much this kind of thing is deplored and denounced, trial by newspaper will continue because, as here, it is unmistakably and beyond all question a public service.

For another example in a totally different context, take the night of March 25, 1965, when Viola Gregg (Mrs. Anthony J.) Liuzzo was driving back to Montgomery, Alabama, after having returned some civil rights marchers to Selma. A car came up from behind and, while passing hers, erupted in a fusillade that killed Mrs. Liuzzo. Her only companion, a young black, said that her car went out of control and stopped off the highway.

The next day, President Johnson, speaking from the White House, with Attorney General Katzenbach and FBI Chief Hoover by his side, announced the arrest of four members of the Ku Klux Klan for the crime. The President was careful not to call them guilty of the murder. He referred to them only as being charged "with conspiracy to violate the civil rights of the murdered woman" —murder not being a federal crime. But the President told a nation watching on television:

> Mrs. Liuzzo . . . was murdered by the enemies of justice who for decades have used the rope and the gun and the tar and feathers to terrorize their neighbors.
> They struck by night, as they generally do, for their purpose

cannot stand the light of day. My father fought them many long years ago in Texas, and I have fought them all my life because I believe them to threaten the peace of every community where they exist.[15]

The words were technically correct, by pre-trial standards. Yet they left little doubt that the four arrested so swiftly after the crime were indeed the murderers. How, indeed, could it be otherwise? The idea of keeping members of the public, from among whom jurors will be drawn, from getting into their heads anything that might give them an opinion as to whether the accused are guilty or not is a noble one. But often it is unrealistic. It is as though the medical profession, concerned lest patients come into surgery contaminated, were to insist on sterilizing the entire outside world. Mrs. Liuzzo's murder, being at that time but the latest in a series of similar outrages, shocked the nation. Because the states of the deep South did not prosecute white murderers of blacks, or murderers of whites aiding blacks, it was important to the entire American people that the guilty not get away with murder. To have the President himself assure the nation unmistakably, if not quite in so many words, that those who were guilty of the murder had indeed been caught was a tonic. The fact that it had been done swiftly and precisely, through FBI infiltration of the KKK, made it the more certain that the suspects were indeed guilty. Here was proof, which the nation longed for, that racism would not always triumph over justice. Nor was there any sign later that the glare of national and even world publicity that resulted from this example of trial by newspaper, as directed by the President himself, affected the actual trial of the men one way or another.

Trial by newspaper can, and often does, serve a public purpose.

## Journalism by Judges

If the journalist's desire to tell all at times strays into excesses that prejudice trial, censorship is no solution. Yet members of bar and bench, concerned over the integrity of the judicial process, become fired by the ideal of avoiding even the suspicion of prejudice. And this at times drives them to withhold facts the public ought to have.

Indeed, much of America's legal profession looks with envy upon Great Britain, where fair trial is exalted over free press and no argument about it. In recent years the British courts have made even more stringent their already stiff prohibitions against publication, notably as regards pre-trial proceedings. There is no need here to examine British practice, which has developed out of traditions and conditions that differ markedly from ours. But a single example, typical of British fussiness in these things, is illuminating because it shows how far protecting fair trial can go when there is little countervailing pressure to publish.

The example in question revolves around one Michael Abdul Malik, a British Black Muslim leader also known as Michael X. A previous trial on a charge of inciting racial hatred having ended in mistrial, he was awaiting a second trial. A few days before the trial began, the *Sunday Times* (no relation to *The Times,* though both are Thomson properties) published an article on race relations in Britain. One of the accompanying illustrations was a small picture of Malik, run over a four-line caption that identified him as "having had an unedifying career as brothel keeper, procurer, and property racketeer."

In the trial Malik, who had no lawyer, argued that the caption made a fair trial impossible. The court did not agree, and it sentenced him to twelve months in prison. One would think that would settle it—but not in Britain. For the first time in its 150 years the *Sunday Times* was charged with contempt of court. Its editor, Harold Evans, was likewise charged, and the Attorney General himself took over as prosecutor. When the contempt trial was over, the Lord Chief Justice and two other High Court judges fined the paper £5000, or $12,000, for having been in contempt by publishing the caption before trial.

Curiously, so severe a judgment, which in this country would be most unlikely, was hailed as indicating a trend toward a liberal attitude on contempt. Why? Because the editor, Mr. Evans, had not been put behind bars.

So strictly are British newspapers forced to mind their judicial manners that, as was brought out in the proceedings, the paper had a meticulous system to prevent just such an error. Mr. Evans himself had not seen the caption before it was published. Yet in the editorial chain of command there was provision for careful review, including scrutiny by the paper's own lawyer—who had let the caption stand on the theory that it was libel-proof because true, and not in contempt because it bore no relation to the issue on which Malik was being tried.

Lord Chief Justice Parker agreed that, though the editor took full responsibility, he could not be expected to see every word of so large a paper before publication. Not only that but the editor "had devised, so far as humanly possible, a system to prevent this sort of thing." Hence no jail for Mr. Evans.[16] The fine against the paper was presumably a lesson to others not to print anything about crime except what the judges say they may.

American practice is mild by comparison. Still, legal unhappiness has continued over careless and often callous disregard for fair trial on the part of press and radio, a situation made even less happy by the advent of television.

The shattering experience that brought the issue to a head was the assassination of President Kennedy. The Warren Report, published almost a year after the event, served to satisfy the nation's hunger to know every last detail about the tragedy—a need that a trial would have filled had not the murderer, Lee Harvey Oswald, himself been murdered. The Warren Report did not find any substantial error in the immediate, on-the-spot reporting of the tumultuous events of that four-day tragedy. But it did cite that reporting as dramatic evidence of the need "to bring about a proper balance between the right of the public to be kept informed and the right of the individual to a fair and impartial trial."[17] It did not hesitate to lay down a lawyer's concept of where that balance lay:

The American Bar Association declared in December 1963 that "widespread publicizing of Oswald's alleged guilt, involving statements by officials and public disclosures of the details of 'evidence,' would have made it extremely difficult to impanel an unprejudiced jury and afford the accused a fair trial." . . . The Commission agrees that Lee Harvey Oswald's opportunity for a trial by 12 jurors free of preconception as to his guilt or innocence would have been seriously jeopardized by the premature disclosure and weighing of the evidence against him. . . .

An informed public provided the ultimate guarantee that adequate steps would be taken to apprehend those responsible for the assassination and that all necessary precautions would be taken to protect the national security. It was therefore proper and desirable that the public know which agencies were participating in the investigation and the rate at which their work was progressing. The public was also entitled to know that Lee Harvey Oswald had been apprehended and that the State had gathered sufficient evidence to arraign him for the murders of the President and Patrolman Tippit, that he was being held pending action of the grand jury, that the investigation was continuing, and that the law enforcement agencies had discovered no evidence which tended to show that any other person was involved in either slaying.

However, neither the press nor the public had a right to be contemporaneously informed by the police or prosecuting authorities of the details of the evidence being accumulated against Oswald. . . . The courtroom, not the newspaper or television screen, is the appropriate forum in our system for the trial of a man accused of a crime.[18]

This counsel of perfection reveals why it is not possible to achieve a balance that gives full and equal value to both rights. The notion that a cataclysmic shock, the like of which the country had not experienced since Abraham Lincoln was shot, could be dismissed by confining information to the civilian equivalent of name, rank, and serial number, is naïve. In the first place at such a time the authorities, from the corner cop to the commissioner of state police, and on up to the FBI and United States Attorney General, have other things to do besides thinking ahead to what the Supreme Court might say years later, if the case should bring the bar-press conflict before it. In the second place the public should not, and indeed will not, tolerate virtual silence. Man abhors a vacuum of information. If he doesn't get the facts he will invent substitutes, in a flaming spiral of rumor and fantasy. A self-governing people must have as much of the truth as it can get, in the administration of justice as in all else. And the truth is the truth, whether prejudicial or not, and whether later admissible as evidence or not. When the Warren recommendations came out, five of us on an ASNE committee issued a report, largely prepared by the chairman, Alfred Friendly of the *Washington Post*. It said:

> Merely to state the idea that there could or should have been less than complete disclosure is to indicate its impossibility. It is worth letting the imagination run for a moment on what the consequences would have been to the persons and property of both right- and left-wing groups in the United States, to Oswald's widow, to his and her former associates and indeed to the public attitude about relations with the Soviet Union, had any areas in the whole ghastly episode been hidden behind a curtain of official secrecy during the first 24 to 72 hours after the fatal shots. For the public to have been left speculating, guessing and ultimately inventing for the several weeks, or more probably months, before Oswald could have been brought to trial would have been a course fraught with the greatest dangers.[19]

A detailed and convincing analysis of the undesirability and indeed futility of such an attempt can be found in the appendix to a dispassionate study of bar-press relations, *Crime and Publicity,* written subsequently by Mr. Friendly and a lawyer, Ronald L. Goldfarb. Suffice it to note their conclusion:

> We have guessed at the consequences for Oswald [including a "voluntary" confession extracted via third degree] had the Dallas law enforcement officials confined their public statements to the items under the Warren Commission rubric. What guess may one make about the consequences for the nation? . . .
> Our guess is that they would have been dreadful.[20]

Through the years before the Warren Report was published newsmen and lawyers had, for the most part, been content to re-

main each on their own side of the fence, issuing occasional denunciations of the other. But beginning with a pilot project in 1963,
the American Bar Association undertook a survey of "the entire
spectrum of the criminal justice process." So it was natural that,
when the Warren Commission urged joint bar-media action toward
establishing ethical standards for reporting crime, the ABA should
set up an advisory committee on fair trial and free press.

This committee, manned by experienced lawyers and state and
federal judges, had Justice Paul C. Reardon of the Supreme Judicial Court of Massachusetts as chairman. It spent two years in research, field investigation, and consultation. Representatives of
national press and broadcasting groups protested some of the overtones of censorship that appeared in the committee's work, which
led to modifications. The report was published in October 1966,
and, after further minor changes, the ABA adopted the whole as
part of its new Code of Professional Responsibility in February
1968.

A successor group to Judge Reardon's was charged with the task
of urging the adoption of the new rules throughout the country,
and of encouraging bar and media cooperation "in voluntary measures to protect the rights of fair trial and free press."[21]

What newsmen still tend to call the Reardon report, or Reardon
for short, consists of four categories of standards, grouped under
these headings:

I   Conduct of attorneys in criminal cases.
II  Conduct of law enforcement officers, judges, and judicial em-
    ployees in criminal cases.
III Conduct of judicial proceedings in criminal cases.
IV  Exercise of the contempt power.

The code says nothing about requiring the press to limit publication, though there had been several attempts to do just that, for the
obvious reason that such censorship would violate the First Amendment. And the code's intent was to permit a maximum of information—from the lawyer's point of view—to be made available to the

public. Nevertheless the overriding concern of the report is that nothing be published that might prejudice fair trial. Thus it is held permissible to give out information that a crime has been committed, that an accused has been arrested and under what circumstances, and to permit "what transpires in open court" to be reported. But throughout, whenever there is a possible conflict between the First as against the Sixth and Fourteenth Amendments, the doubt is resolved in favor of secrecy.

It is hard to quarrel with these rules—if one assumes the universal probity and ability of police and law-enforcement officials, lawyers for prosecution and defense, judges, and court officials. There is, for example, nothing against the public interest in admonishing lawyers that it is ethically improper to make out-of-court statements about a trial, the parties, or the issues, beyond quoting from the court's public records. As an ABA commentary explained, the restrictions on news "do not do more than prescribe safeguards against exposure of the jury to inadmissible or prejudicial statements or influences that may affect the outcome of the trial." But there is nothing here about the fact that precisely this concern for the accused may also—if something should go wrong somewhere—conceal from the public something it ought to know. Typical is the way Reardon provisions for pre-trial hearings lean in one direction only. A defendant may move that part or all of the hearing be held in the secrecy of the judge's chambers, with no reporters present, and with publication possible only long afterward, after the trial itself is over. Even if it is a public hearing, the judge has power to caution newsmen that certain information given there, if later inadmissible as evidence in the trial itself, may jeopardize fair trial.

The Reardon report was not the only move the legal profession made to ensure that fair trial and free press might live and let live, while yet resolving any doubt in favor of fair trial. A contemporary of the Reardon committee was another, set up by the Association of the Bar of the City of New York under Judge Harold R. Medina of the U.S. Court of Appeals, Second Circuit. This committee, too, formulated its thesis, tried it out on the customers, and then put it in final form. Newsmen tended to look upon it with a more friendly eye than they did the Reardon report, because the Medina committee said right in the beginning that it had concluded "after exhaustive study, . . . that direct controls on the radio and television industries and on the press by a governmental scheme of regulation are untenable in the light of the First Amendment's guarantee of free speech and free press."[22] It recognized, as the Reardon Committee did in the end, that the key to fair trial lies in controlling lawyers and judges, enforcement officers and police, and in avoiding the fair-trial advocate's natural inclination to tell the press, "You can't print that."

Still another committee, set up by the Judicial Conference of the United States, with Judge Irving R. Kaufman of the Court of Appeals for the Second Circuit, New York, as chairman, plowed the same field. Its aim was to implement the guidelines set down in the Supreme Court's Sheppard decision, and in general to achieve in the federal courts standards to match those put forth by the Reardon Committee and the ABA for the states. In the end it recommended that the federal system adopt the substance of the Reardon standards. Then it added a recommendation that, in highly publicized or sensational cases, each federal court

> . . . may issue a special order governing such matters as extra-judicial statements by parties and witnesses likely to interfere with the rights of the accused to a fair trial by an impartial jury, the seating and conduct in the courtroom of spectators and news media representatives, the management and sequestration of jurors and witnesses, and other matters the Court may deem appropriate for inclusion in such an order.[23]

On September 19, 1968, the Judicial Conference adopted these recommendations. Local federal jurisdictions thereupon adopted them, just as many states adopted Reardon. For practical purposes Reardon became the law of the land.

These attempts to set up guidelines, including the attendant controversy and soul-searching by the media, are all to the good in that they minimize the possibility of excesses by the media in the future. Nevertheless, the widespread adoption of Reardon leaves a residual uneasiness among those whose principal concern is informing the public. Federal and state legal establishments have power, simply by willing it, to adopt whatever restrictions seem good to them. If the Judicial Conference of the United States, or the top court of a state, or whoever else controls a particular judicial structure, so decides, then Reardon or anything else is as rigid and unassailable as any law debated and passed by a legislature made up of elected representatives responsible to the public. Press and broadcasters have no comparable authority to say how things are going to be.

If the motives of bar and bench are the highest, journalists nevertheless fear that lawyers and even judges may be just as human as journalists, and therefore just as liable to error. For example: On March 20, 1968, about six weeks after the ABA's House of Delegates adopted Reardon, a Common Pleas judge in Philadelphia, Stanley M. Greenberg, was indicted by a federal grand jury. He and two others, not lawyers, were accused of having done at least nine banks out of $200,000—shortly before his appointment to the bench—by means of kited checks and other unjudicial devices.

The judge, apparently, was known and respected by members of the bar. Upon news of his indictment some of his distinguished colleagues forgot all about fair trial, and rushed into trial by newspaper in his defense. The Chancellor of the Philadelphia Bar Association, a former Chancellor who was lawyer for Judge Greenberg, the Administrative Judge of Common Pleas, and the Philadelphia District Attorney—on this occasion, when it suited them—thus turned their backs on Reardon. One let it be known that officers of the bar association "have great confidence" in the accused as a "citizen, a lawyer, and a judge." Another, the accused's counsel, said that normally he would say nothing but "I must set aside my policy because the extreme circumstances of this case justify a statement to the public. . . . I am indeed outraged by the return of this indictment because, in my opinion, there is no basis for these charges and the judge will be vindicated." The Administrative Judge was confident that "when this matter is disposed of, which I hope will be done promptly, Judge Greenberg will be completely vindicated."

As for the District Attorney, he was shocked by the indictment, and added: "Everyone is presumed innocent and in my opinion that certainly applies to Judge Greenberg especially." In fact after thinking it over for three days he came out against Reardon, with a blast that no newsman could have phrased better. "The case," he said, "illustrated that the important time for comment is when the incident is first called to public attention . . . not when a trial is over and the issue stale." He added that "Newspapers reflect the reality of public concern. They are concerned when an event happens, not a month later when it is all over."[24] Incidentally, when it was all over Judge Greenberg was convicted despite the prejudicial publicity in his favor, though he went on to endless appeals.

Another worry of journalists is that Reardon may have an effect more powerful than that intended. Despite the ABA disclaimer that Reardon does not forbid publication of facts the public ought to have, it has inspired courts and their officers, and prosecutors and police, with fear lest they overstep the bounds Reardon lays down. No judge relishes the thought of being reversed on such a ground.

The principle involved here is inherent in man. I once saw it at work with dramatic effect when, in 1937, I went to Nazi Germany to see what I could of the way in which Dr. Goebbels ruled the press. His aim was to keep the newspapers from putting into the minds of the German people anything he did not want there. The fact that daily orders went out from the propaganda ministry—as to what news was to be published, and how it was to be played—was notorious at the time. I never did succeed in getting my hands on a copy of those orders. But I found German editors remarkably frank, when out in a car, or off in a corner of a restaurant or beer garden where no one could overhear. One after another these editors, with the Nazi party button prominent in their lapels, would say that it wasn't so much what was ordered that kept them in line as fear of what might happen if they strayed over what might turn out later to have been the line. Self-censorship, rather than censorship, gave Goebbels his power. So much so indeed that he used to complain that the papers were too obviously a monotone, and why didn't the editors show some initiative and variety? The trouble was that, when now and again some editor tried it, he disappeared into a concentration camp.

This principle works not only for evil men like Dr. Goebbels, but also upon the best of men, impelled by the best of motives. Take for example a post-Reardon trial in California. The charge was murder: a bartender had been slain for $136. The details, though interesting enough, are too complex to be detailed here. The net of it is that the judge, citing the Reardon report even though it had not been adopted in California, gave in to the public defender's request for secrecy. The local paper, the *Oxnard Press-Courier,* restive that the trial was in good part concealed from the public, appealed the judge's ruling while the trial was still in progress.

On behalf of a unanimous three-man court, Justice Macklin Fleming of the Second Appellate District, Division Two, of the State Court of Appeals in Los Angeles, reversed the trial court's ruling. His forty-page statement is an admirable exposition of both the conflicting values involved. Even so Judge Fleming came out in a ringing defense of public trial as being required by common law, California statutes, and the Constitution, unless pressing exceptions argue otherwise. He found that, by the time the appeal had come up, more than half the case had been heard in secret. His often eloquent decision noted that the judge, "with the most laudable of motives undertook to protect the rights of the defendant" to a fair trial. But the results were what they always are when men invoke secrecy, whether from the noblest motives or otherwise:

> In the present case it is startling to see the evils of secret proceedings so proliferating in seven short weeks that the court could reach the astonishing result of committing a citizen to jail in secret proceedings, could contemplate inquisitorial proceedings against a newspaper reporter for reporting this commitment, and could adopt the position that the district attorney, the chief law-enforcement officer in the community, was prohibited on pain of contempt from advising the public that someone had been sent secretly to jail. In effect, the court, in seeking the ideal solution to the problem of trial publicity, jettisoned important safeguards of California law by conducting what amounted to a Star Chamber proceeding against Dorothy Castro [a witness] and committing her to jail by an order suspiciously resembling a lettre de cachet. As so often happens, participants in secret proceedings quickly tend to lose their perspective, and the quality of the proceedings suffers as a consequence.[25]

Most of the controversy over news of crime and justice swirls not about secrecy during a trial itself, but about pre-trial events: Don't publish anything at the time a crime is committed, or when a suspect is caught, that might prejudice his trial when eventually it comes along. But there is also pressure for secrecy during trials, despite the fact that the Sixth Amendment stipulates a public trial as well as an impartial one. This is testimony to a principle whose roots go back to Magna Carta—that justice is most likely to be done when the proceedings held in its name are conducted in full view of the public.

There comes to mind an incident that took place midway through a criminal trial in Connecticut's Superior Court in Hartford. The defendant was a policeman, accused of breaking into a business establishment he was supposedly protecting. At one point, when things were not going well for the accused, the defense moved —in the absence of the jury—that the state's chief witness be given a mental examination before being allowed to testify further.

"I will reserve decision on the motion," said Judge James E. Murphy. Then, turning to the press table, he added: "There is to be no mention of this motion in reports about this trial."

During a recess the reporters rushed to the judge's chamber to ask how he could issue such an order regarding something that had taken place in open court. "I have the authority, and I'll jail for contempt any reporter who defies me," replied the judge.

Because this happened shortly before noon it fell to the afternoon paper, the *Hartford Times,* to decide whether or not to go along with the judge's order to suppress. Presumably the judge had in mind the desirability of not casting doubt on the credibility of the witness before it was determined whether he was or was not reliable. Yet the motion had come up in open court. Accordingly the *Times,* its later editions still to be printed, went ahead and reported what had happened just as it had happened.

In doing so the paper was going out on a limb—the more so because Judge Murphy had a reputation for severity. This time it got away with it, however, because during the noon hour the judge apparently thought the better of his decision. When the afternoon session began he denied the defense motion for a psychiatric examination, and then told reporters they were free to use the story. No contest.

Here was an infinitesimal bit of flotsam on the massive tide of news about crime. Yet the principle involved is significant. Let the jury be sequestered whenever the court sees a risk that it might be contaminated by evidence that is not admissible. But unless the public knows what has happened, just as it happened when it happened, it cannot be sure that some error or favoritism is not being concealed, or that the law under which trial is held is not working as intended, or indeed that anything else has gone amiss.

The issue remains two-sided. If it is a constant struggle to keep justice from being contaminated by prejudice, it is equally a constant struggle to keep justice in full view of the public. The centuries of Anglo-Saxon jurisprudence are studded with statements, now classic, to that effect. Typical are three from the writings of that British philosopher of law and morals of the early nineteenth century, Jeremy Bentham. They appear within a few pages of one another in the first of his five volumes on the "Rationale of Judicial Evidence." They deal with "Publicity and privacy, as applied to judicature in general and to the collection of evidence in particular."

The first makes clear why a witness should testify in open court, rather than in chambers or elsewhere out of sight:

> Environed, as he sees himself, by a thousand eyes, contradiction, should he hazard a false tale, will seem ready to rise up in opposition to him from a thousand tongues, many a known face, and every unknown one, presents to him a possible source of detection, from whence the truth he is struggling to suppress, may, through some unsuspected channel, burst forth to his confusion.

If the watching public keeps the witness honest, it does no less for the judge:

> Upon his moral faculties it acts as a check, restraining him from active partiality and improbity in every shape; upon his intellectual faculties it acts as a spur, urging him to that habit of unremitting exertion, without which his attention can never be kept up to the pitch of his duty. Without any addition to the mass of delay, vexation, and expense, it keeps the judge himself, while trying, under trial.

And again:

> . . . suppose the proceedings to be completely secret, and the court, on the occasion, to consist of no more than a single judge, —that judge will be at once indolent and arbitrary: how corrupt soever his inclination may be, it will find no check, at any rate no tolerably efficient check, to oppose it. Without publicity, all other checks are insufficient: in comparison of publicity, all other checks are of small account.[26]

We have learned, let us hope to the point of never again forgetting it, that a civilized society cannot tolerate the excesses of trial by newspaper. But journalism by judges is no better.

### Render Unto Reardon

"We do not want a press that is free, more or less, just as we should not tolerate trials that are almost fair. . . . The paradox is that neither value can be absolute, yet we cannot accept the diminution of either one." That is how Friendly and Goldfarb, the newspaperman and lawyer whose book was mentioned some pages back, sum up the bar-press conflict.[27]

In practical terms, however, need that paradox bother us? An issue exists only to the extent that we allow the First Amendment to rule in court, and the Sixth and Fourteenth to determine what shall be published outside. It seems to me that, except for the excesses on both sides, we have already achieved the nearest thing to a solution. It is this: Let trial in court be fair; let the press outside be free. For, despite their frequent clash, each of the two rights should be supreme in its own area, but not in the other's.

Consider again the grisly Sharon Tate murder case. Long before Charles Manson and three female members of his retinue were brought to trial, the *Los Angeles Times* (and other publications around the world) published a long and detailed statement of just what happened that awful night. It was a blow-by-blow account by one of the accused, Susan Atkins. An introductory note said that the authenticity of the statement had been established, that it was the product of an interview conducted "before a judicial order was issued restraining those taking any part in the Tate murder case from making disclosures regarding it." Susan Atkins's tale, as printed, began:

> One day a little man came in with a guitar and started singing for a group of us in that place where we were living, in Haight-Ashbury in San Francisco. Even before I saw him, while I was still in the kitchen, his voice just hypnotized me—mesmerized me. Then, when I saw him, I fell absolutely in love with him. I found out later his name was Charles Manson.

To read on is to live through a nightmare in which seven persons were shot or stabbed to death. But the tale rings with the sound of truth—told though it is, presumably by a ghost writer, in the limited vocabulary of the naïve, ignorant, and inexperienced drifters among the younger generation. It makes a horror beyond explanation.

For all that the tale is satisfying, as the truth—no matter how monstrous—is always satisfying. If we feel we are really getting the truth, it works a therapeutic chemistry within us. Susan Atkins' tale, published as only a statement—correctly enough—is nevertheless a confession. Because it leaves no doubt as to guilt it is as prejudicial as can be. But also, because it is a believable account of the unbelievable, it filled a public void, a void that otherwise would have been filled by doubts and exaggerations and fears and rumors and untruths. Only the facts, at a time when a public outrage creates a demand for facts, can put the public into contact with reality. And that reality remains the first necessity if society is to control itself.

So much for the public need for facts. What about fair trial? Was the Manson trial prejudiced by publication of Susan Atkins' tale? No one can be sure. But what she said checked pretty well with the facts as brought out in open court, much later. Nor was there any indication that the trial would have run a different course had Susan Atkins's statement been suppressed at the time it helped fill a public need. Is it any wonder that different standards seem natural, depending on whether the need is to inform the public or— much later—to keep a trial fair?

The pursuit of absolute purity in a trial, in the sense of attempting to create a situation free from all prejudice, sometimes makes the administration of justice seem a game rather than what it should be: the deadly serious public business of finding the guilty, if they can be found, and of proving them guilty beyond reasonable doubt. Many a suspect has been freed on appeal because some lawyer or policeman or newsman, doing his job at the moment without thought of a possible trial far ahead, did not split the proper legal hairs. A civilized society will let a hundred guilty go free rather than condemn one innocent. But sometimes one wonders whether the zeal for fair trial has not pushed us to the point at which a fair trial becomes one in which an obviously guilty person is acquitted.

Modern communications make the conflict more difficult than it ever has been. Because news of a spectacular crime now travels fast and far thoughtful men have begun to question whether a trial unsullied by prejudice is possible. Are all the standard protections of fairness—sealed lips for lawyers, prosecutors, and police; moving the trial to another area; delay until furor subsides; the judicious selection of jurors and the sequestration of jurors during trial—are even all these enough any longer? In the days when we had weekly newspapers, distributed on foot or at most by horse, potential prejudice was one thing. It is quite another when the whole world knows at once all about a killing of national import. With immediate saturation coverage by television and radio, wire services that blanket the country's press, and national magazines, is knowledge about a spectacular crime now so pervasive that you cannot find jurors anywhere who have no opinion about who is guilty?

This question became pressing when James Earl Ray was brought to trial for the murder of Martin Luther King, Jr. Before Ray pleaded guilty his lawyer, Arthur J. Hanes, asked the judge in Memphis to dismiss the charges against his client. His argument was that the hatred generated nationally by the immediate and nationwide report of the crime had made it impossible for Ray to get a fair trial anywhere in the United States.

This is the end of the road of prejudiced trials. But surely to allow ourselves to be pushed to that end is to reduce ourselves to the absurd. Such concern for prejudice is, as *Editor & Publisher* noted at the time, "the ultimate technique in avoiding the consequences for one's criminal acts."[28] The cure would have to be either an absolute prohibition against publishing anything about so shocking a crime—a patent absurdity—or else letting the accused off on the theory that he could not have had a fair trial anywhere.

In the aftermath of the assassination of President Kennedy, the American Civil Liberties Union declared: "It is generally conceded that as a result of the conduct of the Dallas police and the communications media when Oswald was taken into custody, he could not have had a fair trial anywhere in the United States."[29] Couldn't he? And what about a fair trial for Jack Ruby, who killed Oswald? And for the assassin of Robert Kennedy, Sirhan Sirhan? These last two murders were, for practical purposes, committed before the eyes of the nation. Millions witnessed the original scene on television, and those who missed it had opportunity, over and over again, to see it replayed. And after the last citizen had seen the action, there remained the still photos, like that shot of Oswald grimacing as he felt the bullet Ruby had just fired into him. Again, when Arthur Herman Bremer shot Governor Wallace of Alabama in the thick of the 1972 primary campaign, the papers—heeding the Reardon rubric—kept referring to him as a suspect. This was silly, because for practical purposes the whole world had seen Bremer shoot the governor.

If TV seems to make us a nation of prejudiced jurors, the fact remains that a trial is not a game, like a handicap match in golf, played under rules designed to leave the adversaries equal. The goal is justice, and in pursuit of it it seems unnecessarily squeamish to call the obvious killer a suspect. The only question is the legal definition of the crime, and whether the killer's act makes him guilty under that definition. Surely jurors can be fair about that, even if they saw the action on TV, and read about it in the papers.

In other areas prejudice does exist. It is still unlikely that a black suspect will be weighed equally with a white by a jury of white Southerners—nor indeed by one of white Northerners. But that kind of prejudice follows from a whole backlog of influences, not from what the papers report when the crime is committed. Just because a juror has seen something about a crime or an accused on

TV, or has read about it or even heard about it, does not necessarily make him biased. Perhaps it may. But it is just as possible
that he and his fellow jurors, according to their lights and limita-
tions, will do their damnedest to be fair.

The bar-press conflict exists because we are dealing with un-
knowns. There simply does not exist a body of research testifying
whether publicity does or does not prejudice trial. Frank Stanton,
president of CBS, once tried to get the Brookings Institution to
gather facts on the issue, but the project got nowhere. Then, in
1967, J. Howard Wood, publisher of the *Chicago Tribune* and
president of ANPA, persuaded the Robert R. McCormick Chari-
table Trust, of which he was a trustee, to grant $150,000 for an in-
dependent study to determine whether there was a factual basis for
the claim that crime news reporting prevents fair trial.[30]

Here was a candle—the only one to this writing—in the darkness
of juror prejudice. Dr. Walter Wilcox of the University of California at Los Angeles, who had done some investigating in the field,
was commissioned to see what he could find out. According to
Chilton R. Bush, former communications department head at Stanford, pioneer of scientific research in journalism, and director of
ANPA's News Research Center, Dr. Wilcox was commissioned
"to make a summary and evaluation of all research which has ever
been conducted which related to the question of whether or not jurors are affected by crime news published in newspapers."[31]

Mr. Wilcox dug through 300 individual reports. But when it
came down to facts all he got was this: "Empirical evidence bearing directly on the effects of pretrial publicity upon the jury ver-
dicts is sparse." He did emerge with the suspicion that, of all the
sources of prejudice, the previous criminal record of the accused—
no matter how conveyed into the jurors' minds—is the most likely
offender. But he ends by doubting the bar's all but universal belief
that, because there has been publicity, we must assume prejudice:

> As pretrial publicity was traced through the jury trial, the most
> noticeable over-all phenomenon was a kind of flaking process, of

dead ends, of self-cancelling propositions, of one concept confounded by another. The results do not add up to a neat and logical and defensible summary conclusion. But a powerful impression remains, best expressed in a letter written by Professor Kalven: "Our over-all impression . . . is that the jury is a pretty stubborn, healthy institution not likely to be overwhelmed either by a remark of counsel or a remark in the press." To which is added the thought: Could it be that the American jury confounds all the subtle nuances of the behavioral sciences and simply does its duty?[32]

One comes back to the rule-of-thumb practice that has grown spontaneously in response to need: When information is needed, publish; when a trial is held, keep it clean. Perhaps we can formulate this into a rule: Render therefore unto Reardon the things which are Reardon's; and unto the public the things that are the public's.

## Happy Ending—Sort of

During the long years of the bar-press war occasional groups of lawyers and journalists sat down to reason together. I recall taking part in one such session, sponsored by the schools of law and journalism at Northwestern University, which met in May 1962. Ten newsmen, two judges, four lawyers, two top police officials, and five professors took part. Each side learned something of the other's values, but the result was still a hung jury. The journalists held out against restrictions on publishing crime news; the lawyers kept insisting that there must be no publication that might conceivably interfere with fair trial.

One of the editors present was John McMullan, then of the *Miami Herald,* now of the *Philadelphia Inquirer.* He offered the suggestion, "with complete confidence that . . . [it] will be ridiculed by both lawyers and newsmen," that much of the distrust between press and bar might vanish if the press would impose a few restraints upon itself. Specifically, he urged the following:

*Avoid deliberate editorialization* even when a crime seems solved beyond all reasonable doubt. Save the compliments for the police and the unflattering characterizations of the accused until conviction.

*Avoid unwitting editorialization* by observing these rules:

Don't call a slaying a murder when it's still up to the grand jury to classify.

Don't say solution when it's just a police accusation or theory.

Don't print that "confession" leaked to the press by prosecutor or police. And if you do, call it a "Statement" and let the jury decide if [the] accused really confessed.

Don't let defense attorneys cozy up to us.

Don't let prosecutors and police use us as a sounding board for public opinion or personal publicity.

Don't call a person brought in for questioning a suspect.

At the time nobody paid much attention. But what Mr. McMullan suggested, modest as it sounded, was a rule of reason. Just as many a libel suit can be avoided if the reporter and his editors are meticulously accurate in gathering facts and in clothing them in words, so much prejudicial news of crime could be avoided if fewer beginning reporters were let loose on the police beat, and if newsmen generally were precise about what they said and how they said it. Such an informed sense of responsibility on the part of the press, if matched by a corresponding appreciation among lawyers and judges of the public's need for the truth, can take the heat out of the press-bar war. In fact, to an encouraging extent it already has.

It has done so, that is, in more than half of the fifty states through adoption, or consideration with a view to adoption, of sets of principles and guidelines spelling out the values involved. Among those early in this field were the press and the bar of Massachusetts. By 1964 they had progressed far enough to publish a *Guide for the Bar and News Media.* It was thereupon adopted by the Boston and Massachusetts bar associations, by the state broadcasters, and by weeklies and small dailies. The big papers in the state, with the exception of the *Christian Science Monitor,* declined without thanks. Nevertheless the idea, which had first been given expression in an Oregon statement of principles in 1962, began to spread.

Some editors are still suspicious of such guidelines, from a feeling that even the vaguest set of principles can be used as a club with which to beat a newspaper, even when there is pressing public reason why that newspaper should publish. As recently as 1967 Friendly and Goldfarb stated the case against press-bar codes in this way:

> . . . we believe that they are without great promise. It is not merely that codes cannot be enforced, but that if they attempt to specify what may or may not be published they cannot be abided by. The real precepts for reporting crime and justice are like French grammar: there are more exceptions than rules. Flat prohibitions are unworkable. To subscribe to them and then be forced to breach them is worse than never to have stated them. As code drafters have discovered, they cannot proscribe the standard *index expurgatorious* as the bar would wish, and declare of the items on it, "The press shall not publish."[33]

If editors dragged their feet, lawyers too were skeptical. Nevertheless by the end of 1971 twenty-three state bar associations had joined with media groups to adopt either joint guidelines or statements of principles, and others were nibbling at them.[34] It is obvious that, despite the impossibility of reducing to rules the infinite variety of circumstances in which the two values may collide, an attempt by both sides to be reasonable is better than hostility.

Typical of the new spirit was a report given before the 1970 ASNE convention in San Francisco by Robert G. Fichenberg of the *Knickerbocker News* in Albany, New York. Mr. Fichenberg was then chairman of the society's press-bar committee. He noted that as recently as a 1966 Associated Press Managing Editors convention in Coronado Beach Grant Cooper, a member of the ABA committee that drafted the Reardon report, had confronted challenging editors in a debate that blazed with indignation. But now both sides were having drinks together and "singing the praises of the voluntary-guidelines approach to the coverage of criminal proceedings."[35] There was a reason for this. On March 24, 1969, representatives of the following national organizations had met in Chicago:

American Society of Newspaper Editors
Associated Press Managing Editors
Radio and Television News Directors Association
National Association of Broadcasters
American Bar Association
National Conference of Chief Justices
National Conference of Trial Lawyers
National District Attorneys Association

This meeting unanimously adopted a statement whose language was already familiar from various state agreements. It began with "the co-equal rights of a free press and a fair trial," went on to urge press, bar, and police to work together in joint efforts on a state and local basis, supported voluntary agreements on agreed principles, and urged "continuing agencies to encourage adherence" to voluntary agreements.[36]

What, actually, do these joint agreements say? A fair sample is the joint declaration issued February 15, 1970, by California's state bar, publishers, broadcasters, and the powerful Executive Board of the Conference of California Judges. Agreement by the media was made possible by the fact that California's bar and bench, unlike some others, did not deem it necessary to rush to adopt Reardon without first asking what the media thought about it. In the end the joint agreement made adoption of Reardon unnecessary. The declaration avoids the word code as having too formidable a ring, as of something whose violation might justify jail for contempt. Instead it first states principles and then outlines policy. It specifies the news media's "right and responsibility to gather and disseminate the news, so that the public will be informed." It notes that "free and responsible news media enhance the administration of justice." It says that "the public is entitled to know how justice is being administered," and stresses the responsibility of the press in giving the public information. At the same time it states the equally obvious values of properly conducted trials in giving the community confidence in the honesty of its institutions. Then it cautions editors as to what it may not be best to publish, using some of the language offered eight years earlier in the quiet plea for restraint that Mr. McMullan presented at the seemingly fruitless Chicago meeting.

This may be no more than spelling out that Mother is good and Sin is bad. But there it is, in black and white, for all those who in the course of their busy lives have occasion to brush up against the problem. The California agreement states its values without any shall or shall not, as in this paragraph on the touchy and doubtful matter of previous records:

> In some circumstances, as when a previous offense is not linked in a pattern with the case in question, the press should not publish or broadcast the previous criminal record of a person accused of a felony. Terms like "a long record" should generally be avoided. There are, however, other circumstances—as when a parole is violated—in which reference to a previous conviction is in the public interest.[37]

Voluntary agreements may be hailed as bringing to a happy ending, insofar as there can be an ending, the press-bar war that has clouded the administration of justice for the better part of half a century. As Mr. Fichenberg told his colleagues of ASNE, "In a time when most of the news seems to be gloomy, it is a pleasure to tell you that at least one national confrontation has been ended."[38]

The only question is, has it really ended? Since Mr. Fichtenberg spoke some judges across the land have simply ignored the bar-press rapprochement. From California to Chicago to New York judges have issued gag orders, sought to punish for contempt reporters who would not betray sources, and editors who printed news of court actions despite judicial orders not to. Some courts simply closed their doors to the press. By 1972 Wendell Phillippi, another Freedom of Information chairman, was telling the editors that "there is a growing, insidious infiltration of secrecy in the very courtrooms of the nation."[39] It is as though the attempt to live and let live, to preserve as best we can the often jarring values of both fair trial and free press, had never been made. But, if bar and bench are willing not to be arbitrary, then the way to accommodation with a press that has learned much in this area will remain open.

### The Camera at the Bar of Justice

There remains a bit of unfinished business, a footnote to the otherwise reasonably happy ending of the bar-press war. This is the taboo against the camera, and its frequent companion the microphone, in the American courtroom.

Consider that day in 1960 when a respected judge of Connecticut's Superior Court, Abraham S. Bordon, took the unusual step of admitting news cameras to a murder trial at which he was presiding. Like all judges, he had control over all that took place in his courtroom. So he made it a condition of the news photographers' coming that they cause no distraction whatever. They didn't.

The next morning two photographs appeared on the front page of the *Hartford Courant*. One showed the defendant, judge, witness on the stand, and others intent upon the business in hand. The second showed the jury. It was evident from both pictures that no one was paying much heed to the fact that pictures were being taken.

For all that the fact that the pictures were published, along with a news story recounting that day's events in court, caused the temperature to rise in Connecticut's Supreme Court of Errors. This final court of appeal in the state is also, through the Chief Justice, guardian of all Connecticut's lower courts. Chief Justice Raymond E. Baldwin, former governor, senator, and distinguished citizen generally, let Judge Bordon know that Canon 35 of the ABA's code of Judicial Ethics was in effect in Connecticut, and that therefore there would be no courtroom pictures whatever.

There was no more photographic reporting of that trial, nor has there been any in the state since. Yet the day the pictures were taken did not differ from the others before and after. There was no hint that photography had hampered the search for justice, had intruded into the proceedings, had distracted the witnesses, or had in any other way affected the trial. All that had happened was that, on that one day, pictures had given citizens a more graphic, direct, and accurate report than on all the other days of the trial.

Canon 35 goes back to that 1935 Hauptmann trial, whose excesses triggered the fair-trial/free-press controversy. At that time members of the press as well as of bar and bench were disturbed over the way in which a mob including reporters, radio broadcasters, photographers, and technicians had turned the trial into a disgrace. So it was that a committee representing the American Bar Association, headed by the eminent Newton D. Baker, met with representatives of the American Newspaper Publishers Association and the American Society of Newspaper Editors. Their mutual goal was not to banish those new instruments of reporting, camera and microphone, from court. Rather it was to set up rules to keep coverage of trial by the news media from interfering with the pursuit of justice.

It soon developed, however, that the split between bar and press that has existed through the years since then was already wide and deep at the very beginning. In particular the lawyer members were adamant against cameras and sound equipment in court, while the newspaper members insisted that "a picture may be as informing as columns of type."[40]

While the newspaper groups still had the matter under consideration, hoping for agreement, the House of Delegates of the ABA acted. It settled the issue unilaterally by adopting Judicial Canon 35 at its sixtieth annual meeting in Kansas City on September 30, 1937. Though Canon 35 originally forbade only photography, a

1952 amendment brought radio and TV under its prohibition. A change in wording that did not make it any less severe was adopted in 1963. Since then it has read as follows:

35. *Improper Publicizing of Court Proceedings*
Proceedings in court should be conducted with fitting dignity and decorum. The taking of photographs in the court room, during sessions of the court or recesses between sessions, and the broadcasting or televising of court proceedings detract from the essential dignity of the proceedings, distract participants and witnesses in giving testimony, and create misconceptions with respect thereto in the mind of the public and should not be permitted.

Provided that this restriction shall not apply to the broadcasting or televising, under the supervision of the court, of such portions of naturalization proceedings (other than the interrogation of applicants) as are designed and carried out exclusively as a ceremony for the purpose of publicly demonstrating in an impressive manner the essential dignity and the serious nature of naturalization.[41]

One may note in passing that the second paragraph of Canon 35 makes an exception in favor of broadcasting or televising naturalization proceedings, while specifying no such exception for news photographs. To me this appears to bar news pictures even of naturalization ceremonies. Even so I am assured that the intent of the Canon is to treat all the media equally—total prohibition in all trials, but an exception, in the discretion of the judge, for all media covering the ceremonial stage of naturalization proceedings.[42]

Most newsmen find it difficult to understand how the courtroom photography and broadcasting that according to Canon 35's first paragraph are automatically, necessarily, and always evil can become benign when used to put on a show illustrating the dignity of naturalization ceremonies. That first paragraph says flatly, without conceding any possible exception, that photography in court does detract from the dignity of the proceedings, does distract participants, and does create misconceptions. Obviously, all this *can* happen, and in a few notorious trials it has happened. Yet it has also been demonstrated over and over again, where experiments under proper control have been permitted, that photography and even broadcasting need not—and in fact do not—necessarily detract, distract, and create misconceptions. The rationale of Canon 35's total prohibition remains unsupported assertion. This unilateral action by the ABA thus goes beyond the evidence. Its contrast to the joint search that led to the principles and guidelines on reporting is galling to journalists. Indeed, one has the feeling one has been through this before. Perhaps it was when the Knave of Hearts stole those tarts and, as soon as the accusation had been read:

> "Consider your verdict," the King said to the jury.
> "Not yet, not yet!" the Rabbit hastily interrupted. "There's a great deal to come before that!"

And again:

> "No, no!" said the Queen. "Sentence first—verdict afterwards."[43]

At this writing, a special ABA Committee on Standards of Judicial Conduct is reviewing all the canons of Judicial Ethics, and it has not yet submitted recommendations. But Canon 35 has previously been reviewed extensively, largely because of complaints from the press. Except for a footnote quoting its first paragraph,[44] it was omitted from the Reardon standards, apparently because the ABA considers Canon 35 to be permanently settled policy for all time, in all courts, federal and state. And no wonder. Just as the federal jurisdictions moved to apply Reardon standards in their courts, so they adopted the ABA's prohibition of camera and microphone. No. 53 of the Federal Rules of Criminal Procedure reads:

> The taking of photographs in the courtroom during the process of judicial proceedings or radio broadcasting of judicial proceedings from the courtroom shall not be permitted by the court.

As though that were not enough, the Judicial Conference of the United States, at the time presided over by the normally liberal

Chief Justice Earl Warren, issued this unanimous pronouncement on March 12, 1962:

> *Resolved,* That the Judicial Conference of the United States condemns the taking of photographs in the courtroom or its environs in connection with any judicial proceeding, and the broadcasting of judicial proceedings by radio, television, or other means, and considers such practices to be inconsistent with fair judicial procedure and that they ought not to be permitted in any federal court.

So that, for the time being at least, is that. Where do we go from here?

Although news photographs and broadcasting stand equally condemned, common experience tells us that, when it comes to a potential for creating disturbances and distractions, television is the chief sinner. It has been demonstrated, for example in the great hall of the General Assembly of the United Nations, that where provision is made for it television can be just as inconspicuous and unobtrusive as a reporter with pad and pencil can. But for the most part TV's impedimenta make it far more obtrusive than taking news photographs and broadcasting by radio. This difference has led some editors and photographers to believe that printed journalism should split itself off from the broadcasters, to seek an entering wedge for the modest 35 mm. news camera at least. Still, differences among the media are matters of degree rather than kind. The principle is the same. Therefore, in the pages that follow, all kinds of picture and microphone reporting are considered as one.

The first thing to note is that the lawyers and judges have a point: there is a problem. For one thing the camera, while not inherently a liar—quite the opposite—can be used to tell a lie. We say that one picture is worth a thousand words, thereby twisting out of shape a classic statement in a Chinese history to the effect that 100 hearings (or rumors) are not equal to a single look.[45] Even so, the fact remains that, at times, a thousand words can be more truthful than a picture—and vice versa.

Then again, a problem exists because news photographers are not shrinking violets. They know they have to be on the spot, ready to push the button, the moment that action takes place. So it is that the judge who goes out to the annual Boys' Club dinner finds—it is hardly an exaggeration to say—a news photographer standing with one foot on his neck, the other on the table before him, to record on film for tomorrow's paper the big moment at the head table— which the judge who was there completely misses as a result. Is it any wonder that he promises himself, "Not in my courtroom!"?

I recall too a time when Nicholas Murray Butler, the nationally prominent president of Columbia University, was announcing the winners of Pulitzer Prizes at a public dinner. He could hardly see the list he was reading to a distinguished audience because a gaggle of news photographers, with the big Speed Graphics of the day, were popping flashbulbs into his face. "Why don't you leave off earning your money for a moment," he said testily, "and learn some manners?"

Such scenes have long since been unnecessary. Long lenses and fast film make possible unobtrusive photography, by available light. Even so the photographer is under compulsion to make sure of a reproducible shot when the moment comes. So, though he will argue with a lawyer or judge that he can take pictures in court without anyone being the wiser, when out on other assignments he often acts as though his aim were to prove the direct opposite.

If their trade makes news photographers raffish, television crewmen are worse. That Boys' Club dinner and other routine affairs are all peace and dignity compared to the same event if TV deems it exciting enough to cover. Cameramen with whirring film cameras, or bulky portable live cameras, stride about in everyone's way. Acolytes with piercing lights and cables take over the affair, whether they distract from the high points of the governor's speech or not. One gets the impression that this is not a public meeting held for its own sake, but a theatrical performance put on for TV.

Consider too such actual courtroom scenes as this one, from the

1962 pretrial hearing of Billie Sol Estes in Tyler, Texas, as reported the next morning by *The New York Times:*

> A television motor van, big as an intercontinental bus, was parked outside the courthouse and the second floor courtroom was a forest of equipment. Two television cameras had been set up inside the bar and four more marked cameras were aligned just outside the gates.
>
> A microphone stuck its 12-inch snout inside the jury box, now occupied by an overflow of reporters from the press table, and three microphones confronted Judge Dunagan on his bench. Cables and wires snaked over the floor.

An indirect influence, which nevertheless helps to set judicial nerves on edge, is the fact that television is show business. It is journalism only incidentally. Partly this is inherent in the medium. But in this country the tendency is exaggerated by the fact that we, virtually alone among the nations of the world, do not tax receivers or use other tax money to help pay the ravenous cost of programming. Instead we require advertising sponsors to pay the entire bill.

This makes it television's supreme goal to pursue ever more dollars, without concern for public service. And the chase for more dollars, in turn, pushes programming toward the lowest common denominator. The tinsel glitter of most of the resulting programs, like the irrelevance and crass taste of many commercials, convinces bar and bench that TV is something alien to our courts.

So it is that the courtroom remains unique among our public institutions as a sanctuary from modern journalism. The status of the press was spelled out in the Supreme Court's multiple opinions of June 7, 1965, in *Billie Sol Estes, Petitioner,* v. *State of Texas.* The five to four majority opinion was delivered by Justice Clark, who was to write the Sheppard decision a year later. The question presented, began Justice Clark, was whether Estes, convicted for swindling, had been "deprived of his right under the Fourteenth Amendment to due process by the televising and broadcasting of his trial." The majority, reversing both the trial and appeals courts below, ruled he had been so deprived.

The scene at Estes' pretrial hearing has already been noted. The spectacle seems to have colored the Court's view of the trial itself, as it would again in the Sheppard decision. There was none of that "judicial serenity and calm to which petitioner was entitled." And pretrial publicity "may be more harmful than publicity during the trial for it may well set the community opinion as to guilt or innocence," and therefore prejudice the jury.

At the trial itself, a month later, the scene had been altered:

> A booth had been constructed at the back of the courtroom which was painted to blend with the permanent structure of the room. It had an aperture to allow the lens of the cameras an unrestricted view of the courtroom. All television cameras and newsreel photographers were restricted to the area of the booth when shooting film or telecasting.[46]

Not only that, there was little live coverage. For the most part silent film clips of the day's activities were used on the evening news shows as a backdrop for the verbal reports of the news commentators. Nevertheless television is to be rejected, said Justice Clark, not because it is new but because "its use amounts to the injection of an irrelevant factor into court proceedings." Did this actually happen, and did it prejudice the trial? It doesn't matter. In other cases the Court "has found instances in which a showing of actual prejudice is not a prerequisite to reversal. This is such a case."

Justice Clark also said that the presence of television "is a form of mental—if not physical—harassment, resembling a police line-up or the third degree. . . . A defendant on trial for a specific crime is entitled to his day in court, not in a stadium, or a city or nationwide arena. . . . Trial by television is, therefore, foreign to our system."[47]

Finally, "the sole issue before the court for two days of pretrial hearing was the question now before us. . . . It is said that the ever-advancing techniques of public communication . . . may bring about a change in the effect of telecasting on the fairness of criminal trials. But we are not dealing here with future developments. . . . Our judgment cannot be rested on the hypothesis of tomorrow but must take the facts as they are presented today. The judgment is therefore reversed."[48]

This forceful statement on behalf of the five-man majority was not punitive enough to suit Chief Justice Warren, Justice Douglas, and Justice Goldberg. The Chief Justice, writing for the three, concurred with added vehemence. Fears of TV in court, he declared, are not abstract fears. Estes was a vivid illustration of the inherent prejudice introduced by broadcasting. Therefore this was the case on which to make a definitive appraisal of what TV does to fair trial. And what it does is have an impact on all participants. It gives the public the wrong impression of what is going on. It singles out only certain defendants, and subjects them to added prejudice. It makes a theater of the courtroom. It does so by equating trial with entertainment, developing personalities in the case to squeeze more drama out of it.

The most these three otherwise liberal justices would grant to TV was the right that belongs to the general public, briefly touched on in Justice Clark's opinion, to go into court any time to see what is going on. This was the right that got newspaper reporters in, with pad and pencil. Reporters did not bring typewriter or printing press into court. Why should TV bring cameras, wires, microphones, lights, and other alien nuisances? Justice Warren concluded:

> The television industry, like other institutions, has a proper area of activities and limitations beyond which it cannot go with its cameras. That area does not extend into an American courtroom. On entering that hallowed sanctuary, television representatives have only the rights of the general public, namely, to be present, to observe the proceedings, and thereafter, if they choose, to report them.[49]

Supporters of Canon 35 seem to find comfort in thus dismissing TV with permission to report via pad and pencil. This leaves all media on an equal basis, doesn't it? And this in turn protects the advocates of Canon 35 from the charge of being against progress, doesn't it? Actually, however, the pad-and-pencil formula remains a denial of television's unique quality as the ultimate in reporting, in that it can transport the citizen-viewer to the scene of action itself. It is a little like saying that it is all right for us to buy automobiles, as long as we keep them locked in the barn. When we want transportation a horse and buggy should do.

The swing man among the multiple opinions sparked by Estes was the late Justice Harlan. His vote made Justice Clark's opinion that of the Court. But Justice Harlan had reservations. In Estes, he said, the Court was concerned only with "a criminal trial of great notoriety," and not with routine criminal proceedings. TV in court does have "mischievous potentialities," but forbidding it totally would prevent the states from experimenting with it, which is one of the valued attributes of the federal system.

In the notorious case at hand, continued Justice Harlan, there is no constitutional requirement that television come in. Nevertheless he was not going to say that the constitutional issue should depend on the kind of case involved. Resolution of further questions should await an appropriate case: "The Court should proceed step by step in this unplowed field." Indeed only the other four members of the Estes majority, not he, "would resolve these questions now."

Here is a crack, opening on the future, in Canon 35's monolithic wall. Estes need not necessarily be the rule in all trials for all time. This theme was picked up by one of the dissenting minority, Justice Brennan. In a brief opinion of his own, he drove home the point that what appeared to be the majority—and therefore the Court—was really a four-man minority:

> . . . Only four of the five Justices voting to reverse rest on the proposition that televised criminal trials are constitutionally infirm, whatever the circumstances. Although the opinion announced by my Brother Clark purports to be an "opinion of the Court," my Brother Harlan subscribes to a significantly less sweeping proposition. . . . Thus today's decision is *not* a blan-

ket constitutional prohibition against the televising of criminal trials.[50]

As for the four dissenters, for whom Justice Stewart spoke, they could not agree that the trial itself, with television coverage more orderly than in the pretrial spectacle, denied Estes' Fourteenth Amendment rights. Television in court, in this early stage, is "an extremely unwise policy." But Justice Stewart found himself "unable to escalate this personal view into a *per se* constitutional rule."[51] Nor, in fact, could he find in this case denial of a right guaranteed the defendant by the Constitution.

The pretrial hearings that disturbed the majority, said Justice Stewart, had nothing to do with the guilt or innocence of the accused. We were not dealing here with "mob domination of a courtroom, with a kangaroo trial, with a prejudiced judge or a jury inflamed with bias." The sole pretrial question was the regulated presence of television and still photography at the trial itself. Television does invite serious constitutional hazards. But the plain fact is that none of the things feared by the majority "happened or could have happened in this case." There was indeed nothing to show that the trial had proceeded in any way other than it would have proceeded if cameras and television had not been present:

> What ultimately emerges from this record, therefore, is one bald question—whether the Fourteenth Amendment of the United States Constitution prohibits all television cameras from a state courtroom whenever a criminal trial is in progress. . . . I can find no such prohibition in the Fourteenth Amendment, or in any other provision of the Constitution. If what occurred did not deprive the petitioner of his constitutional right to a fair trial, then the fact that the public could view the proceeding on television has no constitutional significance.

Justice Stewart detected, moreover, that

> . . . there are intimations in the opinion filed by my brethren in the majority which strike me as disturbingly alien to the First and Fourteenth Amendments' guarantees against federal or state in-

terference with the free communication of information and ideas. The suggestion that there are limits upon the public's right to know what goes on in the courts causes me deep concern.[52]

We come back, then, to that same lack of fact about the effect of news of crime that has for so long strained relations between law and journalism. The Estes majority, and especially the three justices for whom the Chief Justice spoke, did not need facts. For them the fear that facts might exist was enough of a base on which to erect a total prohibition. Thus Estes, at least as concerns its four-man minority that passed as a majority, brought no change from the standard of the past.

Justice Douglas, for example, remained in Estes just where he had stood fifteen years earlier, when he made a speech in Colorado against photography in court. That speech was replete with statements such as "in my view" photography imperils fair trial; "I feel that" trial on TV is quite different; "The very thought" of cameras, no matter how silent or concealed, "is repugnant"; "One shudders to think" what might happen; "Imagine the pressure" judges would be under—and so on, without inquiry into what might turn out to be the truth if thoughts, shudders, and imaginings gave way to facts.

To me it seems likely that the judicial phobia against courtroom photography and broadcasting arises not from these newer instruments of journalism themselves so much as from fear that they may have an invisible and intangible side effect. At one point in his opinion, Chief Justice Warren said flatly:

> . . . all trial participants act differently in the presence of television cameras. . . . Thus, the evil of televised trails, as demonstrated by this case, lies not in the noise and appearance of the cameras, but in the trial participants' awareness that they are being televised. To the extent that television has such inevitable impact it undercuts the reliability of the trial process.[53]

Obviously, this could be. But we do not know whether it always and inevitably works that way, because facts are scarce. Indeed I

wonder whether the legal authorities who share this fear of awareness really know what they are talking about. Have they themselves
ever been witnesses? I vividly recall a time when, as a newspaper
editor, I was called to court to testify in connection with a request
for change of venue. The experience convinced me that the last
thing a witness cares about is whether or not he is being photographed or broadcast. He is painfully aware of the fact that, even
without camera or microphone, he is already a public exhibit. His
every movement is watched, and the court stenographers are evidently thirsting to write down his every "ah" and "er." He is wor-
ried about that lawyer who is trying to make a monkey of him, and
about the judge, presiding austerely from his perch above. The witness has no more time to worry about being photographed than the
football player, trying to snare a pass, has time to worry about
whether he is on camera or not.

In fact I suspect that the real devil behind Canon 35 is the bar's
fear that judges, if televised as they try cases, might not be as judicial as they should. Just as there is fear that a witness may clam
up from knowing that TV is watching, so there is fear that the trial
judge, conscious that TV is exposing him to the public, may ham
up his role. The ABA special committee that investigated Canon
35, and then refused to soften it, let a sizable cat out of the bag
when it said:

> Since most of our state judges still are elected in political cam-
> paigns, in which their success can be affected by the media of
> public communication, it is unfair to subject them to potentially
> powerful pressures for a favorable decision as to courtroom priv-
> ileges, the denial of which may result in open and effective op-
> position of the disappointed media. . . . What the decision on
> Canon 35 should be, when all judges are appointed and enjoy se-
> curity of tenure and freedom from pressures related to the par-
> tisan elective system, is not for this committee to suggest now.
> The achievement of the ideal of non-political judicial selection
> would, however, alter the posture of the problem.[54]

To me this indicates that courtroom cameras and microphones
are scapegoats. They are exiled from court not because they in-

trude upon the proceedings, but because too many of our state judges are still forced to run for office like so many congressmen. If that is true the remedy lies not in Canon 35, but in changes in the machinery for recruiting judges. Why not do what some states already do, and have the governor appoint judges, preferably from a list approved by disinterested professional authorities, with confirmation by the legislature? Why take it out on journalism and the public, when the need is not for fewer cameras but for more independent judges?

To banish cameras, moreover, is to lose something. Colorado, like Texas, some years ago began to experiment with the modern techniques of reporting. After formal hearings weighing the evidence from both sides, it set up certain conditions and restrictions, and then allowed trials to be photographed and televised under those restrictions. Justice O. Otto Moore of Colorado's Supreme Court thus summed up the state's experience:

> Not one judge, not one witness, not one juror, not one district attorney, not one lawyer, appearing in any of these cases has suggested that this visual reporting of the courtroom proceedings has in any degree whatever interfered with the search for the truth, or the ability of judge, juror, witness or attorney to function properly.

Consider too this more recent comment on a Colorado experience, given by Robert Lewis Shayon, himself a graduate of the TV ranks, in the *Saturday Review:*

> *Trial—The City and County of Denvers vs. Loren R. Watson,* a four-program series shown recently on the NET network, represents a commendable and fascinating effort to provide all who are concerned about the issue of free press versus fair trial with some of the necessary evidence. . . .
>
> Defendant Loren Watson, a militant leader of the Black Panthers in Denver, was acquitted by a six-member jury (men, women, all white, middle-class) after four days of trial. Each program represents, according to its producer-director team, . . . "a boiled down rather than edited" version of the full trial, with its "drone of reality," pauses, rather mild flare-ups of forensics,

and occasional tedium. I found viewing the programs completely absorbing, surprisingly suspenseful (the verdict is not given until the last program), and tantalizing in their demonstration of how difficult it is to ascertain the truth—the object of our judicial process.[55]

Judge Learned Hand once told me that the only justification he could see for cameras and microphones in court was that, on appeal, they would provide a more lifelike record of a trial than so many words on paper. Judge Hand remained a supporter of Canon 35 to his death. But it is worth noting that it was for the benefit of an appeals court that Michigan began, in 1971, an experiment with a three-dimensional, video-audio-print, official record of a criminal trial, instead of the conventional transcript.[56]

For practical purposes our state chief justices, or judicial councils, or the Supreme Court of the United States, must be the keepers of our courts. The precious inheritance of a calm, detached search for the truth about crime is in their hands. Yet ultimately their authority too comes from but one source: We, the People. And, as our life grows ever more complex, we the people must know about our life—courts as well as all the rest.

Then, too, suppose that—as is entirely feasible technically—you were to take a small camera in your pocket into the Supreme Court, there to photograph the august tribunal at work without even your neighbors, let alone the Court, being aware of it. Suppose further that, later, the photograph were published. You might find yourself held in contempt. Yet if so you would be punished not for taking a photograph, or for besmirching the legal summit of the country, because the act of taking the picture went unobserved and changed nothing. Any citation for contempt would be punishment for publishing a fact. Surely even our court of last resort, the ultimate interpreter of the supreme law of the land, would have to find such punishment a violation of the First Amendment.

Long ago Russia's Andrei Vishinsky, at the United Nations, drew more fascinated watchers than many a commercial TV show running in competition with him. The endless bits of reality that have paraded across the home screen since then have proved again and again what a superb reporter TV can be. It brought us the drama of the Army-McCarthy hearings, the shattering experience of Dallas, sacred moments in Westminster Abbey and St. Peter's, and the abdication of Lyndon Johnscn. It is hard to believe that the camera must be forever barred from but one public place: the courtroom.

It could be, in fact, that the camera as court reporter has not yet had fair trial.

# 6

# *I Will Be Heard!*

### No Admittance

WILLIAM LLOYD GARRISON was a typical American nut, nineteenth-century vintage. He was born in Newburyport, Massachusetts, in 1805, and died in New York in 1879. The son of an alcoholic sea captain who deserted his family when William was a child, he was largely self-educated. Thanks to William's talents, including a gift for words, it was a successful education. As a boy he was apprenticed in turn to a shoemaker, a cabinetmaker, and a printer. This last gave him his voice. At sixteen he began to contribute anonymous items to the *Newburyport Herald,* for which he was setting type.

Having found his voice, Garrison used it in what turned out to be lifelong battles against war, tobacco, freemasonry, capital punishment, and imprisonment for debt, and on behalf of prohibition and woman suffrage. In 1831, when he was twenty-six, he and a partner established the *Liberator* on a short shoestring and without any audience. This was a four-page propaganda sheet devoted to the instant and total abolition of slavery. In his very first issue Garrison fired a blast, addressed To the Public, that included the challenge that has echoed down through the years ever since:

I am aware that many object to the severity of my language; but is there not cause for severity? I *will be* as harsh as truth, and as uncompromising as justice. On this subject, I do not wish to think or speak, or write, with moderation. No! no! Tell a man whose house is on fire to give a moderate alarm; tell him to moderately rescue his wife from the hands of the ravisher; tell the mother to gradually extricate her babe from the fire into which it has fallen; —but urge me not to use moderation in a cause like the present. I am in earnest—I will not equivocate—I will not excuse—I will not retreat a single inch—AND I WILL BE HEARD.[1]

Extremist and troublemaker that he was, Garrison antagonized many liberals who had essentially the same goal as he. At one point he opposed the Civil War. At another, in a gesture reminiscent of more recent protests, he burned the Constitution, under which slavery was allowed to exist, as "a covenant with death and an agreement with hell." He denounced the churches for not preaching immediate and unconditional freedom for slaves. He did all this and much more with an incendiary zeal that, among other things, landed him in a Baltimore jail for libel. Yet he lived to be received with honor by President Lincoln, and by liberal groups in Britain. Before he ceased publishing the *Liberator,* exactly thirty-five years after the first issue, he recorded in it the Thirteenth Amendment to the Constitution. It said: "Neither slavery nor involuntary servitude, except as a punishment for crime whereof the party shall have been duly convicted, shall exist within the United States, or any place subject to their jurisdiction."

What is pertinent about this tale is that, when Garrison began the *Liberator*, he was one of an infinitesimal minority. Nobody, including many enlightened citizens who opposed slavery, wanted to listen to him. For all that, his strident, lone voice turned out to be the voice of the future. The nut turned out to have been a prophet.

Today, as always, there are incipient Garrisons among us. They complain that, under modern journalism, even the voice that Garrison achieved through the *Liberator* is denied them. They charge that something in the historic equation between people and press has changed, to the point where a minority voice—which may be the voice of a crackpot, but may be that of a prophet—can no longer be heard. Therefore they demand that the door to journalism be forced open on their behalf.

This is the cry for the right of access to the mass media, and thus to the minds of 200-million-plus of the American people. Formulation of this right is generally credited to an article in the *Harvard Law Review* of June 1967: "Access to the Press—a New First Amendment Right," by Jerome A. Barron, associate professor of law at George Washington Law School. This thirty-nine-page statement has been hailed as comparable to the famous 1890 articulation of the right of privacy in an 1890 *Harvard Law Review* article by Brandeis and Warren.

Professor Barron's thesis is concisely stated in his opening paragraph:

> There is an anomaly in our constitutional law. While we protect expression once it has come to the fore, our law is indifferent to creating opportunities for expression. Our constitutional theory is in the grip of a romantic conception of free expression, a belief that the "marketplace of ideas" is freely accessible. But if ever there were a self-operating marketplace of ideas, it has long ceased to exist. The mass media's development of an antipathy to ideas requires legal intervention if novel and unpopular ideas are to be assured a forum—unorthodox points of view which have no claim on broadcast time and newspaper space as a matter of right are in poor position to compete with those aired as a matter of grace.[2]

Professor Barron is not merely the academic troublemaker that some in the journalistic establishment believe him to be. What he did was not so much originate the concept of a right of access as give shape and direction to a feeling that was boiling up naturally in the mid-century turbulence. And that, after all, is just what John Milton did three centuries earlier with *Areopagitica*. Barron's article appeared at the right time to give voice to a growing, and by now powerful, reaction against the mass media as they are today.

Actually Barron's argument had been made as long ago as 1947, in the Hutchins report on "A Free and Responsible Press," which included this point as inherent in freedom of the press in the modern day:

> For the press there is a third aspect of freedom. The free press must be free to all who have something worth saying to the public, since the essential object for which a free press is valued is that ideas deserving a public hearing shall have a public hearing.[3]

Basic to the problem of a right of access is the physical growth and technical elaboration that has turned the press from what it was when the First Amendment was adopted into the multicolored, part electronic, world-wide, instantaneous monster it is today. This metamorphosis, which inevitably intrudes itself repeatedly into any discussion of contemporary journalism, may for present purposes be illustrated by this contrast between 1790 and 1970:

> In 1790, the United States had a total of eight daily newspapers and 83 weeklies. When the Constitution was adopted, 97 per cent of the population lived in places so small that they were not even called towns. Of the remaining three per cent, most lived in towns whose populations were under 25,000—most only a few thousand. Under these conditions, the individual could make his opinions known by giving a speech on Sunday outside the local church or by getting a printer to put up a broadside and by posting it in taverns and in other public gathering spots around town. With relative ease he could have an impact.
> Today, unless the individual has access to formal channels of communication, it is almost impossible for him to have an impact.[4]

This quotation is from a staff report to the National Commission on the Causes and Prevention of Violence, a report not always well informed about or understanding of the realities of journalism. Nevertheless the changes in our press and our society that it describes are incontrovertible. The report's contrast is limited to printed newspapers, beyond which lie the fantastic developments of national magazines with circulations in the millions, photography as a virtually universal reporter, wires and air waves that carry words and pictures around the earth in split seconds, the constant bleating and chatter of radio, and the dominant imprint upon society of television. It is a formidable apparatus for the nut, late twentieth-century vintage, to get a word into edgewise.

That, of course, is precisely the point urged by those who cry for access. A balanced report on the arguments for and against access, prepared at the Freedom of Information Center of the University of Missouri, for example, lists this point in favor:

> The freedoms of the First Amendment must be protected not only against tyrannies of the government and governing majorities, they must also be protected against the non-governing minorities who control the machinery of communication. . . . What is needed is an effective but carefully limited counterweight to the enormous power which has steadily been accumulating in a few private hands.[5]

It is not easy to argue the point away. As Professor Barron put it:

> Sit-ins and demonstrations testify to the inadequacy of old media as instruments to afford full and effective hearing for all points of view. Demonstrations, it has been well said, are "the free press of the movement to win justice for Negroes. . . ." But, like an inadequate underground press, it is a communications medium by default, a statement of the inability to secure access to the conventional means of reaching and changing public opinion. By the bizarre and unsettling nature of his technique the demonstrator hopes to arrest and divert attention long enough to compel the public to ponder his message. But attention-getting devices so abound in the modern world that new ones soon become tiresome. The dissenter must look for ever more unsettling assaults on the mass mind if he is to have continuing impact.[6]

Another critic of the mass media points out that, if such protests take odd forms because the protestors cannot otherwise get a hearing, modern journalism reacts in an oddly inconsistent way:

Minority opinion groups have discovered that whereas media ignore a traditional press release on their activities, they send reporters rushing to cover a picket line or any attention-getting "happening." . . . In psychological terms, the news media have been "rewarding" and therefore reinforcing destructive behavior, by drawing attention to it and making national figures out of those who have learned what kind of behavior keeps them in the camera's eye.[7]

We are all familiar with the basic technique. Malcolm Muggeridge, the British journalist and social critic, thus described a personal experience on a visit to New York:

I was walking back to my hotel, and came upon a little group of people standing in the road. It was, in fact, a demo. There were the usual bearded academics and lib-females carrying slogans, a little group of police with a van, and one or two reporters. Nothing seemed to be happening, and when I asked why I was told that the cameras hadn't turned up. Shortly afterwards they arrived and set up; someone snapped a clapper-board and shouted Action! and the demo began. The bearded academics and lib-females raised their slogans and shouted in unison; the police grabbed one or two of them and pitched them in their van. Then someone shouted Cut! and it was all over. Later in the evening I caught the demo on my television set in my hotel room. It looked fine.[8]

It is of course a basic principle of journalism that the bigger, the more off-beat, or the more bloody the spectacle the greater the news value. This is not because newspapermen are more ghoulish, or less sensitive to the finer things of life, than their fellow men. It merely reflects the ineluctable fact that readers will flock to a story that has shock value but ignore one that is routine.

Resort to the spectacular and the violent to get attention for one's ideas is not confined to the United States. In western Europe there have been riots more spectacular than ours. One in 1968 almost brought De Gaulle down. In Turkey, American servicemen have been taken hostage by politically oriented students. Indeed there, as in South America, kidnapping and murdering foreign diplomats have become instruments of politics. All around this violent world rebels use terror in hope of gaining entry into the marketplace of ideas. When Quebec erupted in the fall of 1970 nationalist fanatics kidnapped a British official and murdered a provincial cabinet minister. Their demands included release of twenty-three prisoners, half a million in gold—and publication of their political manifesto. Thus to insist on publication is becoming the terrorist's standard operating procedure.

Whether violence is effective as a means of gaining respect for one's ideas is questionable. But even the more stuffy among the defenders of the journalistic status quo will hardly argue that the Garrisons of today can readily make themselves heard. No doubt any self-appointed prophet has the same First Amendment right to hire a hall, get a demand printed, or blast forth his ideas through a bullhorn as the President of the United States has to get free time on television for the asking. But one pamphlet, or one sound truck on even a busy street, hardly gives today's Garrison a voice equal to that afforded by all three networks in prime time.

Newspapers, with their far greater space, may offer readier access than broadcasting does to the voiceless, especially for local happenings and issues. But how is the potential Elijah Lovejoy of today to compete with ABC's Paul Harvey, apparently our loudest radio voice in more ways than one? His twice-daily broadcasts are carried on more than 470 ABC-affiliated stations. He has a three-a-week column in 300 papers, and his five-minute news commentaries go via tape to more than 125 TV stations. The subscribing papers, and broadcast sponsors, are glad to pick up the tab for his right to be heard each week by an estimated audience of thirty-five million citizens.

Equal access under law may be a right. But in practice it doesn't exist. The fact that private businessmen decide who among us shall have an overwhelming voice like Paul Harvey's, and who shall remain nameless and silent, is what fires proponents of the right of access to say that we had better look again at the First Amendment. Says Professor Barron:

> What is required is an interpretation of the first amendment which focuses on the idea that restraining the hand of government is quite useless in assuring free speech if a restraint on access is effectively secured by private groups.[9]

Few qualified observers will dispute the view that minorities are most likely to feel themselves bereft of a voice in monopoly towns—communities, large or small, with but a single newspaper ownership. To be sure network radio and television, national magazines, even the misnamed underground press are all free to come in. But as regards local affairs the marketplace of ideas is dependent most of all on the local paper.

Newspaper monopolies can, and in fact do, vary all the way from zero to 100 in their sensitivity to points of view other than their own. Some of our best papers are monopolies—but so are some of our worst.

Recent residence in New Hampshire has made me personally aware of a prime example of newspaper monopoly. With its population growing in the south, toward the Massachusetts line and the Boston population complex, and shrinking in the mountainous and wooded north, New Hampshire boasts but a single city, Manchester, that is large enough to support a state paper—that is, with an advertising base sufficiently large to make possible enough news pages to cover the news from, and to circulate in, communities throughout the state. Manchester's entire journalism—morning, evening, Sunday—is controlled by a single individual, William Loeb. It is a competent professional operation, and it does admit letters to the editor—incidentally, an excellent circulation feature—that strongly oppose the paper's own policies. But in blanketing the state with its news reports and editorials and opinion articles, it feeds on and in turn reinforces the state's endemic right-wing myopia. Small wonder that to this writing New Hampshire is the only

state of all fifty which has neither sales nor income tax. Small wonder that it ranks low in national listings in the quality of its legislature, its education, and its services to the people.

It should be noted in passing that the marketplace of ideas is
not the only one closed to the individual today. Though there is no
record that Emerson ever actually used the word mousetrap in
that famous quotation—he said that a man who had anything good
to sell would have "a broad, hardbeaten road to his house, though
it be in the woods"—the twentieth-century mousetrap inventor
suffers from the same conditions as the twentieth-century Garrison.
No longer can he perfect a better mousetrap and sell it to the world.
First he will have to interest and sell out to General Mousetraps,
Inc.—no doubt by now a division of National Tool Products and
Spaceships. Millions in capital, complete with pretesting the market, are necessary before the better mousetrap can be marketed. In
our mass technological society the individual is less of an individual
than his grandfather was.

All the more proof that a journalistic problem exists. Moreover,
the United States is a laggard in coming to the idea that modern
society demands enforcement of a right of access. Western Europe has been more receptive than we to the concept of an ombudsman to fight for the public, and to press councils to monitor the
press. The right of access, plus what is called the right of reply, are
offshoots of the same root. The Scandinavian countries, especially,
have been willing to heed the pleas of those who complain that they
are denied entrance to the marketplace of ideas.

Closer to home the Organization of American States, meeting
in Costa Rica in 1969, adopted a Convention on Protection of
Human Rights in which was embedded a right to reply. The Convention still has to be adopted, through ratification by a sufficient
number of national legislatures, and one day it may come before
the United States Senate. But ratification by this country is unlikely, because the convention's provisions are alien to those normal to us. Article 13 states the goal, which is unquestionably ideal:

1. Everyone shall have the right of freedom of thought and expression. This right shall include freedom to seek, receive, and impart information and ideas of all kinds, regardless of frontiers, either orally, in writing, in print, in the form of art, or through any other medium of his choice.[10]

The rest of the article spells out conditions, including one prohibiting prior censorship. Then Article 14 gets to the point:

1. Anyone injured by inaccurate or offensive statements or ideas disseminated to the public in general by a legally regulated medium of communication has the right to reply or make a correction using the same communications outlet under such conditions as the law may establish.[11]

This is reinforced by two more paragraphs. One provides that publishing a reply does not get the paper or broadcaster off the hook as far as legal liability is concerned. The other requires, in the interest of enforcement, that every medium shall have a person responsible for what it does, and that he not be protected by any kind of immunity, parliamentary or otherwise. This is designed to get around the old European custom of having a nominal editor who cheerfully goes to jail when necessary, while the real editor and publisher go about their business as usual.

Because both journalism and government tend to be different south of the border from what they are in the United States, we are likely to reject such controls. We still put our trust in free discussion, especially as encouraged in recent years by Supreme Court libel decisions like that in *New York Times* v. *Sullivan,* which gave the press wide latitude for attacks on politicians and public figures generally. This doctrine has been carried still further by subsequent decisions.[12]

Still, we can hardly deny that today's journalism does put private censors in place of the governmental and church authorities of old, and that whether they intend it or not these private censors do have substantial power to keep potential Garrisons out of Justice Holmes' marketplace of ideas.

## The Political Marketplace

As if this were not enough, there is similar censorship on the political front. It may be an equally invisible, and presumably unintentional, censorship. Nevertheless it exists. We can tell that from the demand for access to the public made by those who actually represent the public, or would like to represent the public—our politicians. Both candidates for office and those already in office complain that they have trouble getting enough public exposure for themselves and their ideas.

The principal reason is the advent of television. It has become not only our dominant medium of entertainment, if that is the word for it, but also the most important medium through which to make a political appeal. Ever since it began assuming its place in modern politics—this through its coverage of the 1952 presidential nominating conventions—candidates have scrambled to get on camera. For television has the miraculous power of reaching large audiences, whether local or nationwide, in a direct, intimate way that cannot be matched by print or radio. The catch is that television's costs outrank the costs of other media to an astronomical extent. And these unbelievably high costs have bent the entire American political process out of shape. One can almost put the politician's difficulty into an equation: No TV = failure.

The risk that follows is obvious. Just as no general ever has enough troops or material to fight the battles he is assigned to win, so no politician ever has enough campaign funds. This basic fact has always invited corruption. How much more so, now that television has pushed the cost of campaigning out of the reach of any candidate who is not a multimillionaire? The result is either to limit political office to the rich, or else to force the man of ordinary means who runs for office to owe favors to someone who puts up money because he has some axe to grind. It works all up and down the line because buying time to run in a local campaign is relatively just as expensive as buying time to run for President.

What may be even worse is the opportunity for deception of-fered by the growing use of television. The book about the cam-paign that finally got Richard Nixon into the White House throws light on the extent to which the technics of advertising and public relations have corrupted the process of self-government.[13]

It is the use to which the devices of mass manipulation are put that is evil. Among those devices the chief offender is the political spot commercial. These spots can be innocent, even helpful. But they can also be what Frank Reynolds of ABC, a news-show an-chorman, once had the courage to call them, despite his employer's obvious interest in taking in this kind of revenue. The 10-second or 60-second political commercial, said Mr. Reynolds, is "made to order for trickery, innuendo, implications of treason, smear, and irrelevance." He cited examples, and offered a remedy: a total ban on political commercials over television and radio. At the time he spoke cigarette advertising was about to be prohibited on tele-vision on the ground that cigarettes are injurious to public health. "The slick political commercials now polluting the air," Mr. Rey-nolds said, "are no less injurious to our political health."[14] There is, however, a sad footnote: subsequently, Mr. Reynolds was re-moved from his post as commentator on the evening news show. Suspicion lingers that it was done at the behest of the White House, though ABC denies it.[15]

By 1970 the threat of television's political commercials and costs had grown so great that the National Committee for an Effective Congress succeeded in getting through Congress a bill limiting TV and radio spending by candidates for President, Senate, House, and Governor. The bill also repealed the equal-time provision of the Fedederal Communications Act, which, though waived for the 1960 Nixon-Kennedy confrontation, has consistently prevented American voters from having the modern equivalent of the Lin-coln-Douglas debates.

The effect of the bill would have been to limit television and radio spending in 1972—for time, not production costs—to $5.1

million for each national ticket. This as against $12.7 million actually spent in 1968 by the Republicans, and $6.1 million by the Democrats. The bill left untouched, however, all media other than broadcasting.

If this was hardly perfection, it was nevertheless progress. Even so, President Nixon vetoed it.[16] And even though the bill had substantially bipartisan support, the veto was sustained. The President said that, despite the bill's "highly laudable and widely supported goals," it was worse than no answer at all because it was the wrong answer. He adduced half a dozen reasons of varying degree of persuasiveness, such as that the money saved by limits on broadcast spending would not be saved but merely transferred to newspapers, billboards, pamphlets, and direct mail. The opposition charged, however, with some support through independent newspaper reporting, that the President killed the bill because it would have stopped "the Republican Party's campaign to saturate the public airways with paid spot commercials."[17] And there was inevitable suspicion, again backed by independent newspaper reporting, that Mr. Nixon—who had come off second best in the 1960 debates—wanted to avoid having to meet his 1972 opponent in open debate in virtually every American living room.

Since then we have made modest progress, but the ground rules for political access to the public remain unfinished business. The nation will have to struggle with them in the years ahead. Accompanying this unresolved question, moreover, is a related one. If television is effective in getting a candidate's appeal before the voters, it is equally effective for the officeholder after he is elected. Television can sell policies as well as personalities. The result is that, in the same year in which this first attempt to hold down the cost of TV campaigning was made, critics of the Nixon war policy in Indochina charged that he got national exposure automatically, while they couldn't get it no matter how hard they tried.

An incumbent has always had readier access to the public than a member of the opposition. Anything an official does or even says is news, and the higher the office the bigger the news. This can have unhappy results, in that a vast and tumultuous nation that cannot hear opposition voices clearly enough may miss the course of action it would have chosen had the marketplace of political ideas been as free and open as it should be.

As the Vietnam war began to develop into a major menace to the world, it became essential for the public to have access to all ideas as to what to do about it. It was only natural that at one point Senator Fulbright, whose dovish voice had long been futile against the hawkish acts of two Presidents, should object. "Communication is power," he said, "and exclusive access to it is a dangerous, unchecked power." He urged that Congress legislate a right of access to television that could match the access the President has naturally, by virtue of his office.[18]

Within ten days the Federal Communications Commission, noting that the President had made extensive use of prime-time television to defend his war in Indochina, ordered the networks to give exposure to the President's opponents. It was the first such order in American experience, but it did not get far. By virtue of his election the President obviously has the right, even the duty, to speak. But who decides who should represent the opposition on the air? How decide among doves, or between senators and representatives, or Republicans and Democrats? Congress has no single voice, and senators might want to answer senators as well as the President.

In addition the air was thick with other questions, each with its proponents demanding that the live TV camera's red eye turn toward them. In Florida a meat cutters' union sought access through radio ads to promote a boycott. And in Washington the Democratic National Committee insisted that its fund-raising TV commercials should not be rejected simply because they were controversial. So it went, and so it goes still.

In the background hovers the FCC's Red Lion doctrine of enforced fairness, unanimously affirmed by a seven-judge Supreme

Court.[19] Two cases had come up from the lower courts, both involving the question of whether the rules the FCC imposed to ensure fairness on the air were actually having the opposite effect: specifically, by abridging freedom of speech and press. The dominant case concerned the Red Lion Broadcasting Company of Red Lion, Pennsylvania. Over its transmitter the Rev. Billy Hargis had broadcast an attack upon Fred J. Cook, a writer who had been critical of Senator Goldwater. The Hargis attack was apparently strong medicine, and Cook demanded free time to reply. When Red Lion refused, the FCC ordered access for Cook. And this the Supreme Court upheld.

It is not easy to say where justice lies in this, and endless controversies like it. Is it right, because it is in the interest of fairness, to force access upon an unwilling broadcaster? Or is it wrong because to do so abridges the broadcaster's right to decide what should be aired? Justice White, who wrote the Court's decision, said that because broadcasters operate a new medium, differences that distinguish it from the press "justify differences in the First Amendment standards applied to them." He found the right of listeners and viewers, not that of broadcasters, to be paramount.

Repeated attacks on the fairness doctrine have prompted the FCC to hold hearings on possible changes,[20] and it will no doubt be pressed to do so repeatedly. In fact it is likely that we shall be struggling for a long time with the First Amendment differences between printed journalism and broadcast journalism. Despite the basic qualities they share, as reporters and interpreters, there is as much to distinguish the two media as to unite them. Not least is the requirement that broadcasters be licensed to assure them their exclusive spot on the broadcast spectrum. In broadcasting's first half century the authorities were no doubt too lenient in renewing these licenses, which give private persons, at no cost, virtual ownership of the public's air. There was little inquiry into what public service the broadcaster might be giving in return.

The truth is that the minute one begins to police a broadcaster's programming, one invites Big Brother's ideological control. Thus the emergence of Vice President Agnew as the Nixon administration's chief critic of what the media said about that administration raised fear among broadcasters. The Federal Communications Act of 1934 denies the Federal Communications Commission any right to censor. But now, the broadcasters insisted, not only the FCC but also the Vice President and some elements in Congress were moving to censor them.

Noting the change Julian Goodman, NBC president, said: "There was a time when excellence in reporting won awards. Now it is just as likely to draw a subpoena." And Vincent T. Wasilewski, president of the National Association of Broadcasters, added that FCC proposals that stations carry certain types of programs in certain percentage amounts at certain times would end in a "jumpy, responsive, subservient broadcasting system, eager to do anything and everything to please the commission, and intimidated from doing anything that would displease it."[21] As one knowledgeable critic, John Hohenberg, wrote: "If the testing of ideas is to be resumed as a matter of national policy and public necessity, the independent newspaper is the only available force that can set a proper example.[22]

Always too one comes back to the newspaper's capacity for reporting detail, whether in local news or in the complexities of national and world news. This detail cannot be matched within the iron framework of time that hems in TV and radio. If the public is to be exposed to minority views and obscure facts, it can get them most readily and in largest quantity through print.

Another contrast between printed and broadcast journalism appears in their different ways of paying for access to the public for political candidates. As newspaper habits and traditions were formed over the centuries it became standard practice to cover politics as news. Today candidates do buy newspaper campaign advertising, but the newspapers' great burden of informing the public about candidates is carried by news coverage. This the pa-

pers provide at their own expense. Through news and interpretations of the news they put before the public daily details about the
doings of officeholders and those who would like to become officeholders.

Broadcasting is different. Snippits of free time on TV and radio
news shows do get candidates before the public. But for the most
part broadcasters perform this service only for hire. Each candidate buys what time he can afford, whether to put on spot commercials or to talk to us at length over the home screen, as if in
person. If he doesn't the other fellow will—and so will have opportunity to make an impression on the voters that can be made in
no other way.

This is where the modern problem of access for politicians begins. And here, too, much unfinished business remains. But by now
we have enough experience to conclude that, when it comes to
holding down the cost of campaigning, it is better to limit the total,
leaving it to each candidate to determine where he wants to spend
it. It is not desirable to limit costs on one single medium, using the
doubtful model of the ban on cigarette advertising over TV. Nor,
for that matter, should we set arbitrary limits for each medium.

As for the difficulty of public exposure of a candidate, as against
a man in office, when has an incumbent not had an advantage
over a challenger? Besides, the record shows that sometimes the
electorate is more anxious to throw the rascals out than to accept
their blandishments and keep them in power.

So we get along. But still politicians, ins and outs alike, at times
feel themselves as effectively shut out of the marketplace as do
the nuts and prophets. All up and down the line of public affairs
modern technology has brought into being the problem of access.

What can we do about it?


## Who But the Editor?

The demand for access comes down to a demand that Isaiah's
voice, crying in the wilderness, shall be brought to the attention

of the people whether they care to listen or not. The logical under-pinning of this demand has been mentioned earlier in a quotation from the Hutchins report of 1947: "Ideas deserving a public hear-ing shall have a public hearing." The catch is this: Who decides what idea deserves a hearing?

Professor Barron, in presenting his thesis, included his answer.[23] For one thing, he said, the courts might decide. An appeal to the courts, if sustained, might force the newspaper to publish the plaintiff's opinions in its letters-to-the-editor column, or as an ad-vertisement. Then too there might be legislation to the same end, at least to the modest extent of requiring "that denial of access not be arbitrary but rather be based on rational grounds." He found justification for both kinds of access in the Constitution, by read-ing the First Amendment not only negatively, as restraining gov-ernment censorship, but also positively, as requiring an open door for expression.

While Professor Barron did not find court opinions providing such relief in so many words, he did cite some that point in that direction. He repeatedly emphasized that it was time for a change. As a guide to the courts he would substitute ". . . the sensitive query 'Does the statute prohibit or provide for expression?' for the more wooden and formal question 'Does the statute restrain the press?' "[24]

Professor Barron recognizes that "not every listener's taste pro-vides standing to challenge the applicant for renewal of a broad-cast license," and that "the daily press cannot be placed at the mercy of the collective vanity of the public."[25] But he provides no practical guidelines for administering the right of access in day-to-day journalism. For him it is enough that the long-established doc-trine of the confrontation of ideas "demands some recognition of a right to be heard as a constitutional principle."

The nation's newspaper editors are rarely unanimous about any-thing. But, not surprisingly, they overwhelmingly oppose the Bar-ron doctrine. When it became evident that his law-review article was not a flash in the pan, but that it triggered more and more cries for access, ASNE's bar-press committee asked Robert M. White of the *Mexico Ledger* in Missouri to study the question. When Mr. White reported to the 1970 convention his first sentence was, "Who can edit newspapers better than newspaper editors?"[26]

Even before that J. Edward Murray, then of the *Arizona Republic,* had addressed himself to the issue in a speech accepting the annual John Peter Zenger award for freedom of the press and the people's right to know. He asked the same question Mr. White asked, and then spelled out the difficulty of finding any other answer than that the editor should continue as guardian of the gate to the marketplace:

> . . . Who would have made a sounder decision on what to print or broadcast in the sixties than did the nation's editors?
>
> Mr. Agnew? His Silent Majority with its strength in the fat suburbs and the Old South?
>
> Professor Barron? Or his judges and legislators and politicians?
>
> And who would have decided between them when they disagreed, as they most certainly would have?
>
> Earl Warren's Supreme Court?
>
> News is today, now, not in the good time of the Supreme Court.[27]

A year later the same subject bounced right back before the editors, and they gave it the same answer. Vice President Agnew had complained that the CBS documentary, *The Selling of the Pentagon,* was biased against the Nixon administration and the Vietnam war. In furtherance of this view the House Interstate and Foreign Commerce Committee subpoenaed the network in an attempt to get all films, tapes, notes, transcripts, and other records connected with the program—the raw material that was *not* used as well as that broadcast in the finished product. Here, obviously, was a fishing expedition. Frank Stanton, CBS president, replied that the committee was welcome to the record of the program as edited, but not to the private material that had been discarded in the editing.

This skirmish may portend a continuing war between government and the television industry over the journalistic independence of a medium subject to federal license. To give the committee all the network's material on the Pentagon program would be to invite the government to second-guess the network—in fact, to edit the news. This possibility led the ASNE, meeting in Washington at the time, to protest to the committee against the threat to freedom inherent in a government attack on a program that was not to its liking.

Precisely that is the danger: that government—whether the executive, the legislative, or even the judicial branch—will seek to edit the news according to its own estimation of itself. We seem not to have progressed far from the time the printing press first alarmed authorities of Church and State, and so inspired censorship.

The cry for access, in its myriad forms, continues. But when you look around for an omniscient, omnipresent enforcer of the right of access, there isn't any. The nearest thing to so divine a figure is the shirtsleeved, usually rather undistinguished, and often harassed editor. As Ben Bagdikian of the *Washington Post,* himself often a critic of the press, told the Association for Education in Journalism:

> The answer is simple. Editors must decide what is news. This sounds arrogant and of course it is. Who are we to decide what the world will see and hear? There's no really satisfactory answer. We are frail human beings and we don't have any magical powers of special wisdom. But there is no alternative.[28]

One can even find legal authorities who agree. When for example a plaintiff in the Federal District Court in Chicago sought forced access to newspaper advertising that had been denied him, Judge Abraham Marovitz ruled against him. A publisher, said the judge, has a right to reject any commercial advertising he chooses, on the ground that "the right of free speech was never intended to include the right to use the other fellow's presses."[29]

Another U.S. District Court, in Denver, came at the issue from a different set of circumstances, but it also came out against forced access. Two organizations, fighting a proposed plant for cutting up the carcasses of animals, submitted to the local papers advertisements asking readers to boycott products of the company that wanted to put up the plant. Among other things involved was a state law making it unlawful to print boycott notices. The court, ruling on the right of access, held that "Newspapers are not engaged in an enterprise which is ultimately the responsibility of government to regulate or carry out."[30]

There have to be sure been court decisions that went the other way, to force access for views that did not make it into the marketplace of ideas on their own. One such was a ruling by a United States Court of Appeals that required a TV station carrying advertisements promoting powerful cars also to carry information outlining the resulting harm to the environment.[31] This resembled the anti-cigarette spots that preceded the total ban on cigarette commercials on TV.

These counter-commercials were so effective that the demand for them spread. In 1972 NBC became the first network voluntarily to run free advertisements that answered paid advertisements on a nation-wide basis. It accepted three one-minute spots to oppose commercials urging public support of a Surface Transportation Act, which opponents charged would make it easy for railroads to abandon still more trackage.[32] More recently the Federal Trade Commission has urged the Federal Communications Commission to require free air time for rebuttals to commercials that raise "issues of current public importance."

This sounds reasonable enough. But what if the shoe is on the other foot? Numerous newspapers have refused advertising for X-rated movies. As the *Detroit News* explained: "In our view, a sick motion picture industry is using pornography and an appeal to prurience to bolster theater attendance; quite simply, we do not want to assist them in that process." The movie industry protested that X ratings were not bait to lure those seeking pornography, but a guide to parents as to when not to take children to adult pictures.[33] Should newspapers therefore be forced to grant access to advertisements for X-rated pictures?

For all its plausibility, the demand for forced access somehow twists values out of shape, in that it seeks to enlarge freedom by abridging it. Precisely this point prompted the American Civil Liberties Union, in what might seem a man-bites-dog action, to turn its back on the right of access. In 1968 ACLU's biennial conference had recommended that ACLU file access suits on behalf of "advertising and notices," that it consider litigation to establish a right of reply, and that it help form a national commission to study denials of access by the mass media. But the parent body turned down this suggestion from its own ranks. Whereupon one commentator wrote:

> Its [ACLU's] refusal at this time to commit its considerable legal expertise and prestige to an access interpretation of the First Amendment reflects the organization's substantial uneasiness about the implications to freedom of the press in the Barron thesis.[34]

The point is not to be dismissed lightly. Anyone who has been on the receiving end of letters to the editor on a metropolitan paper knows what a madhouse this world would be if access were granted not only to the deserving few, but to all those who demand it. If the prophet has difficulty getting himself heard amid today's welter of printed pages and amplified voices, how much greater would his difficulty be if the multitude were to join him in shouting in the marketplace? The risk is that an enforced right of access would change journalism from what it is and should be, an edited report on what is happening, into a common carrier like the mails or telephone that has to transmit anything anyone wants it to. Only, instead of our receiving one letter or one phone call at a time, we would be subjected to a confusion of voices compared to which Bedlam would be sanity.

We can glimpse the distorted values involved in forcing access by reading again as Ben Bagdikian reduces it to the absurd:

*Editor & Publisher,* the Old Testament of newspaper printing,
might be ordered by a court to feature the latest release from the
National Association of Broadcasters claiming television to be
a superior medium of advertising. *Broadcasting,* the weekly en-
cyclical of electronic movie-attendance, would be forced to give
equal space to FCC Commissioner Nicholas Johnson. It would
take ten full issues of the magazine to let Johnson catch up, by
which time the Tobacco Institute would have sued *Broadcasting*
for letting this period go by without quoting in full a speech by
Senator Ervin on how much the tobacco industry has done for
the economy of North Carolina. . . . Station breaks on NBC
would urge viewers to switch to CBS and ABC would promote
the New York Yankees. Meanwhile, back at *E&P,* Robert U.
Brown would be composing a poem in praise of the International
Typographical Union while the Guild Reporter would run a
front-page piece saying that George Hearst, Jr., was justified in
trying to break the unions in Los Angeles. Hearst would do a
column in his *Los Angeles Herald-Examiner* telling readers that
Otis Chandler's *Times* was really a better newspaper, while Los
Angeles Mayor Sam Yorty would sue Chandler (again) demanding that *Times* cartoonist Paul Conrad draw a picture of Yorty
looking intelligent.[35]

No doubt Professor Barron and those who side with him answer that such a caricature raises fears so exaggerated as to be
groundless. Nevertheless there is some truth in Mr. Bagdikian's
distorting mirror, as there is in all effective caricature. Professor
Barron keeps reiterating, from his first paragraph to his last word,
that in the modern day the concept of a free market in ideas is a
romantic notion, no longer grounded in reality if it ever was. Yet
those of us who have spent our lives in newspaper work can testify
that, even today, the concept of an ideological free market isn't
as unrealistic as he makes out. Journalistic staffs do try to give a
hearing to ideas and people and facts that deserve it. They worry
along at the task despite all kinds of hazards, from their own
shortcomings to public indifference and to the actual restrictions
sometimes imposed by publishers or owners or governments. It is
a sheer impossibility to do a perfect job, or perhaps even a halfway perfect one. But most of us in the business can testify from

daily experience that we try, anyway. After all, to cover the gamut is our job.

For one thing recognition of the fact that the orthodox view is not the only one the community should know about is what led to the tradition of objective reporting. Let me repeat here that I have never forgotten what was drummed into me, first in journalism school and then in my early days as a reporter. It did not matter what I thought about any event or situation I was reporting, or what I thought ought to be done about it. My job was to get the story—the whole of it, including background facts, plus any viewpoints held by any contending parties involved, whether I or anyone else liked them or not. This tradition of objective reporting, whose long, slow, and still incomplete growth I have traced in another book,[36] was partly the product of natural forces in our history. Insofar as it was deliberately cultivated, it was intended precisely as an antidote to the fundamental fact that man, left to himself, slants the news in the direction of his own hopes and wishes and beliefs, and therefore does not naturally grant access to those whose hopes and wishes and beliefs are different from his.

What the polemics for and against an enforced right of access come down to is a question of fact. Are the views of minorities suppressed, or aren't they? Once one asks this question, it becomes immediately apparent that few have remained ignorant of the views of at least the more contentious of our minorities. We have been made painfully aware of what youth thinks of Vietnam and the draft, of what black Americans feel about their chances in a life controlled by the white majority, of what consumers think about pollution.

The bizarre, disruptive, and destructive activities that have helped bring these views into the forefront of public consciousness are, of course, cited by proponents of the right of access as proof that written and spoken access has been denied. Obviously, there is some substance to the charge. But still, is our situation today really different from that of the past? Rebels have always had to resort to the spectacular to get attention for their viewpoint, and all too often they have resorted to violence to get those ideas acted upon. The difference now is that, over the centuries, we have substituted the marketplace of ideas for the historic pattern of physical conflict.

Moreover, this nonviolent substitute works. What point of view is suppressed today? We suffer a flood of publications, big and little, giving expression to every conceivable doctrine. There are those who still think the earth is flat—or did until pictures of the earth, showing a little ball floating in the black emptiness of space, were brought back from the moon. Here in itself was an example of the marketplace of ideas at work.

Then again the continuing battle over pesticides and pollution, which began with publication of Rachel Carson's *The Silent Spring,* testifies to the fact that no concept that deserves to be brought before the public long remains hidden. Charles Reich, author of *The Greening of America,* was as critical of the Establishment as Rachel Carson was. His thesis was actually an updating of the Manichaean fallacy, which held that all the world is divided into Good and Bad. He argued that we were all undergoing conversion to Consciousness III—the triumph of the Good. If we all became good guys our modern problems would disappear. We would no longer suffer the age-old, insoluble human difficulty of governing men who, since Adam, have been an indissoluble mixture of good and bad. This amounts to an old-fashioned religious conversion in modern dress. Even so, many among us were so unhappy with the world that Professor Reich's idea took fire, making his book a best seller. Which is hardly denial of access.

Religious, scientific, cultural, political ideas—where is there a cause that is suppressed, that does not have its endless meetings and speakers, its publication whether mimeographed or slick? Indeed where is there a viewpoint that does not rate its moment in the newspapers, perhaps even on the national news shows?

Checking the facts as to whether access is denied or not would make material for monumental studies—some of which have in fact been made. Pending definitive studies, however, most of us can find ample empirical evidence in the world about us that few voices are suppressed for long.

Professor Barron himself is Exhibit A. Editors, across whose desks there flows a daily torrent of printed and written matter, do their best to keep up. But few among them, even the more omnivorous, regularly peruse the *Harvard Law Review*. Yet how many of them have been allowed to remain ignorant of the *Review*'s issue of June 1967—which contained Professor Barron's plea for an enforced right of access?

This is the way things work. If we don't see it ourselves, someone will thrust it under our noses. Whether it is Garrison a century and a half ago or Barron today, the fact is that our prophets—big, little, and in between—*are* heard.

Perhaps the reason some among us fear they are not heard is not that there exists a conspiracy to suppress them, nor even that the transformation of yesterday's four-page paper into today's vast and impersonal mass media has made it hard for the individual to make himself heard. I submit that the demand for access springs less from a denial of access than from a denial of subsequent action. When Garrison demanded abolition, the Thirteenth Amendment did not automatically follow. Society has always suffered from a vast inertia. We do not like to put new ideas into effect. This does not prove that there is a plot by media barons to hush up ideas they don't like. It is merely the familiar cultural lag.

For an example, turn again to the long nightmare of Vietnam. A minority in our nation held from the beginning that it was a mistake to apply military force in Vietnam in an attempt to make political events there turn out to our liking. Gradually this minority view came to be accepted by what the polls showed to be the majority, if for a variety of reasons. But, whatever the reasons, this majority came to believe that the only way to right our original mistake was to acknowledge that it was a mistake and to get out of Vietnam without precondition. Despite the obviously growing steam behind it, this simple truth was not acted on by our government. Beginning with 1965 it seemed as though a single man, the one in the White House whether his name was Johnson or Nixon, refused to end the Vietnam war. Both, Johnson by abdicating and Nixon by withdrawing troops, showed that they were aware of the idea dominating the Vietnam marketplace. But access to this idea was denied to nobody. Inplementation was.

The difference is important. If getting ideas acted on rather than merely circulated is our chief difficulty, then the problem is less one of law and journalism than of politics and government. We should urge courts and legislatures and Vice Presidents to take needed political action, not to edit our papers and news programs.

As far as access is concerned the need now, as before, is to let our nuts talk. If we let them talk freely we shall have more than a safety valve. For then we can be sure that the occasional prophet among them will be heard.

How do you tell the prophet from the nut? Not by forcing an unwilling public to listen to every nut, but by a simple test over a period of time. Is the man in fact heard, despite the ever-present cacophony and caterwauling, despite what the big guns of the communications media decide shall not be published? If you yourself know about his idea, through whatever minority channel, then the advocate has been heard.

Thus to be heard is not easy. But there is a reason. Before one can get the nation (or the town or whatever) to accept and to act on one's idea, one has to be right. And how do you tell who is right? By the very fact that, in time at least, an idea is not only listened to but put into effect. The nut is the one to whom nobody listens, no matter how long and how hard he, and Professor Barron, try to make him heard. The prophet is the nut who preaches an idea whose time has come. And if he does that, he doesn't need forced access.

Day in and day out, who indeed can edit the news better than the editor?

# 7

# *A Conscience for the Press*

## Quis Custodiet?

"FEW AMERICAN institutions are as free from responsible and systematic analysis as the American press. The press, which performs the role of reporter and critic for other institutions, has been reluctant to undertake self-analysis."[1]

That comment, made by a study group reporting in 1969 to Milton Eisenhower's National Commission on the Causes and Prevention of Violence, must have been the understatement of the year. Whenever anyone directs Juvenal's question *Quis custodiet ipsos custodes?* toward the press, the press answers that there isn't going to be any guardian over the guardians of the press.

In a fundamental sense that answer is right. The history of the last three and a half centuries tells us that we cannot regulate the press by law, or by any other force from without, and retain our other liberties. Yet the modern world has brought complications. Freedom of the press was won in the eighteenth century by a press so modest yet so relatively numerous that its freedom was virtually a civil liberty of the individual pamphleteer. Today's press is a costly and complex behemoth. It is so unresponsive to the individual that today's citizen is likely to be more interested in making it behave than in welcoming its freedom as his own. And free it still is, as he would soon find out if, like the citizens of twentieth-century authoritarian states, he had to rely on a controlled press.

To be sure our dilemma is hardly new. As long ago as 1815, ex-President John Adams said:

> If there is ever to be an amelioration of the condition of mankind, philosophers, theologians, legislators, politicians, and moralists will find that the regulation of the press is the most difficult, dangerous, and important problem they have to resolve. Mankind cannot now be governed without it, nor at present with it.[2]

More than a century and a half later we are still struggling with the same seemingly irreconcilable conflict. Indeed our transformation from an individualistic, essentially agricultural people into a techno-industrial mass society raises the question insistently: Cannot something be done toward making an impersonal and powerful and virtually monopolistic press more conscious than it is of its public responsibilities, while yet not limiting its freedom?

Lord Devlin, the distinguished British jurist who served for a time as chairman of Britain's Press Council, thinks it can. On his retirement as chairman in 1969 he said: "All professions have a discreditable past . . . their medical quacks, their rascally attorneys and the like. During the past 100 years one profession after another has submitted to discipline."[3]

The implication is clear. Even though journalism must never be shackled by a licensing power like that common in other professions, contemporary conditions require that it discipline itself.

In Great Britain the press accepted a press council, empowered to hear complaints, on July 1, 1953. It had been kicked into it, in response to growing alarm over the rush to monopoly that followed World War II.

This alarm prompted a vote in the Commons on October 29, 1946, that set up a Royal Commission to inquire into things journalistic, notably monopolistic tendencies and press performance under them. Britain's editors and publishers did not like the idea any better than do their counterparts in the United States today. Nevertheless, in due course the Royal Commission recommended that the press itself establish a central organization to be called the General Council of the Press. Not surprisingly the press, thus left to itself after all, dragged its feet. So at last, in 1952, Parliament threatened to act if the press continued to stall. That did it. Phillip Levy, legal adviser to the *Daily Mirror* and historian of the Press Council, put it succinctly:

> After four years of serious doubt and many meetings of the constituent organizations, the Press, more under duress than of its own free will, set up a Press Council of its own making. Had it delayed doing so much longer it was virtually certain that Parliament would have imposed one by legislation.[4]

The reason Parliament threatened to act is given by George Murray, another historian of Britain's council. Parliament was responding, he said, "to the instinctive feeling of the British people that the power of the press had increased, was increasing, and ought to be diminished."[5]

It is a feeling now almost palpable in this country, in which the same question has long been agitated with little result. At one point Norman Isaacs, Louisville editor and 1969-70 president of the American Society of Newspaper Editors, undertook to inspire his fellow editors to adopt a modest experiment in self-discipline. Accordingly he arranged to have the ASNE board hold its 1969 fall meeting in London, where it could have a first-hand look at the British press under a council that was by then sixteen years old.

Out of the experience came what Mr. Isaacs hoped would be a historic step. He and his colleagues recognized that a country as large and diverse as this, lacking a national press like Britain's, might not readily adapt itself to a single, national press council. So he proposed a more modest ASNE grievance committee, "to receive complaints of substance about the performance of daily newspapers."[6]

Past proposals in the same direction had all been slapped down. So it is hardly surprising that opposition within the ASNE made itself felt. The ASNE board, in special session in Chicago on February 24, 1970, backed away from the grievance committee. Instead, it established a committee on ethics, empowered to respond to "broad criticisms of newspaper performance," and to study the whole concept all over again.

At ASNE's subsequent annual meeting in San Francisco the incoming president, Newbold Noyes of the *Washington Star,* appointed still another committee, consisting of five past presidents of the society, to carry the exploration further. The committee was balanced between two proponents, two opponents, and a swing man who was favorable to the idea of a press council but had reservations as to its feasibility. The society's board of directors gave the committee a free hand, but it asked nine sets of questions exploring the whole subject, including the central issue of whether ASNE should have any part in it.[7]

## Why Do It?

The British experience is worth studying. For one thing, it shows that a press council is not an easy institution to contrive. The British version has been reformed twice. And apparently it still leads a precarious existence, at least as far as finances go. But it does respond to a public need. The first Royal Commission, in 1947-49, expressed that need in this way:

> Industrial development . . . has enabled the press to report and interpret more fully; but to the extent that it has given added importance to the commercial aspects of newspaper production, it has tended to divert the attention of newspapers to ends other than those to which the interests of society require them to attend. . . .
>
> If the press is not aware of its responsibility to the public it

cannot perform its functions adequately; but if it is not free it cannot perform them at all. . . . In our view, therefore, it is preferable to seek the means of maintaining the proper relationship between the press and society not in government action but in the press itself.[8]

Other more or less self-governing countries too have sought to persuade their press that, more than any other private enterprise, it has a public responsibility. Visiting American editors have found that even the government-controlled Soviet press holds what it calls reader conferences, give-and-take sessions between editors and their customers.[9] Canada, like other advanced nations, has felt concern over a big-business press that often seems to give its public responsibilities second place. A special committee of its Senate suggested, among other things, a national media council to accept and publicize grievances against newspapers and broadcasters.[10] Because Canada's journalistic reflexes often parallel our own, the Canadian Daily Newspaper Publishers Association rejected the idea.[11] But at least ten other countries, ranging from West Germany to Turkey, already have something of the kind. Even in the United States local councils have been tried experimentally in half a dozen communities.

It makes sense. American newspapers are increasingly not only big business, but monopolies. And our networks, like Britain's big papers, have a national audience. Both are more and more presided over by boards of directors. And to a board of directors there is only one way to measure success—by ever-increasing profits. The result is that the strongest pressure felt by the men who command our journalism is not the historic editorial mission of informing and explaining, but that of earning more money each year than the year before. This is good as far as it goes, because solvency, the ability to stay on top of rising costs, is the first requirement for remaining not only free but responsible. Still, as that first British Royal Commission noted, it introduces an element other than "the interests of society."

### Don't Touch Me!

Because the press supplies information without which self-govern-ment cannot exist, why should not our newspapers, and news broadcasters, have looking over their shoulders some other watch-man beside the gentlemen in gray flannel suits who press the pur-suit of ever more dollars? Why not for example a board of observ-ers representing the public, the whole spectrum of the local community—though without any vote on policy, or any other power except the right to be heard? Or why not a similar public gadfly for radio and television, as Gilbert Seldes once suggested:

> A practical proposal could be made to the local manager. Let him provide a time on the air, every month or oftener, for a panel of representative citizens to meet with him and discuss the station's programs and general service to the community during the pre-ceding period. The presence of a station executive would be es-sential because the purpose would be an exploration of mutual problems. He would be there to receive praise (of which in most cases there would be much), and to explain or defend whatever the citizens might take amiss.[12]

American journalism instinctively and overwhelmingly rejects anything of the kind. Newspapers especially still give off convul-sive reflexes from the trauma suffered in 1947 at the hands of an uninvited interloper, the Commission on Freedom of the Press. This private commission was headed by Robert M. Hutchins, then Chancellor of the University of Chicago, and was financed chiefly by Henry Luce of *Time*. It issued a report that set editors' and pub-lishers' teeth on edge. Not only did it ask such insulting questions as how "press lying" could be lessened, but it dismissed ASNE's admirable code of ethics as of no account:

> At an early meeting the Society drew up and adopted a code of ethics which, if followed, would have made the newspapers re-sponsible carriers of news and discussion. The only means of en-

forcement was expulsion from the Society. Shortly after the code was adopted, a case of gross malpractice on the part of one of the members was reported. After the Society had deliberated long and painfully, the case was dropped. This settled the function of the code.[13]

The commission came up with thirteen recommendations, but the newspapermen's anger tended to center on one urging the press to set up "a new and independent agency to appraise and report annually upon the performance of the press." The commission had been careful to stress the sanctity of press freedom. But it warned that the press, by its attitude of "Nobody's going to tell me how to run *my* paper," might itself invite pressures to limit its freedom. The burden of the whole report was that the press should do something toward living up to the ethics it professed.

I shall never forget the reaction that followed at that year's ASNE convention. As a new member I sat on the back benches as my betters howled and growled at the commission and all its works. In those days the society spent the Saturday afternoon of its three-day sessions debating resolutions. The 1947 transcript reveals twenty-four pages of disputation over how to phrase the anathema to be pronounced upon the Hutchins report.

The final product began by saying that ASNE "welcomes informed criticism of the newspaper press and offers its cooperation to any responsible student of newspaper problems and shortcomings"—a way of conveying the idea that the commission was neither informed nor responsible. Then came the punch: There would be no watchdog whatever, because the ASNE "believes our press is performing with increasing effectiveness and fairness the duties of keeping the American people the best informed people in the world."[14]

The editors had been irked by several peripheral issues, as well as the central one of a watchdog over the press. One was the commission's lumping radio (TV was still in its cradle), magazines, movies, and books together with newspapers under their private brand name, the press. Another was the fact that the commission had the temerity to sit in judgment on newspapers without inviting a single professional into its ranks.

To have asked a newspaperman to join the commission might have been politic, though unlikely to change anything. To this day there is a tendency among journalists to dismiss outsiders as incompetent to judge press performance. Yet the commission members were men of stature, and denigration them as outsiders who were therefore incompetent to measure press performance is of course the argument *ad hominem*. This is a logical fallacy, because what matters is the validity of what is said, not who says it. Even if a drunk preaches temperance, he may still be right. Besides, to have the press judge its own performance is to allow the accused to decide whether he is guilty or innocent, a notoriously inaccurate process.

Our trouble arises from the fact that the two rights involved—freedom of the press and the public's need to be fully and fairly informed—are both precious. Perhaps that is why newspapermen suffer a split personality over the inevitable clash between the two. This is as true today as it was in 1950, when an ASNE committee was still warding off what the Hutchins report had said three years earlier. To my astonishment I find what I had forgotten—I myself had been a junior member of that committee, and had signed its report.

It is characteristic of the endless debate over this issue that we boldly attacked the subject by expressing belief "that the Society, in the interest of the freest possible discussion of all public issues, should welcome critical studies of the press made in good faith by independent agencies." But alas, the press is always thus marching up the hill to do battle for the Lord, only to march right down again. Further on our report said:

> We vigorously repudiate the concept of a referee, or policeman sitting in judgment upon and seeking to enforce, *if only through some appeal to public opinion* [italics added], conformance to a

standard of performance which the referee may deem desirable in the public interest.[15]

Our conclusion was that all was well anyway because the society itself is "a continuing committee of the whole on self-examination and self-improvement." In other words, right back to home base: don't do anything.

## What Is Truth?

One can smile over such ambivalence. But the fear of a watchdog over the press is not lightly to be brushed aside. Nobody has yet answered Pontius Pilate's question, "What is truth?" Nor can we give any referee the final say as to what truth is. We cannot have freedom for the best without allowing it also for the worst. Freedom for our truth is nothing without equal freedom for the other fellow's error.

The danger signals keep flying. In 1970 the psychiatrist W. Walter Menninger again proposed that oft-suggested but hopeless contradiction, licensing for newsmen. And measures toward that end were actually introduced the same year in Michigan and Puerto Rico.[16]

Always there is temptation to give teeth to the watchdog proposed for the press. Thus, the task force reporting in 1969 on the media to the National Commission on Violence would give its supposedly independent Center for Media Study government money and presidential appointments.[17] This is a sure way of making the whole proposal one of political censorship, and therefore unsound to the point of being vicious.

Nevertheless, having said all that, we still have not faced up to the issue: Must we then continue to do nothing? And is it true that even a toothless watchdog will limit press freedom, either in itself or as an advance agent for regulation?

At the time of the 1968 Democratic National Convention in Chicago, the public refused to believe the flailing police clubs, descending on the heads and bodies of street protesters and newsmen alike, that it had seen with its own eyes. Because it was fed up with defiance, disruption, and destruction, it was convinced the protesters must be wrong. So it refused to believe what TV and the papers showed, and sided with Mayor Daley instead.

In the following year, public approval of Vice President Agnew's unprecedented attacks on network news commentators, and on newspapers, was almost palpable. Small wonder that Dr. Gallup reported, soon thereafter, that only 37 per cent of the American public believed that newspapers "deal fairly with all sides" in presenting news of political and social issues, as against 45 per cent who didn't (18 per cent ducked this question). Television news did a shade better: 40 per cent found network news fair, as against 42 per cent who didn't. Still, the fact remains: If this is an accurate sample, and presumably it is, then hardly more than one American in three believes American journalism to be fair. That's hardly a score to be content with.

Anyone experienced in journalism knows that unpopularity is inherent in the business. The American citizen today is no different from the legendary Pharaoh of old, brooding on his elegant couch after having stabbed to death the messengers who brought him bad news. All of us tend to blame the press for the often ugly world it mirrors. But it does not necessarily follow that we must therefore reject all means of keeping journalism aware of society's need for the most distortion-free mirror possible.

It is one thing to set a policeman over the press. It is something else again to set up a group or groups of citizens, whose qualities entitle them to respect, to do no more than investigate specific complaints carefully, and then report what they find. Freedom has always made a fundamental distinction between action and speech. Any guardian of the guardians of the press must be encouraged to speak, but forbidden to act. Any press council or other watchdog must remain powerless to enforce its conclusions except through the moral validity, the public credibility, of what it says.

Also, such a group ought always to include professional journalists from papers large and small—and some younger rebels as well as editors, publishers, and owners—to explain the facts of journalistic life to the lay members. Money comes best from the press itself. But the chairman and a strong minority, or even a majority, should be laymen because they may see the journalistic forest the better for not themselves being trees.

## It Is Already Late

Much of the turmoil of these closing years of the twentieth century arises from popular anger and despair at the sluggishness with which our society becomes aware of the need for change, and then does something about it. There can hardly be doubt that a monopoly press, toward which we have already gone most of the way, requires something other than the absence of self-discipline that served well enough when "the press" meant only printed newspapers, with plenty of them competing for public favor. Surely it is already past time to set up some voluntary guidepost to compensate for the fact that there is no longer enough variety and competition to make the process self-correcting. Whether this is done through a single national press council or through regional or local councils is a detail. However it is done—let us hope with built-in provision for evaluation and change in light of experience—the ball is at the moment in the hands of ASNE. But ASNE's history on the issue makes one suspect that in the end, if left to itself, it may once again decide that all's well after all, and do nothing.

That is not necessarily undesirable, because the issue is bigger than ASNE alone. Despite its power and prestige, ASNE is not the sole journalistic authority in the country. In Britain there was a comparable situation, which accounted for the fact that the Press Council was formed not by one but by all important journalistic groups. Not only the editors and proprietors but regional (Scottish) and other professional and union groups were included.[18]

Equally broad representation, in one form or another, would be desirable here. Indeed in the end it should be even broader, to include television and radio news—something that the semi-public BBC seems to have made unnecessary in Great Britain. As far as printed journalism is concerned, no editorial or business element of national significance should be left out. This might mean, then, not only ASNE but in addition something like the following:

American Newspaper Publishers Association
Associated Press Managing Editors Association
The wire services
Representatives of smaller papers, like the National Editorial Association
Representatives of the magazines
Representatives of the larger journalism schools

Because of its activity in the field, and because of its prominence in the editorial direction of journalism, ASNE might serve as catalyst in getting the project started, if not as its sole creator. Or it might be the pioneer, acting only for the 700 or so dailies that comprise its membership—which includes most of those that matter. In this way it could serve as bellwether for all media, either through a single group, or through separate trade groups, or regionally. For the present no other agency that could get things started is visible on the journalistic horizon—if one excludes that presumably eager volunteer, Vice President Agnew.

Always we must remind ourselves that the media themselves should make the experiment, because anything that smells of law or other compulsion from the outside is a negation of freedom of the press. And the whole idea is to protect and further that freedom, rather than to circumscribe it. What is new is the economic and technical structure of contemporary journalism, and this requires that we make sure that the press's freedom continues to be exercised for the benefit of the public.

It is quite likely that no significant start in this direction will be made in this country, any more than it was in Britain, unless the press feels itself threatened from the outside. Our press's fear of a toothless, self-imposed press council is curiously pathological. It seems no more grounded in reality than was the American Medical Association's phobia against medical insurance. Certainly the experiences of other countries—and Sweden's journalistic Court of Honor goes back to 1916—indicates that press councils help the press as well as rebuke it. Case after case before Britain's council shows precisely that.

As early as in 1958, at the end of the first five years of Britain's Press Council, its chairman said:

> My view, after much experience, is that many of the would-be reformers of the press are in need of the curbs they propose for others, since they themselves are guilty of the offenses they allege—wild exaggeration, distortion of the truth, and the unproved assumptions that they speak for the nation.[19]

More recently, in 1969, 385 complaints were brought before the Council. Of these it accepted for adjudication only 61. And of the 61, it rejected 36, as against 25 it upheld.[20]

Charles J. Bennett of the Oklahoma City papers, one of the ASNE visitors to London in 1969, reported that Britain's council had been responsible for:

> Better performance by newspapers and periodicals.
> Much improved public attitudes toward the press.
> Strengthening newspapers' ability to obtain news from public bodies.
> Heading off numbers of petty but costly libel suits.
> Shielding newspapers from legislated controls.[21]

One of the Americans bold enough to risk and experimental local council, Robert W. Chandler of the *Bend Bulletin* in Oregon, found his paper the better for the experience. And it wasn't all that painful:

We were surprised and pleased when members of the council, after hearing a full explanation from both sides, agreed at least in part with the newspaper in most cases.[22]

So it seems to be whenever any owner or editor is willing to dip his toes into the water. When the Louisville papers assigned a former city editor to be ombudsman to represent rank-and-file readers—who have no ready access to an editor or publisher, as do leaders in business or government—the results were favorable.[23]

There are other signs that the fear of the journalistic establishment that someone will do unto it as it does unto others is a paranoid fear. The success of the various journalism reviews, from Chicago and St. Louis to New York, like the success of local press councils, from Minnesota to Hawaii, indicates that the need for a toothless guardian of the guardians is real.

Perhaps our editors and publishers, and our broadcasters as well, are too much like the man with disturbing symptoms who fears to go to the doctor lest he find out that what ails him is bad. A courageous experiment now might reveal that meeting an obvious public need will not bring, through either the front or back door, the policeman with a club. The fear is indeed groundless, because such a policeman is forbidden by the Constitution. Powerless but respected observers of the press may not be fatal to its freedom, but rather a tonic to it.

The conclusion seems inescapable. Newspapers and broadcasters had better do something themselves before they get further out of touch with their public than they are already. That is reason enough for the press to welcome a still, small voice of conscience whose only strength is the newsman's own willingness to listen.

# 8

## *Mass Man and Mass Media*

### Exit the Individual

THIS IS the day of mass man. At some point in the mid-1960s our population shot past 200 million, and seemingly nothing but the Four Horsemen can keep it from passing 300 million before the end of the century. But even if we shrank back to the 100 million we were during World War I, we would still be a mass. We are not individuals any more, so much as a single, organic whole. We still live on farms and in villages, towns, cities, and suburbs, though the pattern is shifting to megalopo-suburbia. Everything in our lives, from what we eat and wear and drive around in to what we know about passing events, comes prepackaged from some distant, impersonal source.

Clearly, the mass media have helped to make mass man. Newspapers, the big magazines, radio, television, films, and even the flood of books, have homogenized us. Through psychologically based advertising as well as centrally packaged news, they have crammed us all into the same mold—even though as individuals we are not alike. A ghetto child has little in common with a Texas oil baron, or a suburban housewife.

If mass society is thus swallowing the individual, why has journalism not come to the rescue? The free press was not written into the Constitution for the benefit of million-circulation newspapers, or multimillion-circulation magazines, still less for the broadcasting empires that can make the whole nation look at and listen to the same thing at the same time. The free press was established to articulate the yearnings of the individual, through a hand-operated press not unlike Gutenberg's. But within the last generation something fundamental has changed. As long ago as 1959, the sociologist Elisabeth Noelle-Neumann described it:

> To many, the publishing world appears to be an independent, autonomous power that does not reproduce public opinions formed elsewhere, but manufactures them. The press was once regarded as the decisive instrument for the liberation of the individual from absolute government, and nowadays we are more inclined to ask ourselves how we can liberate the individual from the spiritual despotism of the mass communication media.[1]

Throughout its history the United States has depended on a free, multifarious, and variegated press, not only to fight its peoples' battles, but to give them the information they need to govern themselves. The minimum goal for the future must be to continue a report to the individual citizen on his world that is so free, full, and varied that nothing significant can long be ignored or suppressed. Can it be done?

## The Coming of Monopoly

Throughout this century there have been fears that the coming of monopoly, which has killed everything from the corner grocery to the independent auto manufacturer, would kill the free press as well. The danger is obvious, because monopoly of the news makes it possible to transform journalism from the uninhibited cacophony it was into a single, overpowering voice.

The fact is that, for all the seeming variety of print, picture, and sound that surrounds us, a substantial monopoly in journalism is already here. In 1910, when our population was 92 million, there were 2600 daily newspapers. Since then, despite a population explosion to more than 200 million, the total number of dailies has declined sharply. True, since World War II the decline has all but stopped. The total keeps hovering somewhere near 1750—while the population still grows. Moreover, with a handful of exceptions, we are down to one paper per city, so that the surviving dailies speak with that much more powerful a voice. And to a considerable extent they all say the same thing.

Then, too, there are the newspaper chains. The better known ones are big chains, but the number of lesser multiple ownerships of two or more papers each has grown astonishingly large. All together these publishing units now total almost 160. Finally, only two wire services give the nation its basic information about the world.

Broadcasting is by nature even more monopolistic than printed journalism. True, there are many more broadcasting stations than newspapers—almost 7000 AM and FM radio stations, and almost 900 television stations. But relatively few of them maintain news staffs that amount to much, in comparison with newspapers. Television doesn't have time for detailed, local news. Besides, by nature, broadcasting lends itself to network programs. Yet television has become our dominant medium of communication. By 1970, for example, the president of NBC could say:

> Television has developed an audience in nearly 60 million American homes, more than 95 per cent of the households in the country. Week in and out, it has the attention of some four-fifths of the national population. It is significant that year after year surveys find that if the public were faced with the prospect of having only one mass medium, most people, by a large majority, would prefer that medium to be television.[2]

This is hardly the historic free press. It is geared to the mass, and the newspapers and national magazines are but a step behind. Small wonder, then, that mass communication seems to dominate the citizen, rather than the other way around. Small wonder, too, that the citizen no longer thinks of either daily newspaper or television as his private civil liberty, through which he can express himself.

When all that has been entered into the balance, however, bigness and near-monopoly still do not seem to be the source of our discontent. For all their mechanization, neither the newspapers nor the news programs of radio and TV speak in quite that monotone that critics insist must follow from limited numbers and concentrated ownership. The tradition of objecting reporting still lives, despite the new journalists' scorn for it. This gives the news media a sense of obligation, however imperfectly observed at times, to report both sides of controversies, or more if there are more than two sides, and to dig out skulduggery wherever it may hide.

The result is that little of significance is ignored or suppressed. If the American citizen takes the trouble to be well informed, he has better opportunity than his like before him.

Why then the change from the days when our predecessors called their newspaper the tribune of the people, or the palladium of their liberties? Why the common feeling that big papers and big television are all the same—that they constitute a vast, remote, power complex that, far from liberating the individual from government, has largely teamed up with government? The press and the government, while outwardly the familiar institutions of old, both seem to have become despots beyond the individual's control.

Our basic trouble is that democracy doesn't seem to work any more, at least not the way it used to. Everything from inflation to Indochina, from campus explosion to crime in the streets, seems to materialize spontaneously, without our being able to do anything about it. Is this because the technological world we have contrived has triumphed over Jeffersonian democracy? Have the myriad intricacies with which President or Pentagon or Congress must contend—plus those with which state and local governments must contend—become so numerous and so confusing that we no longer get enough information to understand them, and therefore cannot control them?

Beyond question the world is infinitely more complex, and more changeable, than it ever was before. In George Washington's day, the New England farmer or Virginia planter or Philadelphia merchant could judge the issues before the country almost as well as the President himself. There were, of course, momentous problems like the American Revolution and American Constitution. But the issues that our forbears had to struggle with were for the most part simple, near, and familiar. Should the town build a new bridge? Should Congress buy weapons for the country's minuscule navy? A bridge was a bridge, and a cannon, a cannon.

Today who knows enough to say whether or not we should build an FX-111 or SST or ABM? Or how to measure the cost of a space station against the cost of national health insurance? Or how to contrive, and how to pay for, schools and police forces good enough to lessen the fire of racial hatred? It is all too big and fuzzy and complex to come to grips with.

## Communication = Change

It may be that our bafflement results less from our ignorance of the countless details of our affairs than from a new phenomenon so far little reckoned with. This is the fact that modern mass communications not only report the world, but change the world in the process. And this change is even bigger, and more fundamental, than the change that covering a news story sometimes makes on the news itself.

The late Canadian economist and historian Harold A. Innis studied communication, going back to the clay tablets of cuneiform writing and papyrus. He concluded that a society's means of communication had an effect on its knowledge, and that "a monopoly or an oligopoly of knowledge is built up to the point that an equilibrium is disturbed." Written codes imply uniformity, justice, and a belief in laws, he said, but they also imply an element of rigidity. Methods of writing, requiring as they do tools and training, preserve traditional ideas and outlooks. But "sudden extensions of communication are reflected in cultural disturbances." All in all, "We can perhaps assume that the use of a medium of communication over a long period of time will to some extent determine the character of knowledge to be communicated."[3]

From this one can proceed to the thought that every revolutionary change in the means of communication is followed by a revolutionary change in society itself. Could it be the coming of radio, and especially television, that precipitated today's turmoil and trouble?

It seems unbelievable. Yet precisely that is implicit in the doctrine preached by that other and better known Canadian, Marshall McLuhan. Mr. McLuhan, though originally a teacher of English, fights a losing battle with the English language. He is also something of a showman. Yet for all his exasperating obscurities and unsupported pronouncements, he has given us an insight that is as penetrating as it is new. Scholars of communication seem persuaded that he is essentially right in saying that the medium is the message.[4] As he put it in one of his less turgid presentations: "Societies have always been shaped more by the nature of the medium by which men have communicated than by the content of communication."[5] So it isn't what *The New York Times* prints, or what ABC-TV broadcasts, that matters, so much as whether the report is printed or broadcast. The difference between the two is transforming our life.

This is a startling thesis. But the more you look into it the more persuasive it becomes. And it requires that, despite the surface similarity of the news we get via printed page and electromagnetic waves, we stop thinking of our mass media as a single behemoth. Even radio and television, McLuhan insists, have sharply different impacts on us.

The first thing to note is that in this country there is no Establishment that, after the fashion of Hitler's Dr. Goebbels, uses all the mass media to ensure the triumph of Middle America, or any other America. Nor are newspapers, television, and all the rest ruled by that Eastern, liberal cabal that Spiro Agnew sees in his nightmares. Our trouble is not that simple. It derives instead from the fundamental fact that, even though we get substantially identical news from radio, newspaper, newsmagazine, and Walter Cronkite, the various journalistic mechanisms through which we get the news change us without our even being aware of it.

### Television = the Mass

Consider the fact that, thanks to television, too many of us now know too much about one another. That surviving exemplar of nineteenth-century individualism, the Maine lobsterman, knows all about riots on campus and in the ghetto because he has seen them for himself, without leaving his own house. And the Orange County John Bircher knows enough about the ghetto to fear and hate it, for the same reason.

Perhaps because all of us are battered ceaselessly by an endless surf of breaking events, we seem no longer capable of taking in stride a world that for all its teeming population, and extraordinary talent for violence, isn't really any more cruel, bloody, or difficult than it ever was. Said Charles L. Bennett of the *Daily Oklahoman* and *Oklahoma City Times:*

> One of the mirages of today . . . is the belief that better communication necessarily results in better understanding. . . . Information becomes useful only when organized, analyzed, and rationalized. This requires self-disciplined, unemotional thought and, too often, it's far easier to dismiss the day's news with an emotional, all-encompassing reaction and let it go at that. . . . Public discussion becomes public argument, recrimination, and name-calling.[6]

S. I. Hayakawa, the semanticist turned gamecock president of San Francisco State, added that "Television tremendously magnifies everything that goes on television."[7] That is why students in recent years became more involved in the world than any before them. With their own eyes they saw such things as the struggle for civil liberties in the South, the assassinations of the Kennedys, the riots that followed the murder of Dr. King, and the endless, meaningless, purposeless violence in Vietnam. No wonder they felt themselves to be an integral part of all that is happening.

It was not so when adults sat quietly reading a newspaper, and students were all but oblivious to off-campus news. Newspapers of those days reported war, pestilence, and disaster, just as television does today. But those newspaper stories, mostly from distant parts, still left us undisturbed. It all took place far away from where we sat.

Can we recapture such equanimity in a world whose flames television brings to within a few feet of us every day? In the midst of the Cambodia-Kent State upheaval in 1970, the *Wall Street Journal* said:

> When you feel the emotions rise from the riots and burnings on television, turn the blasted thing off, go out in the fresh air and take a walk around your own block. You will make a comforting discovery that you are not personally threatened at all.[8]

Unfortunately we are not disposed to turn the blasted thing off for good. Therefore we shall have to ask whether newspapers, which used to carry the burden of informing the country, and in so doing made self-government possible, can hold up their end in the shapeless, felt world of mass man that electronic circuitry has created. More than that, it makes us wonder whether our eighteenth-century Constitution, which in the past has been adapted to a changing world, can endure in a United States in which television is the dominant medium of communication.

### Newspapers = the Individual

McLuhan says that before writing was invented "man lived in acoustic space: boundless, directionless, horizonless, in the dark of the mind, in the world of emotion, by primordial intuition, by terror. Speech is a social chart of this bog." Then came the goose-quill, and that put an end to talk as the decisive element in shaping society. Writing, that "step from the dark into the light of the mind," brought civilization. It created towns and architecture, roads, armies—and bureaucracies.

In due course it also brought printing. And printing, in turn, let loose a revolution of its own.

Aristotle concluded that a democracy must be small if it is to work:

> If the citizens of a state are to judge and to distribute offices according to merit, then they must know each other's characters; where they do not possess this knowledge, both the election to office and the decisions of lawsuits will go wrong.[9]

Thus it was printing that, by spreading knowledge beyond the range of personal contact, made possible the expansion of self-government from a fifth-century Athens of perhaps 40,000 adult males[10] to a United States of more than 200 million people.

Not only that, without printing's power to spread ideas, there would have been no Reformation. And the Reformation, by battling for the right to dissent, played a crucial part in clearing the way for modern democracy. It was not today's McLuhan, but the Thomas Carlyle of 1840 who said:

> Literature is our Parliament too. Printing, which comes necessarily out of Writing, I say often, is equivalent to Democracy: Invent Writing, Democracy is inevitable.[11]

And what is democracy, when given life through representative government? Before World War II, during the years of the rise of totalitarianism, José Ortega y Gasset put it well:

> The political doctrine which has represented the loftiest endeavor towards common life is liberal democracy. It carries to the extreme the determination to have consideration for one's neighbors. . . . Liberalism is that principle of political rights, accord-

ing to which the public authority, in spite of being all powerful,
limits itself and attempts, even at its own expense, to leave room
in the State over which it rules for those to live who neither
think nor feel as it does, that is to say as do the stronger, the majority. Liberalism . . . is the supreme form of generosity; it is
the right which the majority concedes to minorities and hence it
is the noblest cry that has ever resounded in this planet.[12]

Ortega concluded, however, that liberal democracy "is a discipline too difficult and complex to take firm root on earth," and that,
therefore, humanity soon became "anxious to get rid of it." This
raises a question: If printing made liberal democracy inevitable,
does television condemn it to death?

If democracy does decline, it seems likely that some form of
totalitarianism will be its successor. Twentieth-century totalitarianism, which no matter what its ideology is a marriage of tyranny with
technology, began in Leningrad in 1917. That was before radio
broadcasting existed or television was more than a dream. Also,
India has shown, if tentatively and precariously, that democracy
can function without literacy. Yet there is a ring of truth to the thesis that the individual and his private thoughts are at home with a
newspaper, magazine, or book, but lost before the all-seeing eye
of TV.

"Print technology created the public," says McLuhan. "Electric
technology created the mass. The public consists of separate individuals walking around with separate, fixed points of view. The new
technology demands that we abandon the luxury of this posture,
this fragmentary outlook."[13]

The man who views the world through his newspaper can think
about it, bit by bit at a time. The child who grows up with television, to which he devotes more hours than to school, feels that
the world surrounds him:

It was the funeral of President Kennedy that most strongly
proved the power of television to invest an occasion with the
character of corporate participation. It involves an entire population in a ritual process. (By comparison, press, movies, and radio

are mere packaging devices for consumers.) In television images are projected at you. You are the screen. The images wrap around you. You are the vanishing point.[14]

Is television, then, making mass man a cipher—a recipient, rather than a doer and originator?

The thought fits all too neatly into the contemporary scene. What with an increasingly nosy census, ever more official wiretapping, and proliferating data banks that tell Big Brother all about us, the government knows more and more about the citizen, and the citizen knows less and less about his government. Does this, linked with a return to the directionless life of feeling that preceded writing and print, impel us willy-nilly toward McLuhan's world, recreated "in the image of a global village"? Are we becoming a United States in which not the citizen, but a President who commands television at will calls the tune?

We have already gone part way. Television is transforming politics—from election campaign to presidential preponderance over Congress to presidential press conferences—or the lack of them.

In Franklin Roosevelt's day the press conference was likened to the formal, and formidable, question hour in Britain's Parliament. A small group of experienced reporters put the President on the griddle with searching questions, and, despite his skilled fencing and dunce's corner, they kept after him until they got some answer. Today's press conference is a TV spectacular, a ritual of showmanship dominated by the President. Newspaper reporters have become but actors. Their role is to jump up and vie for recognition, with the lucky ones confined to opening the presidential floodgates. They never follow up a question, because time and their numbers forbid. Besides, it would take a brash individual to say to the President, before a watching nation that is already irritated with the press, "That's all very well, Sir, but why don't you answer the question?"

Increasingly, moreover, not only the President but our governors and senators as well are sold to the electorate over TV like so many soaps or detergents. In the 1968 campaign President Nixon avoided the interview programs, ignored the news shows, and, simply by buying time, told the voters only what he chose without allowing anyone to doubt or question him. And so again in 1972.

Once in office, a politician can use TV to keep the mass behind him. The President commands prime time whenever he wants it. This makes Congress restive because, although it is supposedly a co-equal branch of government, it is too sprawling and shapeless and divided to be able to get equal TV exposure. Add to this the fact that television broadcasts not so much images and sounds as emotions, and you come face to face with something new in American history: instead of being independent citizens who control our government, we risk becoming a faceless mass ruled from above. Is that what frustrates all of us, and makes the young ready to silence "the noblest cry that has ever resounded in this planet"?

### Can Printed News Save Democracy?

Not many years ago David Brinkley assured the American Society of Newspaper Editors that TV could never replace the newspaper:

> . . . on a story like a convention, a Churchill funeral, or a Kennedy funeral, or an inauguration or something like that that happens out where you can see it—something that is planned in advance, something that has a strong visual aspect, as opposed to being an abstract conception—on that kind of thing nobody can touch us. But when it comes to covering the news in any thorough and detailed way, we are just almost not in the ball game.[15]

The contrast between the news that can be broadcast in a fixed time slot, as against page after page of newsprint, is striking. In 1971 two UCLA researchers measured the amount of news distributed in one week by television and by the local paper in Bakersfield, a market town at the southern end of California's vast, hot, and fruitful San Joaquin Valley. Three local TV stations, each with a network affiliation, were measured against the 51,000-circulation

Bakersfield *Californian*. The detailed findings were thus summed up:

> Each minute of broadcast news was found to be the equivalent of 4.7 column inches in the newspaper.
>
> The "one hour" dinner time news program presented by two of the local TV stations was the equivalent of a little more than one newspaper page of news; the "one and a half hour" dinner time program of the third station was almost the equivalent of two pages.
>
> During an average weekday, the three stations, on average, presented 63 news items, of which nine were repeated. The average number of general news stories in the Bakersfield *Californian* was 217.[16]

The two researchers, Dr. Jack Lyle and Richard A. Stone, spelled out the consequences in these words:

> Even in a small city, then, where TV news can be more focused than is possible in a metropolitan complex, the conscientious citizen trying to keep abreast of events on both the local and broader scene must continue to rely most heavily upon the newspaper. Here we are not speaking of the specialized functions the newspaper provides in presenting editorial analyses and such things as stock market transactions, sports records and such which cannot practically be presented on television. We are speaking specifically in terms of the surveillance function of the news media in providing a report on significant events—local and elsewhere.[17]

Newspapers, at best, are uncertain mirrors of the world. But when electronic news is compared to them its lack of nourishment for the mind forces us to ask: Can a nation that gets most of its news from television be sufficiently well informed to govern itself? The Pentagon Papers earned their place in history through the cumulative impact of detail after detail in document after document. The whole made a book of almost 700 pages. Television simply could not have performed this crucial service in informing the American people.

It is not that people choose to be under-informed, so much as that they do what comes naturally. The decisive fact is that television is easier to take than a newspaper. Once you have bought the set, the news is free. You don't even have to go to the door, or to the newspaper tube at the end of the driveway, to get it. And once you have switched on the set you don't have to do anything. The machine does it to you as you sit there like so much blotting paper, absorbing what is extruded from the screen. Thinking becomes a spectator sport.

Burns W. Roper of Roper Research Associates has made numerous studies of the field for the television industry. He noted, that while newspapers remain first in informing voters about candidates for local and county elections, television leads in state campaigns. As for national elections, television "has a commanding 41 percentage point lead over newspapers."

By 1968, moreover, television had outscored newspapers, 57 to 23 per cent (magazines and radio were also-rans) in answers to the question, "Which would you say gives you the clearest understanding of the candidates and issues in national elections?" In fact the public says that, if you get conflicting or different reports of the same news story, television is more believable than newspapers, 44 to 21 per cent.[18] Ouch!

The American people then, prefer a medium of information that under-informs them while seeming not to. Despite the high quality of network reporters and commentators, despite the vividness of the camera's eyewitness testimony, despite the brilliant and revealing documentaries (which seem more and more forced off the air by commercial pressures), TV walls us off from much of the world. We do not even know of the existence of most events and conditions, much less their origins and details, the conflicting values involved, the meanings inherent in them. The result is that the American citizen, after having been entertained by the evening news show, thinks he knows what has happened—but he doesn't. Though all the news that fits between the commercials is a starvation diet, he isn't even aware of it.

So the question remains: Can television make an informed citi-

zenry possible? The question becomes barbed when one considers
that what seems like and often is the immediate, overwhelming
reality of an event on television can also be, and sometimes necessarily is, distorted. What appears to be the visible, self-evident truth
is not necessarily the truth, as witness the popular reaction to the
famous battle of Chicago in 1968. At that time the press reported
more police violence than the street films, taken under Mayor
Daley's blackout, were able to show. Yet the public back home
would not believe even such police violence as it had seen on television with its own eyes.[19] Again, did the endless TV snippets of
explosions and whirling helicopters and jungle grass reproduce the
subtle realities that made Vietnam the world tragedy that it was
and is?

One comes away from that anfractuous puzzle, the interrelation
between mass man and mass media, with the conclusion that if
democracy is to be saved print must save it. We surround ourselves
with electronic images and sounds. Our preference for them over
print keeps us starved for information and understanding. Thus,
despite surface appearances, we have actually not gone beyond the
point at which Alexis de Tocqueville found us, nearly a century
and a half ago, when the printed newspaper was all there was to
hold us together:

> When men are no longer united among themselves by firm and
> lasting ties, it is impossible to obtain the co-operation of any
> great number of them unless you can persuade every man whose
> help you require that his private interest obliges him voluntarily
> to unite his exertions to the exertions of all the others. This can
> be habitually and conveniently effected only by means of a news-
> paper; nothing but a newspaper can drop the same thought into
> a thousand minds at the same moment. A newspaper is an ad-
> viser that does not require to be sought, but that comes of its own
> accord and talks to you briefly every day of the common weal,
> without distracting you from your private affairs.[20]

Fortunately, print is too valuable to be allowed to disappear.
Facts, ideas, emotions, and meanings, fixed in print, are therefore
unlikely to give way entirely before the vacuum tube. Printed mat-

ter itself should survive, no matter how much the technics of pro-
ducing it may change. This, presumably, despite the fact that in
western nations, including this one, newspapers are suffering economically from inroads made into their advertising revenue by
television—and by wonder whether generations brought up on electronic images will make the effort of reading.

What matters, then, is not the photo-electronic gadgetry that
will produce the print of the future so much as the product itself.
The familar, believable, paper-and-ink record that we can hold in
our hands, ponder individually and at leisure, and save for reference, must continue to be widely available and widely read if the
American people are not to become a herd of sheep.

This puts a heavy burden on newspapers, on magazines and
books, and above all on those who edit what comes over the cables
of the future. Those in the command posts of journalism will have
to work harder and more skillfully, and spend more money than
their predecessor did, if they are to lure mass man into reading
the stuff he ought to read, and ponder, for his own good.

Walter Cronkite, who started his career in print journalism, once
considered ending his TV news program with the recommendation
that viewers consult their local newspapers for details and further
analysis of a complex issue, for which he had no time. But, he says,
he finally realized that most newspapers themselves offer little more
than headline facts.[21]

What should the newspapers do? A good question, as the lec-
turer says when he doesn't have the answer. Besides, experience has
taught me not to prophesy. Still, the years since World War I, and
the changes those years have wrought in newspapers, surely point
toward the future.

For one thing it seems likely that the familiar categories into
which newspapers divide their pages will continue: general news,
sports, business and finance, the arts, society, home and living,
and so on to the crossword puzzle. Detail, especially local detail,
will remain important because television cannot encompass it. But

because increasing demands on our time leave us ever less time for news, the papers will have to spend ever more skill and sweat condensing the hard news—the bread-and-butter items running from Main Street to the uttermost parts of the universe—that every community must have. Here the two columns headed "What's News" on the front page of the *Wall Street Journal*, and the condensations and wrap-ups of the newsmagazines, point the way.

Compressing essential facts leaves room for the depth reporting for which this century has long cried out. But again, interpretive reporting must explain not by editorializing, but by digging out more facts.

In the future print can make its greatest contribution as a social antidote to the mesmerizing of mass man inherent in television. I have had occasion to see something of the rising generation of activist-journalists, many of whom seem fired by a desire to take newspapers, after the manner of the underground press, into television's psychedelic world of emotionally felt truth. They are impatient with staid print as the repository for factual, objective, measurable, and verifiable truth which, though necessarily imperfect, is at least a crude portrait of the world as it is—warts, halos, significance, and all.

To the activist, what he thinks about the news is more important than the news itself. Hence his impatience with the newspaper as mirror of the world, and his desire to transform it into a sword with which to conquer the future.

This is, however, no formula on which to base self-government by free men. It is a return to the primitive habit of getting an opinion first, and thereafter looking about for facts to bolster it. Truth still wears as many faces as it did in the days of Areopagitica—if not more. Surely it comes more nearly to him who strives to hold his prejudices in check, who gives hostile facts the same weight as friendly facts, than to him who reverts to the fallacy of believing there is only one truth and it is his.

Therefore, if self-government is indeed to survive, the first necessity is a standard of reporting and editing that follows the truth wherever it may lead. It will not assume that a Bobby Seale or a Richard Nixon is either right or wrong before the fact-finding, or even the editorial writing, begins.

We shall continue to need editorials, because we don't know enough to write interpretive news that says all that needs to be said. But effective editorial writing is less a matter of opinions served up in the brimstone and vitriol of old than of competence, integrity, and determination to get needed things out into the open, and their meaning made clear, no matter whose sacred cow is gored.

That is why, in the 1970s and beyond, the editor and his staff should be left on a long leash. They should be professionals, and on any given paper or other news organization they should be of varied backgrounds and talents and outlooks. Ideally they should be free to choose their own way, much as an aerospace corporation will leave its physicists and engineers free in the field of their compenence, or the business office of a hospital or clinic will leave its doctors free.

This may be a counsel of perfection, but what's wrong with that as a guide? Let the editor and his reporters and news analysts and editorial writers be free to examine each issue, each commercial interest, each candidate, and each party as it comes along in the procession of the news. And let them be the ones to decide, where need be, which is on the side of the angels at that moment. Let them be dispassionate rather than Democratic; let them rather be right than Republican.

Here, then, is the challenge: In today's world of mass man and mass media, communication has become so powerful that, ultimately, he who controls communication controls the world. But communication is a power in a sense even deeper than this. For no matter who uses it, or is used by it, communication in itself can be power, changing us as it washes over us.

This means that our problem remains what it has always been:

to democratize communication. Journalism, and first of all print journalism, must fight not only those who use and misuse communication but, where need be, it must fight the mechanics of communication themselves, just as in the past journalism has helped fight every other tyranny over the mind of man. But as our condition is new, so must our response be new.

# 9

## *Farewell to Horace Greeley*

### Buck Rogers, Journalist

ON APRIL 16, 1937, the annual convention of the American Society of Newspaper Editors assembled for its afternoon session. The group, small by present standards, met in Washington's National Press Club. The first speaker was John Martin, managing editor of *Time*. Fourteen years after its founding, this first of the news magazines had outgrown its infancy as a rewrite of news lifted from the week's newspapers. It was having enough impact on the country—the editors' wives read it, if not the editors—to prompt ASNE members to be curious. How did *Time* go about presenting its rounded picture of the week's news, set in orderly yet colorful perspective?

Mr. Martin obliged by explaining what made *Time* tick. Then, suddenly, he altered course:

> I suppose I could go on about backgrounding the news some more, but I am full of something that I think is of greater importance. . . . It is the most fascinating thought that could come before a body of journalists such as we are here today. . . . I am told that the radio people in the course of their television experiments have now perfected a device which will do with the

230

whole newspaper page, . . . with almost the same rapidity, what
Wirephoto can do with a photograph over the wires [i.e. turn it
into electric impulses, transmit it, and then turn it into a photograph again]. They can now do that by radio, believe it or
not. . . .

So, behold, what these visionaries of today have told me, and
probably some of you have heard about it. . . . They say that it
would be possible to set up these machines which they figure they
can make and lease. . . . You become a subscriber to one of
these machines and thereby to a newspaper which would be
printed in your home while you sleep. . . .

I have no idea what might happen to all kinds of news publishing in this country if that machine which I have just heard
about does work. . . . It sounds a whole lot more feasible than
television does and they still think they are going to give us that.[1]

Here was something that startled me, a visitor in the audience.
Why didn't every newspaperman in the place blanch at the prospect? Radio, whose networks were then a decade old, was already
taking millions in advertising dollars away from newspapers that
still were feeling the bite of Depression. Now, if Mr. Martin was
right, radio's expansion into facsimile threatened to wipe out newspapers entirely.

The assembled editors, however, were not impressed. The questions they asked Mr. Martin were all devoted to the manners and
mannerisms of *Time,* none to the facsimile newspaper that might
put them out of business. If the editors seemed obtuse, they were
nevertheless right. Facsimile was not yet anything to worry about.
In a 1939 report to Columbia University, where I was then on the
faculty of the Graduate School of Journalism, I summed up the
difficulties:

Facsimile reception today, when compared with the glowing de-
scriptions one first heard of it—amounting to something like finding the *New York Times* in a little basket attached to the radio
each morning—is disappointing. In the first place the two systems
(R.C.A. and Finch) now being broadcast from about 25 experimental stations are limited in paper size. Finch uses a roll of gray

paper carrying text and illustrations about two newspaper columns (four inches) wide, and R.C.A. a roll with text pages 7½ by 11 inches in size. In the second place the rate at which images are reproduced on these relatively small rolls of paper is slow. Transmission of the facsimile edition of the *St. Louis Post-Dispatch,* consisting of nine of the R.C.A. letter-sized pages, takes more than two hours. In the third place the impressions made are fuzzy and unsatisfactory when compared to letter-press printing, even in the extremely fast and therefore less perfect newspaper form. Finally, facsimile employs a scanning process which breaks the image up into fine lines, tending to blur reproduction of type, at least in the small newspaper sizes.[2]

To this day the facsimile newspaper still waits around the corner of the future. But technologists continue to work on it. In Japan, by the time of Expo '70, *Asahi Shimbun* and two other newspapers were broadcasting fast, clear, larger-than-tabloid facsimile newspapers, though still experimentally rather than commercially. The most authoritative survey of the future technology of mass communication to date, the RAND-sponsored study by Ben H. Bagdikian, puts off the appearance of facsimile newspapers in American households until the 1990s.[3]

Facsimile, however, is but one of many technological advances. The vision Mr. Martin held before the unimpressed editors in 1937 is nothing compared to the Buck Rogers revolution in communication that has finally begun. The advance guard of computers and electronic-optic contraptions has already invaded newspaper plants that, until the 1960s, had seen little technological improvement since the nineteenth century.

Everything we now have—newspaper, radio, television, phonograph, tape recorder, film, cassette, the electronic visual recording device that does for television programs what phonograph records do for symphony concerts—all this and more are to be merged into one vast system. Every conceivable kind of sight and sound and record can be on tap in every home. Computer-controlled electronic signals will be available to bring them to us—via broadcasts,

direct or from satellites; or by telephone; or by television. As
David Sarnoff of RCA told the Advertising Council in 1965:

> With the introduction of microwave channels and the appearance
> of communications satellites and high-capacity cables, there is no
> longer any distinction among the various forms of communica-
> tions. All of them—voice or picture, telegraphy or data—pass si-
> multaneously through the same relays in the form of identical
> electronic pulses.

In 1937 the editors ignored John Martin. But now, when Sarnoff
spoke, not only newspapermen but others began to pay attention:

> Newspaper owners, book publishers and TV officials have a re-
> current nightmare: one morning they learn a competitor has per-
> fected a communications system that will drive them to the wall.
> The nightmare has its basis in reality. In laboratories and re-
> search centers across the U.S., ingenious engineers are developing
> new ways to gather, record and transmit information. At the
> rate communications technology is advancing, muses Edwin
> Smura, manager of systems engineering at Xerox, editors and
> publishers are somewhat like "bush pilots suddenly placed at the
> controls of a Boeing 707."[4]

What will all this mean to us as members of the public? There is
substantial agreement among the prophets. Here is one example:

> By touching a key, I can cause today's headlines to appear on
> the screen and these headlines may well have been revised only a
> few seconds before. By touching another key, I can see any story
> which interests me, but just today's developments. If I need a
> backgrounder, I can call for it, but I need not wade through un-
> wanted rehash. If the story contains a name I don't recognize, a
> touch of a key will produce a biography. If I want interpretation,
> a touch of another key will fetch forth an editorial or a column.[5]

Two devices already in use, the computer and the television
cable, are the source of all this. Indeed, all the communications
revolution lacks today is enough homes and offices connected with
enough computers via the cable.

Most of us have brushed up against computer technology, if not in our work then in such things as the Egyptian hieroglyphs printed on our bank checks to identify our accounts. I recall my own introduction to the computer when, as an editor in the 1950s, I was taken on tour of a military device called SAGE, which served as a warning system against nuclear attack by aircraft. It was housed in a huge building close by what was then Stewart Air Force Base, near West Point. Its function was to receive early-warning information in the form of electronic signals, reporting what enemy bombers (or perhaps geese) were coming from where, from which direction, and how fast. SAGE did the requisite math instantly, deducing a continuing result from a mass of swiftly changing data. It was a task that could never have been done by men. Had the attack been real, and had human beings undertaken the calculations involved by hand, they would have been dead for weeks before they could get the data on paper.

The officers and engineers operating the computer told us that SAGE wasn't bright. All it could do was tell the difference between yes and no, or 0 and 1. It had to be fed information in the language of binary numbers, that befuddling system of mathematics that any twelve-year-old can explain to you though I cannot.

If SAGE was not bright, it was fast. It could receive any number of binary stimuli, blink and whir to itself, and come right up with the answer—so many presumably Soviet bombers coming toward Canada, on such and such a course, at such and such altitude and speed. Word could go out instantly to Washington, to SAC, our strategic offense in Omaha, and to NORAD, the Joint Canadian-American air defense at Colorado Springs.

Apart from its impressive control center, SAGE's vast complex, according to my limited understanding and fuzzy memory, consisted for the most part of endless stacks of metal trays in rows of cabinets, containing electronic gadgetry that looked like the bottom of a hi-fi receiver. But if one of these trays failed it would call attention to itself by turning on a light, so that an attendant could find it, reach across the aisle to a replacement tray, slide it into the slot in place of the defective one, and thus keep SAGE's nervous system whole and hearty.

The communications signals of the future will operate in essentially the same way. All journalistic information, now typed, printed, photographed, punched on tape, pressed on records, or stored in video tape, will be reduced to a simple matter of yes or no. Again, the computer's speed makes it possible thus to cover the infinity of human concerns.

Computer speed is now reckoned in milliseconds—thousandths of a second. Ahead lie microseconds and even nanoseconds—millionths of a second and billionths of a second. At that speed you don't have to be bright.

When I went into newspaper work, the measure of speed in communication was still the Morse telegraph, then already well on the way toward the end of its first century. News from afar, whether stories on the doings of Washington or the round-by-round account of a prize fight, came into the *Springfield Union*'s newsroom by Western Union wire, through the clatter and clack of the magnetic telegraph receiver. I recall to this day hearing, over the partition that hid the Morse operator from the city staff, the familiarly unintelligible dot-dash sounds chattering away. Then, suddenly, the operator's startled "Christ, Harding's dead!" as the news clicked in and he translated it into writing.

That telegraph sent its signals at light's speed, 186,000 miles a second—for practical purposes, instantaneously. But the dots, dashes, and spaces that represented letters and words were cumbersome. A skilled Morse operator could translate them at about thirty words a minute, writing or typing as he listened to the code tapped out by the skilled fingers of a distant sender. Today the standard news teleprinter, essentially a typewriter actuated from afar by electrical impulses, brings in the news at sixty-six words a minute—both on tape that will actuate the typesetting machines and on typed copy for editorial control. But there are already in use devices that transmit 1050 words a minute, with computer-to-computer speeds of 50,000 words a minute to come.

Thanks to television the journalism of the future—indeed all transmission of information—will be visual as well as written. Something like a television screen with two-way sound will be attached to a typewriter-like keyboard in the coming home communication set. Nor will our powers for collecting information through these instruments end with printed news and instant pictures of what is going on as it goes on. Already there is in process the transformation of books from the tomes familiar since Gutenberg's Bible into miniaturized photographs that are as tiny as the computer is fast. The Encyclopedia Britannica has marketed a portable reader on which its Library of American Civilization can be read, or as rapidly scanned, as a printed book. A single 3" x 5" card, to be inserted in the reader, contains as many as 1000 pages, and print-outs at will are coming.[6] A division of the National Cash Register Co. has begun putting collections of books—small libraries —on 4-by-6-inch cards that can hold 3200 printed pages each. Says one account:

> The 3500 new volumes will require no shelf space and take only one tray of a filing cabinet. An oddity of the system is that the Library of Congress catalogue cards that are shipped with the order weigh more and take up more space than the books they describe.[7]

Nor will treasuries of books like these be confined to libraries. The cable will bring them, too, into the home at will. The wisdom of the ages, now treasured up in the libraries of the world, will be available to us all at home at the touch of keyboard or button.

The cable that is to pipe all this into our houses, as we now pipe water or electricity, was not invented for that purpose. In one of those recurring examples of serendipity, it sprang from the desire to make TV signals available in sparsely settled areas far from urban transmitters. Even an elaborate household antenna is no help there. So why not put a community antenna atop the nearest hill, draw the signals from it via coaxial cable (a complex wire), and deliver them to the home sets of viewers for a monthly fee? Nicholas Johnson, the maverick FCC commissioner, once described the cable's potential in these words:

> Technologically, it is just another wire—like the telephone wire or an electric power line—coming into the home. While it isn't much bigger than a telephone wire, comparing its capacity with that of the telephone cable is like comparing a river with a garden hose. The same wire that today carries television signals can also carry the signals necessary to print a newspaper in a home, connect a home information center with a distant computer or teaching machines, or provide closed-circuit television signals for visiting with friends or "window-shopping" from home.[8]

It was not long before CATV moved in from the hinterland to invade the city itself, right at broadcasting headquarters. The steel cliffs of skyscrapers and other urban structures often made home reception in the city as poor as that in the desert wastes. Improved reception became especially important with the advent of color television, because in difficult areas color requires mechanical niceties that are often beyond the powers of broadcasting through the air. So there developed a market, both in rural isolation and in urban canyons, consisting of consumers willing to pay five dollars or so a month for a cable that gave sharp reception.

At first the broadcasters welcomed cable TV, because it promised to enlarge the audience they could sell to sponsors. But now they face a threat not unlike that which facsimile poses for newspapers—namely, that of being put out of business.

This threat is reinforced by the fact that cable can transmit far more programs than can the VHF and UHF broadcast spectrum. Whereas the American metropolis today may have half a dozen local transmitters, some of them bringing in the network shows, cable already has room for a dozen channels, with forty in sight and eighty to come. This may abolish television broadcasting as we know it today, much as TV itself virtually abolished network radio.

It is unlikely that the cable's vast number of channels will be

filled with programs, local or network, that merely duplicate existing ones. Three networks, all vying to say the same thing at the
same time, are enough. Entrepreneurs have already made available over cable supplementary services such as continuous news
bulletins, and stock-market and weather reports. Special events,
like the hockey and other games now blacked out from TV in
their home towns, can also be shown on closed-circuit television.

The future of cable programs has been foreshadowed, in some
of our big cities, by development of the multiple FM programs
that cater to limited but eager audiences. If this kind of thing pro-
liferates, the mass audiences made familiar by TV in its early decades may be fragmented into specialized groups, just as the mass
magazine audience already is.

One result among many could be unedited, fixed-camera—that
is, cheap—television coverage of complete legislative meetings, in
place of the rare edited highlights we occasionally see now. These
may be dull shows—rambling committee meetings or the droning
full sessions themselves, whether of town council or PTA, the state
legislature, or Congress. But there will be some to whom what happens is vital.

In addition to all this, cable duplicates the telephone's capacity
for two-way traffic. Today the reader can talk back to his newspaper only in an occasional letter to the editor, which may or may
not get attention. He cannot talk back to his radio or TV set at all,
short of tuning in another station or turning the whole thing off.
Cable promises to change all this by offering the individual all
kinds of outgoing as well as incoming services.

Then again, it is technically possible to monitor the cable's use.
This means, should anyone want it, a continuous readership survey
or audience rating—or an instant, everlasting public-opinion poll.

If this differs from what we know today, so will the advertising
that cables and computers make possible. Advertising today is a
matter of the seller buying as much exposure for his product as
he can get, whether through newspaper and magazine circulation,

broadcast audience, junk mail, or billboards. He spreads his message before one and all in the hope that a tiny fragment of the vast audience will be in the market for what he offers. A legion of specialized magazines, from *Christian Century* to *National Rifleman,* offer the advertiser a concentrated market. But now the prospect opens for a reversal of the advertising process. Instead of having the seller tout his wares before an audience, large and diffuse or small and specialized, the customer of the future—once he is in the market for a particular item—may canvass a whole battery of sellers to see what they have to offer along the line he is interested in. We already have a prototype in the potential buyer who scans the classified ads in search of a used car, or the housewife who compares prices in the supermarket ads. Mr. Bagdikian has visualized the future of this kind of advertising:

> A central data bank in each community would contain an inventory of goods for each major retail outlet—sizes, prices, colors, and locations where the items can be ordered. The computer would sort these out so that the consumer could ask for pictures or listings of all items in the same category, regardless of brand or store.
>
> A housewife wishing to buy a raincoat for her child could ask to see pictures or listings of all raincoats in the desired size and price range. These might be listed in textual description or in colored photographs flashed onto the TV screen in sequence, each with a code number like mail-order catalogues. From these the purchase could be made by telephone or Touch-Tone buttons on the phone, or on some other signaling device in the home. The order would be received on the store's own computer, the amount of the purchase automatically deducted from the consumer's bank account and registered in the store's running inventory.[9]

How would such two-way advertising be paid for? The store or the manufacturer might pay to be listed in so lively a marketplace, and the housewife might pay a fee for such a complete answer to her quest, much as she might now buy a consumer magazine.

Long ago, before World War I, E. M. Forster wrote a short story called "The Machine Stops." In it he projected the future as the science of the day permitted him to envision it. In some ways that future has still not arrived. In Forster's tale, for example, the whole world lives underground, in mechanical beehives. Everything the individual needs, from food, medicine, and other creature comforts to intellectual fare, is brought to him without his even venturing out of his cell. His contact with his fellows is via a television-telephone system not unlike the Picturephone now at hand:

> Imagine, if you can, a small room, hexagonal in shape, like the cell of a bee. It is lighted neither by window nor by lamp, yet it is filled with a soft radiance. There are no apertures for ventilation, yet the air is fresh. There are no musical instruments, and yet, at the moment that my meditation opens, this room is throbbing with melodious sounds. An arm-chair is in the centre, by its side a reading-desk—that is all the furniture. And in the arm-chair there sits a swaddled lump of flesh—a woman, about five feet high, with a face as white as a fungus. It is to her that the little room belongs. . . .
> And of course she had studied the civilization that had immediately preceded her own—the civilization that had mistaken the functions of the system, and had used it for bringing people to things, instead of for bringing things to people. Those funny old days, when men went for change of air instead of changing the air in their rooms![10]

Forster's metallurgical-electrical beehive was run from afar by an invisible, all-powerful Machine to which the individual owed obedience and reverence. We are not that far along—yet. But the revolution in communications technology now under way is in fact heading us toward a system in which the world is brought to the individual, instead of the other way around.

Perhaps Mr. Martin was right after all. For it seems assured that much of our present communications system, including the centrally printed newspaper, will join the horse-drawn carriage and the trolley car, the kerosene lamp and quill pen, on history's town dump.

## The Reader as Editor

At the ASNE convention in 1963 John Diebold, a management-technology expert, pictured automation of the editorial process in centrally printed newspapers as just ahead. Written copy, edited on a desk with a pencil, would no longer exist. The news would be reduced to digits filed in a computer. From there it could be summoned to an editor's desk, not physically, but as an image on a television screen. On that screen it could be corrected with a light pencil, or tried out in various typographic arrangements. Only when the item or page was in final form on the screen would the touch of a button transform it into an actual plate ready for printing. All this and more, said Mr. Diebold, would make the editorial office of that year, 1963, "quite a different place" by 1973.[11]

Today these innovations, though still comparatively rare, have already begun to invade newspaper offices. Besides, we must remember that, as the historian Daniel J. Boorstin has pointed out, "By a giant leap Americans crossed the gulf from the daguerreotype to color television in less than a century."[12] Therefore not only journalists, but the public, will have to face the fact that before long technical changes in the hardware of journalism promise to force changes in society more profound than those wrought by printing—on which the world as we know it was built. Today we buy a paper or magazine, or tune in on a program, that professionals have prepared. The finished product offers information, or entertainment, or both, in the hope that we will read, watch, or listen. Inevitably we pick up something of what the editor or other professional wants to say. In this way we get facts and ideas we might not have thought of, or even known about, by ourselves. This is especially true of news. But, thanks to the technics of the future, we shall ourselves summon up only that information or entertainment we wish.

What will be the consequences? Listen to one of the growing

tribe of researchers into the sociology of communication, Professor
Edwin B. Parker of Stanford:

> There's a rather significant difference between the kind of media
> we had in the past, which have been all what I call "sender-
> controlled." The source of the information controls what is trans-
> mitted through the information channel. And, as we shall see, the
> main characteristic of the time-shared computer information me-
> dium is that much of the decision of what is transmitted through
> the communication channel passes from the sender to the re-
> ceiver. And this has all kinds of implications for the way the
> communication system itself will work and for the consequences
> on the rest of the society.[13]

The metamorphosis of local journalism into mass media that
began to occur after World War II has already taken us part way
toward a transfer of decision from sender to receiver. It appears
not only in news but in advertising, entertainment, and even the
arts. Said Gilbert Seldes:

> We see here *a shift in emphasis from the artist to his audience.*
> Since the artist—in words, in oil or marble, in music—is trying
> to communicate, the audience has always been present in the
> back of his mind. . . . But the creative artist remained in the
> central position so long as he *said what he wanted to say,* so that
> only *how he said it* was influenced by the thought of the audi-
> ence. With the coming of the mass media, a deliberate attempt
> has been made to discover that the audience *wants said*—what it
> wants to see and hear.[14]

How much more will the audience be in control of what comes
into its mind when we move beyond today's readership survey and
Nielsen rating to the point at which the individual need no longer
turn to the choice of a professional for his intellectual and esthetic
fare? Presumably there will always be mass as well as fragmented
audiences, because there will be broadcasters and publishers who,
cable or not, cater to man's lowest common denominator. But the
nervous system of our society, and through it the course we take
as a nation, will be different from what they are now.

It will not be the first time that new instruments of communication have wrought social and political change. In the 1930s President Franklin Roosevelt took advantage of the new medium, network radio, to invent the fireside chat. He did it to bypass the newspapers, and get his message directly to the public. Television enlarged the opportunity, so that by the time of the 1962 Cuba missile crisis President Kennedy could look us in the eye as he talked to us via the home screen. Or President Nixon and Vice President Agnew could pre-empt the national attention to tell us directly, at will, whatever they chose about Vietnam, or law and order, or the sins of the media. Their messages were subject only to after-the-fact interpretation by commentators, which they did not relish.

With the two-way communication that is coming, and with an infinity of information available to us all, the listener or viewer will still want to tune in the President. But we shall no longer be at the mercy of an editor or broadcaster who selects what he thinks we ought to know, and tells us what to think about it. Indeed, if he wishes, the future newspaper reader can know as much about an event as the editor does. In the same way students will have at their beck and call, if they choose, as much information as the teacher has.

Today we are free to skip news that doesn't interest us, or tune out a program we don't like. But we cannot reverse the process. We cannot get into the paper something we would like to know that isn't there. Suppose, for instance, we are interested in the fate of a bill before the town council, or state legislature, or Congress. If nothing much happened to the bill yesterday, it won't be reported in the paper. Or it may have been crowded out by bigger news. But in the two-way communication of the future we can converse with computers, which will answer our queries at our command. We may have missed something yesterday, but the computer didn't. And if in fact nothing new happened recently, we shall still be able to find out how far along the bill is, and what its chances may be. Or if what we want to know is not even in such a news recapitulation or interpretation, then we can demand still further information out of books or other resources, right up to that universe of knowledge, the Library of Congress.

Already the communications revolution is upon us. In 1969 *The New York Times* announced a computerized service that would permit not only its own staff, but outsiders as well, to have access to all it knows. Most newspapers today still rely on the information-retrieval system which was used by the *The World* when I was a reporter there in the 1920s: filing cabinets full of dusty, musty, crumbling newspaper clippings stored in brown envelopes, available more or less on demand to reporters seeking past information on the man or event they are going to write about.

Not so the *Times* of the 1970s, which stores and indexes not only its own files but also material from sixty other newspapers and periodicals. Said a vice president, Ivan Viet, in announcing the new order: "*The New York Times* intends to enhance its reputation through its information retrieval system, as one of the world's most reliable and authoritative sources of information."[15]

The new system became operational in 1971. To the user it looked like a television screen with a typewriter-like keyboard attached to it. The whole gave access to information stored in disk packs and data cells, with texts treasured up on microfiche—four by six inch films each containing ninety-nine images. The user, whether a *Times* reporter seeking background or an outsider at home or in an office or at a library terminal, punches his query in ordinary English, instructing the mechanism that he wishes, say, to browse through the thesaurus that replaces the familiar *Times Index* in unlocking the past. Then he can ask the data bank to furnish him—either on the cathode-ray tube or in printed form —with what it knows *about* X, *and* Y, *or* Z, *but not* N.

Clearly, the American citizen of the future will have at his command riches of information. But what of the editor, and his counterparts in broadcasting, the arts, entertainment, and advertising? It doesn't look as though the reader who is his own editor would leave much for him to do.

### Come Back, Horace!

Consider Horace Greeley, the bewhiskered founder of the *New-York Tribune,* who helped articulate the thoughts and shape the course of nineteenth-century America. His *Tribune,* like other leading papers of the time, dug out the facts. Reporting them was, for all the inevitable aberrations and omissions and distortions, a public service without which the country could not have functioned. An added service was Greeley's moral leadership through his editorials, which were circulated through much of the country in the *Weekly Tribune.* Wrote one social historian:

> The New York *Tribune* for a whole generation, the fateful generation in which the struggle against slavery rose to a climax, stood pre-eminent among the organs of opinion in the United States; it was one of the great leaders of the nation, and its role in the particular drama which ended with the Emancipation Proclamation was as great as any statesman's save Lincoln.[16]

So it had been with the best in journalism before Greeley's day, so it was after, and so it is still. We need not look to the past alone for models of the editorial leadership we must have in the electronic future—despite the fact that each reader can serve as his own editor. Each generation, each year, each day even brings fresh demonstration of the continuing need for an independent, aggressive journalism. A significant example is the publication, by *The New York Times,* the *Washington Post,* and other newspapers of the Pentagon Papers, that top-secret report commissioned by the then Secretary of Defense, Robert McNamara, when he became disillusioned with America's war in Indochina and sought to find out how our decision-making process had gone wrong.

The report, whose existence was not even suspected by the public or the press, ran to 2.5 million words. Even so the record was incomplete, because it did not include White House and other files. But these forty-seven volumes of texts and analyses, covering much of our step-by-step involvement in Indochina from World War II to mid-1968, documented for the first time how four Presidents had, despite all the evidence that it was a mistake, pushed deeper and deeper into our longest and most unhappy war.

All too often our government had said one thing while doing another. The four Presidents, together with their advisers in the White House, Defense, State, and CIA, had simply accepted without question the cold-war premise that it was vital to the United States to preserve a non-Communist government in Saigon. Because of this our modest aid to a none-too-savory government, in a distant trouble-spot half way around the world, was gradually transformed into a major American war on the Asian mainland—the very kind of war it had been our policy to avoid.

Obviously, under self-government anything as momentous as the decision to make war calls for extensive public debate, followed by a national decision made by President and Congress together. Instead, a little group around our Presidents made clandestine preparations for a covert war, until it was too late for public opinion to force a change. The nation could only thrash about in frustration. Concealment of the truth from the supposedly sovereign public played its part in dividing the country, in alienating youth from much that is best in us, and in troubling our friends abroad.

All this was compounded when the Nixon administration, which bore no responsibility for starting and enlarging the war, and kept saying over the months and years that it was ending it, nevertheless sought to halt publication of the Pentagon Papers. This was probably the first time since Blackstone's day in the eighteenth century that an Anglo-Saxon government sought prior restraint against the publication of non-military, historical information. This gave the revelations more shock value than they would have had if the unauthorized publication had been allowed to run its course.

Within days the government sought injunctions halting publication of the rest of the Pentagon record by *The New York Times* and the *Washington Post*. The issue was swiftly appealed upward to the Supreme Court, which was about to recess for the summer.

The Court, by a margin of five to four, agreed to hear the government's case. This was in itself a landmark, because the obvious implication was that there might be circumstances under which the First Amendment did not apply, and publication might be suppressed before it could occur.

A few days later the Court rendered its verdict: a brief, unanimous, unsigned ruling that the Government had not met the "heavy burden" of justifying prior restraint. At the same time the Court fired an extraordinary legal barrage of nine opinions, one for each justice. Six favored publication, with varying degrees of enthusiasm. Three, including the two Nixon appointees then on the Court, dissented.

So it was that, after an interval of nearly three weeks during which the First Amendment was held in abeyance, the newspapers resumed publication. They were able, in the words of Justice Black's concurring opinion, to serve the governed rather than the governors. Yet they remained responsible after the fact for any abuse of their freedom, as they must under the doctrine of no prior restraint. The whole, including some gratuitous and unjudicial slaps at the press in some of the opinions, remains an impressive reminder: the future reader who is his own editor will need, perhaps more than ever, computer-and-cable journalists who will fight, as valiantly as have the print journalists over the centuries, for a press free to monitor government.

So far, so good. But if government failed us by going to war in secret in Vietnam, where was the press all that time? Where was our Horace Greeley, and why did he have to wait for one of the authors of the Papers to leak them to the press, instead of digging out for himself the facts about what was going on as it went on? When the Pentagon secrets came out, that question was asked by Senator Goldwater, the unsuccessful hawk in the 1964 election. In an article that appeared in the *Times* itself, he wrote that *The New York Times* would undoubtedly win journalistic awards for violating secrecy—as it subsequently did. But:

By the same token I believe *The New York Times* deserves some
kind of a booby prize for its failure to detect the intentions of the
Johnson Administration during the Presidential campaign of
1964.

There was no doubt in my mind seven years ago that President
Johnson intended to escalate the war against North Vietnam by
bombing and by the possible use of American ground troops.
And the indications that such preparation were going forward
were all over the place.[17]

Maybe so. But it is a counsel of perfection to expect that our
press could have published, in 1964-65, the actual record that the
Pentagon study began to reveal in 1971. If the increasingly unchecked Executive Branch does not of its own accord work in the
open, as it should in a republic founded on democracy, there is
only so much that the Horace Greeleys of the moment can pry out.
Actually, much of the essence of what the Pentagon Papers told
had in fact been published as it happened. But it was published as
background, as speculation by reporters trying to get at the truth.
Such information, not attributable to a specific source, cannot have
the compelling authority of chapter-and-verse official fact.

Still, we are left with the uneasy feeling that here was one place
where the journalism of pre-computer days fell down on the job.
What then if the revolution now begun in the technology of communication, with its transformation of the reader or viewer into
his own editor, eliminates Horace Greeley? In the words of one
British writer:

In the computer, the newspaper as a medium of information has
another and perhaps more serious rival than television. Once information can be stored, automatically up-dated, and instantly re-
trieved at the turn of a bedside dial, it becomes unnecessary to
buy and peruse a newspaper, in which nine-tenths of the "hard"
information is of no interest to a given individual looking for a
particular job or stock-price. Once it becomes possible to pre-
select the kinds of information—whether editorial or advertising
—that you actually want new every morning, the market for a
"mosaic" product of wide general appeal will surely shrink.[18]

If such a mosaic vanishes, it threatens to take comprehensive news reports and moral leadership with it. Without both the nation of self-editing reader-viewers is left without a mirror in which to watch itself, and without a signpost pointing the way ahead. No matter that the mirror will, then as now, be imperfect and even distorting, and the signpost all too often askew, if not indeed pointing backward. It is simply a truism that only an independent, comprehensive, aggressive journalism makes it possible for self-government to work. By one means or another, we shall simply have to carry it forward into the electronic future.

The future has a way of turning out to be different from what even our most informed prophets say it will be. Still, from what has happened so far, we can expect that, despite the radical departure from Gutenberg's press, the journalistic hardware of the future will leave the way open for the historic essentials of journalism, including moral leadership.

We have learned that new technical achievements do not necessarily kill old ones, as the automobile killed first the carriage and then the train. The movies did not kill the theater, and television did not kill movies, or the printed newspaper, or radio. The old services were simply forced into different areas, with no doubt fluctuating economic results. But they remained.

With the coming of radio, and then television, newspapers increasingly found themselves delivering stale news to their subscribers. The hair-raising adventures of the first astronauts to try for the moon—Would they make it? Would the attempt end in disaster? Could they get back?—kept the customers at their TV sets as long as live coverage was on. Of what use then to deliver to the subscriber late that afternoon, let alone next morning, a paper telling him what he himself had seen those astronauts do, with his own eyes, hours before the paper went to press?

Well, it does have a use. When an occasional editor complained to the wire services that they were furnishing him with news that was obsolete before it reached his newsroom—let alone his subscribers—the inescapable obligation to present the record remained. "The risk of being overtaken by disaster . . . is always going to be there," commented Roger Tatarian, vice president and editor of UPI. "Anybody's mayor can step into an open manhole ten minutes before the home edition lands on the front porch with the story of his decision to seek reelection." Despite the newspaper's need to anticipate, explain, and interpret, he concluded, "we cannot abandon" the spot-news story.[19]

No more can we abandon spot news when *The New York Times* and the Missouri *Unterrified Democrat* as we know them are gone, and shadows on a cable-fed screen have taken their place. Some who have missed the event itself, or who saw it but want to check it again, will provide a market. The same goes for statistical material like the stock tables, the TV log, the wholesale price of eggs, or any other of the thirty-nine kinds of non-general news the papers give us now. Just so, unless man changes more than his machines, he will still want to know what Horace Greeley thinks about it all.

What indeed is going to be so different about the journalistic future, except its mechanics? The need to know, and to understand, existed before printing was invented. It was met in all sorts of ways, from the wall newspaper of ancient Rome (and modern China) to the handwritten newsletters and town criers and heralds of later centuries. So it promises to be in times to come. The more journalism changes, the more it is the same thing.

### Cable, Computer, and Government

No sooner has one said this than fresh doubts arise. Marshall McLuhan's thesis that the medium is the message is persuasive. Broadcasting and print may tell us the same thing, but they have subtly different effects upon us. Then again man's tendency to face the future secure in his hindsight, ready to fight each war with the lessons learned from the past one, leaves us vulnerable to changes that the two-way journalistic hardware of the future may work upon us. Even now, because tomorrow has already begun, decisions are being made that will shape our future. But we aren't looking.[20]

The past reminds us that we had better look. This country, alone among the advanced nations of the world, drifted absentmindedly into what we call free broadcasting—that is to say broadcasting bought and paid for by advertisers. We knew only that we liked neither the hand of government nor government's taxes on our radio sets. So we let George do it. But letting George the sponsor pay the entire bill for broadcasting inevitably shaped programs to suit the advertisers' needs rather than ours. Here as elsewhere he who pays the piper calls the tune. Sponsors wanted the largest possible audiences for their advertising. And if attracting mass audiences is the driving force, programming standards inevitably suffer.

Recently public broadcasting has begun to offer an antidote in the way of programs more adult than those dictated by the search for the lowest common denominator. But as yet public radio and TV remain undernourished infants.

We would have been wiser, had we been prescient enough, to provide some alternative to sponsored broadcasting from the beginning. Just so we shall be wise now if we scan the communications horizon ahead, so that we may guard against at least those dangers that the past has made evident.

Journalism is a victim of two devils perennially striving, tempting, luring, goading—as the hymnal has it—into sin. The first, which goes back to the beginning of time, is government. All government has a built-in drive to control the governed, and one handy weapon is control of the information the governed get. The second, which became a threat after the Industrial Revolution ushered in the modern world, is Mammon—the god of this world and its riches. Both hamper our fallible Horace Greeleys as they undertake to report the truth to the public and to light its way.

What, then, of these two forces in the cable-cum-computer future? Cable is still being used in American homes as a device to bring in broadcast programs that are hard to get through the air, but it has already begun piping in the future as well. In 1971 New York City began an experiment when it signed contracts with its two cable companies. One reporter described the event as follows:

> The 80,000 subscribers to Manhattan's two cable TV systems will be able to see on Channels C and D a continuous flow of public service programs—ranging from the dance to street lectures on venereal disease. . . .
>
> The experiment, which will permit individuals and community organizations to air their views on a first-come, first-served basis [for a modest fee], is expected, if successful, to set the pattern for the rest of the country.
>
> Supporters have hailed the program as the first genuine "Town Meeting of the Air" and a major step toward the political philosopher's dream of participatory democracy. But spokesmen for neighborhood groups and others termed the regulations announced by the city yesterday for operating the channels "unduly restrictive and suspicious."[21]

It is well to be suspicious, and not only of the restrictions New York applied to its experiment. Because the cable promises to be the conduit through which all journalism (and much more) will reach the public in the future, it opens the way to government licensing of all communication. Western man was able to free the printing press from licensing by fighting directly on the issue. There was no mechanical reason why a printing press should be licensed, because it was physically possible to have a dozen or a hundred in town, each saying what its owners chose without interfering with the printed impressions made by the others.

Broadcasting is different, and wired communication is also different. It was the interference of one radio station with another that prompted the early broadcasters to plead with Secretary of Commerce Herbert Hoover to assign frequencies, as was done by the Federal Radio Commission set up under the Radio Act of 1927. So it has been ever since, even though more and more exploitable space was discovered in the broadcast spectrum as FM, television, and police, ship, plane, and other services began to multiply. The physical facts also require that somebody regulate the cables of the future. Because the cables will transmit what radio and television channels now broadcast, the pattern established for regulating broadcasting is likely to be the pattern for policing the cables of the future.

The physical necessity for licensing has presented us with a dilemma from which there has been no escape. As news and opinion began to be broadcast by radio, the stations and networks naturally sought to take their place beside the printed newspaper in the shelter of the First Amendment. But to this day their right to be so protected has never been officially and unequivocally affirmed—as it should be, once and for all, before we stumble too far into the future.

When the Federal Communications Commission was set up by the Communications Act of 1934, it was little different from the Federal Radio Commission it supplanted, except that the FCC also took over jurisdiction over telephone lines from the Interstate Commerce Commission. The birth of the FCC involved a great struggle against the commercialization of radio—a struggle that was lost in Congress.[22]

From the beginning, the FCC was directed by law to keep its fingers out of programming, lest it violate the First Amendment. But it was also told that, in granting or renewing licenses every three years, it should have in mind whether the broadcaster in question serves the "public interest, convenience, and necessity." For many years the FCC was lenient and friendly about the quality of the service to the public rendered by the fortunate few who held the franchise to the public air without even paying rent. Then, more recently, it began actually weighing broadcast performance. It began even to consider transferring that gold mine, a license to a channel, from a poor performer to another who promised to do better.[23]

The trouble is that the minute the FCC begins to set standards, it starts censoring. Says Wilbur Schramm, the authoritative researcher in mass communication:

> We are willing to have the Commission consider whether a station keeps the programming promises it makes when it applies for a license; to enforce its regulation on given equal time for answer to an attack on the air; and to compare the programming promises of two applicants in broad terms. . . . But . . . we don't want the Commission to pass judgment on what a station says about the government (if anything the station says is actionable in the courts, then let the case be tried there—but not in the FCC). We don't want the Commission to put itself in position to pass judgment on a specific news commentator, or a certain news broadcast, or a particular variety program.
>
> Somewhere between these two kinds of action lies the borderline beyond which we are not satisfied that the Commission can safely go.[24]

The conflict between these two public needs—of holding broadcasters responsible for performance, and of keeping the hand of government off what they say—seems hopeless. Unless there is some mechanical way of making the instruments of electronic communication as plentiful and therefore as non-conflicting as printing, we shall simply have to struggle with it from year to year.

This is, at best, unsatisfactory. We are unhappy with the results of unpoliced commercialism, but we are even unhappier—or we should be—when government breathes down a broadcaster's neck. In these recent years, in which everything seems to be rushing into crisis with greater speed than usual, one passing event has served to typify the difficulty of keeping electronic journalism free. This was the broadcasting by CBS, early in 1971, of a television documentary called "The Selling of the Pentagon." It was a courageous program, designed to picture for the American public the way in which our military forces use taxpayer's money to promote themselves among the taxpayers. Naturally not only the Pentagon but its friends in politics, together with that part of the public which accepts war as a patriotic and noble answer to any difficult international problem, didn't like it. Some of the network affiliates thought it poison; they much preferred money-making pap that wouldn't get anybody's back up.

One result was that Representative Harley O. Staggers of West Virginia, chairman of the House Committee on Interstate and Foreign Commerce, went gunning for CBS. Mr. Staggers demanded that the network furnish him with all the materials that had gone into the making of the program—not only the finished product, but all unused films, tapes, notes—everything the network had collected from which it had edited the final version. It appeared from the resulting controversy that CBS had been guilty of one or two questionable but minor bits of editing. But that merely obscured the real issue: whether the United States Government has a right to censor broadcasting.

Mr. Staggers, threatening CBS president Frank Stanton with jail and a fine for contempt of Congress, insisted that broadcasters, being licensed, were not entitled to the same freedom as newspapers. Dr. Stanton refused to turn over the unused raw material. It was, he said, a simple issue: Whether broadcast journalism was or was not protected by the First Amendment. If the committee's subpoena had been directed toward a newspaper, magazine, or book it would have failed because of the First Amendment. Replied Representative William M. Springer of Illinois, ranking Republican on the committee, "We're not interested in the First Amendment. We're interested in deceit."[25] It was the old question: Is there an official, orthodox truth, to be certified by government?

Mr. Staggers persuaded the full committee to cite Dr. Stanton and the network for contempt, twenty-five to thirteen. But, fortunately, in the end the House administered an unusual defeat to one of its committee chairmen, by refusing to go along on a contempt citation. Had the House done otherwise, it would have set a precedent exceedingly dangerous to the adversary relationship between press and government, a relationship that is essential to keep the American people in charge of their own affairs. Even so, this little turbulence on the mighty stream of history does not augur well for the time when all journalism reaches the public through wire subject to government license.

It may be, however, that the same future that holds this threat will bring an escape with it. At this writing it remains uncertain whether the cable companies of the future will resemble broadcasting companies, or whether they will be content to be common carriers. If they produce, or buy, the programs they send into our homes they will merely take over where today's broadcasters leave off. The networks and station owners will simply transfer their present activities from transmission through the air to transmission through cable. And then the Damoclean sword of censorship that now hangs over broadcasting will dangle on a thinner thread than ever.

If, however, the cables become common carriers, on the model of that half of the Manhattan experiment that leaves channels open to all comers, then there will be no occasion for government censors to move in on what we see and hear. The cables will earn their keep merely by transmitting what others offer the public. Then there will be no more excuse for regulating what is broadcast by wire than there is now for censoring what any of us send over the wires of telephone and telegraph companies. If that is the way it turns out, the regulation of cable can be confined to technical standards and rates, where it belongs.

There may be a further saving grace in the capacity of the cables themselves. What will we get through all those channels? There will have to be, in the first place, what we get now—the offerings of networks and individual stations, commercial and public alike, presumably expanded to offer greater variety than the ratings race now allows. Then there will be the open channels, again like those in the New York experiment—and here minority groups and interests will surely press for more access to the cable than the size of their audiences will warrant. There will also have to be new services, now envisioned as possible and desirable: news headlines, news summaries and interpretations; access to libraries; and advertising that may no longer be broadcast but may instead be dialed by the customer when he is in a mood to buy. Finally, there will have to be room for the facsimile newspaper that is eventually to replace today's printed product.

All this and today's telephone and tomorrow's Picturephone too. But still, when one adds it all up, eighty channels remain a lot. It is at least conceivable that we shall end up with more channels than takers.

To be sure, today's broadcasters see common-carrier status as a threat. At a recent gathering of broadcast lawyers, Richard W. Jencks of CBS warned against making broadcasting "a common carrier of other people's views with no creative or vigorous views of its own." To do so would be to move increasingly, he said, toward "a broadcast press without purpose, without passion, which shuns tough issues and does not lead but merely presides."[26]

Need that be? The broadcasters do now own their stations, each with its transmitter. But the networks are limited to ownership of five stations each. National audiences are put together by linking many local stations into a unit via leased wires or through-the-air relay systems. What is the difference between that and having networks and local broadcasters alike lease time on the cables? Vigorous journalism and dynamic programs spring from the originator and his capacity to serve an audience, mass or minority according to intent. It does not spring from ownership of either transmitter or cable. No doubt it is handier to have your own megaphone (transmitter or printing press or cable) through which to address the public. But in this sense the megaphone isn't the message.

The prospect of as many as eighty channels per community in the future—and, who knows, maybe, some day, even more—makes an interesting analogy. It is as though the mechanics and economics of printed newspaper publishing suddenly made available, at low cost, eighty newspaper presses in place of the one per town that is now the virtual standard. That would not only remove the necessity for licensing program originators; it might also remove the hand of monopoly from today's journalism.

As yet we know too little to be sure whether this will actually happen. But we ought to try to head in this direction. In fact, it seems essential to the future of self-government to make the cable of the future a common carrier, rather than a programmer forever subject to FCC or other surveillance. If we can do this, and if there should be more channels available than there are originators of news, documentary, minority, and other informational programs, then we shall have an electronic press as free as today's printed press. Buck Rogers, journalist, will escape the fate of becoming Buck Rogers, licensed journalist.

### Cable, Computer, and Mammon

If there is hope that we can keep government from controlling the Greeleys of the future, there remains the question of how their work is to be paid for without being corrupted. Here the determining factor remains one often ignored by those who would reform the press, printed or broadcast. It is this: *Since the modern world began with the coming of print no society, at any place on earth or any time in history, has been willing to pay the full price of the information it needs and gets.*

This is why newspapers, ever since they began to appear in seventeenth-century Europe, have depended for their existence on advertising. And this is why broadcast journalism in America, since its beginning in the 1920s, has given us programs continually interrupted and befouled and degraded by pitchmen.

Even today the American newspaper gets only from one-quarter to one-third of its income from readers. The rest comes from advertisers. For generations scholars and critics have denounced the press for allowing itself to be thus subject to corruption by Mammon. But not one of them has offered an alternative method of financing that would make service to the public the measure of journalism's economic reward.

It is true enough that in a competitive situation a paper of skill and integrity stands to be the one that makes money, and therefore survive. But all too often a newspaper, if it is to serve the public by standing for the common good and moral principle, must risk losing income. Moreover, now that we are reduced to virtually one newspaper ownership per city, there is no longer whatever economic pressure toward excellence there may once have been. The pressures are in the other direction: don't stir up the animals. There cannot be a newspaperman who has not had personal experience with this kind of thing. And all because we readers are willing to pay only the two cents, or dime, or whatever else the inflating price per copy may be, instead of the thirty cents to half a dollar or more a good all-news newspaper might cost.

Through the years newspapermen have dreamed of adless papers. But every time someone tries it, as did a handful of bold spirits in the early years of the century, it fails. A relatively recent example was *PM,* the supposed newspaper of the future, which was launched in New York in 1940. It never did live up to its inspiring pre-publication prospectus. But that had little to do with the fact that, when Marshall Field financial support failed, it had to take advertising in a vain attempt to survive.

For years the *Reader's Digest,* founded in the early 1920s, seemed—after a hesitant start—to defy the basic economic fact of journalism and prosper unbelievably on subscription income alone. Yet after World War II, when the cost squeeze struck the *Digest,* it polled its readers as to whether they would rather put up with advertising or pay a high subscription price. The public, true to type, preferred to have advertisers foot the rising bill.

There is of course an alternative to advertising as the principal economic foundation for journalism. It is the familiar one of subsidy. This is the method universally used in totalitarian countries, whether of communism's left or fascism's right. The result is inevitable: journalism says only what government decrees.

Nor is subsidy by a political party or a foreign government or a munitions or other industry any better. The corrupt and slanted journalism that was prevalent in continental Europe, notably before the two World Wars, graphically testifies to this. Even in America we have had, and still have, an occasional press owned by a copper or chemical industry, or other non-journalistic aggregation of capital. The tradition and prevailing climate of independent journalism keeps these owners from calling the entire tune. But the tune they do call is more muted than the one an aggressive independence would make possible.

There is simply no way to get around the fundamental fact that, as Walter Lippmann noted half a century ago, "A free press, if you judge by the attitude of the readers, means newspapers that are virtually given away."[27]

Whatever journalism becomes in the electronic future, the central problem of paying for information will remain. We do have one guideline: we should at all costs avoid the American broadcast pattern. Revenue should not come exclusively from advertisers. To let advertisers carry the entire burden drives us toward Ed Murrow's classic but now forgotten comment about broadcasting's intellectual ghetto. It presses broadcasters into programming that justifies Newton Minnow's equally forgotten observation that American television is a vast wasteland. And it gives point to the complaint Fred Friendly made when matters once came to a head at CBS over whether to put on the nation's screens George Kennan testifying on Vietnam before Senator Fulbright's Foreign Relations committee, or a re-run of "I Love Lucy." Thousands upon thousands of dollars were at stake. Everyone interested in the integrity of journalism, now and in the future, ought to ponder Mr. Friendly's account of those emotion-packed days. What stands out as a warning for the future is the clash between public service and

Mammon. Mr. Friendly, who resigned because Mammon triumphed at that crucial point, quoted Murrow: "There is no law which says that dollars will be defeated by duty. . . . But I can find nothing in the Bill of Rights or the Communications Act which says that they [the broadcasters] must increase their net profits each year, lest the Republic collapse."[28]

Here again, as with government, we cannot anticipate the future. But we can choose the way we would like to go. We should try to preserve some standard of journalistic excellence other than its success in putting ever more dollars into private pockets. Norbert Wiener, inventor of the word cybernetics (the study of effectice messages of control), once said:

> I am writing this book primarily for the Americans in the American environment. In this environment, questions of information will be evaluated according to the standard American criterion of evaluation: a thing is valuable as a commodity for what it will bring on the open market. This is the official doctrine of an orthodoxy which it is becoming more and more perilous for a resident of the United States to resist. . . . The fate of information in the typically American world is to become something with a price which can be bought and sold.
>
> It is not my business to cavil whether this mercantile attitude is moral or immoral, crass or subtle. It is my business to show that it leads to the misunderstanding and the mistreatment of information and its associated concepts.[29]

Surely journalism's low commercial value as a reporter, and its high ancilliary value as a salesman, threaten its integrity as a public service. Must it always be so?

If the cables and computers to come make it possible for groups and individuals to offer a whole regiment of inexpensive information and entertainment programs, may it not turn out that man will be willing at last to pay for them directly? Inexpensive is probably the key word here.

Unfortunately, such few examples as we have of customers paying the full price of the information they want are not happy ones.

Take for example the prize fight between Joe Frazier and Muhammed Ali. Frazier was the official champion; Ali was trying to make a comeback after having been deposed as champion because he had refused to be drafted. The event, instead of being a spectacle free to all on sponsored TV, was sewed up by promoters for broadcast on closed-circuit TV to theaters and other places where admission might be charged. An audience of perhaps two million fight fans was able and willing to pay the astronomical admissions charged by the promoters. But thirty to fifty times that number of others who might have tuned in, had a handful of sponsors footed the bill, were left out in the cold. And the gladiators themselves were guaranteed $2.5 million—something that made even the largesse of sponsors look like peanuts. Wrote one thoughtful television critic, Jack Gould:

> Serious students of communications are not devoid of genuine worries over erosion of the free air waves.
>   Only time—perhaps a very long time—will tell what will be the impact of closed-circuit TV on free TV's economic ability to offer news and information to rich and poor alike, carry political addresses and provide other services not returning a profit. A broadcaster is required to provide a balanced service; a closed-circuit promoter is not.[30]

Yet sponsored TV is hardly balanced either, in any socially desirable sense. So, after straining to see a still obscure future, one returns to the present certain only that there are more question marks than landmarks ahead. The information services that promise to be available in years to come are rich and attractive. But the dangers made familiar by the past remain. If the customers had better be aware and wary now, as decisions are made that may determine the future, so had our information media. If there is in fact a possibility that the networks might divorce themselves from the technical instruments of communication, and become mere producers of information and entertainment, the same is true of newspapers. Today's newspaper managements spend their thought and money on business matters, like advertising, mechanical services, and distribution costs. Again to quote Mr. Bagdikian:

> Newspapers will have to decide whether they are printing factories or analysts of daily political and social information. This will not be easy. Though most managements would deny it, today they operate as though they believed themselves to be essentially industrial manufacturers. They do this not only in the proportion of money they spend on their corporations, which is unavoidable in traditional production techniques, but also in how they select their leadership, reward their corporate hierarchies, and how they plan or do not plan for the future. They would do well to plan for the future by asking how appropriate their present leadership and plans would be if editorial operations instead of taking 10 percent of their budgets as they do today took 90 percent. This is only a slight exaggeration of the probable shift in emphasis in newspaper corporations in the coming generation, but it is one that only a few newspapers take seriously.[31]

In many a newspaper plant the twentieth-century Horace Greeley is a minor character, a necessary headache who has to be watched lest he upset Mammon's applecart. What if technology reverses journalistic priorities? What if it enables electronic journalists to devote their talents and budgets to a Fourth Estate serving all the rest of society, but standing apart from it—especially apart from government and the economic power structure?

We don't know yet whether this can be. But just as we must see to it that government doesn't license Buck Rogers, so we must see to it that Mammon doesn't keep Horace Greeley from doing his job.

# 10

## The Prophet Motive

### Molding Public Opinion

I ONCE wrote a column on Vietnam that brought an angry letter from a reader. It began:

> The consistency with which your editorial comments promote a sense of guilt (and a consequent loss of national self-esteem) impels me to write a protest. The mass media mold the minds and hearts of readers, and those who follow your bent are bound to become emotionally disturbed (even to require some kind of psychiatric care).

The signature was that of an M.D. He was, in one sense, obviously right. We see the world not directly, for ourselves, but as journalism reports it to us. This does help mold our minds and hearts. Nevertheless the newspaper editorial—or column, or broadcast comment, or other expression of opinion, is not as persuasive as laymen fancy. Certainly what I had written in opposition to American involvement in Vietnam was hardly powerful enough to put readers in need of therapy.

Even so, the notion of editorial potency is widely held. One day when I was editor of the *Hartford Courant,* I had a talk on municipal affairs with John M. Bailey, a resident of Hartford who was at the time Democratic national, state, and town chairman. He said to me, "You and Ward Duffy [editor of the *Hartford Times*] are the two most powerful men in town." To non-newspaper people, evidently, when editors and editorial writers write, the public reads, marks, and inwardly digests. Presto! Public opinion has been molded.

This concept is flattering to those of us who write editorials. But experience convinces me that it is nonsense. Editorials do have an impact on public thinking. It can be a powerful impact, helping to crystallize public doubt and confusion into a definite pattern. But editorials simply do not persuade readers against their will. An editorial has influence chiefly as it articulates a public reaction already felt, even though formless and not yet expressed in words. It must capture and put into words what readers feel instinctively.

Certainly I have been disappointed often enough, after slaving over an editorial I deemed important, at the lack of public-opinion molding that followed. Next morning I would await the response that comes if you do strike home—only to be greeted by a silence that was oppressively loud.

If, however, the editorial writer puts into words some reaction to an event that people accept as reflecting the truth, then colleagues in the office mention the piece with approval. Subscribers call up to say Amen. Some of those he meets on the street, or at lunch, will say what a good editorial that was. And approving letters to the editor follow—together with the inevitable objections from those who think otherwise. But all this proves is that an editorial, at its best, expresses the underlying good sense of the community.

That is why I insist that editorial writers do not mold public opinion so much as give it voice. If an editorial says anything that strikes the reader as wrong, you might as well undertake to convince him that black is white. He simply shrugs off what you say, grumbling to himself, and no doubt to the neighbors, too, "The old S.O.B. doesn't know what he is talking about." What kind of molding is that?

Paul Ringler, recently retired as editor of the *Milwaukee Journal*'s editorial page, once defined the purpose of his paper's editorials:

> Basically, it is to analyze intelligently the problems of the people of Milwaukee, Wisconsin, and the United States and to support constructive solutions. It is also to help protect their rights and liberties as American citizens. . . .
>
> Editorials seek to enlighten, influence and persuade. They . . . can . . . be the conscience of a community.[1] (*Milwaukee Journal,* April 27, 1969.)

Who reads editorials? If I remember correctly Adolph Ochs, founder of the modern *New York Times*, used to assure friends that although only 10 per cent of his readers were interested in editorials, he was content because these were the leaders. Through those leaders the editorials—which at one point he had considered abolishing entirely—had an impact on city, state, and nation.

That was in the days before readership surveys, which now give a fairly accurate count of what is read, if not what its influence may be. In the 1940s a Continuing Study of the Advertising Research Foundation undertook the first scientific survey of the newspaper-reading habits of the public. The first 100 papers studied showed that 17 to 77 per cent of men readers—depending on the paper surveyed—and 9 to 63 per cent of the women paid some attention to editorials. Taking the median figures as guides, it appeared that about 49 per cent of the men and 29 per cent of the women read at least one editorial for each copy of the paper they read.

By contrast 80 per cent of the men, and 78 per cent of the women, read comics. Another 80 per cent of the men read sports news or pictures, while 84 per cent of the women read society news or pictures. The women who read local advertising—94 per cent—were evidently really interested.

Surveys of individual papers, not surprisingly, showed varying results. One check on the Sunday *Courant*'s readership revealed that 73 per cent of the men and 71 per cent of the women had at least sampled the editorial page. The best-read editorial of that day drew 57 per cent of men and 45 per cent of women. This was even better than the 45 per cent of both men and women who read letters to the editor—which can be the best-read part of the page if given sufficient space and freedom. The least-read editorial that day scored 35 per cent for men, 21 per cent for women. Even this is high as editorial readership goes—a tribute to the amount of money and energy the *Courant* put into its editorial page.

Editorials, and the rest of the editorial page—and the page opposite if there is one—are read if they are worth reading. Readership surveys show this. But on the job one knows it more directly from what one feels—the reaction of important citizens, the climate around town as reflected in phone calls and letters, the whole circumstances of life on the job as experienced in one's contacts with one's fellow human beings.

To be sure, the strength of the public reaction is not necessarily an index of the social usefulness of an editorial. A crisis in City Hall or the ghetto, a national election at a time of doubt and indecision, a depression, a war, or anything else that has fateful implications can inspire editorials that rise to the heights. Then the reaction will be almost palpable. But sometimes an editorial on dogs getting into people's gardens, or the mere mention of fluoridation, will bring forth an almost pyrotechnic response.

Curiously, along with the popular idea that editorials mold public opinion, goes another one that is contradictory. This is the widely held view that editorials are not as influential as they used to be. This attitude goes back to the New Deal, when Franklin Roosevelt was on one side of many a public issue and the majority of newspaper publishers were on the other. The American people, informed of the facts by the front pages and radio, kept right on ignoring the editorials. They elected Roosevelt four times in a row, smashing the two-term tradition that had lasted since George Washington.

It has also been said that the influence of newspaper editorials has declined with the rise of broadcast journalism, which enables people to hear or see events themselves without having some editorial writer tell them what to think about it. Why should people read editorials telling them what the President's speech means, when they heard and saw it for themselves, looking him right in the eye as he spoke? And how can the dull gray print of the editorial page compete with the dramatic nightly performance—raised eyebrows, changing inflections, and all—of Walter Cronkite, John Chancellor, Howard K. Smith, and the rest? They speak directly to national audiences, and they show moving pictures of some of the events themselves. Besides, TV is easier than newsprint for the customers to take. Listening and looking require little effort or education, and no cost once the set is bought. Newspapers have first to sell a subscription, and then to get people to make the effort of reading them.

Not only that but the fighting editor of old is now an endangered species. Instead we now often have the graying gentleman who is skilled at skirting an issue, even while writing about it, so as not to stir trouble for his publisher. The product, all too often, is not incisive comment that brings people up cheering—or damning if they are on the other side. It is so much boiled watermelon. And, again all too often, it is served up in language that has a narcotic effect. Any list of clichés is likely to make an editorial writer squirm.

Yet despite the changes time has wrought, editorials can be as effective as ever. Politicians, businessmen, social workers, professors, athletes, gangsters, students—all those whose activity attracts editorial comment—are sensitive to what the papers say about them. It all depends on how much literate manpower, free to express moral purpose, understanding, and compassion, is turned loose on the editorial page.

Given a chance, editorials can still mold public opinion. As

A.H. Kirchhofer of the *Buffalo Evening News* once told his fellow
editors, there is nothing wrong with the editorial page that a few
good editorials won't cure.

## Prophet—or Profit?

In this irreligious and therefore anchorless and irresolute age, the
Bible is not read as it used to be—even though it remains the best
seller of them all. It may be a refreshing experience, then, to dip
into a fragment from the Old Testament as translated in the New
English Bible—Ezekiel 33, verses one through nine:

> These were the words of the Lord to me: Man, say to your fel-
> low-countrymen, When I set armies in motion against a land, its
> people choose one of themselves to be a watchman. When he sees
> the enemy approaching and blows his trumpet to warn the peo-
> ple, then if anyone does not heed the warning and is overtaken
> by the enemy, he is responsible for his own fate. He is responsible
> because, when he heard the alarm, he paid no heed to it; if he
> had heeded it, he would have escaped. But if the watchman does
> not blow his trumpet or warn the people when he sees the enemy
> approaching, then any man who is killed is caught with his sins
> upon him; but I will hold the watchman answerable for his death.
>
> Man, I have appointed you a watchman for the Israelites. You
> will take messages from me and carry my warnings to them. It
> may be that I pronounce sentence of death on a man because he
> is wicked; if you do not warn him to give up his ways, the guilt
> is his and because of his wickedness he shall die, but I will hold
> you answerable for his death. But if you have warned him to give
> up his ways, and he has not given them up, he will die because of
> his wickedness, but you will have saved yourself.

Talcott Williams, son of missionaries, editor of the *Philadelphia
Press,* and thereafter first head of what is now the Graduate School
of Journalism at Columbia University, used to tell his students that
Ezekiel 33, 1–9, gave the newspaperman his marching orders.
Like the prophet, the newspaperman was watchman for the people.
It was his responsibility to blow the trumpet as a warning if danger

threatened. Today's Ezekiels—and Isaiahs and Jeremiahs and all the rest—are editors and editorial writers. Their trumpet is the editorial page.

The analogy was more accurate in, say, the last two-thirds of the nineteenth century, and up until World War I, than in the last third of this century. Greeley and the Bennets, Dana and Ochs, Pulitzer and Hearst, Medill and Nelson, each had his own trumpet in the editorial columns of the *Tribune* and *Herald, Sun* and *Times, World* and *Journal* and *American*. In Chicago and Kansas City there were the clarion voices of the *Daily News* and the *Star*. Through these and other newspapers the owners and their associates spread among the people the word of the Lord as they understood it.

It is different now. The editor-owner is increasingly rare. The owner, or manager representing the owner—who may be just an anonymous, powerless, lot of stockholders—is as much the boss as any nineteenth-century journalistic giant. But, with some notable exceptions, his function has become that of presiding over what is essentially not a journalistic trumpet, warning the people, so much as a dividend factory.

The change is noticeable in the fact that the editor and his editorial page—the mind and heart and soul of the paper—have been moved down the hall, to a less conspicuous place than before. Look up, for example, the corporate hierarchy of the *San Jose Mercury* and *News* in California, which I cite as an illustration not because it is unique but because it is typical. This chain-owned morning-evening-Sunday combination is headed by corporate brass consisting of a president and four vice-presidents, complete with secretary and treasurer. Next comes a publisher (doubling as one of the vice presidents), a general manager, and a business manager. Then, down in the engine room among the advertising, circulation, and mechanical departments is buried the editorial department, with its own subordinate hierarchy. This department is headed by an executive director, and he is supported by one managing editor for the morning and Sunday paper and another for the evening paper. In these lower echelons it is now normal to find an editorial-page editor, though this particular operation does not have one. But if you proceed far enough down the pecking order you find one lone Ezekiel who is editorial writer for morning and Sunday, another for evening. It is hardly to be expected that what these un-derlings say to the public makes as authoritative a trumpet-blowing as that of, say, *The World* under Pulitzer.

Cross the country from California and you see the same thing, again in a fragment that represents the journalistic whole. Here is a news item from *Editor & Publisher:*

> Editors of the editorial pages of the two Media General news-papers here have been chosen by D. Tennant Bryan, publisher.
>
> Ross Mackenzie, chief editorial writer of the *Richmond News Leader* since December 1, was promoted to the new job. Macken-zie is 28 and joined the *News Leader* in 1965 as a reporter.
>
> J. Edward Grimsley, who joined the *Times-Dispatch* as a re-porter in 1953, joined the staff of the editorial pages last June. He has been in charge of the editorial columns since mid-January. He is 42.[2]

The editor of the editorial page is a creature of the twentieth century. It used to be that a paper was edited by an editor who ipso facto, without anybody saying anything about it or question-ing it, made editorial policy. As newspapers have become more elaborate and costly properties, with an infinity of expenses in-volved in the sheer matter of manufacturing and distributing them, the stature of the editor has shrunk. The only exception, as always, is that he may survive if he is also the owner.

The principal effect is to split responsibility away from author-ity. The modern editor, of the editorial page or otherwise, con-tinues to bear public responsibility for what his paper says. But because he has been eased out of the seat of power, he no longer has authority over what he says. Conditions vary from zero to 100 per cent, depending on the paper concerned. But by now, except again where owner and editor are the same person, responsibility and authority are divided. Inevitably this mutes the editorial trumpet.

Benito Mussolini, from 1922 to 1943 tyrant of Fascist Italy, had in his earlier days been a newspaper writer, novelist, playwright, and editor of such newspapers as the Socialist *Avanti* and the patriotic *Il Popolo d'Italia*. Later, in building a Fascist state, he used control of the press as a weapon. The inevitable result was that what the papers of Italy said was a monotone, decreed from above. But from time to time Mussolini himself wrote for the papers, and what he said had a bite and a tang beyond the powers of the captive editors of *Fascismo*. They had responsibility for what they said, but no authority to say what they thought. Mussolini did. He was the only good editorial writer left in Italy.

The same principle applies throughout journalism—printed, broadcast, or over the cables of the future; under communism as under any other totalitarianism; or under democratic capitalism. We can hardly expect that any top man, anywhere in journalism, would let some flunky of an editorial-page editor come out, say, for a presidential candidate he opposed.

One surviving example of owner-edited papers are those in Louisville, the *Courier-Journal* and the *Louisville Times*. Asked whether the papers endorse political candidates, Barry Bingham, Jr., the editor and publisher, replied, "We do endorse political candidates. The decision is the publisher's after consultation with members of the editorial staffs."

And what do these papers do when sensitive topics other than elections come up?

> Decisions on sensitive topics are made after thorough discussion in the [editorial] conference. In the end, the publisher must have the last word, but all writers are encouraged to express their point of view. Needless to say, no writer would be asked to write an editorial on any subject if he disagreed with the position the paper was taking on that subject.[3]

As one might expect, it is much the same on the *Washington Post*. Sensitive decisions, says Alan Barth of the editorial page, are reached "by the editor, plus specialist, plus consensus."

A further refinement is offered by C. A. McKnight, editor of the *Charlotte Observer*. Political candidates are endorsed, the decision being made by the editor or associate editor "after interviews with candidates, study of records and platforms, and opinions of reporters and editorial writers."[4]

So it goes across the land. Asked about his paper's editorial attitude toward the local power structure George H. Hall, editorial-page editor of the *St. Louis Post-Dispatch,* answered simply, "Skeptical."[5] From Charlotte Mr. McKnight said, "More progressive." In Washington it is "critical," and in Louisville, Mr. Bingham says, he would call his papers moderately anti-establishment:

> We have taken strong editorial positions against air, water and solid waste pollution, thus alienating the industrial portion of the local power structure. Our strong support of equal rights for Negroes has alienated a large portion of the social power structure.[6]

Thus there are still editors and publishers who take their responsibilities as prophets seriously. And even where that happy situation no longer exists, it is encouraging that the modern owners of multiple newspapers are no longer men like Hearst, who saw to it that, on anything that mattered, the editorials in all his twenty-odd papers said the same thing in words handed down from that monument to eclectic vulgarity, San Simeon. Instead local managements are now often allowed to choose their own way. Says Thomas Gerber of the absentee-owned *Concord Monitor* in New Hampshire: "The *Monitor*'s political allegiance used to be listed as independent Republican, but since I've been editor (three years) it has been more independent than Republican."[7]

So our Ezekiels can still function on their own, if they have the capacity and spirit to put up a fight, and work for owners who let them get away with it. But too many editors match the description offered by Robert W. Lucas, who was an editor in Denver and

Hartford before finding his way to his present post as executive editor of the Yakima *Herald-Republic:*

> Now that I'm again distant from sources of good information, I'm surprised at how many editorials in so-called provincial papers are written off the top of the head. There is a smugness and complacency—a euphoria about ownerships in the outlying precincts that is translated into editorial policy by compliant or dull-witted editors. On strictly local or state issues, they are pretty sharp and careful. But on national or international affairs, too many editorials reflect the *U.S. News & World Report's* sterile commentary, in my judgment. And I find this easy to do out here since so many things that grab you in the big cities or centers of power seem unimportant.[8]

Important they are, nevertheless. One comes back again to the disparity between the editorial writer's responsibility and his authority. One friend, chief editorial writer in a medium-sized city— again with an absentee owner—thus describes his lot:

> I have more responsibility than formally vested authority. In practice I have to exercise both as best I can. No business-management official takes a hand. This separation should be good. But the man who has the editor's title keeps so busy with other duties that I don't see him either unless I go after him. And I do that only to get approval of election endorsements. In daily routine I control the topics and themes for the page, guided a little by what I know of the paper's tradition but with (I hope) a strong consciousness that it's got to be kept up to date.
>
> The weaknesses in a system like ours might be important to an evaluation of editorial impact generally. For example, we're not as strong a voice in the community and state as we could and should be, simply because no one with real authority wants to back up what we say. For that reason I have to use my accrued authority carefully. The few times I have tried to get advance approval of a strong and possibly controversial theme on a local matter I've been vetoed, and thus had to leave the topic alone. What I usually do now is go ahead on my own, but cautiously and therefore not effectively.

That is an ideal prescription for the wrong way to lay down editorial policy. But that is how it all too often is. And that is how it is going to be until such a day as Ezekiel once more owns his own trumpet. The late Tom Storke, outspoken editor (and owner and publisher) of the Santa Barbara *News-Press* until he sold it when he was in his nineties, once said it all:

> A newspaper or magazine is a commercial enterprise. It must show a profit, or die. But if it is only a business, it loses its main reason for being.[9]

### Who Writes Editorials?

Today's editorial writers come in all sizes and shapes, intellectual as well as physical. One scientific sampling in 1971 indicated that the editorial writer's median age was 48.4 years, a bit younger than a decade before. Only 4.7 per cent were not yet 30, but 45.3 per cent were over 51. Women, the women's lib ranks will not be astonished to learn, made up only 2.4 per cent of the lot. Fewer than 20 per cent lacked an undergraduate degree or better. Political leanings were 17.97 per cent Republican, 30.54 per cent Democrat, almost half—48.20 per cent—Independent. Only a handful made such fine distinctions as Independent Republican or Independent Democrat.[10]

Not only editorial writers but editorial-page editors, a relatively new breed, tend to be younger than their predecessors were. This is no doubt in part because editorial writers often used to be broken-down reporters, turned out after their useful years to the pasture of expressing innocuous opinions. That kind of editorial writer dates from pre-pension days, when the idea was to work 'em until they're dead.

A good reporter, in my experience, does not necessarily make a good editorial writer. But the reporter's discipline of keeping his nose to the facts—if it survives the current cry for returning to the passionate and prejudiced reporting of a hundred years ago—is a highly desirable preparation for the editorial writer.

Today's editorial writer tends to be more of a professional than he used to be. Since 1949 there has existed a National Conference of Editorial Writers, a professional association "devoted to the public welfare and to public service," whose chief duty is "to provide the information and guidance toward sound judgments which are essential to the healthy functioning" of democracy. To that end, says NCEW's Basic Statement of Principles, the editorial writer should:

> Present facts honestly and fully;
>
> Draw objective conclusions from the stated facts;
>
> Never be motivated by personal or other special interest;
>
> Realize he is not infallible;
>
> Regularly review his own conclusions in the light of fresh information;
>
> Have the courage of well founded conviction and a democratic philosophy of life, not writing anything that goes against his conscience;
>
> Support his colleagues in adherence to the highest standards of professional integrity.[11]

This is an excellent prescription, subject only to the amount of sap running in the writer's intellectual veins and to the fact that journalism is now run by businessmen instead of editors.

Regrettably, the high calling of prophet to the twentieth century puts on most editorial writers a burden heavier than they can carry. No matter who the editorial writer may be, how enlightened his management, and how many colleagues help him get out the page, the job remains that of commenting each day on the significant, the spectacular, and the colorful in the kaleidoscope of events—in town, in state and nation, and in the world. Even where there are staffs large enough to permit considerable specialization, this calls for more knowledge, time, skill, and energy than most of us possess.

The bigger and more responsible papers encourage their editorial writers to get away from their typewriters, go to the scene of action—whether the local ghetto, Establishment GHQ, a political convention or, for the lucky few, the far parts of the nation and the earth. But most papers are small, and many have owners or managers who never heard of Ezekiel and wouldn't like him if they did. So most editorial writers stay in their cubicles, read the papers, and say what they can about the news. The result is that too many editorial pages are intellectual quick lunches manned by short-order essayists.

No one has statistics telling how many editorials the American newspaper averages per day, nor indeed how many of our 1750 dailies and 7000 weeklies get along without any editorials at all. Some do. But they cannot be many, because the editorial page remains the flag over the advancing journalistic troops, the symbol of a newspaper's essence, its mind and heart and soul.

It is true, however, that the number of editorials per day has shrunk. *The World* of the 1920s, and the dozen or so other New York papers of that day, set the national pace with usually two, two and a half, or even three columns of editorials a day. There might be six or even nine editorials each day, on a smorgasbord of subject matter. This standard applied to the better provincial papers as well, and in some cities it still does.

When I went to the *Courant* toward the end of World War II it boasted a half dozen or more editorials every day, arranged in three columns, not unlike those in the New York *Herald Tribune* of the time. Later, when we went to a more modern arrangement of two wider columns in larger type, I insisted that we hold down the length of individual editorials so as to preserve the same number and variety of subjects. It was not always easy, as more columns and features on the page became desirable, while the demands of legibility, and the continuously escalating price of newsprint, kept cutting down the number of words on a page.

I was fortunate in other ways, too, in that I inherited a four-man staff (myself included) even though at the time daily circulation had not reached 50,000 (it is now more than 170,000). The reason was that Maurice Sherman, the editor who had just taken over as publisher as well, had his heart in the editorial page. He had built it into one that had a national reputation, and not only as an outspoken opponent of the Prohibition that many papers of the late 1920s took in stride. The *Hartford Times* had to go along with a staff of equal size—each paper setting a standard for the other—with the result that the greater Hartford community was the better served.

An editor plus three writers, with secretarial plus proofreading and makeup assistance, is not cheap. I like to think that as the urban-suburban, central Connecticut, capital-region population grew the *Courant* gained acceptance because I was able to continue the same number and variety of editorials, some of them outspoken in ways not always in line with establishment outlook. This acceptance cannot be measured in annual profits. But over the years it finds expression in the hold a paper has on its community, and that hold must have some impact on circulation and advertising.

Experience also convinces me that a newspaper, if it is to serve as today's prophet, ought to average six editorials a day. The world, the nation, the state, the local scene, the cultural and intellectual front, and the passing show of human foibles, require it. But most newspapers now fall short of this standard. A pattern of four, three, two, or often only one editorial a day is likely. To take random samples—if it is fair to rate a paper by a single issue—here is an overview of the number of editorials a day in papers across the nation:

| Newspaper | Daily Circulation | Editorials per day |
|---|---|---|
| *New York Times* | 814,000 | 5 |
| Los Angeles *Herald Examiner* | 506,000 | 1 |
| *Washington Post* | 510,000 | 5 |
| *San Francisco Chronicle* | 457,000 | 2 |

| | | |
|---|---|---|
| *Buffalo Evenings News* | 271,000 | 4 |
| *Tulsa Daily World* | 112,000 | 4 |
| Wilmington *Evening Journal* | 89,000 | 3 |
| *Chattanooga Times* | 62,000 | 3 |
| *Tucson Daily Citizen* | 49,000 | 1 |
| *Augusta Chronicle* | 48,000 | 3 |
| The *Columbian* (Vancouver, Wash.) | 34,000 | 2 |

Circulation size alone, obviously, does not necessarily mean a plenitude of editorials. But because most American papers serve small communities, which allow circulations of only 10,000 or 5,000, or even less, one editorial a day becomes the standard. Fortunately, syndicated columns to back the small-town Ezekiel on his job are readily available. We have also television and radio and the magazines and the out-of-town papers, if we want them. Nor does the quality of editorials depend on their number. In the proper hands an editorial page that is a one-man show can still speak with authority and impact.

Unhappily editorials, other things being equal, are likely to constitute the most expensive words in the paper. It takes more manpower, more learning and experience, to write a good editorial than to write an equal number of words elsewhere. Because publishers can get circulation and sell advertising without a brilliant editorial page, most of them put their budget allocations behind such things as mechanical equipment or circulation drives, not latter-day prophets.

It is only fair to say that many papers—the ones you are likely to hear about—take pride in their editorials. One questionnaire sent to newspapers of more than 100,000 circulation indicated that papers of this size tend to have editorial-page staffs consisting of an editor plus three other writers.[12] A 1971 survey sponsored by NCEW confirmed this, showing that more than half (52.52 per cent) of the editorial writers surveyed were members of staffs ranging from two to four full-time writers. And more than a third (38.58 per cent) came from staffs of three to five or more writers.[13]

As against this only 6 per cent could boast that their staffs included a full-time research assistant—something I found we could have used, but never had. There were times when we just did not have the time to go downtown, to the library or elsewhere, to look up statistics or background, or to question authorities, all of which would have made what we said the more authoritative. You yourself can do a lot with a telephone and a little time, but a qualified young research assistant would obviously be useful in helping to keep the modern Ezekiel, lost in a world of complexities, well informed. The truth is that a researcher costs money, and does not measurably increase circulation and advertising. Accordingly most publishers prefer to leave the money in the till. The same publisher preference explains why one editorial writer recently assured his colleagues across the nation that "Many editorial pages in this country's newspapers are wretchedly understaffed."[14]

The NCEW survey revealed that more than a third of the editorial writers responding, 35.8 per cent, were either unsatisfied or very unsatisfied with the staffs of which they were a part. Complaints mentioned not only the small size of the staff (half of them), but also insufficient competence and versatility on the part of the writers.

Writers on the larger (or better) papers are fortunate in that not every one has to deliver his quota of three editorials, or even one, each day. Each writer can afford the time to do research, to sally forth to interview his quarry, or otherwise to see for himself. *The New York Times* is, as usual, a model. It has an editor and assistant editor for the page, plus ten other editorial writers, plus other officials, to make up its editorial board. Reporters and other specialists may contribute. The *St. Louis Post-Dispatch*, a paper whose standards go back to Joseph Pulitzer's aggressive interest in editorials, has seven full-time writers. The *Washington Post*, counting the editorial editor, has eight full-time writers, the *Milwaukee Journal*, six.

Go to the other extreme, to papers with a circulation of about

5000, and you get a situation like that of Loren Ghiglione, the able and conscientious young editor and publisher (and owner) of the *Southbridge Evening News* in Massachusetts:

> We have one part-time editorial writer—me. At best I spend an hour or two during the afternoon of the day before on research, calling people on the telephone, reading things. That night or the morning of publication day I write the editorial.[15]

Still further down the line are conditions like those recalled from his earlier days by Thomas Gerber, editor and assistant publisher of the *Concord Daily Monitor* in New Hampshire: "I once worked for a weekly newspaper of which I was the editor, ad salesman, job-printing salesman, compositor, and pressman."[16]

### How to Write an Editorial

What distinguishes the editorial from a purely personal expression of opinion is the fact that it is, or should be, to some extent at least an institutional or corporate expression. On the *Courant,* for example, we were aware that the tradition of this oldest paper in the land went back to 1764, a dozen years before the day it printed the Declaration of Independence as the latest news. At times we could almost sense the early Federalists looking over our shoulders. We knew that the radical Abraham Lincoln had once been the *Courant*'s hero. But closer to us was the old-guard Republicanism of the early 1900s, reinforced by a succeeding passionate hostility toward the New Deal.

Inevitably, too, we were aware of the fact that United Aircraft was the biggest employer in town, not to mention the fact that Hartford sometimes boasts that it is the insurance capital of the country. Then again we were aware of the view from the Hartford Club, which has its counterpart in every city of any size. There was a large oval table in the front room of the club, at which the leaders of the local aristocracy gathered during the noon hour. John

Alsop, younger brother of the writing Alsops, called it the shoot-the-poor table.

Mixed with all this was a stubborn streak of Yankee individualism, a latent zeal for reform. We also brought to our editorial conferences, and to our typewriters, the newspaperman's experience of the needs of all sorts and conditions of men, which in those receptive to it prompts a desire to see the human need as a whole. All these influences made a mixture hard to define, but one that made our editorials something quite different from expressions of individual opinion.

On becoming editor I continued my political registration as an independent, even though the paper remained Republican without qualification. Indeed, to me the editor and editorial writer in to-day's United States can hardly fulfill his function unless he avoids identification with any cause whatever, except such as make up what is best in our inheritance of western civilization.

That is why our better papers insist that their staffs be reluctant joiners. Everyone in town wants a newspaperman on his board—or if not that then at least a newspaperman's wife—in hope of getting more publicity that way. But because the newspaperman ought to share with Caesar's wife the quality of being above suspicion, it seemed to me desirable to avoid association even with worthy causes. If you let yourself be put on the board of the local Boy Scouts, for example, and then occasion should arise to run an editorial opposing some practice or proposal of the Little League, or whatever, then the local community will put your opposition down to your personal interest in the Boy Scouts, no matter what the truth may be.

The fact that editorials are institutional more than personal accounts for the fact that they are almost always unsigned. Yet such anonymity irritates almost everyone. I had framed and hung outside my office a cartoon from the *Saturday Evening Post* that showed an irate citizen standing at a receptionist's desk, before a door marked EDITOR. The receptionist was saying, "He's not

in right now. Could you thrash him later?" All of us in the trade
share the experience of Ted Bingham, editor of the editorial page
of the *Dayton Journal Herald:*

> It wasn't long after I started writing editorials—possibly the first
> week—that some woman nailed me at a cocktail party, demand-
> ing to know whether I'd written some editorial she didn't like
> and wondering why I lacked the nerve to sign it.[17]

The fact that the editorial writer is thus shielded from public
view, and represents his paper as he writes, is behind a common
tendency to say "We think that . . ." or, "This newspaper believes that . . ." or, "The *Daily Times* believes that. . . ." No
doubt this formula appears to lend majesty to the pronouncement
being made. But actually it does not make what one says a bit more
authoritative. Besides it is a false modesty, if it is intended as modesty, and a false front as well. Why not simply go ahead and say
what you have to say?

If the page is to have readership, the editorials must not all be
weighty. Chess and astronomy, baseball and botany, and so on
through the infinite catalog of human concerns, all add color and
life to the whole. Fortunate, too, is the editor who has on his staff
one or more individuals who, in addition to their other talents, can
salt the editorial page with humor. During my years on the *Courant*
we had such men. Among them were the late Thomas E. Murphy,
a prolific genius at capturing human interest whose typewriter ran
so fast it almost smoked; and T. H. Parker, a critic of the arts and
all-around newspaper veteran. Both could produce wry comments
on the passing show that brought laughter—and readership—to a
page that is by nature sober. Then there is usually an editorial
writer who, as need arises, can serve as Do-Good editor. Tom
Murphy was such a one, a typewriter virtuoso whose editorials on
the Hartford Foundation for Public Giving, the Community Chest,
the cancer drive, or any other, touched hearts and opened check-
books.

Usually, when there is more than one man on the job, the editorial writers specialize in various broad fields of subject matter. Usually, too, there is an editorial conference. It may be no more than a "What are you going to write today?" Or it may be a formal proceeding attended by a dozen persons. There are papers still that do not have conferences, as the *Courant* did not at the time I went there. One argument against conferences is that no writer should look over his shoulder as he writes, and be tempted to say, "On the other hand . . ." Whatever spark he has in him should not be snuffed out by the cold breath of an opposing point of view.

Still, I often found that two writers, on the same day, would turn in pieces on the same subject—not necessarily saying the same thing, either. Here the conference keeps things tidy, in addition to its main function of examining policy before settling on it.

Sig Gissler, editorial writer on the *Milwaukee Journal,* tells this story about how one editorial was beaten into shape. It shows how the system works at its full development:

> Milwaukee's aldermen, a *Journal* news story reported, were considering an ordinance to shield young persons against sexually suggestive movies, magazines, books and other material.
>
> What if anything should the *Journal* say editorially? The proposed law probably would be popular with many parents, but would it be fair and workable?
>
> The opinion shaping began in the conference room. One writer asked about the proposal's far-reaching language. Wouldn't even the Bible technically violate its provisions?
>
> A lively discussion ranged over many points. . . . No consensus emerged. Finally, the man who broached the topic was asked to ponder it further and try to "pull something together."
>
> This meant word by word scrutiny of the proposed law, a talk with the *Journal*'s city hall reporter, a careful check of Supreme Court decisions, an interview with the assistant city attorney who had drafted the proposal.
>
> Research completed, the writer concluded that the city had authority to pass a special law for minors but aldermen should drop the proposal because:

Its sweeping language could threaten free speech if enforced with Puritanical zeal. Such things as underwear ads in mail order catalogs could be deemed in violation.

Sellers of possibly violative material had to make the determination in advance—at risk of jail if they guessed wrong. Since even judges disagree in smut cases, sellers should not be prosecuted unless they sold specific material after a court ruled it harmful.

The writer prepared an editorial expressing this view and read it at the next morning's conference. Some heads nodded; some didn't. He was pressed to justify several points.

Finally, it was generally agreed that the proposal's defects were serious and should be criticized. It also was suggested that the *Journal* indicate sympathy with the proposal's objective and call for a fairer version rather than abandonment. The editorial was rewritten and the next afternoon it ran in the paper.[18]

On the *Courant* I found our small and casual conference additionally useful when some citizen called up or buttonholed me over something we had said, or something he thought we ought to look into. It was also useful when a visiting dignitary came to town. I would invite such outsiders to the daily conference, and usually we learned something from the exchange.

Visitors can also add color to the day. One afternoon we were backed into a corner and talked dumb by one Lillian Vandevere. She was the chief local crusader against fluoridation, a cause to which she brought a colorful if somewhat irregular past. Because her scientific qualifications were less than zero she called herself, when challenged, a Medical Research Scientist. This time she appeared with a cane for support, and her head swathed in bandages —because, she told us, she had inadvertently sipped a cup of coffee in nearby Bristol. Bristol already had fluoridated its water supply, a fate from which she, with the assistance of well-placed citizens who should have known better, kept Hartford for a decade.

Well, then, having finally gotten to the point of writing an editorial, how long should you make it? Short. Few readers are converted after the first three paragraphs. But there is no rule, and if the subject warrants, and if the public is aroused, there is no reason why a single editorial should not take the entire space that day, replacing perhaps the half-dozen of an ordinary day. The briefest editorial I ever encountered was one by another *Courant* editorial writer, Thomas E. J. Keena. He wrote it because, as one Christmas came on, the local Portuguese community was upset by the fact that the eels with which it was accustomed to celebrating the holidays were not arriving in normal numbers. As none of us had a Portuguese background we were startled, not to say queasy, over the thought of eating eels for Christmas. So Tom started off with a heading that said:

Concerning Eels
For Holiday Meals

The entire text of the editorial read as follows: *De gustibus non est disputandum.*

Other days, other lengths. An editorial of 1500 or 2000 words that fills the entire editorial space can be just as well read as a terse one. It may be a short one mulled for several days, as was William Allen White's classic that won an early Pulitzer Prize, "To an Anxious Friend." Or it may be a long one put together in the heat of the moment by drawing on background and reference material accumulated over the years.

I recall writing one in this way back in Joseph McCarthy's heyday, when there was a threat of suppressing free speech at Wesleyan University in nearby Middletown. Fear was abroad in the land, in Connecticut as elsewhere. First there was fear of communism, shared by large numbers of citizens and exploited by the gravel-voiced Senator when he discovered there was political pay dirt in it. But it was less the Senator than widespread support for him that made McCarthyism. This consisted of an overbrooding atmosphere of oppression and suspicion of anything even slightly unorthodox. It was a denial of fundamental Americanism—if one may use that word to mean the qualities that made this country great.

Here was a challenge to a self-appointed Ezekiel. My piece was buttressed with quotations from history, including everything from Thomas Jefferson and Tom Paine to the Connecticut Constitution's flat statement: "Every citizen may freely speak . . . his sentiments on all subjects, being responsible for the abuse of that liberty." Next day the editorial drew hostile comment from quarters high and low, some of it nasty and some of it right in the building. But the editorial was read, and there were respected voices in the community and in the state who praised it for clearing the air. One of them was the president of Wesleyan at the time, Victor L. Butterfield.

Whether an editorial consists of a single line of text, or takes a column or a page, it is most effective if it is confined to a single idea. Each editorial, long as well as short, should waste no words in driving home one dominant theme. If there are ramifications, or supporting arguments, save them for another day, or days. Not everybody reads every editorial, or even any of them, every day. This makes it doubly desirable to iterate, reiterate, and then reiterate again, as Maurice Sherman used to tell me Horace Greeley used to say.

Experience teaches one final caution. It is an occupational hazard that the editorial writer will pontificate. It is well to remind oneself that one is not a lay Pope, issuing pronouncements *ex cathedra,* which the public must accept. Each of us, persuaded of our own unerring insight, is tempted to exhort, to shout, to beat the opposition over the head until it caves in. This kind of thing has no use, beyond the doubtful one of gratifying those readers already converted before you start. There is such a thing as the emphasis of restraint. Understatement is more effective than violent words in persuading the doubtful or the confused.

Beyond that, it remains the editorial writer's business to remember that all life is change. He must be able to distinguish the enduring values of the past from nostalgia for days forever gone, and the promised land from a mirage. Editorial writing, when you come down to it, is simply common sense reacting to fact. If one does not manipulate the facts to achieve some pre-selected end, they have a way of arranging themselves into a pattern that makes clear the opinion decent men must hold.

### Dear Sir—You Cur!

If the modern editor serves his readers as Ezekiel served the people of Israel, what happens when the readers don't like what their prophet says? It is inherent in man to talk back, and the desire to do so becomes stronger as mass man makes the individual smaller, while the mass media make Ezekiel bigger. And, except as he may be represented by the doubtful mechanism of the audience rating, modern man cannot talk back to broadcast journalism at all. At the same time it is obviously essential to the preservation of democracy that the individual continue to have not only a vote, but a voice.

Pending the two-way cable of the future, the requisite safety valve can best be provided by the printed newspaper. It can be provided through, first, newspaper columns that express views different from that of the paper's own editorials, second, cartoons that do likewise, and third, letters to the editor.

Not long after World War II Ralph Nicholson, then of the *New Orleans Item,* argued before his fellow editors that columns should not talk back to the editor, but reinforce him:

> A good many newspaper editors use the columnists as their hatchet men to belabor a cause or a philosophy more ably, or with less restraint probably, than the editors themselves care to. Some of them have sincerely and conscientiously adopted one point of view in their editorial page and honestly believe that their readers are entitled to the best reading they can get purveying different points of view. So far as I am concerned, when columnists stop being good, sound reporters and become advocates of a cause or a philosophy, we don't print them. But I have no quarrel with those who share the other point of view. Mine is

that if I have coralled a congregation and the pulpit is mine, I am not going to share it with the devil, shall we say. If he wants a congregation, let him go get one.[19]

In the discussion that followed, Jenkin Lloyd Jones of the *Tulsa Tribune* raised a question:

Is it honest and ethical to follow such a policy in a town where the newspapers are controlled by one single management or where there is only one newspaper? Is it incumbent upon the editor, as a matter of being a purveyor of free information and a man in whose hands rests the responsibility of giving his readers diverse opinion, to give the devil a pulpit because the editor owns all the churches in town?[20]

The point is hard to dispute intellectually, though to this day many a management ignores it in practice. Even a paper that has competition is likely to prosper the more it offers readers a daily diet of views other than its own, so that all its customers can find in it something that matches their own point of view. In a monopoly town anything else is hard to defend. But there remain owners, publishers, and editors who own the only pulpit in town, but are so convinced that they speak for the Lord that they see no occasion to hire columnists who preach heresy.

While the early eighteenth-century team of Addison and Steele might be called the first columnists, the breed in its present form came out of the new world that followed World War I. By that time it was an established journalistic convention that news was news, factual and undeniable, while opinion was segregated in editorials. This was before interpretive reporting began to enrich surface fact with background fact—and, sometimes, opinion. But sticking to fact that could be verified, and to sources willing to be identified, left much that was going on unreported. Accordingly, there arose the columnist. Usually he was an ex-reporter, living in in Washington, who wrote up such background gossip and I-hear-that and here's-the-lowdown as he could garner. This made livelier reading than an array of confirmable fact. But because there was less than 100 per cent certainty as to the authenticity of what the columnist reported, it broke through the wall between news and opinion.

Since then columns have multiplied. Everything from the automobile to the zodiac has its syndicated haruspices. Riding the tide were and are the back-stairs-gossip columnists, to whom Walter Winchell showed the way through syndication in fifty states and abroad. Inevitably, the proliferation of columns brought into being the homegrown columnist serving only his own paper. Indeed it is my experience that a local commentator can be as valuable to readers as a top-flight typewriter statesman from Washington or New York. When a local columnist articulates the spirit of his community he can be powerful. Such a one is San Francisco's Herb Caen, who carried readers by the thousands with him when he switched from one paper to another.

A conspicuous pioneer in printing columns that presented views other than his own was Eugene Meyer. This financier bought a moribund *Washington Post* in the depression, nursed it until it surpassed and absorbed the *Times-Herald*—offshoot of the *Chicago-Tribune-New York News* empire—and, with the help of his heirs, made it into a paper of national stature. Surely his willingness to spend money on a high-quality, outspoken, thoughful editorial page, backed by a willingness to give space on the page and on the page opposite to all kinds of views, played a part.

Unfortunately, while the idea has spread, it has not spread far enough. At hand is a copy of the *Augusta Chronicle,* whose editorial page of the day offers, in addition to the editorials, columns by James J. Kilpatrick, David Lawrence, and John Chamberlain —rightists all. Far from being unique, this sample is symptomatic of one of the wrongs that persist in American journalism. "Whoever knew truth put to the worse in a free and open encounter?" asked Milton. But here there isn't any encounter at all. There is nothing but a monotone of orthodoxy, because the owner of the only pulpit in town refuses equal time for the devil—who, in fact, may not be the devil at all.

Curiously, opposing points of view are more likely to be offered by newspaper owners through cartoons than columns. It used to be that newspapers able to afford their own cartoonist would hire one whose views coincided with the paper's editorial policy. That brilliant editorial page of the *World* in the first third of this century was the more forceful because Rollin Kirby's cartoons said in caricature what the editorials said in words. The cartoonist serves as our court jester. He can take liberties that journalistic royalty would not permit in print. An idea made clearly apparent in a cartoon, to use the phrase Joseph Pulitzer used in setting standards for the Pulitzer cartoon prize, can sum up in a single flash of light everything an editorial can say in 300 or 600 words or more. Mr. Kirby's figure of the crepe-hanging Prohibitionist must have been as forceful in getting this country to swing toward repeal of Prohibition as the *World*'s editorials. Since then many another cartoonist has put a punch in pictures behind his paper's editorials.

This practice still survives on our better papers, but the cartoonist has largely ceased to be the alter ego of the editor. Instead he has become one more maverick columnist, expressing himself in his drawings. Many papers make a concession to viewpoints other than their own through cartoons more readily than through columnists. Thus they will buy a syndicated Herblock or Conrad or Oliphant or Mauldin or Haynie—all of them center or left of center—and let them add flavor to a conservative diet of print. Or a paper will buy several syndicated cartoons, and run them at will, much like a spectrum of columnists. If such a variety lacks the punch of the cartoon tailored to the leading editorial of the day, it is still healthier than the monopoly viewpoint.

Useful as both columns and cartoons are, there is no substitute for the letter to the editor as antidote for the newspaper's own view. We joke about the Britisher who, faced with some calamity such as the failure of the nightingales to appear on schedule, sits down to write the editor of the *Times*. But the letter to the editor, which goes back to the beginnings of printed journalism, makes an inexpensive and universal tool for maintaining Milton's free and open encounter. Regrettably, rising costs have tended to shrink the space reserved for letters.

This not only stifles expression but cuts readership because letters, properly cultivated and displayed, are often the best-read items on the editorial page. Studies of the *Courant*'s readership demonstrated this repeatedly. One, for example, showed that the letters in The People's Forum were read by 50 per cent of the men and 52 per cent of the women. This against what was an unusually high readership of editorials that same day—47 per cent of the men and 36 per cent of the women, and 47 per cent of the men and 29 per cent of the women—for the first and second best-read editorials that day. Even so, again and again people who protested something we had said editorially would remain unhappy when I offered them the letters column for rebuttal. The letters do not speak with the authority of the editorials, they insisted. And showing them the readership figures only half convinced them.

Reader interest in what other readers say nevertheless remains strong. When in 1971 the *Daily Sentinel* of Grand Junction, Colorado, polled its readers as to what kinds of news they wanted more of, or less of, 2005 said they read the editorials regularly, against 477 who said seldom. But they were even more interested in their own opinions: 2238 reported reading the letters to the editor regularly, while only 284 said seldom.[21]

A modern version of the letter to the editor is the telephone call. In recent years newspapers have set up what they call Action Line columns, or something of the kind. Their purpose is to allow readers to telephone the paper if they have some complaint—not necessarily about the paper itself, but about anything in their lives. Usually such complaints concern bureaucratic or governmental or business indifference. The paper then tries to untangle the red tape, or otherwise resolve the aggrieved reader's problem. In 1970 the

*Detroit Free Press* went beyond this, and invited readers to telephone their opinions on questions of the day:

> The new wrinkle was added on Sunday, April 19. In May, the first full month, 58,023 called to record their opinions. And in June, 59,036 "sounded off" by calling to vote yes or no on a wide-ranging variety of questions: Cambodia, pot, nudity, legalized offtrack betting, the 18-year-old vote, population control, etc.
>
> That is several hundred more than had ever called or written Action Line in a similar period. And those 58,000 were in addition to those who, every day, were still phoning and writing Action Line.[22]

A variation on this theme has been evolved by the *Milwaukee Journal,* in the form of a guest column called "In My Opinion." In it selected contributions, from readers who are allowed more space than usual—600 to 800 words instead of the normal 200-word limit—may say what they will. At first the column was largely monopolized by local and state officials. But once they had gotten their gripes out of their systems—including gripes at the *Journal—*readers took over to a large extent. Their outspoken comments have a wide readership.

If the letters to the editor at times give the impression that ours is a nation of psychopaths, they are readable because Everyman, when aroused, speaks with candor, and even brutal directness. Even the inarticulate can pack a punch, because there is sincerity and drive behind what they say.

It is revealing to have the human motley that writes letters materialize before one's eyes. Twice the *Courant* held dinners for its letter writers. Selected contributors from city and suburbia and exurbia were invited. At the head table were the Governor, a senator or two, the Mayor, the City Manager, and other dignitaries. It was a meeting of the leading citizens and the leading crackpots in town.

Guests were invited to fire questions at the authorities sitting at the head table. There was a bell, ostensibly to halt the period de-

voted to any one subject, such as Washington affairs or the local
scene, but also in case tempers should wax too warm. Only once
was there occasion to ring it—this to halt an incipient fist fight between two letter writers who relished the opportunity to confront
each other in person instead of in print.

It was fascinating to see familiar signatures take human form.
There was for instance Grace Lee Kenyon, the fiery crusader for
right-wing causes, whom we had visualized as a twentieth-century
Brunhilde. She turned out to be a silent, diminutive copy of Whis-
tler's mother. Then there was Aaron Cohen, a real-estate man who
had done just about everything, beginning with flying an airplane
in 1912, nine years after the Wright's first flight. He was a pest
with a heart of gold, out to do good for the elderly, the prison in-
mates, or whoever else he had in mind at the moment. And so on,
through the hundred-odd present. We had photographers on hand
to snap photographs of those who repeatedly contributed letters.
Next morning their pictures, on the front page together with a lively
news story, stirred the town. No paper could invent a more useful
exercise in democracy—and in its own public relations.

What were the letters themselves like? Most of those fit to print
were sober and sensible, if almost always too long. But almost universally there was a greater or lesser personal bias. For example:

> To the bigoted Editor of the *Hartford Courant*:
> The New Englander is an uncivilized Englishman. The people in
> New England are a harsh and somber people. They do not under-
> stand happiness. You see the false smile and the patronizing busi-
> ness manner, but their faces whenever they are in repose, are
> sullen. Their very laughter is strained. . . .

And so on down to the typed signature, HENRY ADAMS, which not
surprisingly turned out to be false.

There were also constant reminders that the human animal sees
the identical object in sharply contrasting images. Here, for example, is quite a different view of the *Courant:*

Dear Sir:

If your statistics went down one subscription on Aug. 26th, it's only because I finally became too nauseated by your Negrophile propaganda that goes to the extent of placing a publicity photo of a Negro Actress on the front page below the main headline for no reason except publicity. That was the culmination of years of reading daily editorials and hundreds of letters to the editor which glorified the Negro race and vilified the White.

It is not I who is biased. I seek only objective truth. The *Courant* is biased, prejudiced, and discriminates. . . .

Ex-Courant reader

A postcard from a nearby veterans' hospital will begin: "You foul Evil traitorous swine. Your actions have not gone unnoticed. TRAITOR." If that is the product of a sick mind, there are also sick minds still in circulation. I used to get telephone calls from the vice-president of a local manufacturing firm, who would let me know in icy tones that I need not think I was getting away with my communist activities, because people were keeping tabs on me. But there were antidotes, like the letter that said:

After reading your lousy newspaper and your item on the labor rally in Washington, I am wondering:

Do you crawl on your Stomach?

Is your blood red colored?

Are you HUMAN?

How can people describe a man like you?

A REPUBLICAN MONSTER?

Another headache for the editor is the letter factory. Its product, ostensibly a letter to the editor, is either typed with carbons, mimeographed, Xeroxed, or otherwise multiplied, and mailed to papers across the country. Sometimes they are serious, like the concise and professionally slick product put out by the China lobby, in the days when many Americans were persuaded that Taiwan was China. Some are fantasies, like this printed notice of the Second Coming:

Over the past years, We have mailed over two hundred of Our books to editors and publishers all over this country and abroad. Our letters of acknowledgement have been a paltry few—too little to mention.

The cloak of fear that shrouds the newspaper industry has Us baffled. I want this great nation of Ours to realize Our existence together in this dimension of Time and Light. My Son and I are here to stay, 'til death silences Our grip, so there is little the editors or the President—of this vast country of Ours—can do.

Perhaps your fear is of a God Greater than I, but alas, your fears are unwarranted as only I—*your Living God* and *Creater*—can justify.

As *Almighty God*, I ask you to reveal My existence with My Son to countless millions who are unaware. . . .

Many newspapers refuse to print even sensible statements from the letter factories, because they are plainly not so much letters to the editor as organized propaganda. But an astonishing number do find their way into print, which keeps hopeful authors everlastingly at it.

A local variation is the reader who fires a steady stream of letters to his paper. They may all deal with a single favorite cause, or they may take on any subject at all. The writers are likely to be articulate, and often enough what they say is worth printing. Yet they are so prolific that if they were not held in check they would monopolize the letters column, at the expense of those who write only occasionally, perhaps once in a lifetime. Accordingly the normal defense, especially among papers large enough and vital enough to attract more letters than they can print, is to adopt a limit, such as one letter a month at most. But don't let some indefatigable citizen squirm out of that one by getting his wife to sign.

Once the desire to get into print fires a reader, he is likely to invent all kinds of devices to get his manifesto printed. One is to write at the top of the letter "I know you will censor this!" or "I DARE YOU TO PRINT THIS!" At first I made it a point of honor to accept these challenges to print, to show how deep was

our faith in a free press. Later it dawned on me that all too often
we were printing nonsense.

A good letters column requires effort. Whether a letter comes in
with chip on shoulder or not, whether it is legible, articulate, and
brief, or scrawled, long, and obscure, all reflect the reality of hu-
mankind and all deserve an equal chance at the space available. At
times meticulous editing can save some gem in an otherwise rambling scrawl. At the same time one must remember that the more
nearly you allow your contributors to say what they wish, in the
way they want to say it, the more genuine the letters column will
be.

It is a temptation, when some citizen denounces you for an editorial, to argue back. I have seen editorial writers who could not
resist having the last word. They would hitch to a critical letter an
editor's note repeating the argument complained of. Therefore it
seemed wise to cut editor's notes to a minimum. If a critic mis-
quotes you, or complains that you said no when actually you said
yes, state the facts in a sentence or two. But don't argue back. The
fewer editor's notes the better.

Another journalistic habit is to dissociate the paper from a letter,
by putting some comment, often hostile, in the caption over it. This
can be petty, though in skilled hands it can make for controversy
and interest. The soundest rule for headings on letters, and for that
matter on syndicated columns, is to make the headline say exactly
what the writer says in his text.

One final caution: avoid pseudonyms as signatures to letters. To
be sure, the tradition is an old one. It wasn't Madison and Hamilton and Jay who wrote the Federalist Papers in the *Independent
Journal* and the other newspapers of the infant republic, but Pu-
blius. But whatever its justification in those days, it now is a disservice to readers. Before my day the *Courant* allowed its contributors to sign with initials, pseudonyms, or other disguises. The result
was that there were days when few of the letters printed came
from identifiable persons. No doubt this encouraged the writers to

range the more freely. As one reader put it, "Persons who write anonymous letters . . . wish to remain anonymous because they *fear* publicity, favorable or unfavorable. People of prestige have little to fear, but 'little people' of no prestige do have much to fear."

Nevertheless, anonymity makes it possible to shoot from ambush. No harm, perhaps, in letting our downstate fire-eater Mrs. Lillian Hammond Sherwood, sign Hammond Sherwood, even though it was still a masquerade. But what of the priest who regularly plugged the church's political views over the signature Jeffersonian Democrat? Or the aging gentleman complaining about fluoridation, who called himself Mother of Six? And what of the puckish ex-reporter who went to a local bar, found himself a one-armed derelict whose name and address were in the city directory, and borrowed that name and address for letters telling of his extraordinary adventures on his private yacht?

It is not always easy to police these things. I remember the astonishment of a colleague on the Columbia Journalism faculty, who had found a letter over his signature in *The New York Times* one morning. When he complained the *Times* sent him a photostat of the letter, neatly typed on a genuine Columbia letterhead, and complete with a written, if forged, signature.

There are rare circumstances that justify anonymity. Perhaps a prison inmate fearing reprisal, or a home-office insurance girl who doesn't want the boss to know, has something that ought to be said but that can be said only without identification. For the most part, though, it seems best to stay with the town-meeting idea that anyone who asks the right to address the public should first identify himself to that public, instead of hiding behind a "Thoughtful," or "Interested," or some other blind. There are always plenty who will follow the rules to have their say—especially if it is a matter of seting the editor straight.

### Where Shall We Stand?

Once there was an unusual letter in the day's pile. It was from a reader who reported his great interest in the world and its affairs.

He read our editorials diligently, he said, but thought he could do better. As a matter of fact he enjoyed expressing his opinions, so wouldn't we let him have a column to do just that, if only once a week?

Alas, one man's prejudices are so much wind. But the journalistic facts of life are such that a paper's editorials are often little more than the expressed prejudices of the man who owns, or controls, the newspaper. Many an editorial-writing hired hand wishes he could come out from under his paper's wraps and say what *he* thinks. Not that he is forced to say much he doesn't believe in. Still, there is usually an overhanging ceiling, a framework within which one writes, that is not necessarily ideal. The NCEW survey of editorial writers mentioned earlier brought this response to the question, "Do you feel compelled to express ideas contrary to your own beliefs in your editorials?"—

Frequency of Expression of Ideas Contrary
to Editorial Writer's Beliefs

| Response selected by writer | Frequency | Per cent |
|---|---|---|
| All of the Time | 3 | .89 |
| Most of the Time | 3 | .89 |
| Some of the Time | 46 | 13.65 |
| Seldom | 129 | 38.28 |
| Never | 156 | 46.29 |
|  | 337 | 100.00 |

*Masthead,* Fall 1971, p. 7.

The fact that almost half this substantial sample of editorial writers can answer "Never" indicates that we are not badly off when it comes to the honest expression of opinion. Still, there is considerable room for improvement. But it lies not so much in freedom of expression as in the manner in which editorial policy is set. It is no doubt unrealistic to expect that every editorial writer and his editor, expressing as they do not personal but corporate opinion, should enjoy a freedom like that of which Tacitus wrote in the first century A.D., concerning the age of Nerva and Trajan:

". . . the rare good fortune of a time in which you may feel what
you wish and say what you feel" (. . . *rara temporum felicetate
ubi sentire quae velis et quae sentias dicere licet*).[23] But it is not
unrealistic to believe that, were journalistic management and ownership to permit it, editorial policy could be adjusted to public
need more closely than it usually is now.

It is simply a fact that the multiplicity of voices on which the
First Amendment was predicated vanished long ago. Today's individual newspaper must serve the needs that used to be met by two,
three, a half dozen, or even a dozen newspapers in a single community. When there was a multiplicity of journalistic voices, not
one of which spoke the absolute truth, the public could nevertheless get a fair idea of where the truth lay by letting the lot of them
fight it out. This despite the fact that the individual would usually
read only a paper whose prejudices matched his own. Now that we
are virtually down to a single journalistic voice per town, what is
needed is something more deeply and widely grounded than one
man's laying down of policy more or less directly and rigidly, from
above. I can testify that management is sometimes astonished, and
not amused, by what it reads in its own editorial columns. But the
fact remains that day by day, year by year, what a paper says is
handed down from above.

Ideally, how should the working crew that gets out the page decide where to stand? Taking the long perspective offered by the
last century and a half of American journalism, I submit that there
is an answer. We should duplicate, in the formulation of editorial
policy, the long, gradual evolution of newswriting from propaganda to objectivity.

I can think of no better way to advance this thesis than to quote
from an earlier book of mine. Though in today's context I might
phrase it differently, I would still say the same thing:

> The fact that our [journalistic] system works as well as it does
> ought to give us the courage to believe that it holds within itself
> the seeds of all we need for the future. What is conspicuously

lacking is a conviction in most publishers and editors, network executives, and film producers that it is up to them to make a jump into the future like that made by the newspaper pioneers of the 19th century. Where is the publisher with the vision of the 20-year-old Adolph Ochs who, when he took over the sickly *Chattanooga Times* in 1878, saw that success lay in abandoning the universally accepted habit of allegiance to a political party, political idea, religious sect, or industry? Ochs resolved instead to take the entire community for his constituency, and to publish the news as it happened for the benefit of *all* the members of that constituency. The result was that the *Chattanooga Times* and the *New York Times,* with which he subsequently repeated the formula, turned into gold mines. The publishers of today who have Ochs's vision and courage stand to win similar rewards. . . . There is, in other words, a commercial as well as moral reason for a change. But if the managers of today's vastly complicated information system are to win a financial reward and a worldwide esteem like that won by Adolph Ochs, they must take a forward step as positive and as radical as the one he took. They must apply to editorial policy the same standard of service to the entire community that Ochs applied to the coverage of news. Only when an entire newspaper is put together with the thought of reflecting the desires and the needs of society as a whole will the newspaper owners and managers of the 20th century achieve the moral greatness of their predecessors of the 19th.[24]

When I urged this cause in 1949 a handful of publishers and editors were already acting upon it, without any advice from the outside. There are more of them today, notably among the younger men in the smaller towns, which is as far as most of them can get in ownership. It is also fair to say, I think, that the growth of interpretive reporting in our better newspapers, plus the national magazines, plus the network reporting and commenting in broadcast journalism, have moved us in the direction of objectivity in opinion. But the mass of newspapers remain the dominant medium for expressing opinion, above all opinion in the home town about the home town. And here, it seems to me, journalism is missing the boat. The vast majority of ownerships and managements,

though they may protest otherwise, still conceive of their newspapers as partisan political, economic, societal organs, through
which they may preach whatever they themselves happen to believe. But why should not instead a dispassionate, inquiring, objective attitude stand behind every opinion expressed by a paper,
whether the matter in hand is of cosmic significance or concerns
a traffic light?

If once you grant that, then what are the technics of the thing?
How should today's editorial-page staffs and editorial conferences
turn themselves into seekers after truth, wherever it may lead?

The first step, obviously, must be for management to free editorial writers from any rigid, partisan attitude. Thereafter, the
search for an objective editorial policy comes down to nothing
more than a rule-of-thumb method derived from the standard set
long ago by Socrates. Without going into the philosophic niceties
involved, we can recall that the aim of the Socratic method was not
to prove a point, still less to demolish the opposition. It was rather
to inquire, to advance as closely as possible to the always elusive
truth. The idea was not to win over an opponent, but to have both
protagonist and antagonist learn together. This idea, incidentally,
remains the foundation of the theory of a free press.

Socrates himself expressed astonishment that the Delphic Oracle
had pronounced him the wisest man in Greece. It must be, he finally concluded, because while others like him really knew nothing
they were certain of their knowledge, while he recognized his own
ignorance. Hence his method of starting with a hypothesis and
proceeding from it to examine the consequences. Insofar as those
consequences turn out to be verifiable and consistent, instead of
measurably false or inconsistent, they might be accepted as true—
provisionally, of course.

Thus was laid down the rational basis for what later sages, from
Aristotle to Bacon and Descartes and their successors, made into
the scientific method. It simply means getting all the facts you possibly can first, and then basing conclusions on them, instead of

starting out with the mission of arriving at some pre-selected point.

Socrates, of course, ended up drinking the hemlock—a fate not to be wished upon today's editorial writers. Nor is his method likely to commend itself to the tycoons of today's mass media, whether of print or broadcast or cable to come, any more than it commended itself to the elders of fifth-century Athens, who blamed on it much of the decay and disintegration that followed the Athenians' defeat in the Peloponnesian war. Even so, the Socratic method remains the germ of the formula by which the journalist, in these closing years of our century, can best set editorial policy, and thereby serve his fellow men. For it is still true that there is a latent truth on which, given sufficient information and insight, rational men can agree.

### Thus Saith the Lord

When, toward the end of World War II, I came to the *Courant* from New York I found that there was one perennial, unresolved controversy before Connecticut's legislature and its people: birth control. It happened that Connecticut and Massachusetts were the only states left in the country in which physicians were forbidden by law to prescribe contraceptives, even where health or life was at stake. All the other states had in one way or another, by legislation or court interpretation, made birth control legal, under some circumstances at least.

The issue came up every time the Connecticut General Assembly met, which in those days was every two years. The House, which for the most part represented the suburbs and the old Yankee back woods, was ready to join the rest of the country. But the Senate, dominated by an urban constituency that was heavily Roman Catholic, was as regularly opposed.

The result over the years was that, at each session, the House would vote one way and the Senate the other. The resulting stalemate left the question unresolved for another two years. But because both sides felt deeply, the deadlocked state was left with a festering political sore.

In 1947, when the House once more went through its ritual of hearings on the subject, the opposition turned out in regiments. At times the animus displayed was so strong as to be almost a physical force. There were angry growls against speakers in favor that seemed but a step away from mob violence. And it was all made the worse by misunderstanding and misinformation, such as confusion of birth control with abortion, which was then not at issue.

The situation was a sensitive one to comment on, to say the least. Yet there was something out of joint. In the first place the bill proposed was permissive. It would not force birth control upon anyone who did not believe in it. By contrast the existing nineteenth-century Protestant blue law did force upon proponents of change a condition they felt to be intolerable.

Then again it was deeply disturbing that the press of the state, acting as though in concert, never once mentioned the subject editorially. The papers covered the news of the bills and the hearings, as they covered all other issues before the General Assembly. But when it came to editorial comment on birth control there was an unspoken conspiracy of silence.

Was this not a violation of the fundamental principle of American government? Here was a proposed law, up before the people of the state and their elected representatives, that was walled off from the public debate in print that is an essential part of the political process. The great controversy over the Bank of the United States in the early nineteenth century, the Civil War and what followed, two world wars and the great depression—fighting matters all—had been debated freely in the press. But here was an issue so wrapped in brooding fear that the press would not touch it.

Granted that, how does the journalistic prophet decide which is right—to publish an opinion, or to continue the silence before an explosive charge of obviously formidable power? Not birth control, but editorial silence, seemed to me the crucial issue. This was the kind of thing that a press in a totalitarian country does. But a press that is free?

Accordingly, I composed what I meant to be a restrained editorial and took it to the man who had hired me, the *Courant*'s editor and publisher, Maurice S. Sherman. He was a scrappy little man, much like the Foxy Grandpa of the comics of my youth, who in many ways represented the best of Yankee integrity. He read my piece, pondered, and said to go ahead. There appeared in next morning's *Courant* (March 19, 1947) this editorial:

A study of the transcript of last week's hearing on the Birth-Control Bill, H.M. 953, makes the issue concerned unmistakably clear. This bill would allow Connecticut physicians, like those in all other states except Massachusetts, to prescribe birth control where "the health or life" of a married woman is in danger. That is all there is to it. All the storms of controversy that beat about this bill are extraneous.

It is significant that at the hearing fifteen physicians, including obstetricians and gynecologists from some of the state's leading medical institutions, appeared to support it. Of all the opponents only a single one was a physician, and that lone physician offered only one argument material to the subject. This was the observation that no one doctor could say positively that a woman would die if she again became a mother. But then no one state trooper, either, could say positively that a fatal accident would result if a motorist burned up the highway at eighty miles an hour. Nevertheless it is obviously desirable, in the interests of preserving life, to empower the trooper to hold motorists to more moderate speeds. In the same way it behooves the state to empower physicians to use their medical knowledge when, in informed medical opinion, there is a chance that it can preserve health or life itself.

It is noteworthy, too, that according to the unchallenged statement of one of the testifying physicians this is the only existing medical knowledge that Connecticut forbids its doctors to use. Finally, the physicians in the state themselves are all but unanimously behind this bill. According to Clair B. Crampton, chief obstetrician and gynecologist at the Middletown Hospital, the incredibly large majority of 1919 are for it, and only 77 oppose it. So overwhelmingly a verdict speaks for itself. The General

Assembly should make its decision exclusively on the basis of what is germane to the issue, namely the right of physicians to put science at the service of their patients in this as in all other fields. If so, there can be but one answer.

That sounds innocuous today, but the response at the time was instantaneous and violent. The Bishop of the diocese telephoned to let the circulation department know that he was canceling his subscription. One of his parishioners among the *Courant*'s personnel came up to find out who had written the editorial, and the word soon spread. From morning until quitting time, and again part of the next day, my office phone rang incessantly. Most of the comment was unbelievable—hateful to the point of venom, often vulgar, sometimes obscene. There were only occasional protests that seemed normal, such as "I just wanted to let you know I disapprove." Sometimes the generally ugly tone gave way to silence after I answered, as long as I did not hang up. So consistent and relentless was the pressure that the calls did not seem spontaneous, so much as inspired by some central source. Later I was told that, on the following Sunday, the paper and I were denounced by name from every pulpit in the diocese.

There was also, of course, another reaction. Letters and telegrams of commendation came in, many of them from physicians around the state. Through many of them ran a note of approval that at last the conspiracy of silence had been broken. There were other incidents as well. A Catholic printer came up from the composing room, looked in my door, and said, "That's what I think. Let Farmington Avenue [diocesan headquarters] mind its business, and I'll mind mine." And I received a letter from a druggist. His store was near the cathedral, and he reported that after youth meetings there the young people came in to buy contraceptives. The fact was that anybody could buy contraceptives anywhere in the state, despite the law that forbade their sale.

To me what mattered was that the log jam had been broken. Here and there in the state newspapers reprinted the *Courant*'s editorial, though as far as I was aware none printed comment of its own.

Two years later one could sense the changed outlook. At that time our opposition paper, the *Hartford Times,* fired the opening shot with an editorial of its own. It took no sides, saying merely that the issue was difficult. But at least mention of the subject was no longer taboo. Then a few other papers in the state ventured editorials on the subject. The normal process of self-government had begun to operate again. So I sat down to compose another editorial, which said:

This year the doctors' birth-control bill is different. In presenting it yesterday at a hearing before the General Assembly's Public Health and Safety Committee its sponsor, Representative Lawrence Gilman, explained that the words "or injure the health" had been removed. Thus what is at issue is only this: that when in the opinion of a physician life itself is in danger, he may prescribe contraceptives.

The full text of the bill now reads as follows:

"The provisions of Section 6246 and 6562 of the General Statutes shall not be construed to prevent (A) any physician licensed to practice medicine in accordance with Section 2747 of the General Statutes as amended, from prescribing any method or means for the temporary prevention of pregnancy in a married woman, when, in the opinion of such physician, pregnancy would endanger the life of such married woman; or, (B) a married person from using the method or means so prescribed."

In its new version the bill puts the issue even more clearly than did the Alsop Bill of two years ago. As some of the physicians who yesterday testified made clear, it lifts from them the burden of an impossible dilemma. At present they are forced either to violate their Hippocratic oath to serve only "for the good of the sick to the utmost of your power," or else they become criminals.

Both those who yesterday spoke for and against the bill strayed from this point to discuss birth control generally. It cannot be emphasized too often that this large question is not involved in the bill. What is at stake is that Connecticut, alone with Massachusetts among the forty-eight states, still tolerates a law adopted some seventy years ago in the days of Anthony Comstock. The result is to force the evil of hypocrisy upon doctors and people of the State. Birth control is widely prescribed and widely practiced by the people. Under existing law both are criminals. As Dr. Josephine Evarts of Kent pointed out, she came before the Committee "as a self-confessed criminal." She is a criminal, as the vast majority of Connecticut physicians are, because she feels herself responsible for the health and safety of her patients. A mother of four children likewise testified that, because she planned those children, she too was a criminal. And so is many another mother and father in the State.

The bill remains permissive. It would force nothing on any doctor or patient who, in all sincerity, feels birth control to be a moral rather than a medical issue. If it is once more rejected, we shall continue the amazing contradiction of risking life by permitting abortion, while making it a crime for a doctor to prescribe birth control to save a life. But if the bill is passed the entire State can close its ranks without being troubled by this perennial sore. Each of us, in the best American tradition, would be free to go his own way.

Mr. Sherman had died, and I was editor. But this time I was overruled on the ground that the issue aroused strong emotions. Hostility to birth control was so fiery that it would do no good to comment on it. Here was a return to silence in the face of fear, a knuckling under on a vital political issue before the people of the state.

Well, when were we right—in 1947 or in 1949? In such a stormy climate should one publish, or not? It is all very well to invoke the Socratic method, but that still leaves you with no firm conclusion. There isn't any answer. One just has to do the best one can.

There remains also the test of time. And time has brought changes to Connecticut that have achieved the result sought by that controversial legislation in the 1940s. It wasn't action by the General Assembly, or the press, but a decision by the Supreme Court of the United States that finally ended Connecticut's prohibition of birth control. Then too much else has happened. The *aggiorni-*

*mento* of Pope John caught up and channeled the winds of change, winds that have not yet blown themselves out. But they have pointed some straws in new directions.

In 1964 the *Courant* became the first American daily, and as far as I know the second one in the world (after Copenhagen's *Berlingske Tidende*) to celebrate its two hundredth birthday. At that time Hartford's *Catholic Transcript,* the diocesan weekly that had been in the forefront of the attack on me, and because of me the *Courant,* published a warm and generous editorial of congratulation on the anniversary. I wrote a note of thanks, and received this reply, on the Cathedral letterhead, from the editor, Monsignor Kennedy:

Dear Mr. Brucker:
I am glad that the editorial on the *Courant's* anniversary gave your people some pleasure. Particularly am I gratified that you liked it. Some things which I have written in the past did not please you, and with reason. In retrospect, they do not please me, either. There is a slight and heartening possibility that an old dog *can* be taught new tricks.

With best wishes,
Sincerely,
John S. Kennedy

It is healing to experience such magnanimity in the aftertime, when the passions of the past have vanished into the past. But still the journalist must act, from day to day, without knowing whether he is right or wrong, or what the years ahead may say. So there is nothing for it but to assemble all the facts you can, and make an honest effort to eliminate bias as you give the facts searching examination—always being careful not to let the wish father the conclusion. Only then can you decide which course, as of that day, seems to be on the side of the angels. And that gives you the only sanction you can get before you jump into the fray, right there behind Amos, to say "Thus saith the Lord. . . ."

# 11

## *Should an Editor Edit?*

### The Publisher as Editor

SOME YEARS ago Herbert Tingsten, editor of Stockholm's *Dagens Nyheter,* wrote an article for the International Press Institute under the title, "The Editor's Views Should Prevail." In his text he noted that a newspaper proprietor is likely to be a large-scale capitalist—big businessman, we might call him—and that therefore "it can be feared that he will use his newspaper to promote his private interests."[1] Therefore, Tingsten concluded, the public interest requires that the editor have exclusive jurisdiction over what his paper says.

Tingsten was obviously right. The dictionary defines *to edit* as meaning, in this sense, "to supervise or direct the preparation of (a newspaper or magazine, for example)." What indeed is an editor for, if not to determine what gets printed and what does not?

Like other Scandinavian editors, Tingsten felt secure in his authority. He was protected by a contract, which followed the journalistic philosophy spelled out previously by Norway's leading journalistic association: "The editor is personally and entirely responsible for the editorial contents of the paper and he must not allow himself to be influenced to uphold opinions which are contrary to his conscience and conviction."[2]

So far so good. But what if the editor's big-businessman boss has a different conscience and conviction? Here Tingsten's contract provided that the editor should consult with the chairman of the board or his representative. Still, in Tingsten's view, that was just pro forma. In any conflict, he wrote, "It is the view of the editor and not that of the chairman which is decisive."

That's what *he* thought. Not long after Tingsten's article was published, he and his chairman had a showdown. It turned out that the chairman read the contract differently. To him, if there was a difference of opinion, the editor was entitled to press his views in a consultation. But if it came to a clash, it was the chairman who determined what the paper would say. One is reminded of the colonel who was greeted by a newly arrived lieutenant with the assurance that they would no doubt cooperate beautifully. "Yes," said the colonel, "and in this man's army you're going to do all the cooperating."

Because Tingsten was protected by his contract, he was not fired. Still, as he said later, he felt frozen in so he got out. His fate puts into relief the basic dilemma of today's journalism: editors no longer edit.

"I do no man's bidding," Horace Greeley used to say, and "I wear no man's collar." This proud boast has prompted me, over the years, to ask not only lay but also journalistic audiences, "Is there anyone in this room who knows who Horace Greeley was?" The usual reaction is one of wonder as to what the catch is. I have never yet found an audience even now, a century after Greeley's death, that was not familiar with the name of the founder of the *New-York Tribune*. This is because in his day he was as well known as anyone in the country, including whoever happened to be President. It was against this background that I followed my question with another: "Is there anybody here who knows who Horace Greeley's publisher was?" Never yet have I found a single person, in the newspaper business or out, who was familiar with the name of Thomas McElrath, Greeley's partner in ownership of the *Tribune* during the years of its rise to fame. McElrath had bought, for $2000, a half share in the ex-printer's new newspaper. He brought order out of chaos, and suggested the winning formula for a weekly *Tribune*—that it be made up in large part of articles and editorials saved over from the daily issue, which was necessarily local. It was the weekly rather than the daily that was circulated throughout the land, and it was the weekly that made Greeley and the *Tribune* a power that rivaled the national government.

Not only that, Greeley himself was hopelessly improvident in business matters. He had a tendency to fall for varying isms and causes and persons that would have ruined him financially had not the competent, sympathetic McElrath kept him in the black. But McElrath stuck to business affairs, while Greeley remained unchallenged as editor. As he himself later explained:

> . . . my partner never once even indicated that my anti-slavery, anti-hanging, socialist and other aberrations from the straight and narrow path of Whig partisanship were injurious to our common interest, though he must have often felt sorely that they were so; and never, except when I (rarely) drew from the common treasury more money than could well be spared, in order to help some needy friend whom he judged to be beyond help, did he even look grieved at anything I did.[3]

Here is the ideal editor-publisher relationship. It was McElrath who kept the *Tribune* not only solvent but prosperous. But Greeley made that possible. He alone determined editorial policy. He promoted some unbusinesslike social and political ideas, and he also did some pioneering in news gathering that was as expensive to the paper as it was useful to the reader.

Today it is different. The editor, unless he is one of the surviving few who own their own papers, does wear someone else's collar. And, wearing it, he does someone else's bidding. The result is that twentieth-century editors tend to gravitate toward papers offering an ideological climate agreeable to them.

This is not always easy for a newspaperman who is attracted

to the trade by the ideal of public service, rather than by an interest in making money or plugging conservative causes. The basic fact of contemporary journalistic life is that whether the editor agrees with his corporate superiors or not is incidental. It is the businessman of journalism who wears no man's collar.

Note what the chief executive officers of today's newspapers consider important. An ANPA Conference for Young Newspapermen, which might be defined as a conference for journalistic crown princes—those being groomed to be publishers—is an enlightened affair in which young men under thirty-five are subjected for several days to intensive sessions devoted to the following: "Advertising, circulation, *news writing, news editing,* technical developments in communications, business office problems, newspaper personnel and labor relations, governmental relations and other subjects."[4] Those who control journalism today must obviously contend with much that McElrath, let alone Greeley, never bothered with. Labor relations, personnel problems, governmental relations, forsooth.

Nor did Greeley and McElrath ever hear of research in journalism. But not long ago Jack B. Haskins, Snow Research Professor at the Newhouse Communications Center of Syracuse University, sought "to find out what are the great information needs and perceived problems of the newspaper industry." He did so by polling publishers, whose replies ranked the things they needed to know in this order:[5]

|  | Per cent |
|---|---|
| Mechanical/production/technology | 70 |
| Personnel | 70 |
| Newspaper image | 53 |
| Journalism education | 52 |
| Newspaper research | 48 |
| Editing/content/selection | 42 |
| Circulation/markets | 37 |
| Reporting/writing | 37 |

| | |
|---|---|
| Advertising | 35 |
| Promotion | 26 |
| Management | 25 |
| Competition | 25 |
| Economics | 23 |
| Typography | 22 |

Editing, reporting, and perhaps a bit of typography—skills that were once the backbone of newspapering—now rate from less than half to less than a quarter of the interest of the men who control newspapers.

What changed journalism from small business into big business? It is not that owners and publishers are selfish moneygrubbers, while editors are idealists and zealots for public service. Rather the change came, unintended and unnoticed, as the result of a historical accident. During the nineteenth century newspapers were pioneers, not only in news gathering but in adapting a burgeoning technology to their own use. During the first two-thirds of the twentieth century, by contrast, newspaper technology was virtually stagnant.

Thus in 1801, when Jefferson became President, the newspaper's mechanical equipment—a hand press that printed copies one at a time—was hardly distinguishable from Gutenberg's press of three and a half centuries earlier. In 1901, when Theodore Roosevelt became President, huge, power-driven rotary presses were grinding out newspapers of many pages in multiple thousands an hour. Not only that but Gutenberg's movable type, set by hand in metal forms through most of the nineteenth century, was being set speedily—a line of type at a time—by typesetting machines. Photographs, turned into printing plates by the halftone process, had replaced the hand-carved woodcuts of earlier days. And telegraph, telephone, and typewriter had replaced shoeleather, horse, and pen and ink as the tools of news gathering.

Why journalism's technological pioneering came to a halt as this century opened, after it had gone through such spectacular development, nobody knows. It is true that, as other industries of this century spent more and more money and energy on research, the money-men of journalism did not. But no one thought much about it until the coming of radio and television began to make the lag more and more painful.

I well recall my own first encounter with newspaper technology. It was on my first day as a reporter on the *Springfield Union* in Massachusetts, in the summer of 1923. Bill Hatch, the city editor who trained a whole generation of newspapermen, let the neophyte off with a bit of rewrite and a single outside assignment. It was to cover a high-school tug of war, an event not uncommon in those innocent days.

I found it exciting to be a reporter at last. And, having time on my hands, that evening I was determined to become acquainted with all of my new business. So I was able to follow, from beginning to end, the process of turning the report of an event into an item in the paper. Once I had come back to the office, batted out my little story, and turned it in, I followed it through to the printed paper. First it was edited and headlined on the desk, then it was sent by conveyor to the composing room. There it was set into type on a softly whirring Linotype, which tinkled as each brass matrix representing a letter dropped into place at the touch of a typewriter-like key. After the line had been cast the matrix was redistributed to its slot in the magazine at the top. Each line, as set, was thus cast in metal. When enough lines were assembled on the Linotype they were carried by hand to a metal tray, called a galley, and set into it. After a proof was pulled and read in the proof-room several lines of type had to be sent back for corrections. New lines were substituted for the faulty lines in the galley. Later that little block of type, together with a headline set on a separate machine, was fitted with others among the ads on the page, all likewise made of type-high metal. This was locked in its case, a steel frame, and trundled to the stereotypers.

The stereotypers, in turn, laid a cardboard-like sheet or mat over the page, then rolled it under heavy pressure to get a reverse image of the type on the mat. Next came the process of curving the mat into a semi-circle, from which a curved printing plate—half a cylinder—was cast from molten metal. By this means it was possible to print at high speed from a rotating cylinder on the press, rather than slowly and cumbersomely from a flat surface of type.

Next I followed my plate down to the basement pressroom, where it was locked on the press with others, and made ready. At length, after the last plate was in place and all had been adjusted, a warning bell sounded to get the last pressman out from under, and the giant press was revved up. Huge rolls of paper spun through it, each receiving its inked impression on both sides, until printed papers, all neatly cut and folded, came roaring off the far end, then were carried in a steady stream via a conveyor to the mailroom for distribution in the early hours of the morning.

The process that I had watched was the peak of nineteenth-century perfection in newspaper production. What has raised the cost of the process fantastically since then is the fact that virtually the same technique, which requires endless sets of skilled hands, is still basic to newspaper production today.

Now, in the late twentieth century, we are experiencing a fantastic revolution in the mechanics of printing. Type set by punched tape rather than a skilled printer, cold type made photographically rather than cast from hot lead, offset instead of letterpress printing, plus miraculous electronic gadgets that replace pencil and paper, are increasingly in use. And the cable technique that will transform journalism into something unbelievable not only to Gutenberg but to Bill Hatch grows apace. Nevertheless many a paper, especially the ones with large circulations, are still produced by a mechanical process only slightly refined from that which was already long familiar when I first saw it used in the 1920s. Yet newspapers have to pay wages competitive with those of industries in which machinery rather than skilled craftsmen do the work. Such computers and other modern gadgets as have been pressed into newspaper service merely add to the vast aggregation of capital necessary to get out a newspaper. No wonder, then, that newspapering has become a big business, with public service incidental. And no wonder that the twentieth century McElraths have been put in command, and assume as a matter of natural right the power to tell the twentieth century's Greeleys what to say and what not to say.

The results are not happy. Consider the attempt to start a new paper in Oshkosh, Wisconsin, in 1967. In Oshkosh there existed the usual stodgy, don't-stir-up-the-animals evening paper. The new morning paper challenged it, and before long began to succeed. But when a business slump set in, in 1969-70, and the new paper failed to land the grocery advertising that would have pushed it into the black, its publishers killed it. It was still costing money, not bringing it in. The erstwhile editor, Dean H. Shoelkopf, reported:

> We had created a new newspaper, a high quality regional daily, and made it one of the best of its size in the nation [as evidenced by the prizes it kept winning!]. We forced our competitors to become better newspapers. . . .
>
> We had an esprit on the news staff of a kind I never have known before in newspaper work. We felt a common cause and purpose. We were not bound by rules or traditions nor encumbered with sacred cows. We covered the news honestly and with vigor. As a result, we had no problem getting good people—either experienced newsmen or bright, aggressive young college graduates who felt a deep commitment for the kind of journalism we practiced and who were more interested in that than money or location. . . .
>
> Our efforts helped achieve for Oshkosh: a riverfront beautification program; a minimum housing ordinance; a bond issue for a new public high school; bonds for grade school expansion; city bonds for long overdue improvements; a black student center at the University; a new county airport terminal; election of progressive city council members; retention of the city manager system in a recall referendum; establishment of a Boys Club; creation of a family life education center in the public schools.[6]

This blow-by-blow account of the venture is a fascinating revelation of what high purpose, given free rein, can do. But the end re-

sult is equally graphic testimony that it takes, on the part of ownership and management, an interest in something besides dollars to
stay with such a venture until it is safely earning its keep. That can
take a long time.

Consider the situation in Wilmington, Delaware, some years ago
when a new editor, Creed Black, succeeded in modernizing and
revitalizing the jointly owned morning and evening papers. In the
process he both benefited the community and increased circulation
handsomely. But a conservative DuPont ownership preferred to
have him wear its collar. So it sought to put one of its public-
relations men, more sensitive to its outlook on life than Mr. Black,
over him. Mr. Black got out, and in the end, after the Knight
papers took over the *Philadelphia Inquirer,* he found a spot where
his talents were appreciated. As for the Wilmington papers, some
years thereafter the DuPont heirs began to show signs of abandoning control.[7]

Any newspaper man can tell you about money pressures. The
transformation of journalism from an editorial service into a business was typified for me by a chance conversation at an ANPA
luncheon in New York. I found myself sitting by a retired circulation manager, who told me: "I worked for years with Gannett. In
the old days, when the old man was alive, things were good. Nowadays the strongest department they have in the central organization is their accounting department. They know just how many
pencils there are in every one of their papers. But the spirit has
gone out of the thing."

We speak now of black power, student power, woman power,
and other kinds of power. What the modern clash between the
dollar and journalism comes down to is publisher power. American newsmen visiting their opposite numbers in Russia come away
with the impression that the editors and staffs of *Pravda, Izvestia,*
and the rest are professionals whose task it is to put into effect editorial decisions made elsewhere. And that is no different from what
happens in many a newsroom in this country—a circumstance made

ironical by the fact that some of our publishers are among the more frenetic opponents of communism.

Under publisher power the most that can be hoped for is a publisher or owner shaped by his genes or his experiences into being a philosopher-king. Though few of us picture it that way—we simply take what is for granted—publishers have powers comparable to royal powers. So far most publishers have been spared the indignity of democratic challenge from the ranks, and so far none has lost his head in the way Charles I did. They can be and some are philosophers, in the sense that they are sensitive to journalistic intangibles as well as to profit-and-loss statements. Turner Catledge, retired executive editor of *The New York Times,* gives an example:

> When I became managing editor in December, 1951, I was greatly aided in my new job by the knowledge that I had the full support of Arthur Hays Sulzberger, the publisher. He was my boss, my drinking companion, and my close friend. He had groomed me for this job, he had faith in my abilities, and now he was prepared to stand behind me.[8]

A series of Ochs family publishers more interested in news for the public than in money has made *The Times* an institution known through the world. The goal set at the top seeps down through the entire operation, determining what happens in day-to-day operation. Gay Talese, *Times* alumnus and the paper's latest historian, tells of a day when a *Times* editorial took apart an impressive real-estate venture involving luxury-apartment skyscrapers on the New Jersey cliffs, across the Hudson:

> . . . the buildings as seen by *The Times'* editorial writer were a desecration to the natural beauty of that section of the Jersey cliffs. But Green [*Times* advertising manager] did not agree—and besides, he had recently sold the builders and owners of the apartments, the Tishman Realty & Construction Company, a $50,000 advertising supplement that had just appeared in *The Times* praising the project. The Tishman family would be most unhappy about *that* editorial, Green knew, sitting at his desk expecting a

call from them at any moment. They might even wish to with-
draw future advertising, which is not an uncommon reaction
among some big businessmen when a *Times* article or editorial
offends them. A cigarette manufacturer boycotted the advertising
department after a *Times* editorial dealt with smoking and lung
cancer, and this cost the paper several thousand dollars. But with
the possible exception of Green, no executive at *The Times* really
cared. When *The New York Times* cares about what its advertisers think, a few executives have said, it will no longer be *The
New York Times.*[9]

Smaller newspapers, too, can become institutions edited with
integrity. Especially is this true when a younger generation inherits,
buys, or marries into control of a paper. Examples run all the
way from Pittsfield, Massachusetts, and Middletown, Connecticut,
to Riverside and—in the big time again—Los Angeles in California.

Magazines too can have publishers who keep hands off editorial
decisions. When Raoul H. Fleischmann, angel and publisher of
the *New Yorker,* died, the magazine's editor, William Shawn, spoke
of him in words that remind one of Thomas McElrath:

> In a casual-seeming but nevertheless skillful manner, he provided
> a stable, appropriate business framework within which the edi-
> tors were free to go their own way, to create exactly the magazine
> they wanted to create, with total independence."[10]

Unhappily, philosopher-king publishers are as rare in magazines as in newspapers. Over three middle decades of this century
the *Saturday Review* rose from obscurity to national influence under owners who let the editor edit. Back in 1940 an unknown journalist then in his twenties with only half a dozen years of experience, took over as editor of the *Saturday Review of Literature,* an
ailing weekly. It had begun life as a book-review supplement of
the old New York *Evening Post.* But because it could not catch up
with the dominant *New York Times* book section, it was in danger
of death.

The new editor, Norman Cousins, was well aware that under the
folklore of journalism no intellectual magazine in the country

could break the 30,000-circulation barrier. Before he was through the book review had become a review of the cultural life of the nation, the *Saturday Review*. Its circulation, 660,000, showed that the country is willing to consume intellectual fare, edited with a public-service motive, if the editor has what it takes, and if he is free.

Inevitably *SR*'s prosperity attracted the money-men. Two whizz kids from the West Coast, within four years from the time they launched the remarkably popular *Psychology Today,* had gotten into the big time in the conglomerate Boise Cascade. In the summer of 1971 they bought *SR,* and the book affiliate it had developed, for a reported $5.5 million. Said Mr. Cousins, who had sought to buy the magazine himself, at the time: "These are men with serious publishing experience. They understand the kind of selective audience the *Saturday Review* wants to reach, and I am confident they will be successful in further expanding our readership."[11]

One might think that Mr. Cousins himself had been successful enough—spectacularly so—in expanding readership. But this was not enough for the new owners. They dreamed up a plan for aggrandizing the magazine into Saturday Review Industries, a conglomerate. Under it four new monthlies would be founded on the shoulders of a fattened *Saturday Review,* while the new owners would swell their consumer division with book publishing and the Saturday Review Book Club.

Within four months of the sale Mr. Cousins resigned. In an editorial signed with the familiar initials N.C., which for years had become a trademark for a practical idealism, he wrote: "I object strongly to the commercial use of the *Saturday Review* subscription list for purposes that have nothing to do with the magazine. I object to the exploitation of the name of the *Saturday Review* for sundry marketing ventures."[12] The key that unlocks the whole vast subject may be found in this comment by Mr. Cousins: "They thought they were buying a business but what they actually acquired was a human relationship between a few editors and their readers."[13]

Perhaps, over the years, *SR* will continue to make an informed and understanding public its first business. But at the time Mr. Cousins resigned it looked as though journalism had once again fallen victim to merchandisers, interested only in marketing packages that sell.

Everywhere it is the same—even when a chain operator buys an ailing paper and turns it into a money-maker, thus at least keeping it alive. The local management may be free to choose its editorial policy. But its editorial budget is likely to be too small and too unimportant to central business management to enable the local editor to do the job he would like to do. And he had better not pick a fight about a moral issue with a department store or other big advertiser.

It isn't right, and it need not be. When the Knight Newspapers bought the *Charlotte Observer,* and installed C. A. McKnight as editor, a business-office executive suggested that he have some title higher than editor. Jack Knight, principal owner of the Knight papers, who continued his own editorial interest and duties long after retirement age, snapped back: "Hell, there is no higher title than editor."[14]

Look all around the journalistic horizon and you will see the modern need for editor power to counter publisher power. If we do not get editor power the relentless and everlasting pressure to make more profit each year is likely to cut the ground out from under journalism aimed at public service. And it is still true, as Joseph Pulitzer once said, that our republic and its press will rise or fall together.

## The Reporter as Editor

If the republic and its press are in danger from the money-men on the right, they are also in danger from journalistic participatory democracy on the left. An editor may think that he could edit, if he could once get rid of the collar his publisher or owner keeps around his neck. But he may be wrong. Witness the testimony of Dan Rottenberg, managing editor of the *Chicago Journalism Review*, prototype of a new breed of publication put out by editorial staffers convinced that their editors, along with their publishers, are not allowing them to report the truth: "Rules of ownership are especially difficult to enforce upon a generation of reporters who, for better or worse, refuse to commit themselves blindly to their editors' judgments."[15]

Much of what the new rebels say is valid. Too many editors, brought up in the old ways, share the dividend-oriented, politically right-wing philosophy of their publishers and owners. They too are a part of the publisher power that intrudes upon and often prevents editing by editors. But there is a distinction between editor power and reporter power:

> Reporters rejoice and push onward, editors hesitate, publishers cower behind their desks in fearful realization that the day of judgment has finally come. . . . In *Esquire,* in *Time,* in *Newsweek,* we read of numerous cases in which working newsmen are standing up to their bosses by publishing journalism reviews, demanding a say in editorial policy, insisting on a voice in the selection of their superiors, and even talking about taking control of their papers altogether.[16]

So wrote Mr. Rottenberg on another occasion. This time he was putting his finger on the excesses of reporter power, the drive toward which ignores the fact that even monopoly papers do not command a captive audience—but, what with television and other distractions, have to persuade subscribers to buy and keep on buying:

> . . . any idealistic takeover of a newspaper by reporters is bound to fail unless there is someone in the group crass enough to engage in the kind of hustling and salesmanship necessary to attract readers' attention. . . . Someone as crass, say, as some of the very publishers the reporters are now rebelling against.[17]

If reporter power arises naturally out of contemporary America, it is also a consequence of the model set by postwar European journalists. Since World War II many of them have rebelled against the bosses of money journalism, to whom the mission of finding and reporting and interpreting the truth as best it can be found out is secondary.

In this country, Vice President Agnew's angry denunciations of television and the press let loose a public response powerful enough to be felt as though it were a physical blow. It was inevitable that thoughtful journalists, especially the younger and therefore more flexible ones, should become convinced that journalism ought to clean its own house before seeking to brush off Mr. Agnew's strictures and threats. Here was further fuel for the fire already building under reporter power.

One journalism professor, Bryce W. Rucker of Southern Illinois University, went so far as to tell a Sigma Delta Chi (professional journalism) group that working journalists ought "to assume complete, unquestioned control of the news-editorial operations of the news media." As he explained later:

> Undoubtedly, there are working journalists in America who, if challenged, have the desire, the drive, the guts, the ability to make every newspaper in this land a vital force. Only they can produce news-editorial content which can regain public confidence, revitalize the press through imaginative redefinition of newspapers' roles, thwart efforts to impose governmental restrictions on newspapers.[18]

The drive for reporter power boiled to the surface in this country in the years from 1965 on. Those were the years when the ghetto exploded and burned, and when the excesses of the student rebellion made one wonder whether the country would hold together. Though there was some talk of it in the younger ranks, no newsroom in the country was seized and paralyzed and vandalized, as was many a campus administrative office. But it might have been, and might still be.

All of which does not change the fact that an excess of reporter power, no less than an excess of publisher power, can destroy independent journalism. To urge that staff journalists elect the editor and control news and editorial policy may have a noble sound. But as anyone who has read history knows, and as anyone who takes part in an old-fashioned New England town meeting can tell you, government by committee—especially a committee of the whole—doesn't work. Like Lenin's 1917 slogan, Power to the People, it doesn't give power to the people. Mob democracy leads first to chaos, then to dictatorship.

To make self-government work there have to be delegated responsibilities, carefully fitted into a structure of checks and balances. To have the rank and file elect the editor and publisher may sound like the paragon of democratic control. What could be more free, more just? The trouble is that in practice such an arrangement, were it ever possible to set it up, would mean that the editor, publisher, or other boss would spend his days not minding his business but running for office. He would resemble a representative in Congress who, as soon as one election is behind him, has to start cultivating the voters, and the pressure groups, and the fat cats, with an eye to the next election. Anything like this would make accession to the command posts of journalism a beauty contest, in which journalistic excellence would be given floods of lip service and little reality.

Any such people's democracy in journalism is hopelessly unrealistic. Nevertheless there are in the younger ranks some who see it as the answer to the failures of the present. In 1970, for example, there was formed in Minneapolis an Association of *Tribune* Journalists. It was not a collective-bargaining unit, but a device to force management to stay on the straight and narrow path:

> There had been the usual grumbling at the *Trib* about shortages of staff and space, but there was a new element in the talk. As an association member later explained, "There was a feeling on our part of loss of respect. We were being treated like army privates

and the editors were officers; we were to do what we were told
and like it and no one gave a damn if we thought our orders
were sane or insane."[19]

Surely no recruit to a city staff who is worth his pay has ever
doubted that the paper would be better if he ran it. But the hard
fact of human organization, in journalism as in all else, is that you
have to have officers in command of privates, and the privates
must do the work as they are told to do it. The officers have to be
few, and the privates many. You just can't get anything done by
an army of generals, each with a veto power over what he is or is
not to do. Editors and publishers have to have authority, and that
includes not only authority to hire and fire but also authority to be
or to do wrong. Anything else is chaos.

Rebellious European editors, who have made far more progress
toward editor power than their American counterparts, have found
that their own attacks on publisher power have stimulated cries
from others for reporter power. Scandinavian editors have been
pioneers in protecting journalistic integrity against corruption by
orders from the money-men above. But as soon as they detected
groundswells of reporter power below they hastened to protect
themselves from this new assault. They got together to draw up a
declaration of principles, spelling it out that the editor's chair belongs to the editor:

> The chief editors have the judicial responsibility for the content
> of the papers as well as the internal responsibility for editorial
> policy and consequently they are responsible for proper commu-
> nication between the editorial staff and other departments within
> the newspaper house.
>     The rights and responsibility vested in the chief editors act as
> a protection for the independence of journalists in their daily
> work and as a bulwark against outside pressure. It is self-evident
> that employment and dismissal of editorial staff is the respon-
> sibility of the chief editors. . . . The chief editors must be heard
> in all decisions affecting, directly or indirectly, the position of the
> paper.[20]

It is hard for journalism to discharge its high mission in any other way. What we can learn from the various movements toward reporter power is that, just as a changing world found the universities too stuffy and stodgy and set in their ways for their own good, so editors as well as publishers have become insensitive to changes that ought to be made in the interest of journalistic service to the public. This is a day in which the word dialogue appears in every manifesto or disquisition about what ought to be done about anything. Surely there is room for more dialogue, that is to say more free and open give and take, between editors and their staffs than is customary. Where it has been tried, it works:

And in Philadelphia, the senior editors of the *Bulletin* have been conducting regular Monday afternoon "seminars" with some fifteen of the younger—and more activist-minded—staff reporters. The weekly seminars began last March [1970] after managing editor George Packard had heard complaints from staff members that story suggestions and opinions about news coverage were not "trickling upward." A typical meeting allows equal time for a senior editor to explain his particular operation (news desk, photo assignments, etc.) and for reporters to ask questions or otherwise respond. The trickle—some say, torrent—of underclass feelings loosed by the seminars has already resulted in some changes in the way the *Bulletin* handles racial identifications in stories. *Bulletin* editors are also opening up channels so that younger reporters can get story ideas into the paper's new "Enterprise" page, and no one seems more satisfied with these developments than Packard himself.[21]

Once, when the American Society of Newspaper Editors was fretting over this issue, Newbold Noyes of the *Washington Star* was asked what the relationship should be between editorial policy and the news staff's ideas about editorial policy. The question was asked because, at one point, about 10 per cent of the *Star's* editorial staff had signed a letter saying they disagreed with the *Star's* position on Vietnam and Cambodia. Said Mr. Noyes:

My feeling is that the relationship has got to be an informed one. The obligation of the editor—and his editorial writers—is to know as much as he can of what the paper's news staff is finding out, to get in touch with them and to get all the feedback that he can from them. But I do not believe that the editorial policy of a paper can be set by a caucus in the newsroom or a committee function, or something like that.

In the end, somebody has to sit down and decide what the hell that paper is going to say. And I think it gives it more bite and more point if it is an individual who is saddled with that responsibility. If it is not the right individual, you get rid of him and get somebody else.[22]

And who should he be—that individual who decides? Why of course, once again: Who but the editor?

# 12

## Who Should Own Newspapers?

### Who Does Own Them?

IF IN the years ahead American journalism is to fulfill its function as an essential and integral part of our self-governing society, the fundamental need is to return it to the point at which editors once more edit.

The principal obstacle is our conventional economic creed, which controls journalism as it controls all else. That creed remains, despite all the restrictions time has put upon it, laissez-faire: Self-interest is the most powerful stimulus to man there is; let us all therefore put our self-interest to the test of competition in a free market; he who does the job best will come out ahead; thus our affairs will regulate themselves to the greatest advantage of all. The clincher is that this free, self-regulating mechanism works more realistically and more effectively than any other that idealism or government has dreamed up.

The laissez-faire doctrine, radical when propounded in the eighteenth century, worked well until the modern world began, almost a century and a half later, with World War I. But now, in today's mass society, journalism along with much else has become big business. The consequence is that, as Jean Schwoebel of France's *le Monde* says, "Freedom of expression is given only to people who can assemble formidable capital."[1]

Self-government cannot function without an informed public. But the accidental and unintended effect of our faith in laissez-faire is that the public gets only the information that puts money into private pockets. Therefore the mass of men in the liberal democracies, who need more information and understanding than do their counterparts in totalitarian and underdeveloped lands, are under-informed. Says Mr. Schwoebel:

> This widespread under-information, which does not permit citizens to appreciate realities as they are, and to see the problems those realities pose, has the effect of clogging progress and at the same time reinforces the injustices that disrupt the world and the tensions that menace peace.[2]

The Pentagon Papers are a classic example of just such public under-information. Had our reporters and editors of broadcast and print been aggressive enough and nosy enough to ferret out the facts about the Vietnam war as that war was being escalated, the history of not only the war itself but of the world would have been different from what it has been. Said one thoughtful commentator, Richard L. Tobin of the *Saturday Review,* after the facts had finally been published:

> What keeps gnawing in the back of a man's mind, close to half a year after the Pentagon revelations, is why didn't we know about these things long before through normal channels of journalism, both electronic and print. . . .
>
> What really gets you, as you think about it more dispassionately with the lengthening of time, is what *else* don't we know. What other hidden military commitments, real or implied, have been made in the White House since, say, the end of the Korean War? Do we really know anything at all about what it costs the American people per day simply to sustain the largest military budget in the history of mankind—and in what is technically peacetime at that? How many murders of heads of state, how many revolutions, how much unethical interference in the in-

ternal affairs of other nations, small or large, have been planned, carried out, and financed through the simple budgetary device of hiding tens of millions of CIA dollars in the other departmental appropriations? We just don't know.[3]

There is no more profound and significant failure of journalism than this: that in modern liberal democracies the public doesn't know enough to govern itself. Money journalism, obviously, is not the only reason. But because money controls journalism, it is crucial. It can limit reporting as well as freedom of editorial expression.

This is all the more frightening because today freedom of expression is limited not only by the fact that one has to command formidable capital before one can exercise it, but also by the fact that even the rich have few opportunities to acquire a newspaper. Newspapers are more and more being gathered into the hands of corporate monsters that own two or more papers. Even riches cannot buy them.

To be sure, the United States is not yet as badly off as regards single ownership of multiple publications as West Germany is. In that country, in 1968, an investigating commission determined that press freedom was endangered if a single publishing enterprise commanded 20 per cent or more of total circulation of newspapers or magazines. Yet at the time one publisher, Axel Springer, controlled almost 40 per cent of total national newspaper circulation, and more than 17 per cent of magazine circulation as well. When this fact was brought out, and public concern arose lest Germany's new democracy be imperiled by so great a concentration of power, Springer sold some of his magazines.[4]

In the United States we have not gone that far—not yet, at least —but the concentration of newspaper ownership has advanced so far and so fast as to give reason for concern here, too. Typical is this 1970 report, which appeared in the *Wall Street Journal:*

> Rochester, N.Y.—Gannett Co., the owner of 34 daily newspapers, said it plans to buy seven more through an agreement in principle

to acquire Federated Publications Inc., Battle Creek, Mich. The transaction would be for Gannett stock valued at about $52 million at current market prices. . . .

Federated publishes daily newspapers with a combined circulation of 300,000 in Lansing and Battle Creek, Mich., Lafayette and Marion, Ind., Olympia and Bellingham, Wash., and Boise, Idaho. . . .

Gannett's daily newspapers, which like Federated's serve small and medium-sized cities, are located in New Jersey, New York, Connecticut, Illinois, Florida and California. In addition to 34 dailies, Gannett publishes 13 weeklies and owns two television stations, five radio stations and a cable-television facility.[5]

It is necessary to ask whether this kind of thing, which grows apace, is in the public interest. Instead of lumping more and more newspapers under a single ownership, why not give some one else a chance? Those of us who have tried to buy a newspaper (there are perhaps thirty would-be buyers for every seller) soon find that the cards are stacked against the individual. Even a man who is so fortunate as to have access to enough capital to swing a purchase has to use full-sized dollars to bring it off. Someone else who already owns a newspaper or other business can use smaller dollars that are much easier to come by. He can offset the losses involved in buying a paper, and in modernizing it to the point of efficiency, by paying the usually large costs involved out of profits from the paper or papers he already owns. Raymond B. Nixon, formerly professor of journalism and international communications at the University of Minnesota, is an authority on who owns what in the newspaper business. As he once explained it: ". . . Tax Court rulings make it advantageous for a business concern to invest accumulated earnings in related enterprises, rather than to build up larger surpluses or to pay extra dividends."[6] The result is that to those who own newspapers shall be given more newspapers. As for those who don't own even one newspaper, they can remain hired men.

According to Mr. Nixon a variety of economic, social, and political factors have accounted for the growth of newspaper groups. By the late 1950s, he reports, local consolidation into one-newspaper communities had reached a practical end, with fully competing newspapers remaining in only thirty-seven American cities. As newspapers with surplus earnings went further and further afield through the country, to buy up what might be left, groups began buying groups. At last count a total of 157 daily newspaper groups owned 879 dailies, or a fraction more than half of all there are in the country.

We can visualize what is happening by noting one of Mr. Nixon's tables. It shows that, while the *average number of papers* owned by an individual group has not advanced beyond the half-dozen it was in 1933, the *number of groups* continues to shoot upward. This means that ever more papers are taken out of the hands of individual and local ownership:

Group Ownership of U.S. Dailies, 1910-71

| Year | Groups | Papers | Average |
|------|--------|--------|---------|
| 1910 | 13 | 62 | 4.7 |
| 1923 | 31 | 153 | 4.9 |
| 1930 | 55 | 311 | 5.6 |
| 1933 | 63 | 361 | 5.7 |
| 1935 | 59 | 329 | 5.6 |
| 1940 | 60 | 319 | 5.3 |
| 1945 | 76 | 368 | 4.8 |
| 1954 | 95 | 485 | 5.1 |
| 1961 | 109 | 552 | 5.1 |
| 1967 | 160 | 817 | 5.1 |
| 1968 | 159 | 828 | 5.2 |
| 1971 (1/1) | 157 | 879 | 5.7 |

*Editor & Publisher,* July 17, 1971, p. 7.

There are no less than nineteen groups owning ten dailies each, or more. And when it comes to the total circulation concentrated under a single ownership, here are the facts:

| Group | No. of Dailies | No. of Sunday Papers | Total Circulation |
|-------|---------------|---------------------|-------------------|
| Chicago Tribune Co. | 8 | 5 | 26,058,015 |
| Newhouse | 22 | 14 | 21,400,027 |
| Knight | 11 | 8 | 15,696,078 |
| Scripps-Howard | 17 | 6 | 15,394,920 |
| Hearst | 8 | 7 | 14,406,259 |

*Editor & Publisher,* Sept. 25, 1971, p. 70.

These are but the top five among the fourteen groups with a seven-day circulation of five million or more. After them in the big league come other familiar names like Times-Mirror of Los Angeles, Gannett, Ridder, Dow-Jones, Cowles, and so on down.

As if this concentration of ownership were not enough, the pressures toward monopoly, fueled by escalating costs, keep bearing down in communities in which competing papers still survive. It always seemed wasteful to me, for example, that in Hartford the locally owned *Courant* and the Gannett-owned *Times* should each maintain a complex and costly mechanical department, both of which are idle some of the time. Why two sets of mammoth, expensive presses? Why not a single, complete production facility, geared to print both papers at less cost to each?

Over the years some publishers have entered into just such arrangements. But some have gone further, to merge not only printing but circulation and advertising departments as well. This permits setting advertising and circulation rates that are mutually satisfactory. Even that is not the end of the line:

In 1933, in the midst of the Depression, the only two papers in Albuquerque, the morning *Journal* and the afternoon *Tribune,* reached a secret agreement by the terms of which both papers would be printed in the same plant, there would be one advertising department instead of two, one circulation department instead of two, one business office instead of two. All commercial expenses would be shared, and at the end of each year there would be a division of profits according to a fixed ratio regardless of the circulation or the volume of advertising carried in either paper. The arrangement worked. Within a short time both papers had become highly profitable enterprises, a fact which led to their example being followed by hitherto competing morning and afternoon papers in many other towns and cities.[7]

If both papers had been bought by the same owner, no one would have objected to so cosy an arrangement. But when two separate papers in the same town did it they were sailing close to the anti-trust wind. The Supreme Court, on March 10, 1969, ruled that just such an arrangement, one between the *Arizona Star* and the *Citizen* in Tucson, violated the Sherman Antitrust Act.

This was upsetting to the forty-four newspapers in twenty-two cities that had by this time set up one joint arrangement or another. Accordingly they went to Congress with battalions of lawyers and lobbyists, and came away, on July 28, 1970, with what is now called the Newspaper Preservation Act. It might with equal accuracy be called the Newspaper Monopoly Act, because it exempts from antitrust action not only sensible joint printing arrangements but also ostensibly competing papers that don't compete. It is splendid to help keep alive an honored newspaper name, rather than to allow one more newspaper to die. But it is something less than splendid to guarantee profits to a paper, no matter how inadequate its service to the public. This circumstance makes it likely that the courts have not yet spoken their final word on the subject.

Still another trend toward concentrated ownership of the means of public information appears in the growing cross-ownership of various kinds of media. Both NBC and CBS own once-independent book-publishing houses, as well as much else right down to CBS ownership of the Yankees. Not long ago the *Atlantic Monthly* sought to survey these interlocking ownerships. It found that while some newspaper-television-radio holdings spread across the nation, or large parts of it, there was local incest as well:

> One owner may dominate a city's media. For example, one man, Donald W. Reynolds, owns Fort Smith, Arkansas's two newspapers and its only television station. Reynolds is also an example

of one man having great impact on entire regions . . . through concentrated ownership of newspapers and/or broadcast properties in Arkansas and Oklahoma and Nevada. In Miles, Michigan, the Plym family owns the only daily newspaper, the only AM radio station, and the only FM station. There is no local television outlet. According to the information supplied by the FCC to the Senate Antitrust and Monopoly Subcommittee, as of late 1967 there were seventy-three communities where one person or company owned or controlled all of the local newspaper and broadcast outlets.[8]

Another statistic pointing in the same direction is the 1968 figure showing that 127 of 184 television stations in the fifty largest markets were owned in common with another medium of communication.[9] Individual or corporate ownership of a local monopoly, or of multiple media in scattered places, is not necessarily evil. Professional management, backed by adequate resources, may do a better job of serving the public than can a single small owner who may not be up to his financial and professional responsibilities. But the fact remains that ownership of the means through which we see and judge our world is getting to be so concentrated as to threaten the major premise on which our free press is based.

### Money's Divine Right to Edit

None of us dreams of objecting to the fact that the local publisher, or the chief executive of a broadcasting network or multimedia complex, calls the editorial tune. By common consent editorial control is a right that goes with ownership. Still, once we begin to examine this assumption it turns out to be no different from that other assumption—equally unchallenged in other days—that kings had a divine right to rule. "The right divine of kings to govern wrong," Pope once called it. We might call the journalistic version the publisher's divine right to edit wrong. Whatever we call it, it is the right of money to edit.

One can pursue the royal analogy further. Why should a self-governing people allow editorial control of anything so precious to its well being as a newspaper or TV station to be passed on from king to crown prince by inheritance? Or from one man with money to another? Is that really the best way to choose those who control our window of the world?

Kings used to arrange for themselves or their heirs judicious marriages, which might add another province or country to the realm. Today's publishing or broadcasting baron can no longer get far through matrimony, although that has been done too. But he can accomplish the same end by using dollars, or their equivalent in stock holdings. Hence the flowering of corporate marriages, either polygamous marriages to a harem of newspapers or else more heterogeneous ones, as when one man owns every medium of information in town, or in many towns.

Because the traditions of journalism are strong, and because it is to the advantage of the media king to give some service to attract the public he then delivers to advertisers, the information and entertainment the American people get from ownership's divine right to edit is better than one might expect. Still, considering the rapidly growing concentration of ownership, and society's need for ever more public information and deeper understanding, one wonders.

In 1608, when Lord Coke asserted that James I was ignoring the law of the land, the king was deeply offended. If Coke was right, why then the king was "under the law, which was treason to affirm."[10] Through the centuries since then the peoples of the western world have toppled most of their crowned heads, divine right and all, and have substituted various forms of self-government for them. Is there not some way to democratize the government of newspapers? Treason though it be to affirm it, journalism is too important to be left to the publishers.

## Democratizing Journalism

What this requires is some way of choosing those who edit the news that is neither inheritance nor purchase. One suggestion is to go public—to discard the imperialism of a privately held corporation in favor of one whose shares are freely available to all who have the price and the desire.

This suggestion is increasingly put into practice. At last count 216 weekday and Sunday newspapers, or nearly one in every eight, were publicly held through nineteen corporations. Their circulation totaled 14,527,221, or roughly 23 per cent of all daily circulation.[11] If such public ownership were to become the rule throughout the nation it would automatically democratize the divine right to edit—would it not?

There are those who argue that it does. Paul Miller, head of the Gannett newspaper-broadcasting empire that recently made the transition to public ownership, said a few years ago that local, public participation in the ownership of papers belonging to the group could benefit not only the area served, but the parent company as well:

> I used to think that publicly owned newspaper and broadcasting companies would not be able to maintain editorial independence. Over the years, I have learned and observed that this is not so.
>
> Stockholders invest in a company because they believe it will be profitable and increasingly so. Extremely rare is the newspaper with a namby-pamby editorial policy and healthy balance sheets. Readers prefer the newspaper that takes a *strong* stand on a major issue, even if they *disagree* with that stand. True independence and editorial vigor are found most often among newspapers profitable enough to do a good job, *and* to finance improvements and growth.[12]

Why not? Stockholders do invest in hope of return. The better job a paper or broadcast operation does the more it will earn, the more people will want to own shares, and the less its journalistic performance will be subject to lethargy or whim. Ergo, public ownership serves the public.

Unquestionably there is truth in this. Yet it is not the whole truth.

In the first place, as Berle and Means first showed in 1933, in their *Modern Corporation and Private Property,* stockholders have little to say about how a corporation is run. No matter how widely diffused ownership may be, the modern corporation is not democratic:

> In examining the break up of the old concept that was property and the old unity that was private enterprise, it is therefore evident that we are dealing not only with distinct but often with opposing groups, ownership on the one side, control on the other—a control which tends to move further and further away from ownership and ultimately to lie in the hands of the management itself, a management capable of perpetuating its own position. The concentration of economic power separate from ownership has, in fact, created economic empires, and has delivered these empires into the hands of a new form of absolutism, relegating "owners" to the position of those who supply the means whereby the new princes may exercise their power.[13]

Publication of the truth is journalism's reason for being. Yet publishing the truth requires spending more on newsgathering than many an owner or manager of a journalistic medium likes to divert from profit. It also requires the courage to step on important toes and to buck the prevailing winds of economic, political, or social gospel. So one comes back, again and again, to the basic fact that journalism's high mission necessarily and inevitably collides head-on with the pressure to produce ever more of the dividends that once forced off the air George Kennan's dramatic and significant testimony before the Senate Foreign Relations Committee, and put a used *I Love Lucy* on. Fred Friendly, who resigned as president of CBS News over that decision, put his finger on the heart of the issue:

> When Paley suggested that CBS's troubles may have begun when it went public, he was referring to the fact that Wall Street had discovered broadcast stocks. The tragedy was that they also discovered Nielsen and the ratings, and soon a strange formula became the determining factor of what went on the air. The stock

market watched the ratings and, in turn, their effect on advertising sales, expected earnings, the amount of news and serious
programming, and eventually the price of the stock. Thus was the
broadcast diet of the American people determined.[14]

Journalistic service to the public at times annoys advertisers, offends the powerful, leads to boycotts or circulation losses, and
otherwise lowers rather than increases profits. Therefore it is to
the credit of owners and publishers and broadcast executives that
the information about and interpretation of their world that the
American people do get is as reasonable a facsimile of the real
thing as it is. But that does not say that existing corporate ownership of the means of communication allows journalism to be as
accurate and revealing as it should be.

Indeed there is something profoundly wrong with the way we
pay for the picture of the world we get. It is not the money-men
of journalism who are wrong, so much as the system that makes
them what they are. Mr. Friendly, writing of his own experience
when it came to that showdown over money vs. reporting, said:
"Whatever bitterness I feel over my departure is toward the system
that keeps such unremitting pressure on men like Paley [chairman
of CBS] and Stanton [president of CBS] that they must react more
to financial pressure than to their own taste and sense of responsibility."[15] Keeping the Kennan testimony off the air for a single
day saved CBS and its stockholders $250,000, and its affiliated
stations perhaps as much again. The money to be made from using
daytime television to put before the nation retread serials, soap
operas, game shows, and other intellectual sawdust has been estimated at $130 million a year.[16] Granted such figures what network
executive, what publisher of a publicly owned newspaper—however
dedicated he may be to public service—can possibly put the public's
need for information ahead of his company's need for profits bigger than last year's?

The issue cuts more deeply in broadcasting than in newspapers.
With television and radio it is either/or: you put on a show that

makes money, or you put on news that largely costs money. In a newspaper, though the space available each day for news varies directly with the amount of advertising, you can print both news and advertising. Nevertheless, in newspapers, as in broadcasts, the economic pressures are the same, and inescapable. That is why I insist there is something wrong with the economic base and organizational structure that the journalism of our modern mass society has inherited from simpler days.

Because there is no way around this problem, those concerned with the future of our journalism and our government have cast about for some means of keeping journalism's eye on its job more than on its cash register. Once Eugene Meyer had resuscitated the *Washington Post,* he set up a private screening system, apparently since forgotten, to approve or reject future changes in ownership. This kind of thing does not change the rules of journalistic ownership and control, but at least it can save us from the disasters that have often followed from the purchase of newspapers by men more interested in money than in reporting. Others have taken similar actions. Nelson Poynter, owner of the *St. Petersburg Times* and other publishing properties, established a foundation, the Poynter Fund. Its purpose was to prevent the sale and possible prostitution of the paper, and to keep control in the hands of those who get out the paper:

> Mrs. Poynter and I could have cashed our chips and been rich but we thought publishing was rewarding and still do. The Poynter Fund will have no incentive to sell its publishing properties and the active staff has plenty of incentive to improve them through the profit sharing program. . . .
> There is a direct relationship between excellence and profit, if the operators look beyond immediate profit.[17]

That last is the key point: good papers pay off. But to get a good paper, and keep it good, you have to keep on spending money that in any other business would be siphoned off into dividends. And you have to keep on taking risks that might cost money.

Doing this daringly, but successfully, in a long-range program, is an intricate balancing act. To do it, the publisher must go out on financial, political, and social limbs—and that does not come naturally to those whose purpose is money.

In Canada, where worry over these things preceded our own, government itself has acted. In 1969-70 a Special Senate Committee on Mass Media surveyed a Canadian journalism whose concentration and monopoly resemble ours. The study served a purpose not unlike that of our private Hutchins Commission of 1947, and of Britain's Royal Commission on the Press of 1947-49.

The Committee noted that Canadian broadcasting was already being monitored by the Canadian Radio-Television Commission, which has authority over broadcast mergers. It was also evolving a philosophy that held concentration of ownership to be guilty unless proved innocent. Therefore it proposed a companion Press Ownership Review Board, "with powers to approve or disapprove mergers between, or acquisition of, newspapers and periodicals." Its model was a 1965 British law whose terms gave a Monopolies Commission broad powers over the ownership of British newspapers. The Canadian version was this:

> The Commission shall report whether or not the transfer may be expected to operate against the public interest, taking into account all matters which appear in the particular circumstances to be relevant and having regard (amongst other things) to the need for accurate presentation of news and free expression of opinion.[18]

The thinking behind Canada's proposal for a Press Ownership Review Board was that "Newspapers, emphatically, are not just another business." As the report explained: "What happens to the catsup or roofing tile or widget industry affects us *as consumers*. What happens to the publishing business affects us *as citizens*."

The Committee evidently felt that restraints that might keep ownership's eye on public service instead of dollars would not be enough. Accordingly it also proposed what it called a Volkswagen Press. Just as inexpensive, practical automobile imports had offered the public an alternative to Detroit's costly behemoths, so might journalism offer the public a choice as against the established press. The committee proposed formation of a government Publications Development Loan Fund, with not less than $2 million a year at its command, to subsidize an alternative press. It cited several examples of shoestring publications, in some ways like our misnamed underground press though apparently less raffish and more responsible, which already offered an antidote to the big-time monopoly publishers. Applicants could not simply have a free ride, however. First they would have to raise money and start publishing on their own, to prove their worth by surviving for a time—say, half a dozen issues for a monthly. Only then could they seek government funds to tide them over the long gap before advertisers decide that a new publication is a safe risk.

No one in this country has yet proposed steps as positive as these. But the dream of moving in the direction of some counterforce to money power over journalism has burned long, and still lives. The American Newspaper Guild, born during the Depression, was founded with the purpose of being a guild in fact. Its aim was not only to protect editorial employees from being put out in the street, unlike union-protected mechanical staffs, but also to raise the standards of journalism. It did not succeed because it had no real power, and it survives today as a largely wages-and-hours union in which editorial employees are a minority.

So we must turn elsewhere. For example to Britain, where we might suppose conditions and habits resemble our own. Britain is a borderline case. It is a strong union country, journalistically as otherwise. But the mass-circulation dailies remain as free as ours to let public service and revenue fight it out, to the inevitable advantage of revenue. The national quality dailies, the *Times* and *Guardian,* keep their sights higher by clinging to the tradition of service left over from their great days in the nineteenth century. Shortly before the press lord Roy Thomson, Lord Thomson of Fleet, bought the *Times* I inquired about this of Sir William Haley,

then editor. He answered: "The whole strength and influence of
the paper reside in the fact that the people of Britain know he
[the editor] and his staff are left completely free to use their professional judgment, both as regards the contents and the policy
of the paper." To Lord Thomson's credit be it said that he has not
yet allowed the fact that the *Times* continues to run in the red
lower the paper's standards. Alastair Hetherington, editor of the
*Guardian,* informed me in much the same spirit that when he was
made editor he was told only that he should carry on the paper in
the same spirit as before. It was a spirit typified by the professional
competence and unyielding integrity of the great C. P. Scott. This,
he added, was a happily broad directive. He was free to interpret
it as he wished. "There has been no interference from the management side," he added. But it is characteristic of the fundamental
problem of today's printed journalism that the *Guardian,* like the
*Times,* has not found the economic going what it used to be.

## The European Example

In Britain the tradition that the editor should edit still survives—
tenuously. It is across the Channel that we must look for a model
of what might be done here in the United States. While the roots of
this model go back to before World War II, notably in Scandinavia,
in a substantial sense the development came out of the monumental
suffering Europe's peoples underwent during six long years of war.

In 1949, on its two hundredth anniversary, Copenhagen's *Berlingske Tidende* issued a pamphlet declaring, among other things,
that seven principles are necessary to guarantee freedom of the
press. A crucial one is this: "In point of law the editor should be
alone responsible for the contents of the paper, and should be
vested with corresponding authority." An admirable principle,
surely. But how do you apply it in America? Here when a new
owner comes along the editor and editorial staffers along with the
rest of the hired hands simply have to conform.

A possible way out has been demonstrated in West Germany, where the remnants of Kaiser Wilhelm's empire and Hitler's twelve-year malevolence were alike buried in the *rauchendes Trümmer-haufen*—smoking heap of ruins—that Germany was in 1945. After emerging from Allied tutelage during the occupation, German journalism became an integral part of the democratic society that emerged from the rubble.

Not surprisingly, when the staff of *Stern* (*Star,* the German version of *Life*) heard that the magazine was to be sold to a new owner, they got up on their hind legs. By threatening a strike, the editorial workers extracted the right to elect a small council that has power to participate in the choice of any new editor—and even to keep an editor when the publisher wants to fire him. Moreover, to keep editorial policy headed in a progressive-liberal direction, the council also has a voice in formulating that policy.

In the early 1960, when the magazine *Der Spiegel* (*The Mirror*) got into a row with the Adenauer government over defense matters, popular support went to the magazine, rather than to the government. Here was proof that postwar West Germany was as devoted to a free press as we or the British. Indeed the incident at *Stern* is an example of what we might do in this country, if we chose.

Interestingly enough, *Der Spiegel* has also suffered—or perhaps enjoyed is the right word—an internal revolution. At this writing the newsweekly is in an interregnum, going through a transition from single ownership to 50 per cent participation by employees, which is to begin in 1973. It may be that the fact of transition accounts for disagreements among groups of employees, and for a drop in circulation from 1,000,000 to 800,000. The generous concession of 50 per cent ownership by the publisher, Rudolf Augstein, is a step in the right direction. But it hardly seems an ideal arrangement. It looks rather like an invitation to a collision between an irresistible force and an immovable object. And that can hardly be the soundest way of democratizing journalism while still leaving it governable.

It is the French who have done most toward bringing about the change that ought to be made throughout the liberal, western world. The French movement grew spontaneously out of the liberation of Paris in 1944. Its pioneers were a handful of individuals in government and journalism who had survived the war in the underground. They were determined to carry forward into the years of peace the ideals, the consciousness of human needs, that had been born of the long night of war. In particular they wanted to ensure, in France's future, some higher standard of editorial judgment than that which follows naturally from modern journalism's fantastic requirements for capital. Their principal weapon was change in the rules of ownership.

The story centers upon the Paris newspaper *le Monde*. It is a story told in a book, unfortunately not translated into English, called *La Presse, le pouvoir et l'argent*—The Press, Power, and Money.[19] The author, Jean Schwoebel, is diplomatic editor of *le Monde*, architect of its plan for employee co-ownership, and promoter of societies of editors as voices to be heard above those of the money men of journalism. "We are exporting a revolution," says Mr. Schwoebel.[20] Let us hope he is right.

Mr. Schwoebel's book makes fascinating reading. Suffice it here to put what happened into a capsule. *Le Monde* grew directly out of the wartime underground press—a genuine underground press, unlike ours. At the time of liberation *le Temps*, France's prewar prestige paper, went down in defeat with the rest of the Vichy collaborators. This left a vacuum that could be filled by a new major paper. With the help of some former *Temps* staffers who had not gone along during the Nazi occupation, the Information Minister of the new de Gaulle government of 1944 entrusted the task of establishing a new Paris daily to Hubert Beuve-Méry. He had been *le Temps* correspondent in Prague before the war, had not bent at the time of the Munich betrayal or during the oppressions of the occupation, and was above all a man "who had a high conception of the role of the press."[21]

The new *Monde* achieved its present stature because it was set up from the beginning as a paper devoted to a purpose other than money. This was possible because, having inherited the mechanical plant left by *le Temps*, the new paper required only modest capital. The new Information Minister chose the founding stockholders not for their cash but for their moral qualities. To demonstrate publicly what their purpose was, these stockholders drew up an agreement which stated that they did not expect dividends as the paper succeeded, but only 6 per cent interest on their exceedingly modest investment of 200,000 prewar francs each—$400 in 1944. Moreover—and this is a crucial point—they did not plan to leave their shares to their heirs, but rather to surviving or succeeding partners. The idea was independence, so that public-service journalism, in the spirit of idealism fired by the war, might live on.

So it was that *le Monde* took off, and soared steadily in public acceptance and influence. But time passed, and with it passed the lessons born of suffering. The keystone of the venture had been the policy that editorial authority and responsibility should be lodged in a single editor-publisher. But only seven years after the liberation of Paris and birth of *le Monde*, the changing scene brought a crisis:

Because *le Monde* continued to stress the dangers of a politics of alliances and blocs that heated up the cold war, let loose the arms race and already entailed the double consequence of leading the United States to demand the rearmament of Germany and inclusion of Spain in the Atlantic Pact, Mr. Beuve-Méry, accused of neutralism, was the target of more and more virulent attacks. The government for its part was uneasy at this independence of judgment on the part of a French newspaper that was being read abroad more and more. Soon talks began among the groups of associates [owners] opposed to Mr. Beuve-Méry, under the arbitration of a third person, Mr. Johannes Dupraz, Popular Republican Movement deputy from Indre-et-Loire, former secretary-general of the Ministry of Information, who had played an important part in the birth of *le Monde*.[22]

The merits of the dispute are hard to judge at this distance. Perhaps most of us, in those days of the height of the cold war, of the rise of McCarthyism, might have gone along with the restive owners rather than with Mr. Beuve-Méry. He seems to have been a victim of the same vicious, destructive madness that in this country ruined the careers of dedicated and able men who were falsely accused of "losing" China. But the point is not to determine who might have been right. What stands out sharp and clear is the fact that the editor, chosen for his proved competence and integrity, was independent. Such a man may be just as wrong as any right-wing money-man of a publisher. But only an editor who is independent as well as competent can be a journalistic prophet who is likely to be right, whatever the prevailing political and ideological winds may be.

As for Mr. Beuve-Méry himself, he saw the crisis as a departure from the ideals with which *le Monde* had been founded. Threatened with a committee of censors who would review articles on foreign policy before publication, he resigned.

In the past in France, as today with us, that would have been the end of it. Money and orthodoxy would have had their way. But by this time the skilled and dedicated editorial staff of *le Monde* had tasted independence. Its members were outraged at the prospect that a newspaper already great should lose its soul. They insisted that *le Monde* continue to devote itself exclusively to giving the public what was in the judgment of its editors the most objective, dispassionate, and informed view of the world it could—even though that view might not be popular in high places. According to Mr. Schwoebel the departure of Mr. Beuve-Méry, the editor-publisher who represented all this, aroused in the staff of editors "an intense emotion." He adds the significant point that the resignation seemed to readers, as well as to the majority of editors, "an intolerable attack on freedom of information."[23]

By threatening mass resignations, which would have taken the life out of what had become a prestigious enterprise, the staff suc-

ceeded in persuading the shareholders to put Mr. Beuve-Méry back
in command. What happened thereafter is complex, and there have
been changes since the revolt of 1951. *Le Monde*'s present structure
was finally established by agreement, on March 14, 1968. Key to it
is the fact that the men who put up the money share their money,
and therefore their divine right to edit, with the editors and staff.
Non-editorial employees are included, to give them too, a stake
in the paper's independence.

At first the journalists were given 28 per cent of ownership. That
enabled them to veto actions they disapproved because, under company rules, all important decisions had to be taken by a three-
quarters majority. In the end no less than three companies within
the company were established. Capital stock was set at 1000 shares,
distributed as follows:

    400 shares (40%), the editorial company
     50 shares (5%), executives' company
     40 shares (4%), employees' company
    400 shares (40%), founding shareholders and successors
    110 shares (11%), ex-officio to executives—70 shares to editor-
        publisher, 40 to general manager

This arrangement, says Mr. Schwoebel, "amply supports the
rights of authority, at the same time that it permits the journalists to
participate effectively in the responsibility of safeguarding, in the
heart of a commercial enterprise, the spirit of a genuine public
service of information."[24] Again, the key point is this: no one may
inherit shares. And the intricate structure of the several companies
within the company, dividing ownership among them, is designed
to make sure that an editor who knows what he is doing will continue to edit.

In France the system has spread, notably to such other important
journals as *Figaro* and *Ouest-France*. In fact in 1972 another of
France's modern publisher-editors, Jean-Louis Servan-Schreiber,
said that 30 of France's 85 dailies had formed journalists' associations like the editorial company of *le Monde*.[25] It is a pattern any

of us can follow, if we have the vision and spirit to see in journalism something other than a dividend factory. Perhaps in the future the French example will commend itself to American owners who fear the tax laws may no longer allow them to pass on their newspapers to their crown princes. Perhaps too when a threat to editorial integrity arises, American editorial staffs, right up to the top, will insist on some fundamental democratization of ownership.

It is noteworthy that when, by early 1972, rising costs in French journalism, reinforced by television's siphoning off what had been newspaper advertising revenue, brought hard times to French newspapers, *le Monde* was the only Paris paper to stay in the black. Democratized journalism, difficult as it may be to achieve, remains a practical way to maintain a press that is economically healthy but editorially independent, in fact as well as in name. It is a beacon, shining with hope.

## Why Not Here?

Can there be a similar fusion of the ideal and the practical in American journalism?

Though nothing much has come of it the ideal of employee ownership, ownership effective enough to give substantial editorial control, has long been talked of in the United States. There are various partial, if largely ineffective, examples about the country. But two of our better known newspapers, the *Milwaukee Journal* and the *Kansas City Star*, are largely employee-owned—the *Journal* to the tune of more than 80 per cent of the stock.

As yet the two different corporate structures involved do not seem to match the completeness, flexibility, and authority of that which now controls *le Monde*. The catch is that it takes something like an earthquake to open the way toward employee ownership. Lacking a shock like the shattering of Germany and France in World War II, this country must await a fortunate combination of circumstances that will bring to the fore owners and their successors who have an abnormally high sense of public service and journalistic integrity. Indeed it was not William Rockhill Nelson of the *Star* and Lucius Nieman of the *Journal* so much as their successors who brought about the heroic transition—men like Irwin Kirkwood, Nelson's son-in-law, and others; and Harry J. Grant of the *Journal*. They were the ones who engineered the long and complex transition. The employees themselves cannot begin the long and difficult and costly process of taking over majority ownership unless someone in a position of power (or more likely several someones) gives up a good part of this or his children's rights in the property. And that just doesn't happen often.

As things are America seems headed in quite the opposite direction, toward relentless concentration of ownership in ever fewer and larger corporations. But forget for the moment what is, and dream of what should be. It is this: that each of our 1750 dailies, and preferably all other journalistic enterprises as well, should be independent, editor-edited, and under a local ownership in which employees have a voice that cannot be ignored.

In India, a nation that is struggling to enter the twentieth century under parliamentary government, there has been proposed legislation that would give employees a 50 per cent ownership of all newspapers. Any individual's holdings in any newspaper would be limited, moreover, to 5 per cent of the whole. On top of that no newspaper could invest more than 50 per cent of its own paid-up capital in another newspaper.

This would be journalism democratized with a vengeance. But it seems doubtful that, despite India's loosely socialist aspirations, it will materialize even there. Certainly one can be sure that in the United States an explosion of indignation would greet any such proposal. It would be considered indecent, if not obscene. And yet, and yet. . . . Having in mind the national need for a journalism free from not only government but private interests as well—what's wrong with it? If we could get rid of our increasing multiple ownerships, if each community could have at least one newspaper locally owned and controlled by professionals of journalism rather than by money—perhaps on the European model—our newspapers would surely serve us better than most of them serve us now.

While dreaming, one need not indulge in nightmares over what would happen if fuzzy idealists from the editorial side were to assume control of their papers, ride their hobbies, and neglect the stark necessity for hustling income to cover costs. It has long since been standard for our newspapers to have in charge a businessman who hires an editor and tells that editor what he may say and may not say. Might it not work more nearly in the public interest if the editor were No. 1, and a businessman–general manager No. 2? It was from just such a position that Thomas McElrath kept the nationally famous Horace Greeley, with his maverick irresponsibilities, from running the *Tribune* into the red. It is significant, too, that the various European plans for ensuring editorial control of the editorial product specify exactly that pecking order of authority over editorial policy.

It is true that mob democracy cannot run a newspaper, any more than it can run anything else. Somehow, through a system of checks and balances, we have to find a middle way between today's money power in journalism and an army of privates thinking they are generals, attempting control from the bottom.

There must be a way, because the problem of democratizing journalism is inherently no different from that of democratizing government itself. Madison (or perhaps Hamilton) pinpointed the dilemma in that famous Federalist No. 51:

> If men were angels, no government would be necessary. If angels were to govern men, neither external nor internal controls on government would be necessary. In framing a government which is to be administered by men, the great difficulty lies in this: you must first enable the government to control the governed; and in the next place oblige it to control itself.[26]

Under our Constitution this difficulty is resolved through checks and balances. The framers based the Constitution on Montesquieu's principle of the separation of powers. It is pertinent that Mr. Schwoebel, philosophizing on the identical difficulty of too much authority at the top of journalism as against mob rule from the bottom, himself quotes Montesquieu:

> Let us not be afraid to go to the wellspring and pose, with Montesquieu, the problem of authority: ". . . But it is eternal experience that every man who is given power abuses it; he goes just as far as he can until he finds its limits. Who would deny this? Virtue itself has need of limits."[27]

Surely, if there were sufficient motivation, if this country could summon up again the pragmatic idealism that made it what it is, a similar solution could establish self-government in journalism without lapsing into irresponsibility or chaos. By carrying forward the model set on the Continent, and in our own few and partial attempts at employee-ownership, democratization could be extended to American journalism as a whole.

Who knows? The ideal of a democratized ownership of the press, with internal checks and balances designed to keep it headed toward public service, while yet keeping it economically viable, could also be practical. Ever more complete and informed reporting, rather than ever more dividends, would be its guiding star. Again as on *le Monde*, profits would be plowed back into higher salaries and improved mechanical efficiency, instead of being drained off into private pockets.

Such a democratically and professionally controlled press is the best we can hope for. It would, as far as possible, close the gap between today's increasingly intricate public issues and public under-information about those issues. It would take us as far toward an ideal journalism as fallible man can go, as long as he is faced with our existing journalistic technology and its increasing demand for larger and larger amounts of capital.

Perhaps we shall be able to swim upstream toward the ideal. Perhaps something will happen to us, as in different circumstances happened to the Europeans, to unite us in that response to challenge that Arnold Toynbee tells us makes the difference between a civilization that lives and one that dies. It could yet be. But if we are honest with ourselves, we have to admit that nothing like it is in sight.

## Technology to the Rescue

It looks, then, as though a public-service journalism, decentralized and democratized, might never come. Our habits of government, our conventional economic and social wisdom, do not permit us to unite in driving toward such a goal, obviously desirable though it is. So one scans the horizon, and listens for the hoofbeats of the cavalry that must be riding from somewhere to our rescue. Surprise! If one looks and listens carefully enough one discovers that rescue does promise to come, flying the banner of technological change.

Technology has given us our mass society and the troubles that plague it. Technology and its costs are also primarily responsible for making our present journalism inadequate to our need. But it may redeem itself—if we let it—by lowering journalism's production and distribution costs to the point at which the editor can once again outrank the money-maker.

Hope lies in the cable. Though cable was pioneered with no thought but that of enriching the broadcasters, it could open doors to a different future. The prospect is that these cables will be developed to the point of bringing as many as eighty two-way channels of communication into every home. After all, even the poor have television today, so why not this more elaborate gadgetry? Promise lies in the cable's capacity for making available to each of us more channels than there are commercial enterprisers to use them. Already the Canadian Senate Committee that diagnosed the defects and hopes of Canadian journalism has addressed this challenge to the Canadian people:

> Tired of the same old programmes on the tube? There's a channel on your cable system that's reserved for community programming.

That means you. So rally your bird-watchers' group, approach the cable owner, and go into show business. Communicate![28]

One has to visualize the future as one in which television, newspapers, magazines, and even books as we know them no longer exist. Instead a combination TV screen and typewriter and telephone will link us, in two-way contact, via satellites or otherwise, with every source of information in the world. What will make the difference is that multiplicity of channels of communication that does not exist now. Dr. Peter C. Goldmark, inventor of the long-playing record, a color television system, and much else, recently retired as head of the CBS laboratories. Yet he gave up retirement compensation of $75,000 a year, apparently to be in on what he sees as the coming action. He expects the use of satellites and cable together to end the scarcity of communication channels that gave us the Federal Communications Act of 1934 and the troubles we have had ever since with the use and misuse of such channels.

Much of the future is already here. A printout from tomorrow's home communications set, replacing today's newspaper, may still be two decades away. But there is already much that can be done. As one young and enthusiastic advocate put it:

The tools are right around the corner, and we know it . . . We see that the United States has been shifting for over 20 years from a materials-based economy of land, capital and labor to an information-based economy of access to information. An information-based economy is an economy of unlimited wealth. Information never decreases. It always increases with use.

After World War II, we saw industries evolving from hard, energy-generating types such as steel and automobiles to industries that make information-processing machines. IBM, Honeywell, Control Data, Xerox. New companies all around the world soon discovered that they weren't in the business of making machines but of processing information. In the '50s, the investment in hardware [the new machines] was 90 per cent, in software [what comes out of the machines] 10 per cent. Now it's 10 per cent hardware, 90 per cent software.[29]

Crucial to all this is what the Canadian Senate committee told the bird watchers, that "there's a channel on your cable system that's reserved for community programming." No longer will the publishers, the networks, and the local stations monopolize what we get— if we plan it right. In this country too the entrepreneurs of cable are sometimes required to reserve some channels for purposes other than TV programming. While there are now only one or two public channels available here and there, on an experimental basis, they seem bound to multiply. The question is, what use will we make of them? And who will have access to them? The fight of the money-men to control cable for their own profit, a fight that will be fought from the White House to Congress to the home town, is bound to be fierce. And in such a fight the devil will take the hindmost, whose name is likely to be the public interest.

If we are to keep the journalism of the future adequate to the needs of the future, it is essential that we do not repeat our fateful error of the 1920s and 1930s allowing the economics of radio, and therefore of television when it came along, to follow the line of least resistance. We gave the public airwaves, without charging rent and with little other restraint, to the money-men—each of whom, if he was reasonably competent, found that he had in his private possession a money tree that really belonged to the public.

Other advanced nations were careful first to siphon broadcasting revenue into the public pocket, as by the tax on receivers that from the beginning paid the bills of the BBC. The opposite evil, that of government monopoly, lethargy, and Nice Nellieism was eventually avoided by permitting competition from limited commercial broadcasting. But we in this country, instead of achieving some such balance half a century ago, are still struggling to find a way of getting adequate and independent funds into public broadcasting.

We must not repeat that error with cable. The way to do it is to make certain that cable, including all its ancilliary hardware, is set up not as a private possession but as a public service. There are several ways of ensuring this. In the first place network ownership of cable franchises should be prohibited. Beyond that each owner of a cable franchise can be required to reserve channels for all comers. Also, in the future at least, a franchise could be for common-carrier service only, on the model of a telephone or telegraph system. Under this arrangement there must be no power to originate programs or otherwise control content.[30] To do otherwise would be like allocating the only printing press there is to a single owner.

Under such a system the channels would be available, presumably at low cost, to all who want to use them on a first-come first-served basis. Care to get up your own group to discuss local school problems, or perhaps crime and drugs? Care to be the journalistic pioneer of tomorrow?

A multiplicity of available channels, waiting for some one to use them, promises to bring about a revolutionary change in journalism. Its effect may be to carry us, in the future, toward as free and happy a condition as our forbears enjoyed long ago. Gutenberg's printing press was in being long before printed journalism began. But the fact that his press existed made possible not only printed journalism, but a wide variety of other printed voices as well.

In the economy of the seventeenth, eighteenth, and nineteenth centuries a press was no doubt a heavy capital investment. Still, the presses were there, available to all. The printers of the day had little trouble getting their hands on one. This was quite unlike the situation now, when it takes capital beyond the reach of all but a handful of the super-rich to get a newspaper press, and all that goes with it. Before the twentieth century, all it took to start a new paper was a young man with an idea and some drive to put behind that idea. With presses and therefore the opportunity to address the public readily available, a competing free press followed automatically.

The mighty batteries of rotary presses of today, and all the hand craftsmanship plus electronic wizardy needed to feed them, are really something recent. A century and a half ago, a century ago—perhaps even only half a century ago—any journalistic hopeful could earn the right to be an editor by getting his hands on a press and starting his own paper. In doing so he challenged existing papers—something almost impossible to do now. Newcomers were able to tap readers who were neglected by existing editors, as when in 1833 the New York *Sun* and its successors of the penny press opened a new era in journalism. By neglecting the political and economic ponderosity of the six-penny mercantile press, they appealed to newly literate masses of readers who had never read a paper before. This opened a new world in American journalism, and therefore in American history.

Take any of the newspaper greats of the past—Ben Day or Bennett, Greeley or Dana, Pulitzer or Ochs. Or take even that last exemplar of the old school, Captain Joseph Patterson, who with his cousin Colonel McCormick of the *Chicago Tribune* launched the *New York Daily News* as a picture tabloid in 1919. Or take Alicia Patterson Guggenheim, who founded *Newsday* on the explosion of Long Island's suburbia as World War II came on. Each of them, together with other newcomers who did not succeed and therefore have not been heard from since, offered the public a newspaper different from that of its competitors. Those who turned out an editorial product that met a public need were the ones who triumphed. Each earned the right to say what he chose in his paper, without wearing any money-man's collar, by succeeding in the teeth of competition. It was a long century's journey away from today's monopoly town, a still longer one from the crutches of today's Newspaper Preservation Act.

Why shouldn't tomorrow's journalistic pioneers, as well as bird-watchers and PTAs and conservation groups, use the excess of available cable channels in just the same way as our journalistic predecessors used Gutenberg's presses? Here is an opportunity to make a fresh journalistic approach to the public—without first amassing $50 million.

A younger generation, largely frustrated, may now look forward to making an end run around today's big shots of print and broadcast. Cable's technical ability to decentralize and democratize the information offered the public opens this opportunity to them.

Without inquiring precisely into costs, we can accept it as basically true that today's newspapers devote only 10 to 15 per cent of what they spend on the editorial product, the news and interpretation and other services that are their reason for being. But they spend 85 to 90 per cent on getting newsprint, selling and processing advertising, printing the paper, and distributing it. In computer lingo, 90 per cent goes for hardware as against 10 per cent for software. It is this equation, not sheer evil intent, that has put businessmen at the top of the journalistic totem pole and aspiring Greeleys at the bottom. But now we can expect a reversal of values.

If we can summon up the regenerative and redemptive strength to break money's power over journalism, we shall have an alternative to what we have now. If we use them aright, cables and computers and satellites and devices yet to come will in effect duplicate Gutenberg's presses, in the sense that they will be available to all who want to use them. Thus a fresh generation of journalistic pioneers can once more try out news ideas on the public with a minimum of capital investment, and in the process see who serves the public best.

This will mean that instead of today's mass media, or more likely in addition to mass media, there will be once again an open door for any and all journalistic aspirants, brought up on a diet of TV and filmmaking, to try out their journalistic wares on the public. We must look forward to a time not far off when there may be no *New York Times*, no *Hometown Herald*, such as we now hold in our hands every day. Instead there will be riches in video fare, live or taped, in cassettes or on film, or in reading matter in the form of printouts, all beyond what most of us now dream.

These communication channels, we can be sure, will give us the same software that the metropolitan *Times* and the local *Herald*, and the networks and local stations, bring us now. There will be the latest headlines, kept up to the minute. There will be news, interpretation, background, and analysis and opinion, available at the touch of a button. Not only that, we will have access to the world's libraries too. And it will be up to each of us, as readers-viewers-listeners-consumers, to decide whether we want information in the form of talking pictures, or on a piece of paper we can ponder and come back to and store up if we wish, just as we do now with papers, magazines, and books.

Tabloid newspapers and Neilson ratings reveal what most of mankind wants when money is set to tapping the lowest common denominator. But an infinite treasure of specialized programs and services, not now offered because the cost is out of proportion to the price we are willing to pay, will be available too. And what is most encouraging is that, because of the anticipated low cost of distribution, whatever revenue comes in will be expendable chiefly on the editorial product, rather than on keeping today's expensive journalistic hardware in the style to which it has accustomed the money-men of journalism.

It may even be possible, for the first time since Homer was journalist to the Greeks, that man will be willing to pay the full cost of the information and understanding the needs. The low cost of getting news to the consumer through the future's empty channels might make it unnecessary to have the advertiser and his pitchmen pay for our news and entertainment, with all the sleazy and debilitating results that follow.

Throughout history, man has had to know his world. Journalism in one form or another, primitive or sophisticated, adequate or not, has been his means of knowing it. Thus journalism serves man's unchanging need even though, like the society out of which it springs, it must itself keep changing.

If society is to hold together against the forces its own technical prowess has let loose, if government by consent of the governed is to survive no matter how baffling the challenges it must surmount, then each day's journalism must match the need of that day. Our demands upon our system of communication are already great. They will be greater. But if this country still has what it takes to reach the heights, the future is wide open.

# Notes

## CHAPTER 1

1. *New York Times,* Sept. 28, 1964, p. 1.
2. Letter to John Norvell, June 11, 1807, *The Writings of Thomas Jefferson,* Library Edition, Washington, D.C.: Thomas Jefferson Memorial Association, 1904, Vol. XI, pp. 224-25.
3. Edwin Emery, ed., *The Story of America as Reported by Its Newspapers, 1690-1965,* New York: Simon and Schuster, 1965, p. 152 (facsimile).
4. John Reed, *Ten Days That Shook the World,* New York: Boni and Liveright, 1919, International Publishers Co., Inc., 1967, pp. 74, 95, 97, 99-100, 106.
5. *New York Times,* June 29, 1914, p. 1.
6. Sir Alfred Zimmern, *The Greek Commonwealth,* New York: Random House, Modern Library, p. 200.
7. Louis L. Snyder and Richard B. Morris, eds., *A Treasury of Great Reporting,* New York: Simon and Schuster, 1949, p. xxxv.
8. Ibid. p. 3.

## CHAPTER 2

1. *New York Times,* March 22, 1967.
2. *New York Times,* May 19, 1972, pp. 9, 17; May 20, 1972, p. 8.
3. UPI Reporter, May 18, 1972, p. 1.
4. *New York Times,* May 20, 1972, p. 20.
5. Gaillard Hunt, ed., *The Writings of James Madison,* New York and London: G. P. Putnam's Sons, 1910, Vol. ix, p. 103.

6. *New York Times,* Nov. 14, 1967.
7. Rebecca Gross to Herbert Brucker, personal communication, 1968.
8. Speech before Omaha Press Club, Oct. 24, 1969, quoted in *U.P.I. Reporter,* Nov. 27, 1969, p. 1.
9. *Wall Street Journal,* Sept. 24, 1970, p. 1.
10. Quoted in *Wall Street Journal,* Nov. 16, 1967, p. 16.
11. Louis D. Brandeis and Samuel B. Warren, "The Right to Privacy," *Harvard Law Review,* Vol. IV (Dec. 15, 1890), No. 5, pp. 193ff.
12. Ibid.
13. Lord Dunsany, "Fame and the Poet," *Atlantic Monthly,* Aug. 1919, pp. 175-84.
14. James Russell Wiggins, *Freedom or Secrecy,* New York: Oxford University Press, 1964, pp. 7-80.
15. See Herbert Brucker, *Freedom of Information,* New York: Macmillan, 1949, Chap. 9, "Managed News."
16. See Kent Cooper, *Barriers Down,* New York: Farrar and Rinehart, 1942.
17. "Problems of Journalism," *Proceedings* of the 1949 Convention of the American Society of Newspaper Editors, p. 35.
18. Harold L. Cross, *The People's Right To Know,* New York: Columbia University Press, 1953, Chap. XV.
19. Robert O. Blanchard, "The Freedom of Information Act—Disappointment and Hope," *Columbia Journalism Review,* Fall 1967, pp. 16ff.
20. Ramsey Clark, quoted in the *Report of the 1967 Sigma Delta Chi Advancement of Freedom of Information Committee,* Sigma Delta Chi, Chicago, 1967, p. 5.
21. Quoted in Albert G. Pickerell and Edward L. Feder, *Open Public Meetings of Legislative Bodies—California's Brown Act,* Bureau of Public Administration, University of California, Berkeley, 1957, p. 8.
22. Arthur Sylvester, "The Government Has the Right To Lie," *Saturday Evening Post,* Nov. 18, 1967, p. 10.
23. *San Francisco Chronicle,* Dec. 9, 1967.
24. J. Wes Gallagher, "Perspective Reporting Versus Credibility, Gullibility, and Humbugability," 18th Annual William Allen White Lecture, University of Kansas, Feb. 10, 1967.
25. Quoted in *U.P.I. Reporter,* Nov. 9, 1967, p. 1.
26. *New York Times,* Oct. 29, 1967, Sect. 1, p. 57.
27. Ibid.
28. See Victor Bernstein and Jesse Gordon, "The Press and the Bay of Pigs," *Columbia Journalism Review,* Fall 1967, pp. 5-13. See also Clifton Daniel, speech reported in *New York Times,* June 2, 1966, p. 14.
29. Arthur M. Schlesinger, Jr., *A Thousand Days,* New York: Houghton Mifflin, 1965, p. 261.
30. Ibid.

31. Daniel, speech reported in *New York Times, op. cit.*

32. Theodore C. Sorensen, quoted in *New York Times,* Feb. 27, 1966.

33. Arthur Schlesinger, Jr., ibid.

34. Cited by Walter Lippmann, *Public Opinion,* New York: Macmillan, 1929, p. 82.

35. *Wall Street Journal,* July 25, 1967, p. 1.

36. Ibid.

37. Ibid.

38. Ibid.

39. Robert H. Yoakum, "The Dodd Case: Those Who Blinked," *Columbia Journalism Review,* Spring 1967, p. 13; Yoakum, "The Dodd Case," *Columbia Journalism Review,* Summer 1967, p. 51.

40. Yoakum, "The Dodd Case," *loc. cit.*

41. Yoakum, Letter to the Editor, *Publisher's Auxiliary,* Dec. 16, 1967.

42. Jenkin Lloyd Jones, "Problems of Journalism," *Proceedings* of the 1948 Convention, American Society of Newspaper Editors, p. 72.

## CHAPTER 3

1. Stephen Leacock, *Harper's Magazine,* June 1922, pp. 9ff.

2. Reprinted in Snyder and Morris, eds., *Treasury of Great Reporting, op. cit.,* pp. 95ff.

3. *The History of the Times,* Vol. II, *The Tradition Established, 1841-1884,* London: The Times, 1939, Chap. IX.

4. Reprinted in *The Connecticut Courant,* No. 541, May 8, 1775, p. 2.

5. Reprinted in J. Eugene Smith, *One Hundred Years of Hartford's Courant,* New Haven: Yale University Press, 1949, p. 77.

6. Reprinted in Frank Luther Mott and Ralph D. Casey, eds., *Interpretations of Journalism,* New York: F. S. Crofts & Co., 1937, pp. 113-14.

7. *ANPA Newspaper Information Service Newsletter,* Vol. VI (March 29, 1966), No. 3, p. 3.

8. Cooper, *Barriers Down, op. cit.,* p. 18.

9. Herbert Brucker, *The Changing American Newspaper,* New York: Columbia University Press, 1937, p. 11.

10. *From Wall Street to Main Street. The First Seventy-five Years,* New York: *Wall Street Journal,* 1964, p. 33.

11. Ibid. p. 57.

12. Warren H. Phillips, "How the Journal's Fully-Textured News Stories Get That Way," *ASNE Bulletin,* No. 512, Oct. 1967, p. 4.

13. Copy of *Denver Post* memorandum in author's possession.

14. Elmer Davis, *But We Were Born Free,* The Bobbs-Merrill Co., 1934, 175.

15. Eric Sevareid, "Politics and the Press," *Nieman Reports,* Vol. XXI (June 1967), No. 2, p. 21.

16. Letter to author, May 1968.
17. *The New Yorker,* Oct. 21, 1967, p. 173ff.
18. Ibid. p. 174.
19. Gay Talese, *The Kingdom and the Power,* New York and Cleveland: World Publishing Co., 1969, p. 6.
20. See Brucker, *Freedom of Information, op. cit.,* Chap. II; see also Douglas Cater, *The Fourth Branch of Government,* Boston: Houghton Mifflin, Riverside Press, 1959.
21. Kingman Brewster, speech to American Association for the Advancement of Science, in Wall Street Journal, Jan. 19, 1970, p. 12.
22. Bill Moyers, *Bulletin* of the American Society of Newspaper Editors, June 1968, p. 3.
23. Ralph McGill, quoted in Nieman Reports, Dec. 1968, p. 34.
24. Cecil King, "Problems of Journalism," *Proceedings* of the 1967 Convention, American Society of Newspaper Editors, p. 162.
25. Kenneth Stewart, *News Is What We Make It,* Boston: Houghton Mifflin, 1943, pp. 317-18.
26. Ibid. p. 316.
27. Nicholas von Hoffman, "The Four-Ws Approach—So, Who Needs It?," *ASNE Bulletin,* No. 535, Nov. 1969, p. 13.
28. Ibid.
29. Jann Wenner, "Rolling Past the Underground Press," *Bulletin* of the American Society of Newspaper Editors, Sept. 1971, p. 8.
30. W. Stewart Pinkerton Jr., "The 'New Journalism' Is Sometimes Less Than Meets the Eye," *Wall Street Journal,* Aug. 13, 1971, p. 1.
31. Brucker, *Freedom of Information,* op. cit., Chap. XVIII.
32. Leon Trotsky, The History of the Russian Revolution, tr. by Max Eastman, University of Michigan Press, Ann Arbor, copyright 1932 by Simon & Schuster, p. xxi.
33. Eric Hoffer, *The True Believer,* New York: Harper & Brothers, 1951.
34. Sylvan Meyer, "Only One Truth," *Nieman Reports,* March 1970, p. 5.
35. Walter Lippmann, quoted in *Columbia Journalism Review,* Summer 1968, p. 29.
36. Elmer Davis, But We Were Born Free, The Bobbs-Merrill Co., 1934, p. 177.
37. *San Francisco Chronicle,* Aug. 2, 1968, p. 1.

## CHAPTER 4

1. Hal Bruno, "After Chicago," *The Quill,* Dec. 1968, pp. 9-10.
2. *Editor & Publisher,* Dec. 7, 1968, p. 9.
3. Ibid.
4. Walker report, from *Louisville Times,* Dec. 2, 1968, p. A 15.

5. Ibid.
6. Felix McKnight, *ASNE Bulletin,* Jan. 1968, p. 3.
7. Jenkin Lloyd Jones, quoted in *Editor & Publisher,* Nov. 22, 1969, p. 64.
8. *Science,* Vol. 159 (March 15, 1968), No. 3820.
9. Charles McDowell, Jr., "Carnival of Excess: TV at the Conventions," *The Atlantic,* Vol. 222 (July 1968), No. 1, p. 40.
10. *Report of the Warren Commission on the Assassination of President Kennedy,* New York: Bantam Books, 1964, p. 224.
11. Ibid. p. 47.
12. Jerry Landauer, "Does the Press Inspire Assassins?" *Wall Street Journal,* July 18, 1968, p. 10.
13. Quoted in *New York Times Book Review,* Nov. 15, 1970, p. 8.
14. *New York Times,* May 22, 1972, p. 1.
15. Landauer, *Wall Street Journal, loc. cit.*
16. Seymour M. Hersh, "My Lai 4: A Report on the Massacre and Its Aftermath," *Harper's Magazine,* Vol. 240 (May 1970), No. 1440, pp. 77-84.
17. *U.P.I. Reporter,* May 28, 1970, p. 1.
18. Ibid. pp. 2-3.
19. William L. Rivers, "Jim Crow Journalism," *Stanford Today,* Autumn 1967, p. 17.
20. *Wall Street Journal,* March 1, 1968, p. 1.
21. Mass Media and Violence, A Report to the National Commission on the Causes and Prevention of Violence, U.S. Government Printing Office, 1969, p. 152.
22. Report of the National Advisory Commission on Civil Disorders, Otto Kerner, chairman, U.S. Government Printing Office, 1968, p. 202.
23. Nathan Glazer, "The Ghetto Crisis," *Encounter,* Nov. 1967, p. 15.
24. *Kerner Report, op. cit.,* p. 203.
25. *Stanford Observer,* May 1970, p. 4.
26. Otto N. Larsen, "Problems of Journalism," *Proceedings* of the 1969 Convention, American Society of Newspaper Editors, p. 115.
27. *Kerner Report, op. cit.,* p. 201.
28. Rivers, *op. cit.,* p. 16.
29. *Kerner Report, op. cit.,* p. 202.
30. Ibid. p. 206.
31. Ibid. p. 208.
32. Ibid. p. 205.
33. *AP Log,* March 24-30, 1968.
34. *Kerner Report, op. cit.,* p. 210.
35. Ibid.
36. Ibid. p. 203.
37. Ibid. p. 212.
38. Rivers, *op. cit.,* p. 13.
39. *Kerner Report, op. cit.,* p. 211.

## CHAPTER 5

1. *New York Times,* Aug. 4, 1970, p. 16.
2. Ibid.
3. *New York Times,* Aug. 5, 1970, p. 1.
4. *New York Times,* Aug. 6, 1970, p. 34.
5. Quoted in *Editor & Publisher,* Dec. 21, 1968, p. 14.
6. George Waller, *Kidnap,* New York: The Dial Press, 1961, pp. 252-53.
7. Charles A. Lindbergh, *The Wartime Journals of Charles A. Lindbergh,* New York: Harcourt Brace Jovanovich, 1970, p. 187.
8. Waller, *op. cit.,* p. 516.
9. American Bar Association, Annual Report, 1937, p. 861.
10. Louis B. Seltzer, *The Years Were Good,* Cleveland and New York; World Publishing Co., 1956, pp. 270-72.
11. U.S. Supreme Court, No. 490, October Term, 1965. June 6, 1966.
12. Cited, ibid., p. 17, as Patterson v. Colorado, 205 U.S. 454, 462 (1907).
13. U.S. Supreme Court, No. 490, October Term, 1965. June 6, 1966, p. 16.
14. Ibid. p. 27.
15. *New York Times,* March 27, 1965, p. 11.
16. *Editor & Publisher,* Dec. 2, 1967, p. 9.
17. *Report of the Warren Commission, op. cit.,* p. 224; *New York Times/* Bantam Books, 1964, p. 224.
18. Ibid. pp. 221-22.
19. "Problems of Journalism," *Proceedings* of the 1965 Convention, American Society of Newspaper Editors, pp. 226-27.
20. Alfred Friendly and Ronald L. Goldfarb, *Crime and Publicity,* New York: Twentieth Century Fund, 1967, pp. 315-25.
21. *The Rights of Fair Trial and Free Press,* Chicago: American Bar Association, 1969, pp. 1-6.
22. *Freedom of the Press and Fair Trial,* New York and London: Columbia University Press, 1967, p. 1.
23. The Rights of Fair Trial and Free Press, *op. cit.,* p. 28.
24. Quoted in a speech by William B. Dickinson, then managing editor, *Philadelphia Bulletin,* April 22, 1968.
25. For full text see Oxnard (Calif.) *Press-Courier,* April 25, 1968, pp. 8-9.
26. Jeremy Bentham, *Rationale of Judicial Evidence,* 5 Vols., London: Hunt and Clarke, 1827, Vol. I, pp. 522-24.
27. Friendly and Goldfarb, *op. cit.,* p. 346.
28. *Editor & Publisher,* Sept. 16, 1968.
29. Friendly and Goldfarb, p. 385.
30. *Editor & Publisher,* April 29, 1967, p. 9.
31. Walter Wilcox, *The Press, the Jury, and the Behavioral Sciences,* Austin, Texas: Association for Education in Journalism, Oct. 1968, Journalism Monographs No. 9, Foreword.

32. Ibid. p. 53.

33. Friendly and Goldfarb, *op. cit.,* p. 254.

34. Editor & Publisher, April 1, 1972, p. 11.

35. Problems of Journalism, Proceedings of the 1970 Convention, American Society of Newspaper Editors, 1970, p. 21.

36. Ibid. pp. 231-2.

37. Pamphlet, *Joint Declaration Regarding News Coverage of Criminal Proceedings in California,* adopted by representatives of state bar and media Feb. 15, 1970, p. 3.

38. Fichenberg, "Problems of Journalism," *op. cit.,* p. 23.

39. Wendell Phillipi, Problems of Journalism, Proceedings of the 1972 Convention, American Society of Newspaper Editors, 1972, p. 223.

40. Problems of Journalism, Proceedings, Sixteenth Annual Convention, American Society of Newspaper Editors, 1938, p. 29.

41. *Code of Professional Responsibility and Canons of Judicial Ethics,* American Bar Association, 1969, p. 48.

42. Don Hyndman, Executive Assistant to the President, American Bar Association, letter to author, Jan. 13, 1971.

43. Lewis Carroll, Alice's Adventures in Wonderland, Boston, Lee and Shepard, 1969, pp. 166-7 and 187.

44. *Rights of Fair Trial and Free Press, op. cit.,* p. 19.

45. Original reproduced in Herbert Brucker, *Journalist: Eyewitness to History,* Macmillan, 1962, pp. 177-8.

46. U.S. Supreme Court, No. 2560, October Term, 1964, June 7, 1965, p. 3.

47. Ibid. p. 15.

48. Ibid. p. 18.

49. Ibid. Warren, p. 34.

50. Ibid. Brennan.

51. Ibid. Stewart, p. 1.

52. Ibid. p. 14.

53. Ibid. Warren, p. 19.

54. Report to the House of Delegates, *op. cit.,* p. 12.

55. *Saturday Review,* April 4, 1970, p. 40.

56. *New York Times,* Nov. 26, 1971, p. 24.

## CHAPTER 6

1. *William Lloyd Garrison 1805-1879. The Story of His Life Told by His Children,* New York: Century Co., 1885, Vol. I, p. 225.

2. Jerome A. Barron, "Access to the Press—a New First Amendment Right," *Harvard Law Review,* Vol. 80, No. 8, June 1967, p. 1641.

3. The Commission on Freedom of the Press, *A Free and Responsible Press,* Chicago, University of Chicago Press, 1947, p. 129.

4. *Mass Media and Violence,* Staff Report to the National Commission on

the Causes and Prevention of Violence, Washington, D.C.: Government Printing Office, 1969, Vol. XI, p. 68.

5. Cited in *Editor & Publisher,* Dec. 16, 1967, p. 60.

6. Barron, *op. cit.,* p. 1647.

7. Hazel Henderson, "Access to the Media," *Columbia Journalism Review,* Spring 1969, p. 6.

8. Malcolm Muggeridge, "Problems of Journalism," *Proceedings* of the American Society of Newspaper Editors, 1971, p. 179.

9. Barron, *op. cit.,* p. 1656.

10. *Editor & Publisher,* Dec. 6, 1969, p. 68.

11. Ibid.

12. E.g. see *Editor & Publisher,* Feb. 27, 1971, p. 11, and March 6, 1971, p. 13; *New York Times,* June 8, 1971, p. 1.

13. Joe McGinnis, *The Selling of the President 1968,* New York: Trident Press, 1969.

14. *New York Times,* Oct. 14, 1970, p. 95.

15. Robert Sherrill, "The Happy Ending (Maybe) of 'The Selling of the Pentagon,'" *New York Times Magazine,* May 16, 1971, p. 94.

16. *New York Times,* Oct. 13, 1970, pp. 1 and 41.

17. Ibid.

18. *New York Times,* Aug. 5, 1970, p. 10.

19. *Editor & Publisher,* June 14, 1969, p. 15.

20. *New York Times,* March 28, 1972, p. 87.

21. *Wall Street Journal,* April 28, 1971, pp. 1 and 29.

22. John Hohenberg, *Free Press/Free People: The Best Cause,* New York: Columbia University Press, 1971, p. 494.

23. Barron, *op. cit.,* pp. 1667ff.

24. Ibid. p. 1673.

25. Ibid. p. 1677.

26. Robert M. White, "Problems of Journalism," *Proceedings* of the American Society of Newspaper Editors, 1970, p. 244.

27. J. Edward Murray, *The Editor's Right To Decide,* Tucson: University of Arizona Press, 1969, pp. 13-14.

28. *Editor & Publisher,* Aug. 22, 1970, p. 11.

29. "Problems of Journalism," 1970, *op. cit.,* p. 245.

30. American Newspaper Publishers Association General Bulletin, No. 14, March 17, 1971, pp. 77-79.

31. *New York Times,* Aug. 17, 1971, p. 1.

32. *Washington Post,* April 21, 1972, p. A2.

33. *Editor & Publisher,* March 25, 1972, p. 26.

34. Gilbert Cranberg, "Is 'Right of Access' Coming?," *Saturday Review,* Aug. 8, 1970, p. 49.

35. Ben H. Bagdikian, "Right of Access: A Modest Proposal," *Columbia Journalism Review,* Spring 1969, p. 12.

36. Herbert Brucker, *Freedom of Information,* New York: Macmillan, 1949, chap. 18.

## CHAPTER 7

1. *Mass Media and Violence,* Vol. XI, U.S. Government Printing Office, 1969, p. 151.
2. John Adams to James Lloyd, Feb. 11, 1815, quoted on title page of "A Free and Responsible Press," by the Commission on Freedom of the Press, University of Chicago Press, 1947.
3. *Nieman Reports,* Dec. 1969, p. 2.
4. Phillip H. Levy, *The Press Council,* London: Macmillan; New York: St. Martin's Press, 1967, p. 10.
5. *Editor & Publisher,* May 13, 1972, p. 26.
6. *ASNE Bulletin,* Nov. 1969, p. 19.
7. *ASNE Bulletin,* July-Aug. 1970, p. 13.
8. Royal Commission on the Press, 1947-49, Report Presented to Parliament, London: H. M. Stationery Office, 1949, pp. 164-65.
9. *ASNE Bulletin,* Nov. 1969, p. 14.
10. *Editor & Publisher,* Dec. 20, 1969, p. 13.
11. *Editor & Publisher,* April 29, 1972, p. 50b.
12. Gilbert Seldes, *The New Mass Media: Challenge to a Free Society,* Washington, D.C.: Public Affairs Press, 1957, p. 99.
13. Commission on Freedom of the Press, *A Free and Responsible Press,* Chicago: University of Chicago Press, 1957, pp. 74-75.
14. "Problems of Journalism," *Proceedings,* Twenty-fifth Anniversary Convention, American Society of Newspaper Editors, 1947, pp. 231-32.
15. *Editor & Publisher,* April 22, 1959, p. 109.
16. ANPA General Bulletin, No. 11, March 19, 1970, p. 53.
17. *Mass Media and Violence, op. cit.,* pp. 586-88.
18. Levy, *op. cit.,* p. 473.
19. J. Edward Gerald, "The British Press Council," *Journalism Quarterly,* Vol. 36, No. 3, Summer 1959.
20. "Guilty or Not Guilty—Britain's Press Council at Work," *IPI Report,* Aug. 1970, p. 10.
21. *ASNE Bulletin,* Nov. 1969, p. 14.
22. *Editor & Publisher,* Jan. 17, 1970, p. 10.
23. *Time,* July 6, 1970, pp. 44-45.

## CHAPTER 8

1. Elisabeth Noelle-Neumann, "Mass Communication Media and Public Opinion," *Journalism Quarterly,* Fall 1959, p. 402.
2. Julian Goodman, speech before the Rocky Mountain Association of Broadcasters, Jackson Hole, Wyoming, June 23, 1970.

3. Harold A. Innis, *The Bias of Communication,* Toronto: University of Toronto Press, 1951; reprinted 1964, pp. 3-4, 7, 31, 34.
4. Marshall McLuhan, *Understanding Media,* New York: McGraw-Hill, 1964, esp. chap. 1.
5. Marshall McLuhan, *The Medium Is the Massage,* New York: Bantam Books, 1968, unpaged.
6. Charles L. Bennett, Commencement Address, Oklahoma State University, Aug. 1, 1969. Excerpted in *The Quill,* Nov. 1969, p. 4.
7. *San Francisco Chronicle,* March 6, 1969, p. 14.
8. *Wall Street Journal,* May 15, 1970, p. 12.
9. Aristotle, *Politics,* Jowett Transl., Book VII, chap. 4, Oxford: Oxford University Press, Vol. I, p. 215.
10. Alfred Zimmern, *The Greek Commonwealth,* New York: Random House, Modern Library, pp. 174, 429.
11. Thomas Carlyle, *On Heroes, Hero-worship, and the Heroic, in History,* 1889 edition, London: Chapman & Hall, 1889, p. 134.
12. José Ortega y Gasset, *The Revolt of the Masses,* New York: W. W. Norton, 1932, p. 83.
13. McLuhan, *The Medium Is the Massage,* cited.
14. Ibid.
15. David Brinkley, "Problems of Journalism," *Proceedings,* American Society of Newspaper Editors, 1965, p. 43.
16. *ANPA News Research Bulletin,* No. 16, Nov. 24, 1971, p. 103.
17. Ibid. p. 114.
18. *A Ten-year View of Public Attitudes Toward Television and Other Mass Media,* 1958-68, New York: Television Information Office, 1969, pp. 8-10.
19. Thomas Whiteside, "Corridor of Mirrors," *Columbia Journalism Review,* Winter 1968/69, pp. 35ff.
20. Alexis de Tocqueville, *Democracy in America,* New York: Knopf, 1956, Vol. II, p. 111.
21. *New York Times,* Oct. 21, 1971, p. 93.

## CHAPTER 9

1. John Martin, "Problems of Journalism," *Proceedings,* American Society of Newspaper Editors, 1937, pp. 73-75.
2. Herbert Brucker, A Report for the Radio Committee of Columbia University, on Radio and Mass Communication, Oct. 31, 1939, typed copy, pp. 74-5.
3. Ben H. Bagdikian, *The Information Machines: Their Impact on Men and the Media,* New York: Harper & Row, 1971, p. 281.
4. *Newsweek,* June 1966, p. 66.
5. Thomas Billing, controller of Copley Newspapers, speech before the California Editors' Conference, Stanford University, June 1966.

6. *Editor & Publisher,* Sept. 18, 1971, p. 17.
7. *New York Times,* Nov. 9, 1970, p. 49.
8. *Saturday Review,* Nov. 11, 1967, p. 87.
9. Bagdikian, Information Machines, p. 219.
10. E. M. Forster, *Collected Tales,* New York: Knopf, 1947, pp. 144, 153.
11. John Diebold, "Problems of Journalism," *Proceedings,* American Society of Newspaper Editors, 1963, p. 142.
12. Daniel J. Boorstin, *The Image: A Guide to Pseudo-events in America,* Harper Colophon Books, 1971, p. 13.
13. Edwin B. Parker, speech before symposium, "Mass Media and the Educational Scene," Chico State College, Chico, Calif., March 9, 1968, p. 5.
14. Seldes, *New Mass Media, op. cit.,* p. 13.
15. *New York Times,* March 27, 1969, p. 24.
16. James Ford Rhodes, *Historical Essays,* New York, 1909, p. 90. Cited in Frank Luther Mott, *American Journalism,* rev. ed., New York: Macmillan, 1950, pp. 271-72.
17. *New York Times,* June 24, 1971, p. 35.
18. Christopher Driver, *Encounter,* Nov. 1967, p. 91.
19. *UPI Reporter,* March 13, 1969, p. 4.
20. See Stuart P. Sucherman, "Cable TV: The Endangered Revolution," *Columbia Journalism Review,* May-June 1971, pp. 13ff.
21. *New York Times,* July 1, 1971, p. 95.
22. Erik Barnouw, *The Golden Web,* New York: Oxford, pp. 22ff.
23. See, e.g., "Forum vs. WPIX: FCC's Power Tested," *New York Times,* July 13, 1971, p. 67.
24. Wilbur Schramm, *Responsibility in Mass Communication,* New York: Harper & Bros., 1957, p. 118.
25. *New York Times,* June 25, 1971, p. 71.
26. *New York Times,* June 17, 1971, p. 83.
27. Walter Lippmann, *Public Opinion,* New York: Macmillan, 1929 ed., p. 322.
28. Fred Friendly, *Due to Circumstances Beyond Our Control,* New York: Vintage Books, 1968, p. 252.
29. Norbert Wiener, *The Human Use of Human Beings: Cybernetics and Society,* Boston: Houghton Mifflin, 1950, p. 125.
30. *New York Times,* March 8, 1971, p. 67.
31. Bagdikian, Information Machines, p. 283.

## CHAPTER 10

1. *Milwaukee Journal,* April 27, 1969, Part I, p. 18.
2. *Editor & Publisher,* April 25, 1970, p. 38.
3. Barry Bingham Jr., letter to author, July 2, 1971.
4. C. A. McKnight, letter to author, June 18, 1971.
5. George H. Hall, letter to author, June 24, 1971.

6. Bingham, cited.
7. Thomas Gerber, letter to author, June 16, 1971.
8. Robert W. Lucas, letter to author, June 22, 1971.
9. *The Quill,* Feb. 1965, p. 30.
10. National Conference of Editorial Writers, *Masthead,* Fall 1971, pp. 2, 4, 10.
11. National Conference of Editorial Writers, Basic statement of principles, adopted in New York, N.Y., Oct. 22, 1949.
12. *Editor & Publisher,* Jan. 25, 1969.
13. National Conference of Editorial Writers, *Masthead,* Fall 1971, p. 6.
14. Laurence J. Paul, *The Masthead,* Spring 1972, p. 1.
15. Loren Ghiglione, letter to author, June 18, 1971.
16. Gerber, cited.
17. *Masthead,* Spring 1971, p. 8.
18. Sig Gissler, "The Anatomy of an Editorial," Milwaukee Journal, April 27, 1969, Part I, p. 18.
19. Ralph Nicholson, "Problems of Journalism," *Proceedings,* Twenty-fifth Anniversary Convention, American Society of Newspaper Editors, 1947, pp. 132-33.
20. Jenkin Lloyd Jones, ibid. p. 135.
21. *UPI Reporter,* July 29, 1971, p. 1.
22. *Editor & Publisher,* July 11, 1970, p. 14.
23. Tacitus, *Histories,* Book I, Section I, Paragraph I.
24. Brucker, *Freedom of Information,* pp. 278-79.

## CHAPTER 11

1. Herbert Tingsten, "The Editor and Publisher, a Many-Sided Relationship," Zürich, International Press Institute, 1957, p. 12.
2. Ibid. p. 13.
3. Henry Luther Stoddard, *Horace Greeley, Printer, Editor, Crusader,* New York, G. P. Putnam's Sons, 1946, p. 66.
4. *ANPA General Bulletin,* No. 50, Oct. 17, 1968, pp. 391-92 (italics added).
5. *Editor & Publisher,* Aug. 24, 1968.
6. *ASNE Bulletin,* Nov./Dec. 1970, pp. 13-14.
7. E.g. *New York Times,* Nov. 7, 1971, Sec. I, p. 68.
8. Turner Catledge, *My Life and The Times,* New York: Harper & Row, 1971, pp. 188-89.
9. Gay Talese, *The Kingdom and the Power,* Cleveland and New York: World Publishing Co., 1969, p. 75.
10. *New York Times,* May 12, 1969, p. 43.
11. *New York Times,* July 13, 1971, p. 33.
12. *New York Times,* Nov. 17, 1971, p. 53.

13. Letter to the author, Dec. 14, 1971.
14. *Editor & Publisher,* April 17, 1971, p. 78.
15. Quoted in *Editor & Publisher,* Oct. 10, 1970, p. 56.
16. Quoted in *IPI Report,* March 1970, p. 4.
17. Ibid.
18. *ASNE Bulletin,* Jan. 1970, p. 16.
19. *Columbia Journalism Review,* Summer 1970, p. 13.
20. *IPI Report,* March 1970, p. 3.
21. *Columbia Journalism Review,* ibid. p. 18.
22. "Problems of Journalism," *Proceedings,* American Society of News-paper Editors, 1970, pp. 186-87.

## CHAPTER 12

1. *Columbia Journalism Review,* Summer 1970, pp. 8-9.
2. Jean Schwoebel, *La Press, le pouvoir et l'argent,* Paris: Editions du Seuil, 1968, p. 268.
3. *Saturday Review,* Nov. 13, 1971, p. 85.
4. *IPI Bulletin,* July-Aug. 1968, p. 2.
5. *Wall Street Journal,* Feb. 18, 1970, p. 38.
6. *Editor & Publisher,* July 17, 1971, p. 32.
7. Walter B. Kerr, "S. 1312 and All That," *Saturday Review,* May 10, 1969, p. 77.
8. "The American Media Barons, a Modest Atlantic Atlas," *Atlantic Monthly,* July 1969, p. 83.
9. *On the Cable,* Report of the Sloan Commission on Cable Communications, New York, McGraw-Hill, 1971, p. 137.
10. Erwin H. Griswold, *The Fifth Amendment Today,* Cambridge, Harvard University Press, 1955, p. 33.
11. *Editor & Publisher,* April 22, 1972, p. 20.
12. Paul Miller, speech at Journalism Week Dinner, University of Missouri, May 4, 1967.
13. Adolf A. Berle, Jr., and Gardiner C. Means, *The Modern Corporation and Private Property,* New York: Macmillan, 1933, p. 124.
14. Friendly, *Due to Circumstances Beyond Our Control,* pp. 269-70.
15. Ibid. p. 265.
16. Ibid. p. 263.
17. *Editor & Publisher,* Feb. 15, 1969.
18. "The Uncertain Mirror," *Report of the Special Senate Committee on Mass Media,* Information Canada, Ottawa, Vol. I, 1970, pp. 71ff.
19. Schwoebel, *op. cit.*
20. *Wall Street Journal,* Feb. 17, 1970, p. 1.
21. Schwoebel, *op. cit.,* p. 92.
22. Ibid. p. 95.

23. Ibid. pp. 97-98.
24. Ibid. pp. 113-15.
25. *Stanford Almanac,* Stanford Alumni Association, March 1972, p. 3.
26. Alexander Hamilton, John Jay, and James Madison, *The Federalist,* No. 51, New York, The Modern Library, undated, p. 337.
27. Schwoebel, *op. cit.,* pp. 145-46.
28. "The Uncertain Mirror," *op. cit.,* Vol. I, p. 259.
29. Gene Youngblood, "Back to Pictograms," *ASNE Bulletin,* Oct. 1971, p. 24.
30. *On the Cable,* Report of the Sloan Commission on Cable Communications, New York, McGraw-Hill, 1971, pp. 139ff.

# *Index*